Date	Monarch	Event	Keynsham
878			Saxon N Century
901	Edward the Elder	Continuous battles against Danes	
924	Aethelstan	Victor over Scots and Danes	Keynsh;
		943 S. Dunstan	
959	Edgar the Pacific	Union English and Danes	
975	Aethelred the Unready		
	Edward the Martyr	Murdered, Corfe Castle	
1013	Sweyn	England ruled by	
1016	Canute	Danish kings	Pre Conquest estate belonged to Queen Edith (d.1075) wife of Edward Confessor
1042	Edward the Confessor		
1066	Harold II	1065 Westminster Abbey Battle of Hastings	Royal Estate given to William's wife.
	The Normans		
	William the Conqueror	1086 Domesday Book	It records Royal Estate of Caimesham comprised 6 mills, 100 acres meadow, 100 acres pasture, 63 ploughs, 40 cottagers, 70 villanes, 25 colibats, 20 servants, and a wood a mile long and broad.
1087	William II	Killed by an arrow	
1100	Henry I	Only son drowned	
1135	Stephen		
	House of Plantagenet		Strip farming. Feudal system.
1154	Henry II	1170 Death of T. Becket	1166 Death of Robert, only son of William, second Earl of Gloucester.
		1193 Archbishop Anselm	*1170 Foundation of Abbey of St. Mary, St. Peter and St. Paul*
1189	Richard I	3rd Crusade	
1199	John	1215 Magna Carta	Abbots administered law as Lords of the Manor and Hundred of Keynsham.
1216	Henry III	Present Westminster Abbey built	
			1224 Ralph de Willinton appointed Warden of the Forest of Keynsham by Henry III.
			1285 Abbot given right to enclose his deer park.
1272	Edward I	Wales conquered	1270 St. John's Church built.
			1276 King Edward stayed at the Abbey.
1307	Edward II	Murdered Berkeley	County bridge, probably built to replace ford, at Abbey's expense.
			1316 Great ceremony in Abbey hall for knighthood of Richard de Rodney of Backwell.
			1323 John de Kanisham, Mayor of Bristol.
1327	Edward III	Started 100 Years War Black Prince	Pool Barton, the Hams, were Abbey's farm.
		Black Death	1347 Labbott – probably 'road' given to Keynsham by Abbot.
			1348 Black Death – reduced population to a handful.
1377	Richard II	1381 Peasants Revolt	Back Lane – Western perimeter of Abbey.
		Geoffrey Chaucer	Chew Bridge built at Dapps Hill?
	House of Lancaster		
1399	Henry IV	Battle of Shrewsbury	One of the Abbey's several fishponds sited at top of present park.
1413	Henry V	1415 Agincourt	

'KEYNSHAM IN GRANDFATHER'S DAY'

Michael C. Fitter

Foreword by, the late PROFESSOR PATRICK McGRATH

The book commences with an historical introduction beginning with early times, by Mary Fairclough, followed by one of later days by William Gibbons. In the World War One section are the hitherto unpublished letters of Captain John S Parker, O.B.E. But the largest part of the book consists of the personal recollections and memories of an earlier Keynsham, recalled by local people, collected and edited by the author.

THE AMMONITE PRESS
KEYNSHAM

All rights reserved. No part of this publication may be reproduced, stored in a retrieval system, or transmitted in any form or by any means electronic, mechanical, photocopying, recording or otherwise, without the prior permission of the publishers.

Limited edition 1994. ISBN 0 9523202 0 7

The copyright of this book is owned by the publisher.

Published by, THE AMMONITE PRESS, KEYNSHAM,
  'Greensleeves' 6, Avon Road, Keynsham, Bristol, BS18 1LJ.

Typesetting by, Anneset, 25, Back Street, Weston-Super-Mare, Avon.

Printed by, J W Arrowsmith, Winterstoke Road, Bristol, BS3 2NT.

SPONSORSHIP

The generosity of the following local people has greatly assisted in the publication of this book, and their thoughtful benefaction is indeed deeply appreciated.

Mr John Paget.
Mr Ronald Headington.
Mr W. B. Reynolds.
Mrs Susan James.
Edward and David, Cannocks Garage, Bristol Road.
Mr Jack Smith.
Mrs Phyllis Clayfield.
Mr Richard F. Ollis.
Mrs Barbara Ollis.
Mr and Mrs Bryan Williams.
Mr Monty Veale.
Mrs Betty Verrecchia.
Mr B. J. Robe,
National Westminster Bank, Keynsham.
Mr Martyn Whittock,
The Handyman Shop, Keynsham, Ltd.
Mr Chris Wiggins.
Mr Monty Dermott,
Sandison Windows, Brislington.

DEDICATION

This book is dedicated to the warm-hearted people of this former Somerset market town of Keynsham whom I know and have known. Many of them, sadly, are no longer with us. Parish Registers and War Memorials record their names, lest we forget those who formerly lived in this delightful part of our 'green and pleasant land.' It is hoped that this book will also help to keep alive their memory of the town as they knew it, and to preserve it for posterity.

FOREWORD

In this book Mr Fitter has assembled a great range of interesting and miscellaneous material about people who lived in Keynsham in a period he calls 'Grandfather's Day'. In fact, grandfather's day is interpreted freely and there is a chapter by Miss Fairclough on the history of Keynsham. But the introductory survey is followed by an extremely varied collection of essays from people who lived in the town drawing on their own memories and on what has been handed down to them by their parents and grandparents.

It is in some ways a patchwork of reminiscence about bygone ages assembled from many brightly-coloured pictures of Keynsham as it was from the mid-nineteenth century onwards.

It is impossible in this brief introduction to do justice to the variety of contributions, in words and in photographs, or to the wealth of fascinating information they contain. We learn that with the aid of a stick and a pin eels might be caught in the River Chew. There are several eye-witness accounts of pauper funerals and of the remount mules quartered in Keynsham during the First World War.

The purist might argue that this material could be trimmed more neatly into shape and repetition could have been avoided, but this would spoil the effect here presented of a multitude of people telling their reminiscences sincerely in a rather breathless, even slightly rambling way, but building up a composite picture of what life was like here in Keynsham in grandfather's day.

Mr Fitter conveys an infectious enthusiasm for his project. His light touch with the editorial pencil allows the various contributors to speak directly to the readers, who will feel that they owe him a deep debt of gratitude.

    Patrick McGrath.
    Emeritus Professor of History,
    University of Bristol.

September 1991

INTRODUCTION

In the Sunday Times, an Oxford scholar recalled how as a boy he used to accompany his father in visiting one Mr Perry whose home was reached by 'crossing the bridge from Hammersmith to Barnes, beyond the riverbank trees and the towing path. . . . He had a cottage which stood quite by itself . . . opposite Harrod's playing fields. It had a high gable, red bricks, green window frames (to match the railings), a grass bank in front with concrete steps up it, a squeaky gate and a neat flower garden. Behind, Mr Perry's vegetable garden extended – illimitably, so far as I could tell, in a series of square beds surrounded by grass paths.'

Years later, 'Driving up one day, past Harrod's playing fields, I glanced across to Mr Perry's cottage. It wasn't there; just grass and a gap of sky. All that complicated life was now only a shadow in my mind. Even the place where it had happened had been laid bare. That, I know, is how life always vanishes.'[1]

The story has a familiar ring to it. Keynsham likewise has passed through a period of genuine devastation. Much of the old Temple Street has virtually vanished. Many fine buildings in the High Street have been swept away, not to mention the old Vicarage and the houses at the top of both sides of Bristol Road. Where Fairfield Terrace once stood is 'just grass and a gap of sky'. Shops now have a new look and double length. Two roundabouts link Bath Hill East and West. The ancient Back Lane as such has disappeared. Developers have seen to it that the local landmark of the Lamb and Lark has been replaced by an unglamorous supermarket.

What, then, was our lost Keynsham like, the Keynsham of grandfather's day? In answering this question I have necessarily chosen, despite the great attraction of Roman Keynsham, the fine Augustian Abbey and the town in the Middle Ages, (long before grandfather's day of course), to concentrate on the period between, approximately, 1845 to 1935.

Even so, far from this claiming to be a comprehensive and authoritative work on the period, it is rather a collection of individual memories, reminiscences and recollections, which I have found most interesting, and hope that you will too. Compared with this present 'high tech' age, they recall a simpler, rural way of life of a bygone era, even though for many they were hard times.

Professor P McGrath counselled me that there is no chapter on the politics or the politicians of the town, nor even a section on the respected long-serving Clerk to the Council, Mr George Ashton. This was not intentional. With my professional work and many other commitments, there has just been insufficient time. But in any case, despite the dedicated work of many Councillors, what the Council in the 1960s permitted to be perpetrated in the charming old town of Keynsham, is, sadly, obvious for all to see.

---

[1] Professor John Carey, article reprinted in 'Original Copy', Faber and Faber, London, 1987, pp 6 and 7.

Professor McGrath suggested too that I ought to explain the rationale on which I chose my contributors, lest some people feel grieved at not having been consulted. If offence has been given, I offer my apologies. Most of the people that I have consulted were members of the Keynsham and Saltford Local History Society, or of Victoria Church, the Civic Society or other organisations to which I belonged. Typically one person would say, 'You must interview Mr So and So', which I tried to do, but did not always succeed.

Where a contributor would write his own story, I encouraged him to do so. Often, however, it has been a case of drawing out a self-effacing elderly resident, who sometimes would conclude with the injunction 'But don't mention my name'. Yet an historian should name his sources! On many occasions I have consequently had to write up the conversations anonymously. If in such cases I have inadvertently misunderstood or misheard a person, and subsequently have recorded inaccurately or even caused offence, again, I offer a sincere apology.

The research for this book has been long, often fascinating, and always arduous in transforming the sometimes disjointed verbal accounts into a continuous written document. Normally I have then presented it to the contributor for his or her approval and correction.

I am not responsible for the views expressed or the accuracy of contributor's information.

Sadly, some of those who have been a great source of information and who have had chapters or parts of chapters devoted to them, are no longer with us. These include Gwen Newman, Len Ellis, Les Harding, Jesse Stickler and Edward Loxton. At least they saw, and approved, the finished chapters concerning themselves.

I am indebted to Sheila McGrath for her encouragement and advice. My grateful thanks are extended to my fellow committee members of the Keynsham and Saltford Local History Society; to Eric Linfield for initial advice; to Elizabeth White and Barbara Lowe for providing additional information for, and checking the accuracy of, the Time Chart; and to 'Len' Coggins for photographic help and advice. Particularly long suffering has been my mentor on old Keynsham, Mary Fairclough, with her fount of local knowledge, helpful advice and willing perusal of manuscripts. Really it is she who should have been writing the whole of this 'history'. Thank you indeed.

I am grateful too, to Susan James, who thoughtfully passed to me copies of her father's fascinating letters concerning his valuable work in Europe during World War One; and to my son, Christopher, for editing and condensing them.

Where other people have specifically written a chapter, I have placed their names under the chapter headings. In this connection, I am greatly indebted to the following for their essays: Mary Fairclough, Ron Kent, Lily Harrison, Joy Cannam, Isabel Andrews, Monty Veale, Gladys Dyson, 'Bert' Robe; to Bob Milner for permission to quote him; to Jill Renshaw for her poem, and to the late Gwen Newman and William Gibbons for their articles. Mrs. Malcolm Bird generously assisted with my early photography.

A particularly large debt is owed to 'Chris' Wiggins, who so graciously accepted the onerous task of carefully reading through the whole of the book, and for his valuable suggestions. Later, Bert Robe also kindly scrutinized the book and his informative comments will be seen from time to time. He, and Mr D. G. Hiscox, have graciously agreed to proof-read the manuscript.

My appreciation goes out to the many people of Keynsham who so kindly invited me into their homes, and then fascinated me with their tales of Keynsham in Grandfather's Day. I valued the trust that they put in me, and their generosity of spirit in explaining to a Londoner how they used to live many decades ago in beautiful Somerset.

I would record my grateful thanks to the following for permission to quote from their publications:

Brian Woodham, 'A commemorative study of the first 150 years of the Keynsham Hospital 1837–1987.'

Hugh Popham, 'Somerset Light Infantry' 1968. (Hamish Hamilton Ltd.)

Lastly but by no means least, I would express my thanks to my long-suffering wife, who so often looked for fellowship and conversation with her husband, only to find that he was going out to interview people or was in the study typing out his notes.

    Michael C Fitter
    R.K.C. (London), Cert.Ed. (Bristol).
    Keynsham, Bristol.
    December 1992.

CONTENTS

'KEYNSHAM IN GRANDFATHER'S DAY'

Sponsorship	iii
Dedication	iv
Foreword, by the late Professor P McGrath	v
Introduction	vii

CHAPTERS

PART ONE – MAINLY before WORLD WAR ONE

Page

1. 'It started like this,' by Miss Mary Fairclough. — 3
2. The Gibbons Family; and the later 'History of Keynsham', by William Gibbons. — 28
3. 'Burials at St John's Parish Church, 1830–1850,' and the 'Outbreak of Cholera.' — 34
4. 'Occupations, Population and Housing in Keynsham in 1851,' by Ron Kent and Bob Milner. — 47
5. William Charles Ollis, 1850–1935, the last general foreman of the Local Brass Works. — 57
6. 'Difficult Days of Unemployment', and 'The Workhouse,' based on information from C Dowling, Tom Carter, Wm Sherer, Lily Harrison and Leslie Harding. — 61
7. 'The Keynsham I remember before 1918.' Richard Newport. — 76
8. 'Memories of Old Keynsham,' by Mrs Lily Harrison. — 86
9. A Boy's view of School Life in Keynsham, by B J Robe. — 103
10. 'Anecdotes from old Keynsham families,' tales told by Jim Ollis, Phyllis Clayfield, Ron Headington and Grace Ollis. — 113
11. Memoirs of a Poacher's Daughter,' by Mrs Gwen Newman and the author. — 124
12. 'Sights and Sounds of smoky old Keynsham' – further memories of Gwen Newman. — 133

PART TWO – WORLD WAR I and the years before WORLD WAR II

13. 'Happenings in the Keynsham area during the 1914–18 War,' recalled by Susan James, Len Ellis, Jessie Stickler and others. — 141
14. 'The Parkers of Upton Cheyney; and the letters of Captain John S Parker, O.B.E., of the War Graves Commission. — 153
15. 'The Wood Family' and the British Red Cross. — 185
16. 'The Willcox Family', by Isabel Andrews. — 195
17. 'The Somerset Light Infantry.' — 207

18. Chairman of the Council, Mr. Len Ellis, an autobiography. 215
19. 'School Days', 'Early rural Keynsham', and 'Local shops', by
    Miss J Cannam. 226
20. 'Keynsham Town's Silver Band,' with items from Les Harding,
    Jean Williams, H Keeling and others. 244
21. 'Money Comes Slowly,' by Gwen Newman. 250
22. 'Childhood memories of Village Life,' by Monty Veale. 269
23. 'The Harveys of Keynsham.' 272
24. 'The Arrival of the Internal Combustion Engine,' the story of
    Edward A Cannock's garage. 286
25. 'Old Keynsham recalled in verse' by Jill Renshaw. 303

        INDEX   305

PART ONE

MAINLY before WORLD WAR ONE

Chapter 1

'It started like this . . .'

Though my research in this book is with the period of 'Keynsham in Grandfather's Day', and despite the town's so modern appearance today, the village has a long documented history. Its Roman remains are of national importance. Domesday records its wealth compared with its poorer neighbours, as well as its royal connection. With its fine Abbey, its successive Abbots were each 'Lord of the Manor, and of the Hundred of Keynsham' for some 400 years. It has been, indeed, from time to time, a town of some importance and standing.

Therefore, I was delighted when I came across Miss Mary Fairclough's 'Interim Report on the History of Keynsham.' Its charming style compliments its scholarly grasp and interpretation of the history of the village, and of its place in national events. I was even more thrilled when some years ago, she agreed readily to it prefacing my book.

More recently, Mary mentioned to me that though it was historically correct, so far as she knew when she wrote it, she was aware that parts of it have proved doubtful or inaccurate in the light of later research. However, rather than lose its charming style and continuity, it is reproduced here in its original form, just as it was when Mary gave it in a series of talks on 'Old Keynsham.' She says it combines a talk on 'The Parish Church' and a larger general paper first given c.1955/6 to a Ladies Guild in the Old Church Room in Station Road, now, like so many of the fine old buildings of Keynsham, swept away by Philistine development, in this case the By-pass.

Interim Report on the History of Keynsham

by Miss Mary Fairclough

In the beginning . . .

It is easy to see why Keynsham began. The other day a youngster showed me the essay she was writing on Keynsham for a school exam, and she began with the charming phrase, 'The Chew is a happy little river.' It is. In the old days it certainly was – full of fish and eels, otters playing, beavers building dams, deer coming down to drink – Walt Disney would have loved it. And it joined the great tidal river of Avon, with the salt sea water sweeping up as far as Saltford – with trout and salmon and millions of wild fowl over on the Hams. And just above the joining, this nice ridge of hill, not too heavily wooded, several good clean springs of drinking water – it was simply bound to become a place.

This happens when someone puts two or three stones together for a hearth and cooks supper for the family, and then they have breakfast in the same place and it looks just as good as it did the night before. So they keep the fire going. And in a few generations, you build some extra huts and hearths for the great-great grandchildren, and that place is a village.

So by about the time that the city of Troy was being built, I think that we can take it that we had begun too, because by then there was not only the joining of rivers here, there was a joining of roads, of trackways.

A track from the Wells-Radstock direction came down Wellsway and along Avon Road (a little below the present level – never show up on the skyline more than you can help) and it joined the track from Bitton and the Cotswolds just above where the County Bridge is now, where the Avon was fordable. Then it came up the hill, along the line of Station Road, over the site of the International Stores, across into Culvers Road and on up Charlton Road, over Woolard Hill to Stanton Drew.

The Stone Circles of Stanton Drew were raised before Stonehenge – somewhere about 1870 BC. If it is, as we think, a sun-worship temple, then from the way it is set the great festivals of worship for us then were May Day and Halloween.

We had to be at the temple, of course, by festival sunrise. So, the day before, we'd bank our fires carefully over with turf, put on our best things – all our nicest furs and skins and the lovely bright check plaids we'd woven last winter, gold rings and necklaces if we have any – bronze and enamel-work on the chief's horse harness – we were a very prideful, ornamental sort of people in those days. And with our chief and our Druid – our priest – leading, we'd join in the stream of folk coming down from the villages on Cotswold and Lansdown and go to Stanton Drew.

The trouble, of course, lay in the sort of things we did when we got there. I am afraid our Druids were not dignified old gentlemen in Bardic crowns; the whole affair was more like Mau Mau than the National Eisteddfod. Many generations later a Greek traveller said that our habit of decorating our temples with freshly severed human heads 'was really rather sickening until you got used to it.'

It is what you are used to, of course. But strangers didn't like it. In AD 43 the Romans finally mounted a full-scale invasion of Britain. By AD 47, all this West Country was overrun, pacified and settled down to civilian life, and centres like Stonehenge and Stanton Drew had been very thoroughly desecrated and cleaned out by the occupying forces and we could worship any gods we fancied but it had to be done in a decent and civilised manner. And there was a small neat military police post up on Maes Knoll, just over Stanton Drew.

The Roman Occupation

The Roman Occupation lasted from AD 43 to 406 – as long as from Elizabeth I's reign to this present year. And in this district, that meant a good solid 350 years of peace. Except for the small camps – Maes Knoll, Stantonbury and so on – more or less police posts – the nearest legionary headquarters was over at Caerleon-upon-Usk. Bath – Aquae Sulis – was a thoroughly civilian little town. All the villages – Keynsham, Bitton, Saltford,

Newton St Loe, Northstoke, Kelston, Compton Dando, Brislington – were in existence, mostly centres of big farming estates – villas. A Roman villa, such as the great one at the cemetery here, was not something called The Laurels with a privet hedge round it. It was far more like the great plantation house of the Southern States before the American Civil War.

There was the house itself – lead-lined baths, exquisite mosaic floors and painted walls, stone-tiled roof and stone colonnade, gardens, kitchen garden, farm buildings, workshops, smithy, tannery, slave quarters, and so on. Here, with the house tucked into the side of the hill and the Hams liable to flooding,

Miss Fairclough's reconstruction of life in the large Roman Villa at Durley Hill, Keynsham, looking towards Kelston Tump, from the north corridor. It was drawn during the period of 1970 to 1976, and measures 4 foot wide by 3ft 6 inches high.

On the low stone wall, beside the boy grasping his scroll, is his metal stylus and writing tablet, while his father listens to his son's lessons. The parent is seated on a wicker arm chair of local willow, which is authenticated by contemporary sculptures in Gaul. 'We know cats were kept, and the dog is based on a bronze miniature found on Hadrian's Wall', Mary concluded.

a lot of these working parts may have been found in Stockwood Vale, where the old Tanyard and cottages are now. And, of course, there would have been a wharf and boats, probably round by Chequers Ferry. And this great house was the very pleasant home, not, probably, of retired Roman Consuls, but of our own local British Chieftains – the decendants of the man with the gorgeous horse harness who led us to Stanton Drew. But they were also, now, citizens of the Roman Empire; a gentleman of Keynsham might talk the pure local dialect of Welsh Gaelic to his cowherds up on Broadlands and Stockwood Hill, but his dress, manners and formal speech were Roman – and his wife was probably fashionable Roman when she got over to Bath. And we, more or less free crofter farmers, still up here in our village of turf-roofed huts, we also were Roman citizens; and quite a few of our sons were away serving in the legions, anywhere from Hadrian's Wall to Syria, and it was 25 years – not 18 months.

On the whole, Keynsham had not at all a bad time those 300 years – someone who lived here had 'Happy is the bearer' engraved on a ring. In Greek too. By the third century, some of us at least were Christian. Two little baptismal spoons have been found further up the Avon – one for the first anointing in the flowing water, one for the anointing with oils and balm – in a little bower of green branches on the river bank. That little green bower could have been the beginning of our church.

And God knows we needed it. We felt safe and ordinary and peaceful here – but by the middle of the next century Rome, the Empire of which we were citizens, was dying. Rotting, and the barbarian tribes knew it. In AD 367 the Picts broke through Hadrian's Wall in the North, massacred two legions and raided clear down to Kent. Then the sea pirates from the Dutch and Danish coasts began raiding – soon they got bases in Ireland and began hit-and-run raids up the Bristol Channel.

Big villa owners were taxed to the limit – Rome would collect taxes on her death bed – and places like Keynsham had always counted on exporting corn and hides and so on, but it was getting riskier every year; soon you would hear this sort of thing:

'We won't plough Broadlands this year, Daffudd. I've had a word with the Naval Commandant over at Portbury. He is expecting trouble this summer. We may have to get the harvest in quick. Don't get anyone scared but just arrange with the headman to plough as much as possible near the village, and get some storage pits dug where you can keep an eye on them.'

And then the fields go out of cultivation. You must remember, round all these civilised farms was still forest. Leave a field, and the woods began to close in.

The Saxon threat

I think in those years we felt rather as we did in 1939. You knew the worst could happen, but you didn't really believe it would. Well . . . on the night of December 31st, AD 406, a German army crossed the frozen Rhine into Gaul. A galley from Boulogne put into Richborough. Orders for the withdrawal of all regular troops stationed in Britain. No wireless of course, but the main military road of the West, the Via Julia, to the legionary H.Q. at Caerleon runs through Kelston and Bitton, Kingswood way. We probably got the news quite quickly. I think we all know what we felt like.

That was when the men from the homes like the villas of Keynsham, the men who were Roman citizens and magistrates, Christians and our own tribal chiefs, showed what they were made of – and by gum they were worth their enamelled horse harness and mosaic floors and all the rest of it. Under them, we, here, in Somerset and the West, held out against all the barbarians could do to us, for 50 years.

We had some bad patches and then the families from the villas round here were mostly sent into Bath – 23 acres with a wall round it. The Newton St Loe people went there one time – they cleared out everything and laid the roofing tiles over the mosaic floors to protect them in case anything happened before they came back. The tiles were still in place when the villa was excavated a few years ago. But when there was a lull, our people, for instance, did come back. Half the great villa was burnt, but they went on living in the undamaged wing. We found where they had made a cooking hearth in one room on the mosaic floor.

We stockaded our cattle and guarded our crops and buried them for safety when we had got them in and we used the old police posts and hill forts like Maes Knoll, Stantonbury, Winbury and so on all over Somerset for strong points, bases for cavalry patrols – and we hung out – we and our Roman British leaders.

Don't think Arthurius – King Arthur – and his mounted knights were a legend, they were a reality so great they became a legend. But it couldn't go on for ever. In 577 there was a pitched battle over at Dyrham in Wilts. We lost. Gloucester and Cirencester were taken and then Bath. You know what it looks like from Keynsham at night when Bath is on fire – that horrible pulsing flickering glare over the corner of Kelston. We saw it then. I think that was when Roman Keynsham died.

It sounds incredible but one living thing survives now from that time. The great yew tree at Queen Charlton, surrounded at the moment by Mr Dowdney's hen run, was already a sapling then.

And, of course, there were other things unchanged. This was still the meeting place of the rivers and the roads, still a very good place to live in and there were plenty of Saxon warriors looking for likely spots to settle with their wives and families. War is all very fine but what you do really want is a good farm. So quite soon, here's Keynsham again, a good stout wattle and daub, timber and turf village in a wooden stockade, somewhere in the Temple Street–Dapps Hill area I fancy – not too near the main road – we always liked to be able to see strangers coming.

St Keyna, a Welsh Princess

One day a stranger came – a girl from Wales where they were still British and Christian. It seemed she was the daughter of a Prince Bragham of Brecknock. Her name was Keyna. She was one of those Welsh missionary saints who were going about everywhere then. They say she asked our chief to let her build herself a cell in the woods here . . . and the chief said it wasn't safe on account of the snakes. S' thee know, Alfred, I think 'e be 'avin 'er on – there bain't so many znakes 'ere. . . . Aw, 'e wer trying to scare 'er off – an' – 'e – won'r suczeed. I vairly think you *caan't* zcare these yer Christians. They've a-got zummat *to* 'em, look-zee?

And when Keyna built her cell maybe she found some ammonites lying about and put them by the door and said, 'There are your snakes, chief bach!' Maybe – you never know with these saints – we did just wonder a bit . . .

We'll never know for certain, but it's quite likely Keynsham did become Christian again through her. Anyhow, quite early on, we were so, and we carved ourselves a preaching cross to stand at the cross-roads – we still have one stone of it, the only Saxon one left in Somerset – in the arch in Station Road. We must look after it.

In the next few hundred years we had plenty of trouble – just as *we* the Britons had been raided by fierce Saxons, so *we* the Saxons were raided by fierce Danes – poetic justice is *much* more blessed to give than to receive. This time there were not only pirate bases in Ireland but just outside in the Bristol channel, on the Flat Holme – the long ships could come right up the river here. It was worst in King Alfred's time, between 871 and 78. In 871, Alfred became king when his brother was killed over at Moreton in Berkshire, and in the same battle, Heahmund, Bishop of Sherborne, was killed too. We were in Sherborne diocese then, and as we were safely behind the lines for the present, they brought his body back here for burial – it seems likely that there was a priory of some sort at Keynsham. The incident recorded in Ethelwold's History is the first written record of Keynsham – in 871 – 1,104 years ago. Later the Danes invaded all the West – Alfred is said to have had a running fight with them once up Charlton Road which used to be called Dane's Lane, ending in a pitched battle in Woolard. But we got over the Danes, and went on farming, and the next thing that happened was the Norman Conquest – happened very thoroughly.

Keynsham Manor and the Domesday Book

The Manor of Keynsham belonged in 1066 to King Edward the Confessor's widow, Edith Swan-neck, so it passed direct as royal domain to the Conqueror. The Domesday Book shows a lot of the land held by the old Saxon tenants, and the Priest of Keynsham one hide – about 30 aces, including presumably the church and the site of the vicarage, but there is no actual mention of the priory. The Conqueror's son, Henry I, gave Keynsham and the Lordship of Bristol as part of the Earldom of Gloucester to his son, Robert de Melhent.

Robert was rather nice really. He introduced Arabian horses, for instance, to improve the local breed, and founded the Benedictine Priory of St James in Bristol, but when Henry died in 1136 the trouble between Stephen and Matilda blew up and Robert declared for his half-sister Matilda.

For the next eleven years, Bristol was 'the volcano whence the kingdom was deluged with fire and sword' – we were living a dogsbodyish life on the slopes. Still, that also ended, and in 1166 Robert's grandson, who knew and loved Keynsham, being taken ill over at Cardiff and knowing he was dying,

The following two sketches were drawn by Miss M Fairclough in January 1990, to complement her revised text.

The costume of the black Augustinian Canons of Keynsham Abbey, circa 1167–1539. This shows one in his black cope, white rochet, black cassock or pellise, and his sandals. The other figure shows a more portly canon with the hood of his cope drawn up, wearing fur-lined leather boots, or felt-lined boots for the winter.

asked his father, Earl William, to refound Keynsham Priory and let him be buried there.

The Abbey at Keynsham

The legal arrangements and the rebuilding and so on took some time, of course, but in 1170 the Abbey of the Blessed Virgin Mary in Keynsham was founded and about 30 men, ordained priests, Canons of the Order of St Augustine, vowed to Poverty, Chastity, and Obedience, came here and took the final Vow of Stability – their vow to serve God in this place all the days of their lives. That service was continued by them and their successors for 360 years.

For 360 years we, in the village, belonged to them. The whole manor of Keynsham and of Marshfield was given to them – 'in wood, in plain, in meadows and pastures, waters and marshes and fishing rights' – Earl William was very thorough – 'to hold freely, quietly and in peace.'

The Lord Abbot they elected among themselves to be 'the father of the monastery who bears the charge of all of you' was also our Lord of the Manor. The man of whom the Rule of St Augustin says 'In honour before you let him be preferred before you; in fear before God, let him be beneath your feet' – he was also the lord who had the right to hang out of hand any thief caught on his lands; and had for instance the right of Tumbrill – he could order any woman, say, who gossiped too badly, to be dunked in the Chew (happy little river).

Actually, the Abbot delegated most of this secular business to the brother appointed Cellarer – who was not only responsible for 'everything to do with food, drink, firing, carriage of goods by land or water, repairs of houses, purchase of iron, steel, wood, ploughs, wagons, bacon, salt and dried fish, gowns and wine, the care of the monastery inside and out' – he was also 'frequently to visit the manors, ploughlands, folds, keep a sharp lookout on the character, acts and zeal of all servants placed in charge of manors lest they should sell stores, make presents or be addicted to squanderings and revellings and whether their farm labourers' (us) 'are faithful, carefully watching over their flocks even at night', and so on: 'He is the Abbot's right hand in matters temporal' – and heaven help us if the right hand was a heavy one.

The Royal Park and the Abbey's Park

Now, originally canons of this order were supposed to remain enclosed within the covent walls, labouring, praying, meditating, unless like the

The second sketch declares that 'The Abbot of Keynesham claims . . . tumbrell in the vill of Keynesham' (He does not claim pillory) . . . 'The jury find that the abbots have enjoyed said liberties from time immemorial.' Miss Fairclough said that the quotation is dated '3rd [year of King] Edward III' [1330], from 'Notes on Tumbrel, Cucking and Ducking', by Thomas S Bush, Bath Nat. His. & Archae. Field Club', vol 9, 1900.

Cellarer they were specially sent out by the Abbot on business. But by the time Keynsham was founded things were a little less strict and most monasteries had outlying manors – court houses – where members might be sent for a rest, a holiday. Keynsham had Hanham Abbots and Charlton Abbots (Queen Charlton) and our people's main recreation – in fact you could call it a standing temptation – was always hunting.

The Abbey's own park – the area of the present park, plus the entire Chew valley, along to Conygre Farm – was stocked with deer of course. But there was also the Royal Park, or Chace, of Keynsham belonging to Bristol Castle. This was the whole great triangle of land between Charlton Road, West View and Park Road and the Bridle Path from Park Cottages up to just this side of Queen Charlton. All that was walled round, strictly preserved, under the jurisdiction of the Constable of Bristol Castle and the Royal Foresters of Somerset.

It didn't always deter the Abbot. Over and over again the wretched Constable complains about trespassing – the Lord Abbot of Keynsham was just a little too important to be dealt with, so to speak, as any of us would have been, of course. Remember the Chace was important to the Constable, quite apart from sport, in provisioning the Castle, not only with food but also with firewood – Forest Law protected the greenwood itself quite as rigorously as the game.

Twice King Edward I came to Keynsham and stayed with the Abbot for a week's hunting – and each time the Abbot got hunting and firewood concessions from the King – each time there is an official letter to the unfortunate Constable afterwards, informing him of the fact.

No, on the whole the Royal Park added quite a little spice to life in the Abbey. But just think what it meant to us. There we were, strung out along High Street, Temple Street, Dapps Hill – church and vicarage top end, pack-horse bridge at the bottom – some of us still in turfed-over huts, some stone houses, some half timber, wattle-and-daub inner walls, quite nice – and one side of us was the Abbey and our houses were huddled right up against its walls, and the home farm took all Pool Barton and the Hams; and on the other the Charlton Road side of High Street, only a field's length away – Royal Forest. Beyond Queen Charlton was Filwood, Royal Forest. All round Brislington, Royal Forest. And just across the County Bridge (that was already built, by the way) began the great Royal Forest of Kingswood, right round to Bristol, and a most notorious hide-out for outlaws, too.

So all around us lay 'The Peace of the Hunting' – every man-child over twelve had to swear to that peace –

'You shall true liegeman be
Unto the King's Majestie
Unto beasts of the forest you shall not hurt do
Nor unto anything that doth belong thereunto.
The offences of others you shall not conceal
But to the utmost of your power you shall them reveal
Unto the officers of the forest
Or to them that may see them redrest.

All these things you shall see done.
So help you God at his Holy Doom.'

And if you were mug enough to be caught snaring rabbits after that, you were tried at the Forest Court at Wells, without protection in Common Law.

Another thing – for protection of game the foresters had the right to 'taw' all dogs except sheep dogs – cut off three toes from the right fore-paw. It was supposed to be done decently, in the presence of responsible men of the village, once every three years at the Regard, the inspection of forest boundaries; but the foresters about there had the nasty habit of turning up suddenly, galloping down the street yelling and blowing horns so every dog in the place rushed out barking – and then seizing any untawed ones and doing the job out of hand.

Early development of the narrow village

So you see – we were compressed between the Abbey and the forest – and the bulk of our own fields was on the *other* side of the Chew – Wellsway – Manor Road – Stidham – Broadmead area. And to get to it we had to go right down Dapps Hill – the Bath Hill road and bridge didn't exist – cross the pack horse bridge and then either up Poggam's Lane (Fairfield Terrace) towards the Talbot, or Goosberry Lane, straight up the middle, or Steel Mills to the Manor Road area. The Grange – sort of headquarters for the Abbey farm officials – stood in the middle of it – and there is as you may know a farm still called 'Eastover' – corrupt Norman-Keynsham French 'Estoffer' – the place where we could cut our firewood. If you lived the top end of High Street you had a long way to go.

Well, in 1347, Abbot Nicholas thought he would do something about that. He owed us something for having landed us with absolutely the worst vicar we had ever had – Richard atte Wood – always in trouble, absent without leave, up for perjury, misappropriation of funds, goodness knows what – a pest in the parish – so Abbot Nicholas decided to give us a new right of way. First we got Royal permission to close the section of the old highway here from the church end of High Street to Culvers Road, so he could build a new Guest House for the Abbey – the Hospice of St John, now the International Stores. Then he gave us his new path, The Labbot, right across the Abbey's Park – from Temple Street straight down to the river at the bottom of Bath Hill, handy for the mill, passable ford, may even have put in a bridge, only a step up by the Fox and Hounds to Avon Road. Very useful. But in doing so, he has landed us *now* with Keynsham's choicest traffic problem. There still had to be a road to Queen Charlton, of course, so we gaily made ourselves a new lane from Culvers Road straight down into High Street at right angles – the bottle-necked bottom of Charlton Road. Dear Abbot Nicholas . . .

In 1347 it didn't matter. We had other things to think about. The crops weren't too good. Having very little winter fodder except hay we always had to slaughter and salt down much of our stock in the autumn, which meant we never had enough manure to dress our fields properly. But the Abbey were keeping a lot of sheep – they had three shepherds – John Tankard, Robert Grindere and John Twynere – all rascals – and we were skilled cloth weavers

Another 'Abbey' find? Behind the fireplace in this 17th century Steel Mills Cottage, its owners found this beautiful carved oak lintel, presumably from Keynsham Abbey, and they said the wood was so tough that you couldn't knock a nail in it.

and raised woad for dyeing. We had a weekly market on Thursdays and a yearly fair. We can't have been doing too badly because we were enlarging the church, building the South aisle – it was finished all but the windows and the porch, in spite of the vicar.

Oh, and some of us – really guaranteed respectable females – took in the Abbot's and the Canon's washing – once in 3 weeks in winter, once a fortnight in summer.

Black Death

But then came January 1348. A particularly ghastly form of plague spread from China by the caravan routes to the Black Sea ports and from there by ship to pretty well every sea port in Europe. And in January 1348 it hit Bristol. There were hardly enough living left in Bristol to bury the dead. It raged out all over Somerset. We hadn't the faintest idea how to cope with it. One of the first symptoms was a violent fit of sneezing – Lord help us, we took to carrying little posies of flowers and herbs about to smell. It could hit you as you were coming home down Steel Mills and set you staggering round in rings until the haemorrhage started and you dropped. And you never got to Dapps Hill. Maybe the vicar found you before the end – whatever we thought of him he stuck by us, he wasn't one of those priests who ran away – but he died early on. So did Abbot Nicholas. So did a great many of us.

The children started a new singing game that summer – just as they played round the bomb craters a while back:

Ring a ring a roses – A pocket full of posies – Atishoo atishoo atishoo – we all fall down . . .

That was the Black Death. It took us a good thirty years to recover. But after a while we did, and we began building again. The old 'Forester's Arms' – Vickis that is now – and Beale's bakery and the houses next to it, some of the old ones at the far end of Temple Street and Dapps Hill went up then. And at last we really finished the church – the North aisle complete with gargoyles, the west front and South porch – and we decided we had planned too small on the South aisle windows, so we enlarged them to match the North – you can see by the stone work over them what happened. Over the next 50 odd years we made a really lovely thing of it. And we kept it so for another 80. Then the world began to change for us rather quickly. The Tudors came to power.

The Dissolution and the Bridges Family

Our first contact with them was quite pleasant – Jasper Tudor, Duke of Bedford, uncle of Henry VII, came to Keynsham and liked it and left a note in his will that he was to be buried here and 'on the day of his burial 2d was to be given to everyone who would accept it.' The day of his burial *began* very properly – 'William Regent, Mayor of Bristol, with 2000 townsmen clad in black met the dead corpse of Jasper and accompanied him to Keynsham,' but I'm afraid that when the 2ds were distributed it may have got a little festive. The White Hart at least was already in existence . . .

But in 1534 Henry VIII quarrelled with the Pope and all religious houses had to acknowledge the King's supremacy as head of the Church of England. Well, the Abbey and Convent of Keynsham did that, although it meant rendering unto Caesar practically everything in sight. But I think Abbot John Stourton, the last of our Abbots, knew what was coming. During the next five years he sold off or leased a tremendous amount of the Abbey estates, and the offices of sub-seneschal and bailiff of the parish and Hundred of Keynsham – those rather overwhelming jobs that used to fall on the Cellarer – he leased to two brothers I think – John and William Panter.

And in 1539 came the final Dissolution – quite quietly, as far as we were concerned, although there was terrible trouble elsewhere. The Abbot and the Canons signed the Abbey and all its remaining possessions over to the king, accepted pensions and left. The Abbey church was stripped down to the bare stone. The very reason for its existence was gone, you see.

The estate was leased to various people for short periods – Queen Katherine Parr had it as part of her jointure, along with Charlton Abbots which then became Queen Charlton, but the Panters continued to manage things, and then – 14 years after the Dissolution – appear the Bridges family; well connected at Court, through three different reigns and three changes of religion, which must have taken some doing – cousins of the Duke of Chandos, and so far as I can see a piece of good luck for Keynsham.

At first they just built a country house – sorry, 'a superb and elegant seat' – on the site of the Abbey, incorporating all the old domestic buildings and adding an impressive front. They held the rectory of the church – they appointed our vicars for 200 years – and like the Abbey before them they owned the chancel – where they began setting up their monuments. Sorry about that . . . But for the first forty years or so, they seem to have been more closely connected with Bath than Keynsham. We don't hear of them for instance in connection with the anti-invasion measures in Elizabeth's time. We're apt to think of that invasion trouble as centring around the Spanish Armada in 1588. Actually it hung over us for nearly forty years before. During all that time a sort of Home Guard was kept standing, in about the same plight for arms as ours was in 1940. In the 'General Certificate of Soulden in Somerset 1580' Keynsham Hundred has 240 able men, only 77 armed, only fifteen horsemen. In March '84 Somerset had 3000 men sorted and furnished for coast defence, and costing the equivalent of £400 per day. Keynsham provided "15 shott, 14 bowmen, 10 Billmen – 30 corseletts between them – and the shott needed training. A halberd was to be sett up, every shott was to pass in what the French call 'a la file' but we tarm 'in rank as wild geese'" – first learning to handle their weapons 'so as to avoid endangering themselves and their fellows.' Lot to be said for pikes after all . . .

Queen Elizabeth and Charles I

In addition to all this we had Queen Elizabeth passing through here to Bristol – they say she was rude about our dirty High Street, and I don't blame her – and we had several outbreaks of plague, floods, bad harvests, famine. The glorious Elizabethan Age was a very hard one in Keynsham. But we managed to do a good deal to the church – terribly stripped in the first rage of Reformation. We got our present altar and our three oldest bells – we were evidently keeping things in decent order at least – until January 16th 1632.

Brief from King Charles I: 'The Parish Church of Keynsham being a very fair large substantial church and a great ornament to the said town, is lately most lamentably ruinated by reason of most disastrous misfortune by tempestuous weather – which happening on the 13th day of January 1632 . . . continued in a most fearful manner, being intermixed with hideous claps of thunder and flashes of lightening about six of the clock in the afternoon of the same day, and by reason of the force thereof in a moment threw down the steeple or spire of the tower which in the fall thereof crashed down likewise the greatest and principallest part of the body of the said church . . .' (the tower, remember, was on the North where the ladies' vestry is, not the West end) 'And the tower being therewith crashed from the top to the foundation' – And it was pitch dark with a roaring wind and stones and rubble sliding for hours – that was a night! Next morning, of course, we all rolled out to see what had happened – so many of us gave a hand it cost the churchwardens 8/2 in bread and cheese and beer that first day. We have the wonderful luck to have the complete churchwarden's account for 1632–39 covering the whole rebuilding. They tell us an amazing amount about us – about Gorslett the Blacksmith and those two good carpenters, Miss Bowden's ancestors the Sheppards, and Old Joe Bessie who had various odd bobs and coppers from the churchwardens for errands, and then on another page you find 'Recd. of Joe Bessie 5/- which he gave to the church' –nice old chap. We took our oxen off the ploughing to haul timber. We borrowed somebody's scale beam to weigh the roofing lead and broke it – we collected money on the strength of that Royal Brief all over the South of England – and the landlord of the White Hart seems to have done a sort of 'Penny on the drum for the Spitfire fund' – he turned in quite a handsome sum – and someone else gave us quite a sum of bad farthings, anonymously.

Various people gave us timber – one of us had to go, choose the trees, get them felled, topped, barked and hauled here – from Kingswood and Hunstrete among other places, quite a haul for oxen. Various villages over Bath way sent us loads of stone – and then Mr Bridges, who had already given us £5 and repaired the vestry himself, told us we could have all the stone left of the old Abbey church. And so the ruins of the dead church were built back into the living one. That was good.

And we'll never know who proposed it or how long we argued – but we resolved, instead of just restoring, to build ourselves a really fine tower at the West end, with space for a full ring of eight bells – the old tower only held five – and we did it. Just in time. We'd only patched the chancel arch, and all that was left of our lovely screen was the bit in the South aisle. The floor was flagstoned where the tiles were broken and we'd put in a truly dreadful plaster ceiling like a box lid over the nave – but the tower was finished. And the Civil War broke out.

The Civil War and our County Bridge

The main West road to Bristol was, of course, through Keynsham – by way of the County Bridge and Kingswood, *not* through Brislington; that was still only a cart track between villages.

Whoever wanted to get at Bristol needed our bridge intact, and whoever held the city wanted it smashed. What we thought about it just didn't matter. As a matter of fact I think we must just have 'laid low an' said nuffin'.' The Bridges family were Royalist – young Thomas Bridges held Bath for the King – but Bristol was held at first for Parliament by Col. Fiennes, who duly smashed the bridge in 1643, and then yielded the city after all, and was courtmartialled for it. And the whole district was probably mildly Royalist until 1645. Then Bath fell and General Fairfax and Lieut. Gen. Cromwell and the Parliamentary forces were quartered on Keynsham while they felt their way around Bristol, which they took a couple of weeks later. And we still laid low. But the Bridges family escaped into exile.

I must warn you that I have done hardly any research yet on this period – things may come to light later; all I know at present is that in 1654 we acquired No. 3 bell and in 1655, the first year of the Commonwealth, we indulged in the weathercock – the date is on its tail. Then Charles II was restored to the throne in 1660 and the Bridges family came home again. They weren't, by the way, Lords of the Manor – that belonged to the Whitmore family in London, who seem to have built the old **Manor House, Bristol Road**, in James I's time, but never lived there – I fancy the Panters continued to manage the estate. The Bridges only had their great house and the present park, but they were The Family. Sir Thomas and Lady Anna were really rather dears. They seem to have taken us on and looked after us. We needed a bit of looking after.

The Monmouth Rebellion

In 1686 came Monmouth's Rebellion – it rolled up through Somerset collecting men like a snowball, and the advance guards got as far as Keynsham – aiming for the bridge again, to get at Bristol. And they got the bridge – if they had had the sense to go on, they would have had the Port of Bristol, and the Rebellion would probably have succeeded – but they spent the night at Keynsham, camped on Sydenham Mead just beyond the White Hart, and eleven of our men joined them just in time to be caught when the King's Dragoons dropped in on them the next day. There was a running fight all along Avon Road from Dragon's Hill – and then the retreat started – and our eleven finished up at Sedgemoor. They were taken and duly brought back. Judge Jefffries called in on his way to Bristol – stayed at the Old Court House on Bath Hill, now the library – and our poor eleven were hanged up at the cross-roads by the Talbot.

And Sir Thomas Bridges founded the Bristol Road Almshouses mainly for widows.

That was the last time we had actual fighting in Keynsham – dousing incendiary bombs with a stirrup pump doesn't count – and the last time the County Bridge was of strategic importance.

The Royal Coat of Arms above the fireplace at Chandos Lodge, Keynsham, bearing the date 1663, three years after the Restoration and the crowning of Charles II. An old undated newspaper-cutting referring to Keynsham, said of the unfortunate Charles I, 'It is recorded that he hid in what is popularly known as "the stud farm" but which was originally a hunting box on the estate of the Chandos family.'

When these photos were taken, daylight was streaming in from above as a new roof was being built and debris from the old plaster had piled up on the mantlepiece, which the foreman brushed off with his hand. Unfortunately the lower photo shows only too clearly the deposits of dust and rubble.

The stage coach and the turnpike roads

Some time fairly soon after this, the regular stage and mail coaches began running through Keynsham to Bristol and from being a quiet lane just leading to the mill at the bottom of what is now St Ladoc Road and the Tanyard, Sir Thomas' Almshouses were on the main turnpike road. And the Bath Hill Road and Bridge were made, at the other end, cutting out the Dapps Hill bridge.

It was a pretty bad road – I've heard they used to plough it in the spring to

The following four sketches by Miss Fairclough were drawn around 1946 and were based on pictures from the Farmer's Weekly, at a period when, as she says, 'Horses were still widely used in Keynsham'. The top picture features spring ploughing, with sheep enclosed nearby. Below, sowing seed by the time honoured method of broadcasting by hand.

level out the ruts – but there was plenty of traffic – has been ever since.

Two hostelers at the Crown, later on, both made fortunes and retired. One built Uplands House, opposite the old Manor, and the other hanged himself. Don't know why.

Disc-harrowing prepares the ploughed glebe for sowing, while rabbits look on at a scare-crow there to keep the birds from newly-sown seed. Below, a reaper and binder at work, men stooking sheaves, while dry ones hoisted by an elevator are stacked, and the stack then thatched to keep out the rain. Note the lovely old waggons, familiar to some of us, with horse-drawn shafts.

Keynsham began to be quite lively and in 1705 Sir Thomas erected and endowed our first regular school – 'For teaching 20 poor boys of the town grammar, the Latin tongue, writing, arithmetic, the Christian Religion, the Church Catechism, good manners and morals' – very nice curriculum. I think either he or his son Henry built the old school house in Station Road for it, though at first it was an outbuilding of the vicarage – and the vicar was expected to run it.

Our brass mills and the beginning of change

And the first big industry came to Keynsham. Up to that time we had imported all our brass, mainly from Holland. Now a man named Champion learned the technique – secretly they say – in Holland and brought it back to England, with some eight families of skilled workers – Ollis, Frankhams, Frays, Cramers, Hollisters, Steagers, Krinks, Fudges.

The Bristol Brass and Wire Co. was founded in 1702. Soon they had half the mills in the district, the main three being Avon Mill, where the Chew joins the Avon, the old Battery Mill in the park, and Saltford Mill. For a long while, the brass workers formed a little separate community at Avon Mill – 'furriners'. We called them the Intruders. There is a long document signed by our Parish Council and the Company, laying down that they shall by no means be allowed to become a charge on the parish – and also that certain local youngsters shall be taken on as apprentices – we wanted it both ways. We got it – by the 19th century they were the Gentlemen Brass Workers of Keynsham, and went to work in top hats, so they did, and the pubs set aside special rooms for their use.

They turned out some lovely work, though, and inspired the great Mr Handel to write the Hallelujah Chorus – he came to stay with the Bridges and I'm afraid the Battery Mills at the bottom of the garden must have kept him awake, but it was a superb rhythm. Right up until 1922 that work and that rhythm continued in Keynsham.

In 1768, Sir Thomas Whitmore dismembered Keynsham Manor estate – sold it off in lots to the various tenants. In 1776, the Bridges family, monumental to the last, but very nice, died out. Their estate passed to the Duke of Chandos and the great house in the park was pulled down.

Our hand-weaving industry began to die out on us as mechanical weaving developed. Our population was small – 1,591 in 1801 – but it was increasing and we were mainly poor.

And there seems to have been a sort of dull blight on us – there was no Ruling Family, so to speak, to act as a focus after the Bridges were gone. And the church – it has been said that the Church of England at this period settled down to 'quiescent mediocrity' and Keynsham was no exception.

John Wesley's concern for Keynsham

John Wesley was riding the country then – he doesn't strike me from his journals as being much given to 'viewing with alarm', but he was much troubled about Keynsham. Mind you, it wasn't the *worst* place in Somerset – he

Miss Fairclough's sketch of inside Jarrett's bakery at the bottom of Bath Hill West, around 1945, showing a sack of flour being emptied into the mixer, flour being kneaded, and tins of dough being placed in the new electric oven. Behind the baker is a supply of tins, and a spare long wooden peel for use in the oven, suspended from the ceiling. Steep wooden steps lead to the floor above, where flour was stored.

A composite picture of a local scene, which Miss Fairclough based on Keynsham lock, near The Lock Keeper. She wanted to incorporate Brunel's bridge, pollarded willows, and barges. 'There was a terrific lot of heavy traffic by river in the 1930s. In addition to craft from Bristol, many barges came from Bath to deposit their rubbish opposite the Polysulphin', she recalled.

said of another village, 'It was the dullest place in the country – I preach on Death in the evening and Hell in the morning, and it seemed they were the very subjects they wanted' – well, he didn't say that of us. And after a while he says, 'At length we begin to see some fruit of our labours' and 'not without *hope* of doing good even here.' By October 1778 there were two schools here and he says, 'I verily think the spirit and behaviour of these two sets of children gradually affected the whole place, which now retains scarcely anything of the brutality and savageness for which it was prominent some years ago.' Although the body of volunteer cavalry from Keynsham that joined the original form of the North Somerset Yeomanry was known as 'The Cossacks', I'm afraid we weren't completely saved.

Keynsham still consisted as it always had, of one long street – from Dapps Hill bridge to the church – but if you look along it – stand anywhere in its length and look at the upper storeys and roof lines opposite – you will see how, especially in the late 18th and early 19th centuries, the bulk of it was, if not rebuilt, at least refronted. A very great many of the houses, large and small, have the very nicely-proportioned, squarish windows of that period and pleasant plain fronts. At some point – I think in Charles II's reign but I can't find when – the Royal Park was disafforested and became farm land. There were, besides the Old Manor, at least three big farms in that street. One at the bottom of Charlton Road – Stokes' old place, now the garage, is its remnant – one at the turning to the Recreation Ground, and one, still a farm in 1920, now Gould Thomas' yard at Albert Road. Plenty of the houses stood in gardens – and they began to build on their gardens. Slowly, High Street and Temple Street became solid, continuous lines of buildings. You can see it in all those roof lines and levels.

The dawn of the railway age

In 1836 the railway began to be built – that great embankment right across the Hams and cutting through the hill made an incredible difference to our landscape – try imagining it without them. (It also nearly ruined some of us, because through road-traffic and the trade it brought nearly ceased).

In the 1880's we began at least to spread out on the Charlton Road side of High Street – Albert Road was built, Rock Road, St Keyna Road – odd houses began to crop up, little lines of houses – we began to be recognisably what we are now in appearance. Or rather, what we were until ten years ago.

Now Keynsham is changing more quickly and drastically than it ever has. Up in the new housing estate that was once the Royal Park and Chace of Keynsham, someone asked me the way the other day. Honesty compelled me to reply, 'Sorry, I'm a stranger here myself.'

But seeing what we have got through in the last 4000 years, and with probably even more time ahead of us, I think we shall cope with it somehow.

This good sharp lettering captured a moment of history in time. This tablet is at the rear of Brass Mill, Saltford, which is now in the process of being restored. (Author's photo.)

THE PICTORIAL MAP OF KEYNSHAM

4ft 9in wide by 5ft tall, it shows a little of the history of Keynsham from the 1st Century AD, to 1945. Miss Fairclough designed and painted this masterly historical sketch map of Keynsham at the request of Mr Walston Vowles and his sister Jane (Mrs G Corbett) to accompany their gift in memory of their father and mother of 1,000 books for the Children's Library, when it was below the Old Library in the former Liberal Club on Bath Hill, after its release from being the Home Guard Headquarters during World War II.

The left and right hand borders of the map are based on a motif from a local Roman mosaic, the four corners being of medieval carvings embedded in The Archway in Station Road. The top shield contains the De Clare's six clarions, adopted in reverse by the Abbey and by Keynsham UDC in the 1950s. Left of the shield is the Norman period, with a kneeling William of Gloucester offering to the first abbot the manorial rights of Keynsham. Behind him is a fugitive Welsh prince who claimed sanctuary at the Abbey and lived to be 100. Behind the Abbot, peasants till the land.

On the right of the shield, below a standing Sir Henry Bridges, two children from the village's first school, which his family endowed, sit reading on the Abbey ruins. Below a top-hatted 19th Century brass worker is a centuries old figure – a woman scrubbing; and a demobbed soldier returning to tractor driving in Keynsham's timeless farming year.

The side panels around the circular map

Top left – the Roman presence. Top right – the coming of Fry's, below which is the Paper Works, a coalminer, Keeling's lime works, and the emptying of an eel 'hully' [trap] at night.

Bottom centre – The Seal of Keynsham Abbey, (now in the British Museum), flanked with two pictures of the Saxon stone from the Station Road Arch and a frieze of wild animals then found locally.

Bottom left – Albert Mill's (the 'South Mill' of Domesday Book) grindstones in action. King Alfred looks down from Dane's Lane (Charlton Road). Above him are signs of the farming year which surround the village, and market gardening at Stockwood Vale.

Inside the circular map

Above the railway line

On the Hams, St. Keyna, with the now harmless ammonites, towers in importance above Fry's factory, where a Roman helmet identifies the site of the smaller villa. Below is the site of the Civil War battle, near which is a top-hatted brass worker and one wearing the brown paper hat in which they worked. Above them, across the County Bridge, is the Gloucester coat of arms, and a farmer in a rowing boat rescuing sheep from the flooded Sydenham mead fields, remembered by Miss Fairclough's father.

Below the railway line

Above the arched Abbey is a scene from Sir T. Bridge's school in Station Road. To its right, the tiny figure of a World War II Civil Defence trainee with his stirrup pump, who enters a smoke-filled hut to extinguish smouldering paper. Left of the school are the Bridge's Alms Houses, with the Bridges and the Rodney [Sir Thomas's wife's] arms. To the left of the footballer, on the route of the old Bristol Road, the stage coach drives down the toll gate for London, having passed the site of the big Roman villa, marked by another helmet above it at Durley cemetery.

The Manor House is featured by a Tudor and a medieval figure, 'too early really' commented the artist, 'but there had been older buildings there'. On the basis of Charles Abbot's suggestion that Room Robes was originally the Hospice of St. John's, the Abbey's guest-house, the seal of the guest-house appears. In the farming area to its left, a fine scroll represents Broadlands School. Below it, the roads for the final Council House estates are laid out but not built on.

Beyond the orchard, the allotments and the fields to the West of the High Street and Temple street, The Royal Park and Chase of Keynsham depicts the huntsman (King Edward I, who stayed with the Abbot) with his hounds and leaping deer.

To the East of High Street the NFS figure of a fireman with a small pump identifies the Fire Station, while the Liberal Club is marked by a member of the Home Guard and two children reading. Below them, at White's Mead allotments (Chew Park), a man is digging potatoes. Off Bath Hill, Dragons Hill is depicted by a derivative dragon and a dragoon side by side. Above them, Handel is composing the Hallelujah Chorus to the beat of the blows of the brassworkers' trip-battery hammers.

By the Talbot Inn, eleven ropes are suspended from a hanging tree, recalling Judge Jeffrey's execution of that number of local rebels of Monmouth's army. Nearby, Mr. Trott the Blacksmith applies his trade. Along Bath Road are the pens of Cooper and Tanner's live-stock market.

At the end of Temple Street a boy and a milking bucket indicate the farm site that was replaced by the school, while the allotments on the west side have been replaced by the Hawthorns and the recreation ground.

In the Dapps Hill, or 'Crox Bottom' area, the Albert Mill is represented by a peasant with a sack of corn on his back for grinding, while above one of the old men of the Workhouse in his washed-out corduroys sits on a bench.

At the top of Steel Mills Lane, across Wellsway, a cricketer indicates the sports playing field.

Chapter 2

The Gibbons family and William's later 'History of Keynsham'

Jonathan Gibbon's wrote of his great grandfather, 'Henry Gibbons, like many local families, came from farming stock. He and his family have been connected with Keynsham for four generations. He had four sons, John, Augustus, Philip and Robert.'

Augustus Froome Gibbons

Jonathan continued, 'Augustus had four children, Arnold, William, Margaret and Phyllis'. A keen life-long Methodist, at his decease a plaque erected at Victoria Church declared, 'Now thank we all for the life and friendship of Augustus Froome Gibbons, called from among us June 13, 1929'.

Writing of one of his children, Jonathan stated, 'William had four children and lived in Saltford and latterly in Keynsham. He was for some years the Chairman of Saltford Golf Club and had business interests in the Wholesale Grocery trade in Bristol. His son Peter was for many years the organist at Keynsham Parish Church.'

William compiled a 'History of Keynsham', being as it says in its introduction, 'Facts collected by W R Gibbons Esq, and its literary composition and general arrangement were by his brother, P Arnold Gibbons, Esq BA 1912'. Jonathan added, 'Arnold was, I believe, a teacher. Both brothers served in World War I in the Somerset Yeomanry'.

Philip Froome Gibbons, 1856–1927

Philip married Miss Ada Scears, the sister of Mr Martin Scears of 6, Avon Road, at the newly-built Victoria Methodist Church opened in 1886. Jonathan wrote of his grandfather, 'Philip was a Justice of the Peace, and lived in Keynsham. Of his five children, Mary, Charles, Martin, Kenneth and Elizabeth, they all lived in Keynsham for most of their lives, apart from Elizabeth. Philip also had business interests in the Wholesale Grocery trade in Bristol.

'Charles served in the Tanks Corps in the 1914–18 war. All three brothers were in the local Observer Corps in the 1939–45 war. Martin also served in the Signal Corps in World War Two.

'Kenneth and his son Jonathan were both in business as Accountants in

Keynsham. Martin and Charles followed their father in the Wholesale Grocery business in Bristol together with other interests.'

A second plaque in Victoria Church records, 'In thankfulness to God for the life of Philip Froome Gibbons, J.P., who died Oct. 10 1927, aged 71'.

The later 'History of Keynsham' by Mr William Gibbons

The original MS was lent out and never returned, but Mr R Headington had a duplicate copy which he allowed me to photostat. Its eighteen pages of scholarly research cover the Roman and Saxon periods, and particularly the early Rolls regarding the Abbey, not to mention the Bridges family. These lengthy medieval matters are outside the period of this book.

Mainly I have extracted some of the later and humbler matters which I hope will be of a wider local interest.

Extracts from the 'History of Keynsham'

'Keynsham, 'smoky Keynsham' as it is called owing to its foggy climate, is a large country town on the high road between Bristol and Bath at the junction of the Chew and the Avon. Its history is longer and more varied than one would expect from a town of the character it now presents [in 1921], and few towns have more completely lost all trace of their past history.'

In Keynsham the house of St John the Baptist is thought to have stood on the site of the new Post Office [now demolished: it stood beside the Old Manor House]. It was at first separate from but afterwards gradually assimilated into the Abbey when it was a hostel. The Abbey being noted for the way in which it entertained strangers, such a building would be useful if not an actual necessity.

Keynsham bridge and causeway

As early as 1540 we find mention of this structure and it is more than probable that there was originally a ford across the Avon here, afterwards superseded by a bridge. Journeying from Thornbury, Leyland tells us that he came to Keynsham where were bridges, one composed of 6 arches of stone wholly in Gloucestershire then almost in ruins and close by one of 3 great stone arches over the Avon. The Bridge and Causeway consisted of 15 arches, many of which can be seen at the present time. (The county seat is a niche out of the Abbey).

Old records say that the tide regularly came up to the bridge bringing with it quantities of that small fish called elvers. (Leyland was appointed King's Antiquary in 1533 and travelled over England for six years collecting histories and antiquities.)

Keynsham . . . was much noted for the salubrity of its air, being quite a noted health resort for Bristol. Particularly was this the case in 1574 when the plague killed about 2000 citizens and many of the survivors built temporary villas here until the effects of the plague had been destroyed.

The dissolution and later Royal visits

[After 6 pages of closely typed A4 paper, dealing in detail with Keynsham Abbey, its foundation, appearance, Abbots and monks, possessions and vicissitudes, and finally its Dissolution, Mr Gibbons knew that Keynsham was again at the crossroads and wrote accordingly.]

So ends Keynsham Abbey. Its history is never anything other than a very misty picture of monasticism and the same uncertainty shrouds its dissolution. But how very real it must have been to this place and how great a difference must its dissolution have made. The history of Keynsham now loses the picturesque character which has so far distinguished it and becomes that of a dirty little village between Bristol and Bath. [Oh!]

With regard to the visits of Royalty since the Dissolution, Queen Elizabeth passed through on her journey back to London from Bristol, for we find a writ of Purveyance issued for finding entertainment etc. for the Queen and her retinue. Also Charles II slept at Chandos Lodge (The Stud Farm) at some time or other, for the Royal Coat of Arms can still be seen in one of the bedrooms over the fireplace. Nothing very worthy of note has happened here really since the Dissolution . . .

John Wesley

He preached in Keynsham several times in 1775, 1776 and in 1781. . . . As he says in his Journal, 'Not without hope of doing some good'. I will leave you to draw your own conclusions as to the state of the place at that time. In 1804 the first Wesleyan chapel was built but that was replaced by the present chapel, which was built in 1886. On the site chosen, formerly stood the house where Wesley used to stay when at Keynsham, a school kept by two ladies.

Wesley mentions that the road near Keynsham was the worst in Europe. Only a short time before he came through, a lady of good birth who resided in Bristol had to walk through the fields to Keynsham as her coach had got stuck in the mud. . . .

The Brass Mills

Keynsham has long possessed Mills, its position at the junction of the Chew and Avon being favourable for cheap motive power in the shape of water. In Domesday Book mention is made that there were 6 Mills in Keynsham and there is evidence that there has long been one where the Brass Mills now stand. Before 1702 (in which these were founded) there was probably an Iron Mill there, owned by a man named Pearsall, who made iron hoops. The Brass Mills are some of the oldest in the country. Up to the beginning of the 18th Century all the brass in England was made in Holland and no one knew the secret until Richard Champion, a native of Warmley, disguised as an ordinary working man, went to Holland and learnt it. As soon as possible he returned to England bringing with him 10 or 15 Dutch, whose names still survive here in Seger, Ollis (Hollis) and Frankham.

He at once started a mill at Warmley, and Warmley Towers is still pointed out to visitors to that place. He soon removed to Baptist Mills and from there to Keynsham, where he bought up all the mills on the Chew and Avon that he could get hold of. The brass made here is the finest obtainable and the work turned out had been of a very high stamp.

The Colour Works used to be the old Battery Mills where the brass pots and pans were made and most old Keynsham families have one or more of these old utensils in their possession. The Battery afterward removed to Saltford where they are still today. [In reality the roof of the Mill is about to fall in!] Also in this connection were the Mills at Pensford and Thomas Bilbie of Chew Stoke, the noted bell founder. For nearly a century this family were named [famed?] for bells, and many bear interesting inscriptions.

There were also a Steel and a Cotton Mill, but the site of the latter is uncertain, but they were probably bought up by the Brass Works. Until recently (until the end of the 18th century) Keynsham people used to be engaged in the clothing trade of this part of the country but that has since passed away.

An 1808 town guide

The following is an extract from 'Capper's Topographical Dictionary' published in 1808. 'Keynsham, a market town and parish in the Hundred of Keynsham, Somerset, is 5 miles from Bristol and 113½ from London. It stands on the south side of the Avon and consists principally of one street a mile long, containing 278 houses, and 1501 inhabitants of whom 183 were returned as employed in various trades. The town is built upon a rock replete with fossil ammonites. . . .

'Here formerly was a considerable woollen industry, but its chief trade is now malting. Here is a good charity school. At the spring of the year the river swarms with little eels about the size of goose quills which are caught by the inhabitants, and by an art they have caused them to scour off their skins when they look very white. They are then made into cakes or balls and fried. Here is a good market on Thursday Friars [?] 24 March and 15 August. The living is a vicarage rated at £11.19.7d.'

St John's Church

The old entrance used to be from Station Road, and several cottages stood round in front of the present door. The screen in the church is very fine and is almost unique, whilst the tomb of the Bridges is worth noticing.

Market and Fair

Until quite recently an annual fair was held at Keynsham in August, the Monday after August 15. This was a regular 'old time' fair with Roundabouts and Coconut Shies besides the horses, cows etc. Originally there was a weekly market but that disappeared on account of the one held at Bristol. . . .

Volunteers and Territorials

In 1817 the first body of Volunteer Cavalry from Keynsham joined what is now known as the North Somerset Yeomanry and continued to serve until disbanded in 1842. They served several times in local disturbances, particularly in the Bristol Riots. When they were disbanded they were called 'The Cossacks' from their somewhat undisciplined condition and their promptitude and efficiency in emergencies. This of course was only a nickname for the Keynsham Troop.

The Great Ham Custom

[The Hams consisted of the low lying land originally on both sides of the railway lines, comprising the town's rugby pitch on one side, and on the other the land below Cadbury's stretching down to the Avon.]

That all stock be removed out of the mead by 12 March. That from 12 March to the 24 June the land be laid up for mowing. That from the last Saturday in August, the mead be stocked for every 3 weeks with one horse, two cows or 4 yearlings or 8 calves for every acre of land owned in the mead. That at the end of 3 weeks all stock be removed for 5 weeks and then restocked at the same rate for 2 weeks after which it is closed for the season for stock. But the gate will be reopened for sheep only in the proportion of 2 sheep or couples for every acre from 20 November until the 12 March ensuing. There was always a hayward appointed to look after the rights of the mead owners and indeed until recently, when Cooper, the last hayward, died.

There was an action in 1908/9 tried at the Bristol County Court as to whether a tenant had a right to put up fences in the mead. The Judge decided that he had not and that the fence must be removed.

In connection with the Bristol Riots in 1831 the troops [presumably not the Cossacks?] were ordered out of the city and quartered upon a local innkeeper at Keynsham, where many houses were searched for booty that was supposed to have been taken from Queen's Square, which the mob had burnt. (The Recorder, Sir C. Wetherell, on arriving at Bristol, was met by a hostile crowd which grew until he reached Queen's Square. Here the mob became unruly and burnt the Square and adjacent buildings.)

Roads

Since the passing of the Turnpike Act a great part of the main road through Keynsham has either been diverted or altered. Starting from Hicks Gate, coming towards the town, the road at the top of Durley [Hill] has been levelled down many feet and a new road made down through the fields much wider than the old circuitous road round by the Tanyard. The houses then standing in front of the church were pulled down and rails put up on a part of the site. These were removed in 1879 and the whole space thrown into the road.

As to how the road originally proceeded towards Bath, there are several opinions. It is thought that the main road went down Temple Street and over the top of Dapps Hill, down to the ford over the Chew close to the Logwood Mill. It then proceeded by Shallard's Lane, round by the old Manor and out to Saltford just opposite Mr. Locke's Farm. Here there was a Turnpike Gate and the road proceeded through Saltford village, the new road up the hill and past the Crown not having been made.

Another theory is that the road used to go down Back Lane past the Parochial Schools down to the Chew by the spring, across the ford and up over the brow of Dragon's Hill to the pound, which is situated near Fairfield Terrace. The hill was so called on account of an old public house that used to crown the brow called 'The Dragon'. Sometime afterwards a road was made from the Lamb and Lark down to the river where a bridge had been made and the road levelled up on both sides. This road turned abruptly down from Temple Street but since then the corner has been rounded off and a wide road made down from the hills. Although one cannot quite conceive how Queen Elizabeth was on the main Bristol and Bath road, yet there is the remains of an old way from Queen Charlton straight down the valley to the Tanyard [at Stockwood Vale].

Chapter 3

Burials at St. John's Church, 1830 to 1850

William Harvey, the local carpenter who made coffins, kept what he entitled his 'Burial Book', and recorded on its rear brown stiff cover, 'Twenty leaves, 16 inches long' [and 6 inches wide].

An interesting entry in it records:
'1838 Dec. 27. For tolling on Nell for Mrs. Ollis, £0.2.0
1839 Jan 17. To tolling the bell 6 hours for the Duke of Buckingham 6..0.'
According to Mr R Headington, a horizontal stroke through the amount signified that it had been paid.

A few local residents still remember the practice in the town for the 'death knell' to be rung soon after a soul departed, one toll for every year of the deceased, so that labourers in the fields could work out for themselves which of their aged neighbours had died. This was quite separate from its use later at the funeral service. The practice seems to have been discontinued around 1930.

Mr Gordon Jarrett recalls the local ringing of the Angelus bell in the evenings, inviting the faithful to say their prayers.

One wonders how much were the customary charges for grave digging and tolling last century? Writing in 1874, Thomas Hardy, in 'Far from the Madding Crowd', explained the charges of dying a pauper, as it affected destitute Fanny Robin.

'And so she's nailed up in parish boards after all, and nobody to pay the bell shilling and the grave half-crown.'

" 'The parish pays the grave half-crown, but not the bell shilling, because the bell's a luxury, but 'a can hardly do without the grave, poor body. However, I expect our mistress will pay all,' said Joseph Poorgrass."

An analysis of the Burial Book, despite its partial illegibility and absence of commas and apostophes, produces the following data:

Year	Number buried	Refs to Wife	Child	Pauper	Times Tolled
1830	18	0	7	2	2
1831	19	1	5	1	2
1832	53	2	15	7	15
1833	41	4	11	5	23
1834	41	3	11	6	28
1835	43	1	9	4	21
1836	24	1	9	1	19
1837	63	3	15	7	48
1838	58	2	16	11	44

1839	35	0	8	7	25
1840	30	0	6	8	21
1850	44	3	6	15	25
Totals	469	20	118	74	273

When analysed, these figures produce some interesting local information, as follows:

Pauper Deaths at the onset of the Victorian era

Over the 12 year period from 1830 to 1841, and the year 1850, out of a total number of 469 deaths, 74 were those of paupers, that is, approximately one out of every seven deaths.

As there was no one to pay for tolling the Death Knell, no such charges are entered. However, the parish paid 2/6 per child grave and 3/- per adult grave and occasionally 3/3.

The first such entry is as follows:

| 1830 | May 12 | Willm Whitey | Child | pauper | 2/6 |

Then come the following representative names, with many in between,

1830	Oct 16	Bettsey Williams		pauper	3/-
1832	Aug 7	John Eashat	Bastard	pauper	3/-
1832	Nov 7	Betty Jones		pauper	3/-
1833	Sept 27	Willm Lanes	Child	pauper	3/3
1837	Jan 29	John Carpenter		pauper	3/-

Names chosen at random of paupers buried in 1839 include Thos. Holbrock, Billy Webb, Charles Godwin and John Bees.

1840 records Charles Abbott, Henry Hicky, Wm Willington and Ann Berry.

1850 Ann Godfrey, Caroline Boulter, John Gilliard and Samuel Harding.

The expense of tolling the bell

In the 12 year period, the 'knell' was used on 273 occasions, which averages 23 times a year. As with most things in life, there are the exceptions, so with the payment of the knell in the burial of children. Most people paid 1/6, but in 1839 some started paying 2/- while others kept to 1/6. However, in

				KNELL	GRAVE
1837	Jan 4	John Veils	Child	2/-	3/9
	Dec 10	Henry Wyatt	Child	1/6	3/3
1838	Oct 31	Thos Baker's	Child	2/-	3/10
1841	June 17	Frances Smith	Child	1/-	2/9

It is with the death of the adults that the length of cost of tolling increased, viz,

1833 Aug 7 To Mrs Williams Nell Tolling 2/-
1850 Jan 24 To tolling the Bell for Mrs Thomas Child 4/-

A page from William Harvey's 'Burial Book' for part of the years 1838–39 showing the cost of 'Tolling on the Bell for 6 hours for the Duke'.

Though the average of 2/3 to 3/6 was common, there were payments of 4/-, 5/- and even 5/7, almost double the norm.

Occasionally grief demanded yet even more, as follows:

1832	Oct 9	Trustee? Swanburn		8/0	12/-
1833	Jan 27	Sarah Dowdell	Grave	8/-	12/-
1835	May 20	James Woods	Wife	10/-	14/-
1832	Aug 4	James Williams	Child	Bastard	3/9

Apart from any financial consideration, there is other information:

1832	May 12	Marking? a plate for late Wm Parsons			0/9
	June 17	Making? a plate Lewish Child			0/6
1834	June 8	Willm May	the Sweep	3/-	4/9
	Nov 16	Mrs/Mary? Ball	Grocer	10/-	11/3

Particularly sad must be the story behind the following entries:

1832	Nov 4	Thos Frankham	Child	2/-	4/-
	Nov 11	Thos Frankham	Child	2/6	4/6
	Dec 9	Thos Frankham	Child	1/6	3/6
1834	Dec 14	Thos Frankham	Child	–	3/3

With two rivers flowing through the town, the following form of death is recorded more than once:

| 1831 | July 3 | Willm Acres? | Drowned | Nell 1/- | 7/- |

This lady of some substance was still a stranger in Keynsham, though one wonders how long she had lived here:

| 1835 | May 26 | Mrs Collins | Bath | 6/- | 9/6 |

Very much a local was:
| 1833 | May 14 | Cantle of the Oak | | 7/- | 11/- |

A grave matter for everyone

Perhaps you could have a grave dug in Hardy country for 2/6 but not in Keynsham, where we have already seen that the customary adult pauper grave was 3/-. Many hardworking citizens only paid the same or a few pence more.

| 1832 | Oct 2 | Williams Collier | 3/- | 5/6 |
| 1832 | Oct 4 | Ann Hurley | 3/6 | 5/6 |

But of course, many felt that love required a greater expenditure. The farmers appear to have been men of substance, as

| 1830 | April 17 | Farmer Hicks | Grave 4 | 8/6 |
| 1832 | June 24 | Farmer Scammell | Daughter | 7/6 |

But they did not have the monopoly of wealth.

1832	Oct 31	Miss Shallard		6/-	10/-
1833	Jan 28	John Harvey Wife	Grave 3	7/-	
1833	June 12	Mrs Wingrove Daughter			10/-

A few weeks later we come to

1833	Aug 1	To a man found Drownd	3/-
1836	Sept 27	Mrs Henderson Grace Nell 3/10	8/-

Even today most people know the whereabouts of Milward House and Milward Lodge, so it is not surprising to see that his family excelled all others in his funeral expenses, as in:

1833	Nov 25	Mr Milward	£1.0.0

Many names well known today occur, though they are not necessarily connected. An exhaustive list is impossible, but here are a few:
Dunford, Martin, Adams, Sheppard, Fray, Chapman, Wiggins, Wills, Reed, Deft, Philips, Howard, Hill, Nott, Wickham, Lewis, Glass, Palmer, Willcox, Brookman, Day, Ford, Godwin, Cox, Dolman, Chewton, Dyer, Rex, Thomas, Fear, Malpas, Strange, Bowles, Light, Pitman, Oldfield, Simmons, Weymouth, Atkins, Brassington, Tippett, Boucher, Granger, Allen, Steager, Bees, Mitchal, Holbrook, Fray, Veasey, Masters, Lippett, Chipper, Hoare, Evans, Briant, Lomas, Hudd, Hale, Rees, Chard, Caukin, Johnson, Woodman, Chappel, Emett, Foux and many others, whose names, we trust, are all written in 'The Lamb's Book of Life'!

The Poor Rate

It is not my intention to record how much was paid out and to whom. That research is for another.

Yet in William Harvey's Burial Book, part of a page, which has been photostated, records just how much he had to pay to help those 'on the parish'. He recorded:

Paid Poor Rate
1836	£0. 5.10
1837	5. 5
1838	9. 9
1839	12. 5
1840	6. 6
1841	17. 6
1842	7. 9
1843	11. 7½

Returning to burials, Mr Headington drew my attention to what he described as a change in William's writing on April 9, 1839. 'It became spidery, as if he had something on his mind. The entry of April 21 explains why, 'Wm Harvey, Child, no charge'. His own child had been ill and had finally died and presumably dad had made the small coffin.

He passed away some time after 1850, his last year of entries, and another made a coffin for him and arranged for the knell and the grave. Sleep well, Father William. We are greatly in your debt.

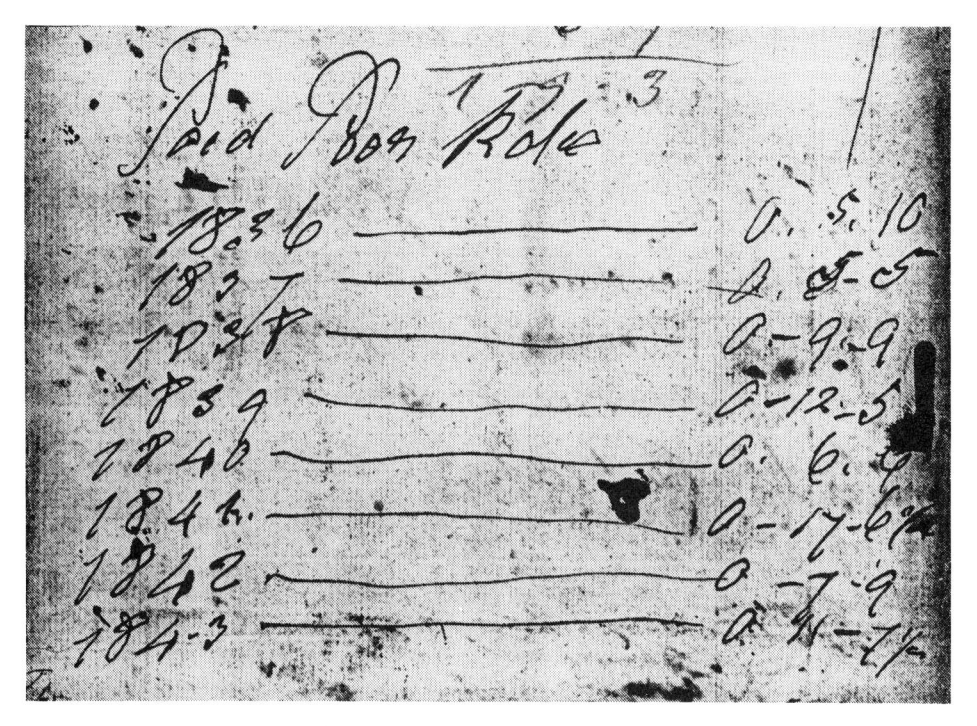

William Harvey's record of what he paid towards the Poor Rate in 1836.

A lovely photo of Hickling's Ironmongers shop, with its wide range of wares. It illustrates the lovely buildings that once graced the High Street.

Addenda – How the epidemic swept through the Union

The first reference to the above building is the entry:

1836   Nov 15   Ann Lewis   Child   Union   3/-

Miss Fairclough quotes Charles Abbot as saying that the row of houses in Dapps Hill that face the Hospital, with a date stone of 1840, but built in 1824 [see B Lowe's, The Poor in K'm and S'ford] were in 1831 bought for the poor, but were overtaken by the opening of the Union in 1838.

I completed the above research on the 12 year period and typed it all out and sighed with relief. But before I returned the Burial Book, I decided to have a last look through the final years, and my attention was arrested at the year 1849 where I discovered that 40 paupers had been buried that year alone, a large number indeed.

More significant still was that on June 2, 5 paupers were buried. Next day 6 were inhumed, with 2 next day, 3 the next, then 4 and so on. In the 22 days between June 2 and June 24, 28 paupers, 4 being a 'Child', were buried. Mrs E White commented that there was an outbreak of cholera in this area around that time, which was the most likely cause of the numerous deaths.

However, that is not the end of the matter. In the past, as we have seen, paupers were inhumed in individual graves, for which the council paid the 3/-. However, with the numbers involved, individual inhumations seem to have ceased and no payments were made for any of the 28. One supposes then that large communal graves had been dug, and the poor bodies placed side by side. Mrs White mentioned the practice in some places of having one communal coffin for paupers that was used over and over again, which meant that when the body reached the grave, it was removed and buried simply in a shroud, and the coffin reused.

An elder from the Keynsham Baptist Church mentioned that there were some four hundred of their members buried in the forecourt of their church, three hundred and fifty of which were documented, and there were certificates for others, bringing the total up to around four hundred.

An elderly Methodist gentleman, who asked not to be named, recalled that he could remember seeing gravestones at the front of both 'Bethesda' and the Chapel almost opposite.

Miss Fairclough said that land for a new cemetery at Durley Hill was not purchased until 1876, so the victims of the epidemic, and those which the other churches could not accommodate because of their limited grounds, must have been inhumed in the churchyard of St John's. This, according to Mrs White, was larger than it is now.

Mr Headington said that his grandfather was one of the last to be buried in the cemetery there, in a now unmarked grave near the church's main West Door. In doing this, the ground was so full of coffins that he was finally placed between his wife and his sister-in-law, with a further coffin near by at an angle.

In 1960 the Council took over the expense and the responsibility of levelling the churchyard and its future upkeep.

A page from the Burial Book of 1849, recording the large number of daily deaths of paupers at the Union, and that they were not buried normally.

Details of the Keynsham epidemic

I wrote to Mr R J E Bush, the Deputy County Archivist at the Somerset Record Office at Taunton, and received the following helpful reply:

'The Keynsham Guardians Minute book (ref D/G/K/8a/7) contains a graphic and extremely detailed account of the cholera outbreak. It apparently began in the Workhouse on 5 May 1849. A Committee of Health for the parish was appointed but did not include the vicar, the Rev G R Harding, mainly because they thought that he was terrified of the disease and proved to have caused unnecessary distress by spreading unfounded rumours. Irate at not having been appointed to the Committee, Harding refused to bury those who had died in the epidemic without an inquest, which resulted in corpses accumulating for several days at a time when the weather was quite hot. Parishioners even threatened to leave corpses at his house if he did not proceed. Eventually the bishop was appealed to, who duly ordered Harding to carry out the funerals immediately.

The epidemic engendered much ill-feeling in the parish – particularly as the Baptist minister, Mr Ayres, and the Wesleyan preacher, Mr Sheppard, regularly visited infected houses while Harding never went near them. The minutes include lengthy depositions by members of the families of those who had died in a tenement block called Swan River.

The Medical Officer, Mr Edwards, reported on 25 June that there had been no new cases in Keynsham since 19 June. There had been 92 cases of cholera, 180 of diarrhoea with choleraic symptoms, and 110 cases of simple diarrhoea – a total of 382 cases in all. The minutes do not appear to supply the total number of deaths.'

'The tenement block called Swan River' has to be the ancient Poor House Terrace almost touching Dapps Hill bridge, which still has a Swan cemented on to the front of it. So it appears that though the outbreak presumably started in the Union, it spread to the homes of paupers still receiving 'outdoor relief', and to other poor families.

A photostat copy of four pages of the Parish Register of Burials kept by the vicar shows that between May 27 and June 12 there were 32 inhumations, 29 conducted by Rev. Harding and 3 by Rev. Astley. Ages of most of the deceased are given, apart from the tragic May family, where Elizabeth and Hannah were buried on June 2, Emily on June 4, and on June 9 John May aged 2 and presumably his father, Samuel May aged 58. Also Elizabeth Lane, whose age is not given.

The other ages were 1 at 9, 1 at 10, 1 at 11, 1 in her 20s, 5 in their 30s, 3 in their 50s, 2 in their 60s and four in their 70s, the oldest being 79. Unfortunately, as Mr Bush pointed out, the Rev. Harding does not specify which of the deaths were due to the plague. But as William Harvey designated most of the deceased as paupers, it would seem reasonable to ascribe most of the deaths to cholera.

The Board of Guardians

On a fine morning in April 1991, accompanied by Margaret my wife, I motored down to Taunton, and there managed to squeeze in a brief visit to

Name.	Abode.	When buried.	Age.	By whom the Ceremony was performed.
William Goddard No. 1241.	Keynsham	June 4th	52	G. R. Harding
Ann Williams No. 1242.	Keynsham	June 4th	15	G. R. Harding
Emily Mais No. 1243.	Keynsham	June 4th	—	G. R. Harding
William Tipney No. 1244.	Keynsham	June 5th	20 mo.	G. R. Harding
Frances Lane No. 1245.	Keynsham	June 6th	77	G. R. Harding
Zipporah Parnell No. 1246.	Keynsham	June 6th	—	G. R. Harding
Thomas Godfrey No. 1247.	Keynsham	June 7th	3	G. R. Harding
Elizabeth Phillips No. 1248.	Keynsham	June 7th	13	G. R. Harding

A photostat copy from the Register of Burials of St. John's Church, Keynsham, for June 4–9, 1849, all of whom were paupers apart from William [Henry?] Tipney. Compare this page with that of William Harvey's Burial Book!.

the Somerset Record Office, to research the events of 1849. A thick leather-bound book recorded in copper-plate handwriting the minutes of the Guardians. Dated June 4, 1849, it recorded:

'At the weekly meeting of the Board of Guardians of the Keynsham Union held in the Board Room of the Workhouse on Monday the 11 of June, present,

Rev H T Ellacombe, Chairman   J B Stanley, Esq VC
J J C Ireland, Esq   J Hughes, Esq
Rev J Phillott   Captain Emerson
Mr Green, Mr Grigg, Mr Lyme, Mr Parker, Mr Pritchard, Mr Procter and Mr Wooley [with not a woman in sight!]

The detailed minutes, running to several pages, were duly read and signed. The clerk reported that he had examined the books of the Master [of the Workhouse] and of the Relieving Officer, and that the latter had expended in the week as under.

'District. First, Second and Third, loaves 840 to the value of £15.1.5 and a farthing. Goods of £16.13.4; Money £93.11.1. Total expenses were £125.5.10 and a farthing.

A 'nuisance caused by a foul and offensive drain' was reported in the Dapps Hill area and ordered to be removed. Further, 'A load of lime to be ordered for the purpose of placing in the drain which runs through and beyond the building called the Labbott'. [Then a row of cottages situated in the park].

The Rev Maunder reported that the cases of cholera in the neighbourhood of Kingswood had, during the week, assumed a milder form.

A letter from the Board of Health acknowledged the Guardians' letter informing them of the Rev Harding's refusal to bury the corpses until an inquest had been held on the bodies.

A further letter was read from the Poor Law Board, approving the arrangements made consequent upon the outbreak of cholera. The PLB also raised the matter of the salary claim [of arrears?] by Mr and Mrs Monk, the Schoolmaster and Mistress. The Guardians ordered that, 'Consequent upon the large number of pauper cases [seeking admission, or dying?] . . . consideration to be postponed.'

Earlier minutes contained a copy of the Guardians' letter to the Bishop of Wells concerning the Rev Harding's refusal to bury the cholera victims, and the Bishop's reply by return of post, peremptorily ordering the inhumation to be carried out at once.

Also recorded was a verbatim report of the confrontation on the one hand of the above minister, and on the other hand of Mr Lyme and a fellow Governor, in which the Rev Harding again adamantly refused to bury the corpses himself or to let anyone else do so, 'in my churchyard', until after a coroner's inquest upon the causes of death, despite Mr Lyme's firm but reasoned request.

The Keynsham Board of Guardians certainly appear to have been the most powerful body in the town, and probably in the district too. Not only did they control the admission to the Union and in effect the lives of those in it, but also as we have seen, the oversight of expenditure by the Relieving Officer of some £500 a month, a vast sum in those days. They ordered material for the lime

Page: 157.

BURIALS in the Parish of Keynsham in the County of Somerset in the Year 1812

Name.	Abode.	When buried.	Age.	By whom the Ceremony was performed.
John Shaw No. 1249.	Keynsham	June 5th	2	G. R. Harding
Samuel Shaw No. 1250.	Keynsham	June 7th	58	G. R. Harding
William Veal No. 1251.	Keynsham	June 9th	4	Rd. Astley Off. Minister
Samuel Cox No. 1252.	Keynsham	June 9th	4	Rd. Astley Off. Minister
Elizabeth Lane No. 1253.	Keynsham	June 9th		Rd. Astley Off. Minister
William Williams No. 1254.	Keynsham	June 10th	66	G. R. Harding
William Chappell No. 1255.	Keynsham	June 10th	7	G. R. Harding
Thomas Dod No. 1256.	Keynsham	June 12th	77	G. R. Harding

[R r]

A second page of burials, showing the handwriting of the Reverend G. H. Harding, when he finally complied with the Bishop's injunction.

washing of an infected property, possibly consisting of but one room! Dissatisfied with the local coffin maker, they decided another supplier in Brislington was to be contacted, to present one [or two coffins?] at the Union by tomorrow by 12 o'clock without fail! [So Keynsham's paupers at least had their own coffins for burial!]

Disciplinarians and autocratic they might have been, the products of that Victorian age and possessing so much authority, but they certainly worked hard in the interests of the Union. On June 4, because of the volume of matters to be decided, it must have been evening when the acting chairman, Mr C C J Ireland finally proposed 'that we adjourn until four o'clock tomorrow.' The board met almost daily during the epidemic.

The Board Room was on the left hand side of the Hospital's foyer, and included the receptionist's area and the room behind it. Beyond the Board Room was the Committee Room, with an enormous table, where during the closing years of the Union, Mr C Dowling would sit at one end of the table, being involved in the running of the Workhouse.

Chapter 4

The occupation, population and housing of Keynsham in 1851

'Daddy, what was grandfather's job in the Victorian period years ago?' asked young Tom. Well, what was Keynsham really like in grandfather's or even great grandfather's day? How did most people earn their living? Did most men really work at the Brass Mill? Were there more women than men living in the village? Did any of them live to be 70 or more? Were there more grown-ups then than children? Was the population growing, decreasing, or stable?

Most of the houses were small, but how many were there, and what was the average number of people living in each? Was the elongated village of Keynsham in 1851 essentially a dormitory town for professional people who commuted daily to Bath and Bristol on the newly-built railway? Or was it more a self-sufficient farming community?

The remaining 'KEYNSHAM PARISH' Boundary Stone, still in situ, in Park House Lane. Some 2ft in height, it is incised with the two large capital letters, 'K P'. In the days before ordnance maps, disputes often arose as to the position of parish boundaries, and the extent to which distant hamlets were liable for the repair of the parish church, hence the practice of 'beating the bounds', mentioned in Tudor times.

Work in the village

Mr 'Ron' Kent, of the Bristol and Avon Family History Society, using the Keynsham 1851 Census, kindly produced for me a detailed answer to Tom's question. Painstakingly, he divides the information regarding 'Occupations' into seven groups, starting with 'Professional and Gentry' and ending with 'Tradespeople'.

Occupations of persons in 1851 Census for Keynsham

1. Professional and Gentry

Men		Women	
Solicitor	2	Matron of the Workhouse	1
Attorney	2	Land Proprietor	8
Surgeon & Apothecary	1	House Proprietor	12
MD	1	Independent	1
General Practitioner	3	Private Governess	1
Master of the Workhouse	1	Annuitant	16
Accountant	1	Fund Holder	6
Magistrate	1		
Vicar	1		
Curate	1		
Parish Clerk	1		
Baptist Minister	1		
Railway Superintendent	1		
Gentleman	1		
Land Proprietor	1		
House Proprietor	1		
Annuitant	1		
Fund Holder	4		

2. Upper(?) Middle Class

Men		Women	
Retired Farmer	1	Farmer's Widow	1
Farmer	40	Farmer's Wife	8
Solicitor's Clerk	1	Farmer's Daughter	1
Banker's Clerk	1	Retired Schoolmistress	1
Engineer	6	Schoolmistress	6
Schoolmaster	3	Assistant Matron at Workhouse	1
Surgeon's Assistant	1		
Retired Pawnbroker	1		
Commercial Traveller	6		
Clerk to Keynsham Union Workhouse	1		

3. Farmworkers and 'House' workers

Men		Women	
Farmer's Boy	4	Housekeeper	5
Farm Bailiff	1	Cook	10

Ag Labs	189	Parlourmaid	3
Ploughboy	1	Housemaid	7
Gamekeeper	1	Chambermaid	1
Groom	4	Nursemaid	5
Servant	9	Laundress	7
Coachman	4	Gardener's Wife	1
Gardener	10	Servant	101
Ostler	1		
Footman	1		

4. Shopkeepers etc.

Men

		Women	
Publican	1	Auctioneer's Widow	1
Innkeeper	2	Butcher's Wife	6
Victualler	2	Baker's Wife	1
Maltster	2	Innkeeper's Wife	1
Beerhousekeepr	5	Milliner	6
Shopkeeper	3	Bread Carrier	1
Grocer, Baker and Draper	2		
Grocer	8		
Butcher	12		
Baker	9		
Clothier	1		
Chemist & Druggist	1		
Tailor	11		
Hatter	2		
Merchant	1		
Post Office Keeper	1		
Barber	1		
Book Maker	1		
Milk Seller	1		
Errand Boy	1		
Felmonger (hides and skins dealer)	1		

5. Army, Police, Railway etc.

Men

		Women	
Lt. Colonel (army), unattached	1	Nurse	1
Captain (army)	1	Workhouse Nurse	1
Lieutenant (army), ½ pay	1		
Chelsea Pensioner	4		
Greenwich Pensioner	4		
Sailor	1		
Disabled Soldier	1		
Master Mariner	1		
Policeman (GWR)	2		
Ticket Collector	1		
Railway Porter	1		
Railway Labourer	5		

Watchman (Police)	1
Constable and Basket Maker	1
Superannuated Excise Officer	1

6. Men of Brass

Brass Manufacturer	2
Brass Worker	26
Brass Tube Maker	2
Brass Roller	1
Brass Smelter	1
Brass Caster	1
Brass Wire Drawer	11
Brass Batteryman	2
Brass Turner	1
Lime Burner	1

7. Tradespeople

Men		Men (contd)		Women	
Carpenter & Undertaker	2	Basket Maker	11	Shopkeeper	1
Sawyer	4	Retired Basket Maker	1	Dressmaker	24
Joiner	4	Saddlemaster	1	Seamstress	4
Mason	25	Saddler	1	Needlewoman	1
Mason's Boy	3	Harness Maker	1	Straw Bonnet Maker	5
Stone Worker	1	Master Shoe Maker	1	Shoe Binder	5
Carpenter	12	Shoemaker	13	Boot Binder	1
Cabinet Maker	1	Bootmaker	2	Charwoman	2
Wheel Wright	2	Cordwainer(leather wkr)	8	Washerwoman	18
Mill Wright	2	Tanner	8	Stay Maker	34
Cooper(barrel maker)	1	Farrier	2	Stay Stitcher	1
Thatcher	1	Blacksmith	13	Sand Seller	1
Cotton Weaver	1	Waggoner	1	Match Seller	1
Carrier/haulier	13	Cattle Dealer	2	Water Cress Seller	1
Miller	6	Plumber & Glazier	2	Mantua(dress) Maker	1
Coalminer	6	Plasterer & Painter	3	Barm(yeast) Seller	1
Engine Driver	1	Painter & Glazier	3		
Coal Haulier	3	Plasterer	1	Pauper	30
Dry Salter	3	Glazier	1		
Dyewood Manufacturer	3	Painter	5		
Warehouseman	1	Tiler & Plasterer	1		
Wax Modeller	1	Chimney Sweep	2		
Flour Dresser	1	Lamplighter	1		
Hawker	1	Senior Scholar	1		
Labourer	76	Workhouse Porter	1		
Pauper	4	Pattern Maker	1		

Mr Kent concluded,
'There are not so many Paupers in my analysis because most said 'Pauper and Labourer', or some such. I have put them "in their trade" if possible.'

It is interesting to see that only three ministers were recorded, the vicar, his curate, and the Baptist minister. No Methodist minister is mentioned. Though only a small village, surely it is of some significance that never the less five doctors and one magistrate lived here?

41 farmers seem to have existed with only 8 wives and one widow! Three schoolmasters and 6 schoolmistresses saw to the educational needs. By far the largest single group of workers were the 189 'Ag Labs' (Agricultural Labourers), followed by the equally impressive number of 101 women servants and 9 male. In today's town, both of these groups have virtually vanished. The well-known brass workers, with their distinctive top hats, then actually totalled only 48.

One of the most significant matters highlighted is the multitude of different occupations listed, and the fact that so many no longer exist today. One imagines that a list of the trades followed in 1775 would not have been too vastly different from those recorded in the 1851 Census, compared with today's totally different technological world.

The population of Keynsham in 1851

Mr 'Bob' Milner was for nine years the secretary of the Keynsham and Saltford Local History Society. His fascinating work on the 1851 Census, which he kindly agreed to me using, has produced a summary of the ages of the villagers, in spans of five years, which he then applies to the local workhouse (now the hospital). He then records the names, ages and precise occupations of those engaged in the well-known local brass mill.

As Mr Milner mentions, the Ollis family were 'descendants of the original skilled Dutch workers', brought over from the Continent for their 'brass' skills in the 18th century. He records the descendants' ages and occupations a century later, in 1851. Miss Fairclough commented that, 'when they arrived around 1720, they were probably regarded as intruders, and that it was not until the following century that they were regarded as 'the Gentlemen Brass Workers of Keynsham', who appropriately went to work in top hats'.

Mr Milner plots the slow rise of the population through the nineteenth century, culminating with a summary of the number of houses and the average number of people in each.

Paupers in Keynsham

I questioned Bob Milner regarding his figure of 9% of the village being paupers, mentioning that some people felt this was misleadingly high, as the catchment area for the workhouse included the poor from several local villages. But he did not accept this and felt his figure to be accurate, pointing out that Bristol and Kingswood catered for the poor of other areas.

Bob then explained the cause of the village poverty, declaring, 'Keynsham was primarily a farming village, but the Lord of the Manor had long neglected the area, so that the style of farming was quite out of date and people barely survived from their small plots of land. Things looked bad'.

Mary Fairclough agreed and commented that, 'There was much grinding poverty in Keynsham in the 1850's, but added, 'We were terribly well provided for with shops'.

KEYNSHAM 1851 CENSUS — AGE STRUCTURE

Age Groups	0-5	6-10	11-14	15-19	20-24	25-29	30-34	35-39	40-44	45-49	50-54	55-59	60-64	65-69	70-74	75-79	80+	Sheet Groups	TOTALS
Males	22	22	19	19	10	17	8	9	11	8	9	8	8	5	3	4	3	3	185
	45	41	33	29	29	19	28	21	12	18	10	10	24	6	11	12	5	1	353
	21	29	11	21	14	9	18	19	10	11	10	8	2	4	3	3	2	2	195
	74	45	26	39	27	26	25	12	18	15	12	14	12	9	2	4	5	4	365
Total Males	162	137	89	108	80	71	79	61	51	52	41	40	46	24	19	23	15	=	1098
F'males	22	19	21	20	28	16	6	9	8	13	11	9	13	3	1	3	5	3	207
	62	41	36	33	35	28	24	13	18	15	15	11	18	8	5	8	8	1	378
	34	25	17	11	19	28	22	11	15	11	5	9	10	6	5	4	3	2	235
	70	41	31	33	31	39	30	20	19	14	14	16	13	10	5	8	6	4	400
Total F'males	188	126	105	97	113	111	82	53	60	53	45	45	54	27	16	23	22	=	1220
Total of Males and Females in each Age Group	350	263	194	205	193	182	161	114	111	105	86	85	100	51	35	46	37		

GRAND TOTAL
Males   = 1098
Females = 1220
====
2318
====

Children under 15 form 35% of the total population.

How interesting to note that in this village of 704 women of 20 and over, there was work for 34 stay makers. Truly they would have kept the local ladies upright.

The 76 labourers would have included those who were a familiar sight in old Keynsham, the corduroy-wearing stone breakers. They would sit by the roadside with their hammers, cracking large rocks into smaller pieces for repairing the local roads. Their grandchildren live here still.

Abstract of the population of Keynsham for each of the 10 year periods from 1801 to 1901 with the addition of the years 1951 and 1971 for comparison:-

Year	1801	1811	1821	1831	1841	1851	1861	1871	1881	1891	1901	1951	1971
Population	1591	1748	1761	2142	2307	2318	2190	2245	2482	2811	3152	8277	19258

Number of houses and density of population per house for the year 1851 for the four different areas covered by the Census:-

Area	Inhabited	Uninhabited	Density
1	113	2	5.16*
2	88	6	4.89
3	86	3	4.56
4	153	5	5.00
Total	440	16	4.93

*Excluding the Workhouse and occupants.

For comparison, the figures for 1951 and 1971:-

Area	Inhabited	Uninhabited	Density
1951	2405	–	3.44
1971	6378	–	3.02

Notes
- Population figures from 1801 to 1901 from the 'Victoria County History'.
- Figures for 1951 and 1971 from the Keynsham UDC 'Abstract of Accounts' for the year ending 31st March 1971.
- The area numbers 1 to 4 have no special significance.

The Keynsham poor – 1851

Age Group	Outside Workhouse		Inside Workhouse		Total Outside and Inside	
	M	F	M	F	M	F
80+	3	4	3	4	6	8
75–79	3	9	4	1	7	10
70–74	2	4	4	1	6	5
65–69	2	2	3	1	5	3
60–64	0	5	6	4	6	9
55–59	0	1	2	0	2	1
50–54	0	2	2	1	2	3
45–59	0	1	3	3	3	4
40–44	1	1	2	3	3	4
35–39	0	2	1	0	1	2
30–34	0	1	1	4	1	5
25–29	0	0	1	10	1	10
20–24	0	0	2	6	2	6
15–19	1	0	4	7	5	7
11–14	0	3	19	8	19	11
6–10	4	4	8	7	12	11
0–5	3	2	11	11	14	13
TOTAL	19	41	76	71	95	112

All figures compiled from the 1851 Census

The Keynsham 'poor' as given above are all those classed in the Census as PAUPERS (nearly 9% of the total population)

The Keynsham Brass Mill Industry in 1851
Names, Ages, and Forms of Employment

Name	Age	Form of Employment	Name	Age	Form of Employment
Rich. Brookman	57	BW	⎡Jos. Ollis	80	Retd. Brass Neater
Isaac Buck	70	WW	⎢Nicholas Ollis	75	BW
Jos. Carpenter	67	WD	⎢Wm. Ollis	48	BW
Thos. Carpenter	65	BW	✱ ⎢Chas. Ollis	40	BBM
Jos. Carpenter	60	BW	⎢Wm. Ollis	24	BW
Chas. Carpenter	23	WD	⎢Abel Ollis	15	BW
J'thon Carpenter	33	WD	⎣John Ollis	14	BW
Thos. Evans	37	WD	Geo. Reed	55	BW
Wm. Frankham	51	BW	Geo. Reed	29	BW
Geo. Frankham	25	BW	Ischar Sheppard	61	Brass Roller
⎡Wm. Frankham	18	BW	Robt. Sheppard	46	Brass Roller
⎢Luke Fray	57	WW	Saml. Sheppard	46	WD
⎢Jon. Fray	52	WD	John H Sheppard	18	WD
⎢Chas. Fray	30	BW	Edw. M Sheppard	17	WR
✱ ⎢Wm. Fray	21	BTM	Francis Smith	49	WD
⎢Edw. Fray	18	BW	Frank Smith	15	BW
⎢John Fray	17	BW	Robt. Shortman	42	Brass Melter?
⎢Geo. Fray	15	BW	Jos. Welington	28	BW
⎣David Fray	12	BW	Saml. Wellington	28	WD
John Giles	40	BW	Robt. Williams	46	BW
Thos. Green	41	BTM	Edw. Williams	18	WD
Jos. Gregory	29	BBM			
Thos. Hall	49	WD			
Wm. C Harper	51	BW	BW		Brass Worker
Wm. C Harper	14	BW	BTM		Brass Tube Maker
J Martin Harper	12	BW	BBM		Brass Battery Man
Jos. Hudson	77	WW	WW		Wire Worker
⎡Wm. Krinks	68	BW	WD		Wire Drawer
✱ ⎢Wm. Krinks	46	BW	WR		Wire Roller
⎣Danl. Krinks	46	Brass Turner			
Jos. Malpas	59	BW			
Jos. Martin	56	Brass Caster			
Mathew Monks	81	Brass Founder			
Rich. Mortimer	55	Brass Manufacturer			
Edw N Mortimer	28	Brass Manufacturer			

Total Number Engaged: 56

It is likely that many of those listed above are actually RETIRED even though the Returns do not list them as such. To assess those actually engaged in 1851 it would be safer to discard those over 64. Say, a total of 50 actually engaged?

✱ Descendants of the original skilled Dutch workers - early 18th century.

The Ollis Families in Keynsham, 1851

Ref. in Census	Ages M	Ages F	Occupation	No. in each household
1/5		29	Housekeeper	2
		12	Daughter	
1/7	37		Grocer & Railway Lab.	8
		35	Wife & Grocer	
	13	5	Child	
	10	3	"	
		1	"	
		2mnths	"	
3/29	80		Brass Worker, Retired	3
		67	Wife	
		36	Daughter, Stay Maker	
3/35	75		Brass Worker	3
		77	Wife	
		48	Daughter	
3/71	48		Brass Worker	5
		48	Wife	
	24		Brass Worker	
	15		" "	
		13	Daughter	
3/83		50	Grocer & Housekeeper	2
	38		Gardener & Brother to above	
4/24	45		Agricultural Labourer	11
		45	Wife	
	21		Agricultural Labourer	
		17	Daughter, Stay Maker	
		15	" " "	
		13	" " "	
		11	Child	
		9	"	
		7	"	
		3	"	
		3mnths	"	
4/29	40		Brass Worker	7
		40	Wife	
	14		Brass Worker	
	12	5	Child	
	9		"	
	3		"	
4/50	59		Boot & Shoe Maker	7
		65	Wife	
		28	Stay Maker	
	22		Patten Maker	
		8	Child	
	5		"	
	3		"	
1/3	25		Servant of Farmer	1

49 People in 10 different households.

Note The "Ref in Census" column refers to the area group returns (nos. 1 to 4 in red) and the households schedule reference no. in these returns.

A reminder of hard times, this 3ft high bier, made by Taylor and Cray of Melksham, possibly was purchased when the new Durley Hill cemetery opened in 1878. Above the metal frame was the wooden base, 92 in by 30 in, with 3 metal rollers and 4 leather belts on it. Below the base, wing nuts enabled the steel bars to be removed. There were no brakes.

It seems to have used up to the late 1920s. Patrick Morris, the Keynsham cemetery attendant, or sexton, featured above in April 1994, commented then, "It has not been out for the 20 years I've been here." It was used by the Workhouse for pauper funerals, and by local people unable to afford the expense of a horse-drawn cortege. The springs and turning mechanism still functions excellently. Solid rubber tyres fit into iron frames on the wooden wheels.

Chapter 5

William Charles Ollis, 1850–1935

Born in a cottage at the original Labbott in the park, he later moved to Spring Cottage, Bath Hill, another of the many properties owned by the Mill. First he married Mary Ann Carpenter and in his 60s, Lucy Baker. Of his nine children, only three survived to maturity, his eldest son Frederick John and two daughters, one becoming Mrs Guyan and the other Mrs Headington. His grandson Ronald described him as, 'A very popular, jocular man, a real character, who had been a great dancer in his time. On his second marriage, he moved to his new wife's cottage on the Avon Road/Fox and Hound's junction, the house being demolished a few years ago.

'He was the last general foreman at the Harford and Bristol Brass Company's Avon Mill works, Keynsham, and retired in 1923, some three years before its closure. He was a "hard hat" man, which signified his authority and standing among the workforce. He was nicknamed "Muller" as he wore a half height style of top hat, the tall ones being out of fashion, and their smaller version known as "Muller"s cut down".

'If there was a shortage of work at the Keynsham Mill he would go and help at the "Battery Mill" at Hammer Lane, Saltford, known today as "The Shallows". Only brass pans were made there, and the incessant loud hammering-out of the brass made William and many other employees deaf. In recognition of his years of service, when the company closed down and everything was shut, just before all the moveable machinery was sold and removed, he and the Saltford foreman, both in their 70s, were given permission to make a final pan for themselves. "We can't supply the brass, but if you have any, you can make a keepsake for yourselves".' They did, and the deep, wide and beautifully-made pan is one of Ronald's prized possessions.

He mentioned that, 'Another privilege granted William by the Mill Company was the right to catch eels by the Keynsham sluices. Mr Tyler, the basket maker who lived in Stockwood Vale near the tannery, made special cages similar to crab baskets. These were known locally, in our North Somerset dialect as an "ully", which allowed the eels to enter but not get out. These were placed in the river below the sluice gates. The eels would lie in the mud, and when the gates were opened, they were washed into the baskets. This franchise was quite a lucrative affair, and the catch, still alive, would be given to the guard on the early morning train for Billingsgate, London . . . Today eels are still caught at Saltford.'

WILLIAM CHARLES OLLIS, 1850–1935

The last general foreman of the Harford and Bristol Brass Company's Avon Mill, at Keynsham. He retired in 1923 prior to its closure in 1926.

A slippery business

Ron recalled that, 'Adult eels could be up to 2 1/2 feet long and as thick as your arm. You seized them with great care from the ully, or they would have your finger off. Grandfather had a nasty scar on his thumb from being bitten by a young one. If it had been an adult, he would not have had a thumb! You first got them out of the ully with a net, then with mutton cloth over your fingers, you seized them behind their heads by putting your fingers into their gills.

'To skin an eel, mother would put it on the wooden table in the kitchen of our Spring Cottage home, and having stunned it with a blow, would put an old-fashioned two-pronged fork through its head, which pinned it to the table. Then with a sharp knife, she would just cut through the skin at the neck, without entering the flesh. Then with her fingers, she would pull the skin back to its tail in one piece, the eel still alive. They could live for hours out of water. It was a horrible business; I hated it and never did it. Then it would be washed in salt water and cooked.

'They were considered a great delicacy, like the snails they also used to eat. Both my parents and grandparents ate both eels and snails. They would collect snails locally from non-ivy covered walls and from under stones. They would be dropped alive into boiling water, so they came out of their shells. Then they would be cleaned out, and rewashed with hot water, then back into cold water [A good thing they had their own well!] and served with vinegar and pepper. Dad ate his with brown bread and butter, but mother swallowed them whole like cockles and mussels. Possibly this special appetite was a hang-over from their European origin.'

Mr Richard Newport said, 'The Chew was famous for its eels and there were traps all the way up the river. Keynsham was famous for its eel pies, though I never tasted any. Elvers were common here then. On one occasion there was a terrific catch of 15 hundredweight of eels at Saltford at one go and the catch was sold at Bath.'

Primogeniture

To return to Ron Headington's account of his grandfather, 'It was William's surviving son Frederick John Ollis that at Spring Cottage started the baker's business, and also the haulage firm, and who later owned the field off Avon Road known as "Ollis's Field", where the local summer fetes were held. Later the land was bought by Frys, who in turn sold it, until finally its Abbey National owners sold it to developers, who built the Meadow Park Housing Estate on it.'

'Bert' Robe elaborated on the use of the Ollis' field when he wrote that it 'was used variously as a soccer, cricket and rugby ground and annually at August Bank Holiday for the Keynsham Flower Show, Sports and Carnival.'

Evidence of the skill of Keynsham's earlier craftsmen.

Mr 'Ron' Headington holding the last brass bowl made by his grandfather, the foreman Mr William Ollis, prior to the sale of the closed Brass Mills. The site is Ron's delightful cottage at Saltford.

'Roger-James, Basket maker, 1, Bethesda Cotts. Temple St', Kelly's Dir. 1914. He had lived at No 1 from at least 1906. There Gwen Glover nursed his dying wife or mother, and was presented with this basket, which many years later she gave to me. It was probably made from the local willows: Mr Jeff Whittock recalls being taught wicker work at Bath Hill School during WWII. Both photos are the author's.

Chapter 6

The difficult days of unemployment, the workhouse, and tramps

'Finding a photograph of her father, Mr William Henry Penetta, brought back memories to Mrs Violet Saunders, of Keynsham, concerning stories he had told her of the hard life he and others had to endure during the last quarter of the 1800s and early 20th Century', records an article in the Keynsham Chronicle of July 3 1987.

It continues, 'Known as Chibby to many, Mr Penetta could remember when Keynsham was little more than a village.

'Chibby had no schooling and started work at the age of eight in the Henbury Mills near where the waterfall is now in Keynsham's Memorial Park. His wage for helping with the processing of glass and emery papers was just three shillings (15p) per week. One of Mr Penetta's earliest memories was the time he was led by a dog to a huge 36lb salmon lying on the banks of the River Chew. The fish was so strong it pulled Chibby over and help was needed to properly land it.

'When work was hard to get, Chibby got himself a pair of clappers and worked on a farm scaring birds off the wheat fields from 4 am to 9 pm for which he was paid three shillings a week. He recalled one farmer who had to care for a wife and eight children on a mere 15 shillings (75p) a week.

'Another source of income was breaking stones for paving country roads or for laying in Bristol's cobbled streets.

'Times were so hard Chibby used to buy dog biscuits at a shop for his dinner. Women and children would glean wheat from the fields after the harvest, then carry it to Brislington for the grain to be threshed, take it back to Willsbridge for milling and then carry a couple of large sacks of flour to Keynsham. Housewives would make the dough and take it to the bakehouse before the product was ready for human consumption.

'Mr Penetta's nickname Chibby was given to him because he saw an eel at the mills and promptly cut off its head with a shovel he was carrying. 'Chibby' means the 'head of an eel'. Eel catches of four hundredweight were often caught at a mill in a night. The eels, a delicacy, were sold by the mill management to a Bath fishmonger for one shilling (5p) a lb.

'Recreation for Chibby and his friends was shooting birds or collecting bird's eggs, which, he said, were 'very tasty' when fried. Chibby told his daughter about the 21 lime kilns at the bottom of Dapps Hill, which was then the industrial centre of the village. The Logwood (Albert) Mill dye works was then a flour mill.

'Just before Christmas, a fair was held at the Crown Fields [opposite the

Crown Inn on the Bristol Road]. This was in the form of a large market where villagers replenished their food stocks. The present day fatstock show is a descendant.

'There being no public transport many people, including Chibby, used to walk to Bristol and back every day to work. They had to be careful. Thieves snatched valuables in the dark and "roughs" might set upon anyone. Gas street lighting was a new innovation and used only in the village. Keynsham had street lighting before Bristol.

'The only building not to have changed in Mr Penetta's life was Keynsham's parish church, although the road has taken about 30 ft off the churchyard.

'Except for a short time in the Militia, Chibby never left Keynsham. In his retirement days he gave himself a 'luxury' – lying in bed until 7 am. He loved gardening and listening to the radio. His only regret was he never went to school so could not read in his spare time', concludes the Chronicle.

Edward 'Tom' Carter, JP 1885–1962, of Paulton

Mr P M Bonsall, writing in 1988 a biography of Edward Carter, headed 'A life of service', described how, 'During the economic depression of the inter-war years, mass unemployment was a major social problem of such dimensions that few working people, whether 'respectable' or 'rough' ', escaped its consequences completely.

'Numbers employed in mining fell by over 50% in the inter-war years. The closure of Farrington Pit put Ted Carter out of work in 1921. Following a short-lived boom at the end of the First World War, the mining industry entered a period of rapid decline. Widespread unemployment, short-time working and extensive poverty were common in the coalfields, until the economy began to pull out of the recession around the mid 1930s. . . .

'The last resort for people in dire need was to apply to the Poor Law Guardians (the Public Assistance Committee after local government reform in 1929) for "out relief" which was the contemporary equivalent of supplementary benefit or family-income supplement. Money raised by a local rate was distributed by the elected Guardians of a group of parishes (which constituted a Poor Law Union), either as "indoor relief" in the workhouse (usually inhabited by those too old, too young or too infirm to support themselves) or as "outdoor relief" in the form of payments in cash or in kind to people living in the community. All relief was given on loan (and signed for as such by the recipients) at the discretion of Relieving Officers, under the supervision of a Relief Committee made up of members of the Board of Guardians.

'Labour leaders urged those in need to apply for relief with no sense of shame or humiliation . . . Ted Carter and the Labour Guardians of Clutton did not encourage "scroungers", or have any sympathy with people "on the fiddle". They did take legal action to recover debts when they considered that the loan could be repaid without causing undue hardship. . . . What they did not do was harass the impoverished to repay their debts, for they did not regard poverty as a crime to be punished', wrote Mr Bonsall.

The General Strike

'When King George VI came to the throne in 1936, Britain had been passing through difficult times. Industrial unrest had characterised the years immediately following the First World War . . . the number of those without work began to mount ominously from 1920 onwards. In 1926 there had been the grave General Strike which it was estimated had cost the community £150,000,000 and within a few years of its collapse, the country was faced with a financial crisis (1931) by which time unemployment had mounted to nearly three million. The situation was still serious when King George VI came to the throne and certain industrial regions of the country had become known as 'depressed areas'.' (Newnes Pictorial Knowledge, vol 2. p 245).

Mrs I Andrews has an interesting memory of this event. Her father, Benjamin John Ollis, was a civil engineer who worked in the drawing office of the Great Western Railway in Bristol. On the outbreak of the strike, he was given the added responsibility of helping to man the local railway bridges and level crossings, to ensure that they were not wrecked by those on strike. Isabel recalled him going out at night on duty, wearing a special armband, but she was not sure about that.

Mr Leslie Harding remembered hearing at that time that the local railway lines were getting rusty as no trains were running, and a gang of men going down to see if this was so.

Work and unemployment in Keynsham

Leslie recalled that between the wars, 'There was quite a bit of unemployment in Keynsham. The Labour Exchange was half way between the Charlton Road turning and next-door-but-one to the Fear Institute. There were long queues in those days that stretched up as far as the Conservative Club for the weekly dole.

'All fit men were given a pick and shovel and sent up to Burnett to dig out the road to lessen the steepness of Burnett Hill, so in effect you were paid for working instead of the dole. You were told 'Do that or you're getting nothing', which was how people talked to you then.

'The man in charge of the dole was Fred Dorey. He was a hard man, but he was the son of the master of the workhouse, so he had been brought up to be tough. His wife was a piano tuner. I was a boy then and worked for him and did odd jobs and he was nice to me. I expect he had to be tough with the labour force.

'It was only men who queued, and they lined up quietly. There were some lazy men who were always on the 'labour' and you never saw them work. It used to be about a dozen, but then it grew larger. The more energetic men tried to keep their jobs.

'I recall seeing groups of men stood around talking as they had nothing to do. Then they would go off to their gardens. Most people had large gardens and grew their own vegetables. Most cottages had fruit trees in their gardens. Women would drag along the dusty road large branches of trees that they could not carry, for fire wood. Some would do this regularly. My dad had a

KEYNSHAM

SOMERSET

An appreciation and practical Guide to its most Interesting Features

by

W. B. BUSH, M.A.
and
C. G. EWINS

THE OFFICIAL GUIDE of
The Urban District Council
of Keynsham

All rights reserved

THE HOMELAND ASSOCIATION LTD.
WELLINGTON HOUSE, WELLINGTON STREET
LONDON, W.C.2

Printed in Great Britain

CULVERHAY BOARDING AND DAY SCHOOL
FOR GIRLS

CULVERHAY is situated in the healthiest part of Keynsham. There is every facility for such games as tennis, hockey, etc. Pupils can attend swimming baths in Bristol or Bath. The tuition covers all branches of a first-class modern education, with preparation for any examinations desired. Special attention is given to French conversation and Music.

KEYNSHAM, Near BRISTOL

Terms on application   Principal : Miss Messervy

R.D. HICKLING & SONS

Ironmongers
and
Plumbers

'Phone & 'Grams:
No. 13

KEYNSHAM

28

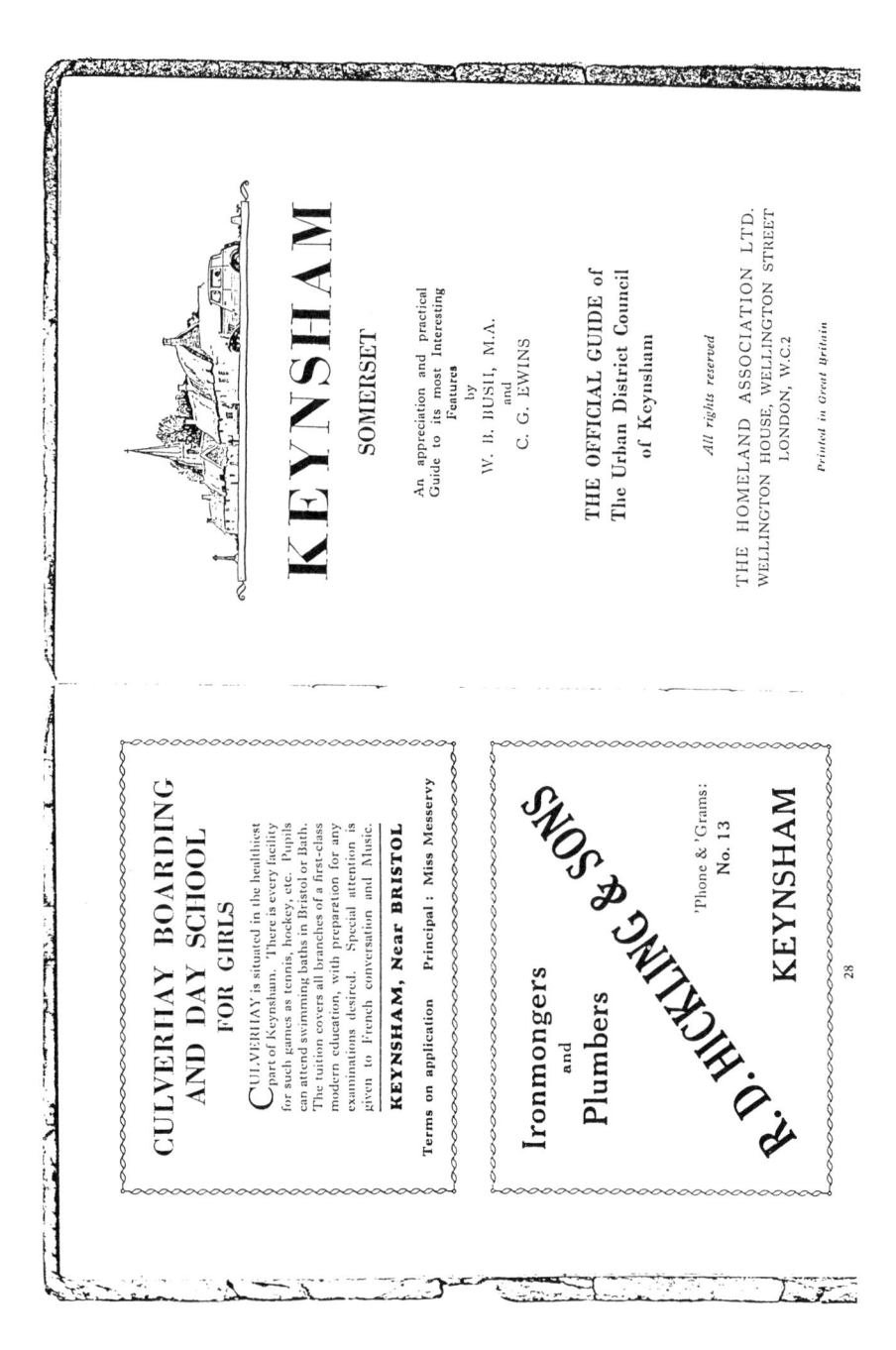

Pages from the 1930 Keynsham Guide. Culverhay School was off Station Road, facing the railway. Hicklings of the High Street was a very well-known firm that supplied nearly everything in the ironmongers' trade.

barrow so if he saw wood hanging about he would wheel it home, so mum never needed to do it, as he had a trade as well.

'You could drag timber along anywhere in the road. The road was theirs. There was nothing else on it.

'There were only just enough shops for the district, so I can't remember any closing. The Brass Mills were working in my time but I only just remember it. Before World War II it was taken over by E S & A Robinsons. That's where paper sacks, instead of hessian, were first made.

'We all wore caps and jackets and scarves, some had corduroys. Other people wore leather leggings. People were poor. We were always poor. Most people were poor, but we never went hungry. The women could always make stew, and keep adding vegetables to it.

'Girls who went into service earned about ten shillings (50p) a week, which for females wasn't too bad as they were kept in food, clothes and were housed by their employers. Some men earned less!

'Between the wars I was a building trade apprentice and got five shillings a week. An unskilled labourer, working with a pick and shovel, using only effort, earned a shilling an hour for many years. Some employers would get them to work for 10 pence (5p) an hour. My boss, Mr Wiggins, was a good fair man and paid a shilling an hour. So a labourer, working an 8 hour day, for 5 days, and 4 hours on Saturday would receive £2 4 shillings. He was lucky if he got £3 50 shillings. A tradesman would get one shilling and six pence (9p). Having served my apprenticeship, I got one and seven pence ha'penny an hour in my first pay packet,' said Mr Harding.

Keynsham born Doreen Gyles remembers that between the wars there were many tramps and beggars on the streets of the town, asking for food or money. Mrs Gyles thought that some were ex-servicemen, and that some had come from the north of England.

William Sherer's recollections

Mr W Sherer comes from a line of successful Christian business men. His grandfather William John Sherer had a confectionery business on Bath Bridge, Bristol, and even the bridge is gone now. He was a local preacher. John's son Herbert William had a wholesale and retail butcher's shop at 30, Bedminster Parade, Bristol. Later he opened a butcher's shop in Temple Street, Keynsham, under his name, H W Sherer, which his son Courtenay Sherer later took over.

Young William came to Keynsham in 1911 when he was but three. His family lived in what today we designate 'Courtenay Road', off Wellsway. In those days it was called Jack Hicks Lane, after a well-known cattle drover who lived there and who came to an untimely end. Either he committed suicide or was hanged, and definitely buried, at Gibbet Lane at the top of Pensford Hill.

Mr Sherer recalled that there were only four houses in the Lane, all with their own wells, with lovely cold water. 'The pump only went dry once, and that was in 1921 when we had a terrible drought. We would go down to the River Chew for water two or three times a week at Chewton Keynsham Bridge, where the local farmers would go daily to water their cattle.

'Though the town had electricity so early (originally generated in a shed I am told), it was not until 1951 that it arrived at Courtenay Road. Our house was called Smisby, with stage connotations. . . . I was told by an old SWEB man, now dead, that the tall cast-iron lampstand in the road outside the Parish church, was the first one to be erected in Keynsham. Up to the early 1930s, all the street lighting went off at eleven o'clock. Later they kept it on longer, but certainly not all night.

'I started school at five in 1913 at Longton House. The teachers were Miss Knowles and Miss Corkquindale. In 1915 after the First World War had started, they closed the school and went nursing, and the school never opened again. I then went to St Mary Redcliffe, where they were very strict. I used to go by train and on my first day I got on a troop-train bound for Salisbury Plain, but an Inspector saw this and a soldier put me off. Later I was at a Business School at Clifton.

'In those days Burnett Lane [Wellsway] was a narrow road with high hedges both sides. . . During World War One I can recall buses from London going through the town on the way to Avonmouth and the Front. On the destination board at the front were messages such as 'Berlin' or 'Kaiser, here we come'. A British Observation Balloon came over, rather like the later barrage balloon. People were frightened and dad said to me, 'Run up to the top of the field out of harm's way'.' [The field was part of the 8 roomed house and 5 acres that his father had bought in 1911 for £500, their home 'Smisby'.]

Mr Sherer said that the General Strike of 1926 did not affect Keynsham much. 'The shops remained open. Ollis the carrier carried on with his work. This was an agricultural village. There were always odd jobs to be had on the farm. My father employed men at haymaking time and it was quite a social occasion. He would provide bacon and ham sandwiches and flagons of cider.

'The average farm worker was ground down and paid low wages, but most grew their own vegetables. Many people in Temple Street kept pigs a little distance from their homes. There was not much unemployment in Keynsham as it only had a population of 3,000 and there were the Brass Mills, the Colour Mill, the Albert Mill and the Soap works' [The Polysulphin].

William said that despite any local hardship, people were honest. It was customary for a butcher's shop to stay open until 11.00 pm on a Saturday night. From Bedminster his father Herbert would then drive back to Keynsham with £500 in gold sovereigns on him, quite unmolested in his pony and trap, with his faithful horse Dolly. He was sufficiently secure to pick up local lads who had been courting in Bristol, and, there being no buses, were walking back to Keynsham.

'There were many horses to be seen in those inter-war years. I recall one bolting in the High Street, and people scattering in all directions. There were a lot of accidents involving horses. Some dealers would buy hay ricks and take the hay to Bristol to sell. One night a man was standing on the shafts of his cart going up Burnett Hill, without a rear light. Unfortunately a lorry coming behind him did not see him, so he was knocked off the shafts and killed. Really he should not have been riding in that position, but people took all sorts of risks.

'The RDC built a lay by beyond the Crown Inn for steam waggons to obtain water from the brook. At first these waggons really frightened the horses. However, the lay by was built right at the end of the steam engine period, so that it was hardly used at all as petrol driven cars had arrived. . . . Horses had for many years been used to the dirt roads so that when they were eventually tarmacadamed, the horses slipped on them. Their annoyed owners complained to the local Highway Surveyor. Later rubber shoes were attached to the horses' hooves, which was especially helpful on icy roads.'

Mr Sherer recalled that there were then local poachers. 'They were not violent. They were good-natured rogues. Foxes kill chickens, so if they shot one, they would bring it up to father, who would give them half a crown. I remember Charlie Glover as one. He was a good-natured man, and his sons. He would build and thatch our ricks at Courtenay Road. He built them round as it is very windy up there.

'At one time Mr Travers owned Chewton House, and he kept chickens. One night someone broke in and stole many of his dead birds ready for market. If that was not enough, the following rhyme was scrawled across the wall of the shed,

'We rob the rich to feed the poor,
We've left a cock to breed some more.'

'Rather cheeky,' concluded William and he chuckled heartily.

The early days of Keynsham Workhouse

Prior to the Civil Registration Act of 1837, each parish had kept its own records and was responsible for its own poor. The late Mrs Gwen Newman spoke of the houses at the bottom of Dapps Hill which had been used to house the destitute prior to the coming of the workhouse. This was not the row dated 1824, but the Chew Cottages row, dated 1685. In a recent brief conversation with the lady who owns the last house there, she confirmed that this was indeed so, adding that her deeds recorded that the houses were for the poor. These cottages were contemporary with the Bridges' Almshouses on Bristol Road, built in 1686, which originally stood above road level!

Mr Ted Carter, mentioned earlier, was a fine Christian man, a local preacher and a great champion of the poverty-stricken working man. His daughter Hilda, later Mrs Clifford Dowling, writing in the book, 'Keynsham Hospital, a commemorative study of the first 150 years of Keynsham Hospital, 1837–1987', edited by Brian Woodham, wrote,

'In 1926 my father was Relieving Officer and the work connected him to the Clutton and Keynsham Workhouses. Sometimes I went with him and became familiar with both places. Often I, with other children and adults, would visit the workshouses to entertain the inmates. I felt it was a part of Christian work to bring a little sunshine into their lives'. (page 16).

Subsequent to the publication of the 'Commemorative Study', Mr and Mrs Dowling kindly gave me a fascinating, unsigned and undated document on the Workhouse, typed on three large sheets, each 12 in. by 17 in. (30 cm by 43 cm), the contents of which now I reproduce.

INDEX OF ADVERTISEMENTS

	PAGE
Accountant and House Agent	
William F. Upton, 35 High Street, Keynsham	26
Auctioneers and Estate Agents	
Messrs. Cooper & Tanner Ltd., Beech House, Keynsham	29
Baker. Messrs. Pearces', High Street, Keynsham	30
Builders	
Messrs. Green & Hodge, Bath Road, Keynsham	32
J. C. Hutchings, Esq., Longreach, Main Bath Road, Near Keynsham	23
H. Willcox, Esq., 86 Bath Hill East, Keynsham	1
E. L. Woods, Esq., "The Uplands Estate, Saltford	24
Edward Wiggins, Esq., Kelston House, High Street, Keynsham	21
Builders, Decorators and Sanitary Engineers	
Messrs. W. Cooper & Son, West View Road, Keynsham, and Highgrove Street, Totterdown, Bristol, 4	27
Carpenter, Builder and Funeral Director	
Herbert W. G. Ibelsten, Esq., 10 Charlton Rd., Keynsham	29
Chemists	
Messrs. Mills & Mills, 37 High Street, Keynsham	31
Chemist and Optician	
B. J. V. Nicholls, Esq., Bath Road, Saltford	25
Draper, Milliner and Furnisher	
T. C. Parson, Esq., 46 High Street, Keynsham	31
Compo-Seal. Messrs. Oliver Keeling & Sons, Keynsham	2
Educational. Culverhay Boarding and Day School for Girls, Keynsham	28
Electrician. H. J. Gill, Esq., Church Square, Keynsham	30
Hairdressers. E. M. Halliday, Esq., High Street, Keynsham	27
Hardware, China and Glass	
Messrs. Carter, 50 High Street, Keynsham	1
Ironmongers and Plumbers	
R. D. Hickling & Sons, Keynsham	28
Laundry	
"The Bath Hygienic Laundry Co. Ltd., Oldfield Park West, Bath	Inside front cover
Ophthalmic Optician	
A. E. Mills, Esq., 37 High Street, Keynsham	31
Printers	
St. Keyna Press, 54 High Street, Keynsham	26
Psycho-Theurapahy	
Augusta Burton-Smith, 12 Bladud Buildings, Bath	Inside back cover
Quarry Master and Stone Merchant	
John J. B. Perry, Esq., 24 High Street, Keynsham	Outside back cover

---

MODERN LABOUR-SAVING
HOUSES FOR SALE
From **£650** *95% arranged*

J. C. HUTCHINGS
Builder and Contractor

LONGREACH, MAIN BATH ROAD
Near KEYNSHAM

Six miles from Bristol, Six miles from Bath

Call and Inspect or write to
ALHAMBRA, 280 BATH ROAD, KEYNSHAM

Car always ready to fetch prospective buyers

Telephone—KEYNSHAM 51 or KEYNSHAM 350

Special Vitrolite Panelling in all Bathrooms and Sculleries

HOT AND COLD WATER IF REQUIRED

Houses built at Stockwood Vale, Keynsham, to suit all intending purchasers, from £495
Ground Rent £3 12s. 6d. per annum. Arrange 95%

The 'Advertisements', from the Keynsham Town Guide, form a succinct list of many of the town's important business people around 1930.

'The Keynsham Union Workhouse completed in 1837 was built to comply with the regulations of the Poor Law Amendment Act of 1834. It was not built in the best part of the town. It was sited near the Mill, the Gas Works, a large number of lime kilns and some very poor and multi-occupied cottages. It served the Parishes of Keynsham, Brislington, Burnett, Compton Dando, Corston, Kelston, Marksbury, Newton St Loe, Priston, Queen Charlton, Saltford, Stanton Prior, Bitton, Hanham, Kingswood, Mangotsfield, Oldland Common and Siston.

Gradually the old poor houses, run by the individual parishes, like the Queen Charlton one still extant on Charlton Cross Roads, were sold off and the poor had either to get out-relief in their homes (if they could – it was in theory illegal) or come to the Union in Keynsham.

Householders who had rateable property worth £30 per annum voted to elect a Board of Guardians who, until the Board Room at the Union was finished, met at the Lamb and Lark Inn. Daniel Cave J.P. was the first Chairman, and for many years Thomas Oxford was the clerk, and kept the records in an immaculate copper-plate hand-writing.

From the early records the Guardians met frequently and worked hard. For instance, the documents show their concern for the inmates' welfare. In 1839 they rebuked the Supplier over the quality of his bread. In 1838 they allowed the inmates to have visitors every Wednesday from 9 to 12. They took special care of lunatics, boarding them out in private asylums, and inspecting their conditions. The Workhouse in Keynsham does not seem to have borne much resemblance to the dreadful workhouses of Victorian fiction. The regime was drearily disciplined, not harsh. Unlike the Workhouse at Andover where the inmates starved, the diet at Keynsham seems to have been stodgily sufficient, plenty of oatmeal porridge, potatoes, bread and cheese, but with meat, bacon, tea, sugar and vegetables (from the Workhouse Gardens) appearing on the menu. In fact the Guardians seem to have been criticised for their provision to the inmates, for they found it necessary to explain in the newspaper that the Roast Beef and Plum Pudding Christmas Dinner was provided out of the Guardians' own pockets, not out of the rates.

The inmates were provided with uniforms, in which serge, calico and Welsh flannel predominated. Underclothes were not at first provided but the women were given stays. Many inmates were described as 'filthy' on admission; some were described as suffering from the 'itch'.

Children were separated from their parents. Visiting was allowed on Sunday afternoons. In 1864 there was a near riot when the Master would not allow the mothers to go to the Girls and Boys Rooms and give them bread and dripping or whatever they had kept from their own meals. Four unruly women broke several panes of glass.

The children were to be educated in the Workhouse School, presided over by a Master and Mistress. The School Mistress was to be between 25 and 45 and 'without encumbrances'. Her salary in 1841 was £20 and 'such provision as the House affords'. She had to reside in the house and 'make herself generally useful'. The poor Schoolmistress had a hard time of it; the children were ill-disciplined and very difficult. Miss Sully was constantly exhorted by the Guardians to enforce her commands but seemingly without much success.

There was no corporal punishment allowed in the School and to be confined to the 'Refectory Ward' for a couple of hours on bread and water (the usual punishment) seems to have had little effect.

The maintenance of discipline, although it was not regarded as a serious problem, must have been difficult. The Punishment Book records offences and the punishments meted out, though the dates indicated these were not daily occurrences. The Master and Matron of the House, the School Master and School Mistress were the victims of verbal and physical abuse.

'Throwing gruel over the Matron' is one offence recorded. Swearing, fighting, abusing the officers and refusing to work, breaking windows, disorderly conduct, attacks on other inmates, especially the physically-handicapped, all are recorded. What Ellen Ford got up to to be punished 3 times in a fortnight for 'Filthiness' we shall never know.

Despite its common title 'Workhouse' there was little work provided, apart from the maintenance of the house, gardens and grounds. Most of the inmates were not able-bodied. They were the old, the infirm, the handicapped, the sick, and women and children, widows, deserted wives, unmarried mothers, and orphans. Keynsham was better than most workhouses in that lunatics were not sent there but were paid for privately at an asylum at Box, prior to the establishment of County Asylums. One of the greatest difficulties for staff and inmates alike was that, apart from segregating the sexes, all categories of pauper were lumped together, a situation that remained virtually unchanged till 1948.

In the early days of the Keynsham Union inmates came and went with an ease not intended by the original Act. One woman entered and discharged herself 20 times in 7 years. The Workhouse filled up in the winter months. A night's lodging could be had in the Casual Ward in return for some work the next day. Some entered the Workhouse to get medical help. Edwina and Louisa Clark entered the Workhouse, having been on out relief, at least 5 times and 5 of their children were born there. The Medical Officer had to attend all confinements or he did not get paid. Workhouses were used as lying-in hospitals, not only by unfortunate girls making a first mistake, but by regulars, who came in to have their 3rd, 4th or 5th illegitimate child.

Another function filled by the Workhouse was the registration of Births, Marriages and Deaths. In 1836 when this was introduced only the Workhouses had the necessary system of national organisation. They also undertook the organisation of vaccinations.

Although the conditions in the Keynsham Union were probably as good as in any workhouse it was still a dreaded place. The purpose of the 1834 Act had been to shame the poor into self-reliance. Entering the Workhouse had a terrible social stigma. It was difficult for an inmate to find work. Children reared in the Workhouse were shunned when they attended ordinary schools and found it difficult to get work later on. Some children at Temple Street School were told by their mothers to stay well away from the workhouse children. Fear of having to go into the Workhouse was a constant dread, especially for the old. Too often it was their fate. Until the introduction of Old Age Pensions, in 1908 a third of all old people died in the Workhouse.

The Keynsham Union, judging by the records, seems to have been humanely run and administered, but its inmates, paupers and officials, were the victims of the kind of life the Act enforced. After the Royal Commission on the Poor Law reported in 1909, attempts began to be made to tackle the causes of poverty, sickness, unemployment, low wages and old age. Keynsham Union changed its name to St Clements House in 1930 and became Keynsham Hospital in 1948, when the National Assistance Act swept away the old Workhouse system. 'It cannot have been much lamented,' concludes the document.

The summary of paupers in the Keynsham 1851 Census, listed in detail elsewhere, records that in that year 19 men and 41 women were receiving out relief. In the Workhouse, a total of 76 males and 71 females of all ages were receiving in relief, of which a combined 31 males and females were over 60, and a total of 75 were under 20.

A fascinating book. 'A commemorative study of the first 150 years of Keynsham Hospital 1837–1987' was produced to mark the occasion. One of the writers was Brian Woodham, who contributed an informative section entitled, 'From Workhouse to Hospital, 150 Eventful Years'. He wrote, 'Years ago, when known as 'the Poor House, Workhouse or Poor-Law Union . . . the majority of Keynsham residents viewed the cold, austere place with almost total horror. Tales of mystery, intrigue, a cruel master and stone floors set shivers down the backs of local people.'

He continued, 'Before St Clements Road was developed and houses built, Keynsham 'Workhouse' was bordered by allotments, a high-hedged picturesque lane and a market garden to the west, a lovely orchard with ducks, duck pond and a little stream to the north, while to the east and south were the green water-meadows and sloping woodlands of the Chew Valley and its winding river.

'Beside the lane was the mortuary, past which we used to run like hell, and nearby the washhouse, where tramps and other down-and-outs or 'out-door patients' were cleansed. The drab interior of the Workhouse felt stony cold and looked spartan. Flagstone passageways exuded an atmosphere of foreboding as though leading to rooms and wards of sinister mystery.

'The Workhouse was ruled with king-like authority by the Master and Matron. Vagabonds, tramps, people of nothing, would call here for supper, a night's sleep on straw and an oatmeal breakfast. But first they had to crack a quota of stones (used for roads) or cut up wood, then have a naked scrub and wash down.

'But the Union was not the sinister hell-on-earth place it was made out to be. Sure there was an instance, told me by Mrs Claudia Brown, who used to live in Temple Street of old, concerning a master and matron who kept the Workhouse's meat rations for themselves. Their dog lived better than the inmates, who were fed the proverbial dry bread and water. And conditions were pretty hard. Yet in many ways the Workhouse was in fact the only refuge paupers had. Going back a hundred years, or less, times were extremely hard; illness, starvation, violence and a no-hope attitude were rife. The Workhouse was a comparative haven for the destitute. Without it many would have laid by the roadside and died.

'The Union provided shelter, food – meat three times a week – medical staff, church minister and a teacher. Yet still some people considered it 'the end of life' to go there. This stigma persisted right up to fairly recent times and even when it became Keynsham Hospital. . . .

'Initially there were 120 inmates. In September 1841, for the quarter ending on that date, there were 183 'in-door' patients and a staggering figure of 1486 'called at the door'. Average weekly cost per head of indoor paupers was: food 2/6, clothing 5d, total 2/11. Salaries came to £18 in 1841 September's quarter. Maintenance of books, stationery, advertising cost about £4.10.0, vaccinations 15/2, mops, brushes £5.15.0, petty expenses, postage, carriage of parcels, £5.17.0, purchase of two pigs £4, vetches for the garden £1.11.4, in maintenance, master etc £11.7.6.

'The Workhouse was in many ways self-supporting. For example £33 was made from selling oakum, £12.13.0 from potatoes grown in the garden and the charge of stones broken by the tramps and overnight stayers brought in more cash.

'And they seemed to have ate plain and simple but well. During that quarter in 1841 they got through 51 sacks of potatoes, 395 lbs of bacon, 441 lbs of oatmeal, 9,768 4 lb loaves of bread, 1,815 lbs of beef and mutton, 619 lbs of cheese and 278 lbs of butter.

'They all must have been scrupulously clean, for the Workhouse then got into a lather with 406 lbs of soap; it also lit 59 lbs of candles, consumed 54 lbs of Congou tea, burnt 24 tons of brush coal (at 62½p per ton) and sampled the 'sweet life' with 346 lbs of sugar, while 544 lbs of rice and 83 lbs of treacle made the saying 'Pop goes the weasel' a kind of reality,' wrote Brian Woodham.

Tramps and stone breaking at the Workhouse

Mr William Sherer remembers how in the 1920s he used to accompany his father from their Courtenay Road home, down Burnett Hill, through Steel Mills Lane and up Workhouse Lane, round along St Clements Road and in the back entrance to the Union, or 'the Spike' as some people called it. They would take two horse and carts to collect stone, broken by the tramps. 'It was like Portland Prison, with a supervisor walking round all the time. Father used to slip them a shilling. There was hardly any talking', he said.

William explained, 'Keynsham being a stony place, the slabs of stone would come from the nearby ploughed field. The pieces would be about 2 ft square, and the men, standing to use their 14 lb hammers, would break the stones into pieces about 4 in square. The old full-time stonebreakers who sat by the roadsides used special hammers. There were some four or five men working when we were there, and when they had finished, they loaded our carts using shovels.

'Father needed the stone to improve the rough track that led to Smisby, our home. Then he put gravel on top of the stones. Later he bought a further 6 acres of pasture above us, which flanked Wellsway. Then he added 18 acres below us, where the Lytes Carey estate now is. He used the land for grazing sheep and cattle. He was, of course, in the meat trade. Sadly Smisby was demolished in 1966 for the Courtenay Road Estate.'

He recalled that the tramps, though roughly dressed, were knights of the road. 'When they entered the Union they were searched for money, so they would hide their few pence in their 'bank', removing stones from the wall on the hill up to 'the Spike', and retrieve it when they left, when they would be given a voucher to spend on food. They usually went to Clutton next. In the 1920/30s if they had two stamps on their National Insurance cards, the Workhouse excused them from work, as they were classed as 'diligently seeking work.

'They were perfectly harmless, oldish and some spoke quite well. They would call at mother's for hot water to make tea, and ask, 'Any old shirts, Missis?' They would put a secret sign on the gates of those who were very good to them, but I never found out what it was.

'The men who lived in the Workhouse wore corduroy trousers and coats. The girls were given grey dresses and white aprons. At school they were treated very kindly by the teachers and other children, who gave them sweets and chocolates. The teachers told the other children that they should be very thankful to have their own homes and parents. Most of the Workhouse children were orphans, and I believe they had to rise early and scrub round their beds before school.'

Mr Sherer thought that, though husbands and wives were separated at the Union, there were not many married couples there. Mainly it was men, he thought.

Mrs R Gyles remembers girls from the Workhouse walking up Dapps Hill for school, in a crocodile-line, in their boots and black dresses and white aprons.

Three Workhouse characters, Percy, Frankie and Johnny

Keynsham born Mrs Lily Harrison, brought up in Temple Street, recalled that, 'As time went by, we small children got to recognise some male inmates from the Union, who almost became characters in Keynsham. One was called Percy, a tall man who carried a wicker basket down the High Street to Dr Harrison's to collect medicines for fellow inmates at the Workhouse. He didn't seem very intelligent, and people just called him Percy [instead of the more polite 'Mister' of those days]. He wore a type of uniform that all the men wore, so you knew where they were from.

'Another one was a short man that we children got to know as Frankie. He always had a sort of grin, instead of a smile. He would dance in the street if you asked him. He was a little simple but harmless. Sometimes you saw both of them walking through the town together.'

Doreen Gyles' eyes lit up when I mentioned him. 'I remember him! He was a bit simple and wore a trilby hat that probably some one had given him. For a bit of a laugh people would ask him to dance, and he did. Everybody loved Frankie', she said.

Hilda Dowling, drawing on her considerable knowledge of the inside working of the old Workhouse, wrote in the 150th Anniversary 'Study', 'I remember Percy Seeney and 'little Johnny', who were always together, coming to Zion Methodist Church at the bottom of Albert Road on Sundays. Percy would pump the organ handle up and down smiling to the congregation so happy to be of use. Their outfits, caps and boots still stand out in mind. Although they were moved to Clutton during the changeover in 1948, they would find their way back to Keynsham sometimes, both still smiling.' (page 16).

She went on to say that in January 1940, her husband Clifford 'was transferred to Keynsham as Relieving Officer, when the 'Workhouse' was known as St Clements House and had an office in the front part of the building.'

Mr C Dowling explained to me that after 1930, different 'Workhouses' catered for specific needs. 'After that date, all the children were gone from Keynsham. We had to look after adults who were sick or handicapped [hence Percy and his friends]. Avon Ward and Harrison Ward at the back of the Union had always been used for those who were ill.

'My responsibility was the administration of 'outdoor relief' in Keynsham. I used to visit people in their homes to assess their needs. I made a weekly payment in cash, according to a laid-down scale of fees. Once a month I had to supply a report on what money I had given out. Another of my responsibilities was to admit people to St Clements, or take them to another home, during the period 1930 to 1948.

'While the men in the old Workhouse worked in the garden, the women helped with the washing and in the kitchen. There was a large allotment just outside the Union where Balmoral Road is, and our men grew food there until the 1948 changeover', concluded Mr Dowling.

Unsure of the exact number, he thought there would have been some 70–100 adults at St Clements in its last days in 1948, made up of a roughly equal number of men and women.

One imagines that when he called on local people as the Relieving Officer, he would be widely welcomed. Yet human nature being what it is, no doubt some hard-up people would feel that they should have had more.

'And Death shall have no Dominion'

A few days after my conversation with Mr Sherer, I met him again unexpectedly in Avon Ward. Our thoughts turned to the theme of Dylan Thomas's poem on death. Mr Sherer said, 'I feel sorry for the paupers who died in the Workhouse years ago. They were put on a covered waggon, and taken to Durley Hill Cemetery, where they were buried in unmarked graves next to the road, beneath the row of trees still there, with nothing to show for their lives.'

". . . .When their bones are picked clean and the clean bones gone,
   They shall have stars at elbow and foot. . . ."

'For those who were poor, but belonged to local families, things were different. Theirs was the sad but ignominious experience of following, all of them on foot, the undertaker and his men, who pushed the coffin through the narrow High Street on a bier, with a few flowers on it. The weeping family would walk behind the bier to Keynsham Cemetery Chapel, while passers-by would stop and take off their hats in respect.

'The last time I saw this was as late as 1933, though I saw it several times before that. It was advertising your poverty before the world', William said.

[But if you could not afford a horse-drawn hearse, then there was no option.]

". . . .Though they go mad they shall be sane,
   Though they sink through the sea they shall rise again. . . ."

'The most impressive funeral that I ever saw was that of Sergeant Downey, who was given full military honours at his funeral in 1913. Aged 80, he was the only Keynsham man who had taken part in the Crimean War [1853–56], where he lost one eye. A widower, he lived in Bath Road with his son-in-law Mr Pike. He was carried through Keynsham on a horse-drawn gun-carriage, his coffin draped in a Union Jack, accompanied by the Regimental Band, who played the Dead March, the first time I had heard it. The soldiers looked very smart in their red tunics, and the Town Council joined the procession. He was buried in Compton Dando.

'The last horse-drawn funeral that I remember was in 1928, and was that of Mr Frank Packer, a successful Bristol business man on my maternal side. The whole turn-out, with black horses and a black hearse, was most impressive,' concluded Mr Sherer.

". . . .Split all ends up they shall not crack,
   And death shall have no dominion."

A few days later on a wintry February morning I met Mr L Harding in his front garden, and asked him if he could remember the deceased of impecunious families being pushed to Durley Hill Cemetery on a bier. 'Oh yes, it was quite a common sight. They had a good service at the Cemetery, and the funeral did not cost them anything. The Council paid for it. We were well provided for in Keynsham. In fact I think the bier is still down there now,' he said, smiling, as he energetically carried on clearing the snow from his foopath.

Poor people paid insurance agents one old penny a week as premium to provide them with sufficient funds, on death, for a proper burial and to avoid a pauper's grave.

Chapter 7

'The Keynsham I remember before 1980'
as related by Mr Richard Henry Newport

'I was born in 1906 at 55 High Street, Keynsham, in one of the upstairs front bedrooms. Though today it is owned by Mr Joll, in 1896 it was leased by Mr Loxton, a draper, who used to breakfast in the cellar below the shop with his family, with its only light from an oil lamp. Why else was a proper fireplace there which naturally reached to the roof? On the floor were beautiful large ammonites . Coal was delivered through a small opening at pavement level straight into the cellar. We only used it for coal. The steps down were dangerous as they were steep and there was no light and no hand rail.

'From being in business in Bristol, my father, Joseph Edwin Newport and his brother, as 'The Newport Brothers', took over the lease from Mr Loxton, who continued his business from a shop just across the road. Above the shop front, which today is virtually unchanged, were the words, '4 yards to Newport – 4 miles to Bristol'. In 1898, when the population of Keynsham was about 2,002, father bought his brother out.

'My mother, Ellen Eliza Newport, was the kindest mother one could ever have. She had a very hard life in bringing up seven children, on just 25/- a week. Gerald the eldest was born in Bristol, migrated to Canada and died in 1912. Jessie married Fred Gullis and died in 1986 aged 93! Margaret only lived one week. I lived at the back of the shop with my parents and my elder brother Thomas and my younger sister Joan. She married an Air Force Pilot who was killed in the Second War and then she married the Rev Easton, who died in 1985. Joan is now 76.

'We had a gas stove in the kitchen for cooking, and gas lighting in the shop and house. Coal from the cellar was used for heating. On washing day mother used a big coal-heated copper bowl and for drying the clothes had a hand-turned mangle kept in the shed at the side of the house.

'In the kitchen we used a pump from the well with a long curved iron handle and a large knob at the end. We had to prime the pump with tap water to get the flow going. The water was fine for washing, but we used Company water for drinking. We had a long tin bath by the pump which father covered with a wooden top which we used as a table, and just removed it for baths. He made a hole in the bottom of the bath, and inserted a plug, and put a pipe under the floor boards which simply drained the water to outside the house.

'The dining-room floor was made of stone, which father covered with linoleum which he glued down. Also he made his own billiard table.

'When my sister Josie was a clerk in Bath at Elands, she would come home for the weekend by train. But because she could only afford the fare from Bath

The tailoring business of Joseph and Ellen Newport, at 55, The High Street, Keynsham, next to the Eyelet Factory, circa 1905. Today the business of Edward Joll, the lower front of the shop is largely unchanged except that clothes no longer hang outside the shop.

Walter Carter's china shop was opposite the Newport tailor's, and the double doors led beside the house to the rear stables and garden. After the Carter's pony died the doors were blocked up and the passage made into another room with a large front window. Notice the jugs and kettles suspended either side of the front door.

to Saltford, she walked from there to Keynsham. My other sister Jessie then used to take Joan in a pram, and with me by her side, would walk and meet her halfway.

'Mother's motto was 'Nothing succeeds like success' and 'Do it now'. This I try to do, and answer letters and pay bills the same day as I receive them . . . My dear mother took out an insurance policy against funeral expenses, and the first and final payment was, I think, £6.00. She lived to be 90, and had no fear of dying because she had a true faith. When she was about 75 she made herself a beautiful white night-gown and knitted a long pair of white stockings, ready for the great day.

'On a Wednesday afternoon, being early closing, father would cycle to Badminton to the Duke of Beaufort, to measure and make breeches for his staff, in appreciation of which the Duke permitted father to inscribe over our side door 'Beaufort'. Father used to sell socks at 6½d a pair, caps 1/- and 2/6, ties 1/- and shirts at 3/6. If at 9.30 on a Saturday night a customer came in and bought a pair of trousers and found them to be too long, father would tell him to go and buy a drink, and would throw the trousers over to mother, who had to stop whatever she was doing, and have the trousers ready for 10 o'clock, at no extra charge.

'During the war I remember Mr Pocock near the Fever Hospital looking after 60–100 mules for the army. If people wanted a new suit and were unable to pay for it out right, father would let customers pay for them at 1/- a week. Of course, some people got behind in their payments, so on a Monday morning during school holidays, father would get the ledger out, and see who owed him money. Then I had the job of cycling up to Mr Pocock, or to Bitton or Compton Dando or the other villages to try and collect the arrears.

'On a Saturday morning I used to take a bowl and a 6d to Mr Parsons the baker at the top of Bath Hill. He would fill it with yeast, which I would take home, where mother would mix it with flour and dried fruit. I would return the mixture, with a further 6d to Mr Parsons, who would bake it for 2–3 hours into a delicious dough cake, for me to collect.

'If father wanted some new suits, he would engage Ollis the Carrier who would take his horse and cart into Bristol to fetch them. Father always had an errand boy who would come in the evenings after school and deliver clothes parcels to customers' homes. On a Saturday the errand boy would come in the afternoon and work until nearly 10 o'clock. About 9.30 mother would make him a mug of cocoa to drink and give him a large slice of her fresh dough cake. He'd love that. Of course the boys were paid for their services, and when they were old enough for better-paid work, they'd pass the job on to their younger brothers.

'Father was an atheist. He also used to drink too much, though mother made sure we children were in bed before he came in. Father used to say his drinking enabled him to do more business. Anyway, mother had a hard life with him and in 1918 she finally left him, taking Joan and myself with her. He carried on with the shop, living alone, until 1932 when he died. Mr Peters then assumed the lease for two years, until Mr Joll senior took over the premises. I was one of the three men present at father's funeral at Durley cemetery, and there were no women present. He was carried there in a motor-driven hearse.

All I got from my father's estate was a bookmaker's bill, which arrived on the day of the funeral.

'Mother, a fine Christian lady, made sure that I went to St John's Church, where I was in the choir and was paid 2/6 a quarter. The Rev Hatcher chose me as choir boy to pump the organ on a Sunday morning, for which I was paid 3d a service, which was reduced to 2d if I went to sleep during the sermon. It was quite easy work. Only the wealthy were permitted to sit in the centre aisles near the front, for which I expect they paid pew rents. Traders had to sit in the side aisles. There are three mentions of our Newport family in the church.

'The leaders in the choir were Mr Cotterell, Mr Prosser, Mr Taylor, Mr Bartlett, and Mr Philip Bush, who had a strong voice, and in the absence of loud-speakers, always read the lessons. The choir ladies were Mrs Cottrell, Mrs Bartlett, Miss Prossor, Miss Philip, Mrs Bush, Miss Shellabear, Miss Jacobs, Miss Harvey, Miss Newport and Miss Fairclough. The church was lit by gas chandeliers.

'In my time we had three doctors in Keynsham, Dr C Harrison, Dr Willett, and Dr Peach Taylor.'

The 1914–1918 war

'My earliest memory was what we used to refer to as the Russian Bear dancing on the weighbridge near the Lamb and Lark Hotel. To a small boy like me it seemed enormous when it stood on its hind legs. It seemed as big as an elephant. It was on a chain, but there was no whip nor cruelty. When it had finished its dance, the man would put his hat down. Then they would go off on their tour. They would come two or three times a year.

'I started school at six, at Longton House in the High Street, under Miss McCorcall and Miss Knowles. I was with the younger children downstairs with one teacher, while the older children were upstairs with the other teacher. There was a playground at the back which seemed large and was great fun. I was there for three years. At eight I was sent to St Mary's Redcliffe, the endowed boys' school in Bristol. I dreaded the idea of going as there they used canes!

'I used to catch the 8.10 train there and the 4.10 train home, and the season ticket for three months was 11/11d. On reflection, I cannot speak too highly of the school.

'As a boy I used to play with a metal hoop, also spinning-tops of many shapes in the road, and at marbles in the gutter. Indoors was billiards, snakes and ladders, ludo, draughts and cards. I was taught to play chess when 9 by my uncle, who promised me a shilling the first time I beat him. This took me another 9 years, but then he paid me 2/6d.

'During the 1914–18 war, Belgian refugees fleeing from the Kaiser's occupation of their land came to Keynsham and lived in the large old house between Milward House and the Old Manor House, now demolished. We felt very sorry for them as they seemed nice people.

'Wilkins and Pearce were the two bakers in the High Street on the opposite side of the road from us, towards the church. During the war, troops which we thought were from Salisbury Plain came through the town in convoys of trucks en route for Avonmouth and France. Of course this was very exciting for us, and we all turned out to cheer the troops. Somehow Pearce knew in advance of their coming, and would bake a special batch of buns, which he would then throw individually to the passing troops, who slowed down as they passed his shop.

'My sister and I caught scarlet fever and were sent to the local fever hospital for six weeks. My elder brother Thomas Cyril was eight year older than me and joined the Gloucester Regiment's Cycle Corps, and used to cycle over

Private Thomas Cyril Newport, eldest son of Joseph and Ellen Newport of 55, The High Street, Keynsham. Here, in 1914, is Tom in The Gloucestershire Regiment's Cycle Corps uniform with his army issue of a heavy bicycle with its front and rear wheel oil lamps, a pump and repair kit, and a rain cape neatly folded on the strong carrier over the rear wheel. His putties would keep his trousers away from the oily chain when cycling.

Sadly, he was blown up by an enemy shell on active service in France, on his nineteenth birthday.

to see us at the shop, possibly from barracks in Bristol. He was a wonderful brother, and when I had recovered from scarlet fever he brought me home on the handlebars of his army-issued cycle. That was the last time I ever saw him. He went to France, where on active service he was blown up by an enemy shell on his nineteenth birthday. They never found his body.'

Some of the local shops in those early days

Number 1 the High Street was still the Electric Works, with the Railway Inn next door run by the Baileys. At 31 was Bert Harding the postman, while Longton House School was 33. 35 was the house with the village pump, and next door at 37 the post office. 41 was Lloyd's Bank and at 43 Mr Hickling, the manager of the Colour Works, with his seven children.

45 was a house that later became Percy Baker the Outfitter. Near us at number 47 used to live Mr and Mrs Kohler. He was the barber and though he was a German he was never interned during the war, possibly because he had an English wife. Later they moved up to number 21.

49 was the Picture House, which was 3d a show on a Saturday morning, sitting on hard forms, but it was great fun. Later it became the Mattick Brother's garage, with a petrol pump on the pavement.

51 was the Bowdens. Really he was a chemist, but he was also the local dentist. For this work, at 1/- a tooth, he would take you into the back room where, without any anaesthetic, he pulled out the offending molars. He would tuck his long beard in his white coat, lest a pain-driven patient should grab it in his moment of agony. Mrs Bowden would stand beside the patient with a bowl of hot water to soothe the gum, clean the face and wash the tooth, which would then go on display in the front window of the shop, joining the gruesome line of teeth. Some advertising!

53 was the eyelet factory, now the Halifax, where an extraordinary number of people seemed to work. We were 55, and at 57 was Michael Cook the watch mender, who was also the verger.

John Carter the undertaker plied his trade from 61, and his son Geoffrey, born six days after me, was my first friend. At 63 was Heal's oil shop, with Miss Withers the Draper at 67 and Shepperd the Cobbler next door.

[On that side of the High Street were six cottages and four houses, with two more across the road, still in use as purely private dwellings. These few constituted almost the final stage of the some 300 years of gradual decline and conversion of the High Street away from private houses spaced out from each other, with front gardens and railings and having just a few shops in between them. Now there are no spaces between the buildings, none are purely domestic dwellings, most of the imposing Georgian homes are demolished and increasingly many new businesses are being transformed into long narrow purpose-designed shops. And in Temple Street, already the tower blocks have arrived, which do nothing for the aesthetics of the centuries-old town. What have succeeding KUDCs permitted developers to do in the name of progress, to this once so attractive town?]

On the even number side of the High Street, Loxtons at 46 have been mentioned. Number 10 was Barrow and Bath the veterinary surgeons. 12 was the

Queen Victoria's Jubilee Memorial drinking fountain at the top of Bath Hill East, where children cheered lorry loads of troops off to Avonmouth for France in 1914. The houses on the left and right remain unchanged. Two sections of the central pillar are cemented into the front garden of the house on the left, down the drive where the two stone pillars stand.

Keynsham's fine stone-built police station, between the wars, showing the more modern rear extension where the sergeant and one of his constables lived. The station also housed the court and had its own well. The path beyond the extension led to the tennis court complex.

well-known George E Chappell, grocer. 14 was Shellabears, another drapers. 28 was Bosley the outfitters. The two dairies were Exon at 4, and Watts at 34. Stokes and Son at 38 and Hicklings at 40 were highly-respected firms. 'Fishy' Fry was a character, who at 42, sold fish on one side of his shop and sweets on the other side, and would bring his small cob horse through the shop. Mrs Fry sold the sweets.

At 44 lived the famous Dr Charles Harrison, whose wife was the sister of the cricketer, W G Grace. Dr Harrison possessed a brougham and would use a megaphone to call out, 'Jones, Jones, bring round the brougham', which was kept in Back Lane. At 48 lived Mr E Wiggins the builder.

At 50 lived Walter Carter, brother of John, who was a very kind man, with a hardware and china shop. On a Saturday morning he would allow me to go with him in his pony and trap delivering paraffin at Stockwood and Chewton Keynsham and the other villages. Like a number of the High Street houses, he had an archway beside his shop enabling him to drive his trap to the rear of the house. There, like his neighbours, he had an enormously long garden that stretched down to the far wall of the Ashton Way car park. The stone side walls were about 5 feet high. The garden enabled him to have sufficient pas-

Two tennis courts in Mr M Scear's limestone quarry. Beyond is not a high wall but the quarry face, then some 12 feet high. Mr Newport recalled that in his boyhood clay was extracted there for making bricks, though there were still two lime kilns there when the tennis and croquet lawns were laid out, between the two great wars.

The lily pond was exceptionally beautiful. Today the site houses Dragon's Hill Court, and remnants of the quarry face can still be glimpsed there behind the row of garages.

ture to feed his horse. When the animal finally died, Walter closed the archway, made it into rooms and inserted a large window to display his china.

[On the subject of who kept horses in those long gardens, we know that Mr Carter and Mr Fry did. Mr C Wiggins said his father did not, but possibly his grandfather did. However, he said that there was a 'hauling way' at the side of the house for a pony and trap, and was shown a pulley used for hauling pigs up to be killed. Miss Fairclough said that the Stoke's garden was massive as it had originally been a farm, and had stretched down as far as West View Road, with barns, stables and a hay loft, and horses too. The gardens at the rear of High Street varied considerably in length, as some went behind others, hence 'Fishy' Fry only had a small garden. Most of the gardens were orchard and grass, though all the vegetables one needed were also grown. Mary said that Mr Tyler had a lovely garden and grew every fruit you can think of.

The other shops consisted of a further draper, another greengrocer and a grocer, plus another baker and a pork butcher. Perhaps most interesting because of what it reveals of the nature of old Keynsham in the time of the First War, was '54, Brushmaker – Mr Tyler' who had no shop front and sold his brushes from the house door. At 56 was 'Saddler, Mr Cornelius Anstey', with its lovely smell of leather!

As we have seen, Mr Newport left Keynsham in 1918, aged twelve, though now this octogenarian lives here again. Like his mother in character, his clear memories are most helpful in recalling what Keynsham was like over seventy years ago.]

The Back Lane

He wrote 'Dr Harrison kept his brougham at the top of the Lane, in a stone barn joined to the garden wall of the Baptist church, now a pathway. Mr Hickling always went down the Lane to the Colour Works and wore a boy's cap with a button bobbin on the top. Mr Cook always went up the Lane as the verger to church. Mr and Mrs Clapp had a small cottage, a sort of two up and two down, in Back Lane. Number 55 had the tin sheds that earlier belonged to the eyelet factory, which my father used to keep fowls and rabbits. At the bottom of the Lane, right next to the cottage, was the shed where Brownsey the butcher slaughtered the animals. Today this is Ogborns, and the passage and the shed at the rear are still there.

'Most of the shops had gardens over Back Lane, which were used mainly to grow vegetables, though a few had apple trees.'

Mr Newport did point out that while the Back Lane faces the river, on the opposite side of the High Street, at the end of where the long gardens finished, was originally another Back Lane with similarly high six-foot stone walls, that led from Charlton Road to Albert Road. Sections of this 'scoutway' can be seen near Charlton Road and beyond Rock Road.

Miss Fairclough mentioned that the Lane continued on past the hospital and joined the overgrown track to Parkhouse Farm, and was, in effect, part of the ancient mediaeval grid of footpaths that linked Keynsham with Pensford in one direction, and over Dapps Hill bridge to Chewton Keynsham in the other direction. Thank goodness parts of these centuries-old packhorse lanes still survive – just.

The stone walls beside the Hollies off Charlton Road would seem to indicate that the packhorse lanes were very narrow, but as Mary pointed out, when the brambles on the pathway up to Parkhouse Farm are cut back the route is quite wide. But in any case, she feels that the stone walls are possibly only a little over a century or so old. The track they enclose is indeed ancient, but the walls not necessarily so. Centuries ago a wall was required to keep in the villagers' pigs and poultry in their long gardens, but with only fields beyond them a second wall would have seemed superfluous.

Local employers

Mr Newport pointed out that prior to the advent of Fry's in 1922, the Eyelet Factory, the Brass Mills and the Colour Mill were the largest employers in the town.

He said that Mr Stokes, the respected business man, was also the captain of the town's famous lacrosse team.

Richard Newport confirmed what Ron Headington had said earlier, that there was a local outbreak of diphtheria, on the strength of which the local wells were closed.

Richard's father bricked over the yard at the rear of his shop and in a greenhouse there grew special yellow tomatoes, for which he always received a First Prize in the local August show in the Unusual Fruit class. When the Eyelet factory closed down the tailor used their tin sheds behind Back Lane in which to keep chickens and rabbits.

Chapter 8

Memories of old Keynsham
by Mrs Lily Harrison

Mrs Lily Harrison, born in Temple Street, most kindly agreed to draw on her excellent recollections of Keynsham in Grandfather's Day to write her 'Memories of Old Keynsham'. That was in July 1987. Later she added a fascinating section on 'Schools in Keynsham', which is included.

* * *

Temple Street Infants School was built approximately in 1890 by a man named Hyde. It was there at the age of five my school days began. October 1894 saw the opening of this building by a Miss Ireland and the then Rural Dean (Rev W B Doveton).

Prior to 1890 it was a farmyard owned by a Mr Paget. Mr Hyde married a Miss Dorey, related to Mr George Dorey who kept the greengrocery shop in the Church Square.

My grandparents Mr & Mrs William Cantle lived on the opposite side of the road to the farmyard, and kept a sweet shop.

Mrs Alfred Harvey of West View Road was the first Headmistress of the above school. Another much-loved teacher was Miss Fussell, who cycled daily from Warmley, in all but the most severe weather.

My education afterwards continued from about the age of eight at the Bath Hill Church School. Mr Mansey was the Headmaster, a strict disciplinarian, and all pupils leaving school at the age of fourteen were well-equipped with knowledge of the three 'R's'.

Activities during school holidays were many and varied. Each season of the year found us gathering either wild flowers, berries, mushrooms or nuts from fields and hedgerows. Likewise games of all kinds were to the fore.

* * *

Traders mostly owned small shops or businesses, and delivered their goods around the streets from door to door with the use of a horse and cart. Some milkmen could be seen carrying milk by means of a wooden yoke across the shoulders, with a chain hanging down on either side where the milk pails were attached. Others used a horse and cart wherein were two or three large churns containing the bulk supply. From them an amount would be poured into a pail for easy handling. The housewife, having brought her jug to the door, would then have her requirement ladled into it from the pail by means of a metal measure. This had a crooked handle so that when not in use it could be hung on the side of the pail.

Bread was carried in large baskets, often still warm, with replenishments kept under a kind of hessian cloth stacked in the pony cart.

Most homes were lit by paraffin lamps; heating and cooking accomplished from the use of coal. Open-range type grates were the usual, which needed black-leading, a very messy and dirty job. There were two hobs and an oven. The hobs, one on either side of the firebasket, were used for kettles and saucepans, the oven being below one of the hobs. All cooking and heating of water had to be done over the open fire. Too hot an oven could result in a 'burnt offering'!

Two very welcome tradesmen were the Oilman and Coalman on which all families were dependent. The former carried a selection of wares, the main item being paraffin. Also for the lamps, wicks and glasses, firelighters and candles to name but a few.

Reverting to the mention of games! Traffic in those days was not a problem, it being the occasional horse and cart or bicycle, which had to be allowed passage. Children could play in the road or on the pavements. *Whips and tops*: this was a piece of string on a stick and you whipped the top to make it spin. *Hop-skotch*: you needed a smooth flat stone or pebble, not too heavy, because you hopped on one leg, pushing the stone over the square pattern drawn with chalk on the ground. Occasionally an irate neighbour would come out and

Tom the carthorse, fine with woolly bobbles on his mane, at the annual Keynsham Carnival at 'Ollis's Field', [Gaston Av] c. 1920. Mr Frank White holds the reins, while his father, Mr Ernest White, holds Tom's head (Mrs Harrison's)

tell us to do the chalking in front of our own homes. Skipping ropes were popular. Either a length for one person to use, complete with wooden handles, or a long length for team use. The soles of shoes suffered from skipping, so parents tended to discourage too much of that exercise. *The hoop*, wooden or metal, was bowled along by means of a stick. Ball games – rounders etc, were mostly played at the Recreation Field, which is now the site of Hawthorns Old Peoples' bungalows. A game we were taught at school and supervised by a teacher was *STOOLBALL*. It was similar to cricket, having two teams. Fielders were all positioned as in cricket and scoring was by runs. At each end of the run we had a post, approximately 3 × 3″ driven into the ground, and a square flat piece was attached to the top. That piece was about 12–14″ square, the height from ground level approximately 3½ to 4ft: the bats used were similar to those for table-tennis. Since my school days I have never heard of that game being taught or played.

Before leaving the subject of leisure activities it is worth mentioning the spring which was near the river in the now-named MEMORIAL PARK. When we ran short of water on our picnics in Gaston's Field we would take our empty bottle and fill it with this lovely cold, crystal-clear water, which was always running. It was also a source of supply at one stage during the Second World War. When the Park was laid out in its present form the spring was diverted into the River Chew.

Whether the location of Keynsham had anything to do with this spring I am not experienced enough to know, only that it lies in the valley of the Cotswolds, the Mendips and Lansdown Hills. Wells were evident in Keynsham, there being one in the back garden of the house where I grew up. It was quite deep, possibly 30ft?

My father decided for the safety of the children (we were a large family), not to use this water well. Its iron framework of four legs supported a wooden roller around which the rope went when water was being drawn. It was operated by means of a handle to one side of the roller, with an egg-shape type of bucket for the water. The roller was protected from the weather by means of a zinc canopy,, like an inverted letter V. The well was put out of action by the removal of the frame, and a huge flattish stone was cemented over the opening on to the plinth. Several years later my father made a small aperture in the side of the well (ground level), in which all empty tins, bottles and rubbish were deposited in an effort to fill it in (another safeguard!!) but had not been accomplished when the premises were sold in 1961.

Also in the garden near the house was a soft-water cistern. A great asset. It was as large as a room, brick-built, and collected rain water from other cottages as well as our own dwelling. This water had many uses, the exception being drinking purposes as company water was laid on. Its softness and clearness was lovely for the skin.

As all water had to be heated, baths were taken from cistern water. It was also used for washing hair, household laundry, and watering of the garden.

During a few exceptionally hot summers when the water level in the cistern dropped to less than a foot, my father and two elder brothers would clean it out. A short ladder would be put down into the cistern and one person would fill up buckets with the silt and hand it up to the people on top, who would

Three White girls at the rear of their home, 32 Temple Street. Lily holds her niece Sheila, with Muriel (Mrs W Bees) above; late 1940. Behind, the opening to the rainwater cistern and the roped drawing-bucket. (Mrs Harrison's)

dispose of it. The human chain process was kept going until all was bailed out. Then the hosepipe and hard broom would come into operation to scrub up the floor of the cistern, leaving it nice and clean ready to receive water from the next rainstorm.

The opening had a square stone framework on to which a strong wooden cover with handle rested. To draw water a bucket was attached to a very stout length of rope, and whilst holding the rope firmly by the right hand you turned the bucket upside down and threw it into the cistern. As it touched the water you gave a flick of the wrist so that the bucket tilted and water began to fill it. You then drew it up and repeated the operation according to the amount of water required.

Fridges for home use were years away, but with a piece of butter-muslin cloth you could wrap butter, meat, bacon or any perishable food into it, put the package into a bucket (kept for the purpose), and suspend this just above the water in the cistern. It was anchored by the rope on the bucket being fastened on to a spike which had been driven into the framework of the opening. Should a thunderstorm or heavy rain descend, you quickly rescued the package because of the water rising. Once again strict discipline was enforced for younger members of the family to prevent accidents.

You will gather from what has already been said the house had a large garden well-stocked with fruit trees of various kinds. Cooking and eating apples; pears; damsons; greengages; with black, yellow and Victoria plums. Soft fruits; black and red currants, loganberries and gooseberries. A touch of humour at this point:- my father and I always had an agreement that when gathering soft fruits I would pick the gooseberries and he the currants: you may think it should have been the other way round, as did he, but the scratches I received were few and the bargain kept!!

Vegetables were grown in abundance, with only a small patch reserved for flowers – this for economic reasons. Horse manure was available from the stable which kept the ground in good condition. Two well-built pigstyes proved useful for rearing hens, as well as any breeding of pigs.

The garden was mostly tended by my father, with occasional help from my two elder brothers. In later years as my father grew older, my sister Muriel and I would look after the flower section. One last item to mention – a large stone-built garden shed, tiled and with a window. When weather was unsuited for outdoor activities, this became the children's play area.

My father was Mr Ernest White, well-known in Keynsham through his Retail Coal business, and a Haulage Contractor. His second son Frank entered the business and it became known as E White & Son.

At the outset a horse and cart or long trolley was used, but eventually motor lorries took over.

He ordered coal from colleries in many parts of the country, according to requirement. By that I mean certain grades of coal from different areas: slow or quick burning; cobbles as opposed to large lumps; anthracite; boiler-nuts or steam coal etc.

In the early thirties, five hundredweights of coal could be bought for nine shillings and sixpence (in old currency), 47½ pence in decimal.

Time was always allowed for harnessing the horse in the mornings.

A White family group, Edwin White with his cap on, with his arm round his nephew Graham White, while Edwin's sister Kathleen holds the doll. The date was around 1930, at Edwin's home at 32 Temple Street, Keynsham. Behind them is the tall boundary wall, while they stand on the top of the underground water cistern, with its wooden door just visible below the stone parapet. Notice the water-bucket by the flower pot. (Mrs Harrison's)

Grooming, feeding and watering in the evenings, with a daytime supply being carried in the horse's nose-bag. Chaff-cutting was another evening job, with a double amount being done on a Saturday, as work on Sundays was kept to a minimum. The care of the horse was a necessity for the Sunday.

Both my parents had strong views about the observance of Sunday, and standards for the family were taught during childhood. Mother always liked the family together for lunch on Sundays, this not being possible during the week.

A strong relationship of trust existed between trader and customers. Business was carried on six days a week, but should a customer call on a Sunday, through some emergency, they were always given sufficient fuel for their need, and a promise that delivery would be made first thing on the Monday morning. An amount of fuel was always kept at the house of business to meet such circumstances.

Roads in some part of Keynsham were bad and even un-made. In severe weather this made travelling with a horse and cart difficult and dangerous. It also meant using frost nails for the horse's shoes.

My mother had an excellent hand for writing, and this she used helping with the book-keeping within the business.

In those days the recognized Bank Holiday was the first Monday and Tuesday in August. The Keynsham Flower Show and Carnival was held on these two days, and was an occasion looked forward to, not only by local residents, but people in the surrounding villages. Most residents, young and old, male and female, took part in some way.

It was held in The Hams field before Messrs J S Fry & Sons came to set up Somerdale. Afterwards, the venue was Ollis's field, Avon Road, now known as Gaston Avenue.

Large tents would be erected a day or two prior to the show, by Yeo Brothers & Paul of Bristol. Charles Hill or similar firm with roundabout and side shows would arrive with 'ALL THE FUN OF THE FAIR'.

With the arrival of Monday morning, exhibitors would take their fruit, flowers and vegetables to the appropriate tent. Schoolchildren with woodwork models, needlework and other items would do likewise.

Friendly rivalry existed, but tempers were known to get the better of their owners at times.

The afternoon of the Monday would see a variety of sport for all ages, male and female. Musical chairs (with bicycles); egg and spoon; three-legged race; flat-racing – one for Veterans; whilst others would be keeping an eye open for the marathon runners' return. Keynsham Town Band played their part during the tea interval, when the prize-giving would take place afterwards.

On the Tuesday all show exhibits would still be on display, but the afternoon would see a very colourful fancy dress parade, for individuals, and the tradesmen's turnout.

Many of them took part, including Ernest White & Son. The morning would have been spent preparing for the 'Turnout' so that the animals with their vehicles looked splendid for the parade and the judging.

Several members within my own family took part in the fancy dress.

The evenings on both Show days ended with a spectacular display of Fireworks. Alas! all good things come to an end, as did the Keynsham Flower Show before the Second World War.

Keynsham Gas Company, as it was known, had its works with two small gas holders at the bottom of Dapps Hill. People could go there and buy coke. About the year 1925 a Mr Ted Summers became works manager, but the company had been operating for many years prior to then.

With the coming of Fry's, Somerdale, they needed gas, and afterwards Bristol Gas Company followed and bought up Keynsham Gas Company in about 1928. Some homes had gas for lighting.

Keynsham can also be proud of the fact she has a place in National History, being one of the first towns to have electric street lighting in 1890. Messrs Parfitt & Webber started the Electric Light Company in sheds behind The Railway Tavern (now the present Electricity Show Rooms). Works supervisor was Mr Bill Webb.

The plant was later augmented by the mill at Chewton, the water of the River Chew being used as an auxiliary force. Eventually it was handed over to the Bristol Corporation Electricity Department.

I remember the excitement when paraffin oil lamps were replaced with electric lighting. The filling of lamps, trimming of wicks, cleaning smoky lamp glasses all ended with the future pressing of a switch. Cooking by gas or electricity came later. It was with a mixture of pride, fear and apprehension that one embarked on cooking their first lunch with either of these types of fuel. My father's comment when the gas cooker was installed – 'He would not eat anything cooked from it', but time heals many things including prejudice!

Coal was still a very necessary commodity in the household. Heating of rooms still had to be done by coal fires, as did the drying and airing of clothes.

Now into the Twentieth Century with its central heating, yet nothing can quite match, on a dark, cold night, the sight of a glowing coal fire. Its flickering flames and crackling sounds stir memories and bring into the room a sense of companionship.

Between the two World Wars the Victoria Methodist Chapel had a thriving Brotherhood, and from its members sufficient talent was found to form a Male Voice Choir. Its able Conductor was Mr Jimmy Lewis. About 1930 the Choir provided the inmates of Keynsham Workhouse with a special tea consisting of ham, cakes and other items, ending the evening with a concert of musical pieces rendered by the Choir. Two of my brothers, Frank and Herbert, sang in the Male Voice Choir, and my sister Muriel and I helped with preparations for the tea.

My recollections of the interior of the workhouse were long bare stone corridors; clanging iron gate-type doors, and a depressive atmosphere.

Vagrants after being given a night's lodging had to do a certain amount of work in the grounds before being allowed to leave.

Another building quite near this area was the Isolation Hospital. This had a lodge at the drive entrance, and by use of a bell the keeper could be alerted, who would then receive any gifts or parcels brought for patients. The isolation period was six to eight weeks.

People now living in the St Ladoc Road area may be surprised to learn that

Station Road many years before the bypass. Note the abundant use of stone. What splendid lamp stands! The Church Rooms were just off the right hand wall. The fine arch and one of the turreted houses remains.

Not 'the Victoria Male Voice Choir', but one of its sisterhood groups, taken around the time of World War One, in Keynsham, according to Mr J Stickler, who gave me the photo.

the Peace Celebrations after the First World War were held on the site – then fields.

Building began in the area in the 1920's with the erection of council houses on the left-hand side of the now St Ladoc Road. As the site developed it was named Pittsville, and remained so for many years. Older residents will still refer to it by that name. Many mining pits had been in the area, hence its chosen name.

Schools in Keynsham

Late nineteenth and early twentieth century

The British School was opened in 1860, and my mother together with her brother and sister attended, and were taught there. It was situated in the High Street where the present Baptist Church now stands: next to the premises occupied by Lloyd Bank. Their Headmaster was a Mr 'Jimmy' Usher, who was there until the school closed in 1894.

It was my uncle Mr Charles Cantle who supplied me with these details before he died at the age of 91 years.

Parents paid one penny (before decimalization) per week for their children to be educated. This was quite an item in those days especially if there were several children in the family. A child's education suffered if their parents could not afford the fee.

Scholars were well-taught, especially in the three R's, and their writing was much admired throughout their lifetime.

The closure of the school was brought about by the Government's introduction of Play Areas for all schools. This requirement was not able to be met by the school, hence the closure.

As a direct result of the British School being closed came the opening of the Temple Street Infants School.

NB Details re: the Temple St School I previously gave in
'*MEMORIES OF OLD KEYNSHAM.*'

My (Mrs Lily Harrison's) primary school days started with the use of a sand-tray; progressing then to a writing slate. These slates had a wooden surround, and we either used slate pencils or chalk. Rubbing cloths were needed for cleaning them off before writing something else. The school had three classrooms so in the third one, known as Standard (1), we were instructed in the use of pen and ink. One basic rule was to keep your hand on the pen whilst forming a word – up, down, round, and not lifting your hand until the word was completed. The pens we used had a long slim handle with a holder at one end where the nib was fitted into position for writing.

The early use of pen and ink took much practice before the small pupil grasped the idea that only the tip of the pen (nib) had to be inserted to pick up enough ink for writing. Otherwise, the nib-holder became covered with ink resulting in blots falling onto the exercise book, inky-fingers transferring it to one's clothes, which meant trouble at home!! How well I remember having my fingers rapped with a ruler by the teacher, before I finally overcame this difficulty. It was reasonably easy to cross the nib by pressing too hard with the pen, or by holding it badly. The tip of the nib had a split in it, and when it became crossed this would open and writing was almost impossible, the result being a replacement nib.

Inkwells were made of a china/pottery ware, and thus breakable although fairly stout. Ink was poured into them from a bottle made either of glass or earthenware. From time to time it was necessary to wash them as they became very messy, particularly if not in use as the ink would dry up. This unenviable job was detailed to be done in turn by the pupils, at the washbasins in the cloakroom.

Seating at the Infants School for the first two years was on small chairs, then wooden desks followed. At Bath Hill school these were long, with sitting forms attached, and would seat about eight to ten. Each desk had roughly the same number of holes in the top for the receiving of the inkwells.

As the years passed, these long desks were being replaced by the two-pupil type, where the top of the desk opened upwards for the storage of books, pens etc; also the seats would lift up (like theatre seats) for easy access in getting in and out.

Classes were known as Standard's, not Forms or Groups as is the modern reference. So! Temple St School housed Standard (1), and Bath Hill from Standard's (2) to (7).

The school leaving age was fourteen, and occasionally two or three children,

'E White's' of 32 Temple Street, early 1930. 'A safer and more contented place than it is today', commented his daughter Mrs Harrison. Left, the middle of the 3 arches leads to the Dr's; beyond, the 3 Horseshoes Inn. (Mrs Harrison's)

having reached Standard 7, but whose fourteenth birthday had not yet been reached, had to continue at school pro. tem. and they were referred to as being in Standard X7. I myself with one boy named Charlie Bishop were two of these X7 pupils.

Teachers had their scholars for a whole year, and instructed them in all subjects other than Cookery, Gardening and Woodwork. This exception was due to required facilities. Only girls were taught cookery. This lesson was held at the Victoria Methodist Schoolroom in Charlton Road, but an elder sister of mine went to the Church Room in Station Road – the latter being demolished to make room for the Keynsham By-pass. The former was years before the coming of The Key Centre, and was suitably equipped for our use.

Cookery had to be on a rota basis simply because it was not possible for all the girls to attend at the same time. Miss Morgan was our teacher, very efficient in every sense of the word, and commanded a high standard of hygiene for pupils and the cleansing of their cooking utensils.

Similarly a rota system was arranged for the boys. Gardening was done on school plots at the bottom of Bath Hill near the River Chew. The ground being on a slope backed away from the river towards the present-day blocks of flats. The Headmaster was usually in charge of this activity. Woodwork lessons took place at The Drill Hall adjacent to the school building. It was necessary for a separate teacher in woodwork as this again had to be alternated with gardening.

It is worth mentioning that there was a school house on the site of the school premises, and it is still there, although used for a different purpose. This was for the caretaker and his family, and the legendary Mr 'Sapper' Clark lived there, afterwards to be a pillar of strength with the Keynsham Cricket Club.

In previous notes I mentioned the names of two teachers at Temple Street School, the third was a Miss Newell – all women. Bath Hill had five women, and the Headmaster and acting Deputy Head, whose names were Mr Mansey, and Mr Griffiths. Recalling names of the lady teachers, they were Miss Davis, and her supporting help, Miss Lake, for Standard (2); then came Miss Garrod (or maybe Garrett), Standard (3); Mrs Jones who lived at Brislington (S.4) (nicknamed 'Ginger' Jones because of her colour hair), but never used within her hearing.

Standard (5) was taught by Mrs Reed, who was the mother of Mr Gordon Reed. He became well-known in later years as a grocer with a shop in Temple Street, and a staunch member of the Baptist Church. Mr Griffiths sorted out (S.6), and the Headmaster took (7) and any X7 pupils. Women teachers were addressed as MISS and the men as SIR.

There would be up to forty-plus children in each standard, and because of them being under the supervision of one teacher for a whole year a relationship was built up between scholar and teacher. There was an understanding of temperaments, nervous, shy, unwell, unhappy, but ALWAYS a strict discipline was maintained, and accepted. Lessons continued in an atmosphere of quiet and calm acceptance; of learning and teaching. No homework was given in those days, and only a few, whose parents could afford it, went on to Merchant Venturers held in Bristol. Any professional business man would apprentice his son/daughter to a suitable career. There were no grants (monetary) available. It meant everyone making, and learning their own way through life according to their own willingness to learn, listen, and be receptive of knowledge. Work was hard, and hours long, but you did it uncomplainingly. There was no Welfare State; only the Workhouse for the sadly-unfortunate ones.

Each day began with the whole school joining in Morning Worship. There was no assembly hall, but the lay-out of the school was such that with all the class room doors opened everyone was able to hear the piano, and the Headmaster's voice. This act of worship would last about ten minutes, then all doors would be closed, and each teacher devote the next thirty or forty minutes to Scripture study. Even today, now as a Senior Citizen, I can remember special passages of the Bible, and hymns that we were taught to memorize in school days. We were frequently told – 'You have a brain, use it'. This advice proved valuable as we were required to do quite a lot of mental arithmetic. I think our minds became a mini-built-in television screen. What a useful asset it has proved in adult life!

Although in mixed classes, boys and girls, as far as possible, were kept apart. Seating arrangements were girls in the front, and boys at the back. Toilets and play-grounds were separate.

Teachers would appoint a monitor for minor duties, such as giving out or collecting books, pens or pencils; cleaning off the blackboard or standing in front of the class to report any misdemeanour whilst the teacher absented the room for any reason.

Blackboards rested on two pegs inserted in holes on a tripod type easel.

There was no grading of pupils for examinations. The subject to be taken would be set for the whole class, and over a period of days or weeks every subject taught would be included. This would apply to the whole school. These exams would be conducted and supervised by the Headmaster, with the Vicar of the Parish being actively involved in the Scripture knowledge.

Ash Wednesday saw pupils and staff soon after 9 am parading along the High Street to the Parish Church for the Service which would begin the season of Lent. After the march back to school we would be given the rest of the day off as a holiday.

Shrove Tuesday preceded the start of Lent, and we knew it was Pancake Day. A bell was rung at Church on that day known as the 'Pan-on-bell', and we children, amongst ourselves, used to sing a little ditty:- 'Pan On; Pan On; pea soup and bacon!' Similarly for a church funeral a muffled single bell would be tolled; but on National occasions, such as Armistice, a muffled peal would be rung from the Bell Tower.

Digressing from school to weddings for a few moments, it was quite a thrill for little school girls to stand outside the Parish Church in order to watch any special weddings. The Bride or Groom would be from a member of Keynsham's more wealthy citizens. A wide red carpet would be laid down from the West Door of the Church to the end of the pavement, where the vehicle would deposit its passengers. Covering the same distance would be an awning; thus the Bridal procession was protected from getting dirt on their dresses, and from inclement weather.

Back to school, and punishment for misbehaviour. This could vary from being kept in after school; having to write so many words or lines (possibly for talking during lessons); being made to stand out in front of the whole class, or the Headmaster administering the cane. Punishment existed for both sexes, but rarely was a girl caned. I think we realized it would be painful, and pride and fear held us in check. One incident I well remember of a boy receiving the cane, and after reporting back to his mother (a widow) she arrived at the school. Entering the classroom and shouting at the woman teacher, she then picked up and threw the inkwell from the teacher's desk at her, causing her to look very shaken. Meanwhile someone had been sent to fetch the Headmaster. On his arrival this large woman confronted the small-statured Master, seized the front of his collar, and proceeded to shake him. Whilst this was going on other teachers had been alerted, and we were marshalled from the classroom. Expulsion from the school resulted for the boy.

Something a little more humorous was a prank of some boys on a wet day to twist their hair in the shape of two horns protruding each side of their forehead. On arrival in class a giggle would, rather silently, be heard, which attracted Mr Griffiths' attention; the boys would be reprimanded, and told to go to the cloakroom to tidy up.

Only the children from the outlying country districts, Queen Charlton, Burnett, and Chewton, were allowed to partake of meals on school premises at midday. Local children returned to their homes.

From Queen Charlton came the families named Ford, Baber, Loxton, from Burnett the children Owen, Wheeler, and from Chewton, those named Price and Tuck. There may have been others whose names do not readily come to mind.

They would bring their own picnic type meals, and either sit around the stove or at a desk; clearing up from the meal afterwards was all part of discipline.

Just a word about the stoves which were the source of heating throughout the school. They were cast iron, and circular, about two to three feet high. Fuel used was coke, with an outlet fume pipe. For chewing in class many a child's sweet was ordered to be dropped into the stove. There was one heater in each of three classrooms, and two in each of the two double classrooms. The double rooms would have teacher and pupils at each end, where both classes would carry on their individual lessons without interrupting the other. Occasionally a child's eyes might glance to the other end of the room, and should the teacher spot this – say, during a reading lesson – the pupil already reading aloud would be told to stop and the offending one asked to continue. If unable to do so at the right place in the book, this would result in punishment for 'not paying attention'.

Apart from having their lunch at school, the country children would be allowed the small concession, in wintertime, of leaving school about ten minutes early to enable them to reach home before it became too dark. They always walked to and from school in all weather. Just before my school days ended, a taxi service was started to convey them during the winter months. As far as memory serves me, this was either free, or sixpence a week per family was charged – I cannot be absolutely certain.

Two playgrounds at the school were provided, divided by a stone wall. Toilets were situated on each area of ground, one section for boys, the other for girls. It was only possible to see what was happening on the other side by climbing the wall, which was forbidden, but – 'He who dares'?

Should the call of nature arise during lessons, scholars had to go halfway up the playground in all weather. These toilets had plain wooden seats about a yard wide stretching from wall to wall, with a hole in the middle where one sat down. I do not remember any flushed cisterns; buckets of water were used. Privacy was maintained by a door and a roof.

Young Doris White on the knee of her big brother Herbert White, in the garden of their home at 32 Temple Street, in the later 1920s. They are sitting on the large stone slab that their father put over their well. Pebbles pushed in, by Herbert's right foot, could be heard to splash below. The abundance of blossom indicates just how beautiful, and productive, these long narrow gardens could be (Mrs Harrison's)

We had a break from lessons mid-morning and afternoon for about ten minutes or so, which was brought to an end by the ringing of a handbell. Everyone formed into lines at this signal, and with the order to march, proceeded back to their respective rooms. At the end of morning, and afternoon lessons, this bell would be rung, teachers would give the order for dismissal, and marching smartly one behind the other, the children would leave the room. Anyone caught trying to do a quick get-out, would be brought back, warned or possibly kept in, writing lines as another alternative. Any one of these could be substituted for your mid-morning break the next day. Respect was always shown to teachers whenever you saw them out of school hours.

Only at a private fee-paying school would there by any kind of uniform dress. Keynsham had, to my knowledge, four such schools – with from six to twelve attending. One was in The Avenue, others in Culverhay and at Miss Jollyman in Charlton Road, and at Mrs Boston on Bath Hill near where Mr Beale had his bakery shop. One of my brothers was a pupil for a short time at this last one mentioned.

At the parochial schools, children were tidy, and well-dressed – at least for school, each wearing what their parents could afford. Girls frequently wore a cotton pinafore, made with a frill over each shoulder, and worn over their dresses. This was for protection, as a cotton apron could be washed or replaced more easily, and less expensively, than a dress. Shaping of girls' hair had not yet arrived, so the long tresses were held in place by the use of a ribbon. Boys wore short trousers just above the knees until they finished school at fourteen. With their first pair of long trousers they felt very 'grown-up', as did girls when they wore stockings instead of socks.

Protective clothing such as macs, and wellington boots had not yet made their appearance for school children. On a wet morning you might have seen two or three small girls all trying to keep dry under one umbrella. Parents would be heard saying – 'Hurry now, and get out of the rain!' Likewise if you were very wet on arriving home – 'Where have you been to get so wet?'

From time to time School Inspectors would call to check on any absentees. It was law, then, for all children over the age of five to be educated, and any who absented themselves, other than through illness, had parents visited by the Inspector as to the reason for non-attendance. For persistent lawbreaking, parents could find themselves in trouble.

Periodically pupils had to visit the school dentist. For this we went to a room in a shop on the right-hand side of Bath Hill, just past the Old Liberal Club building. To the villagers this shop was known as 'Coffee Rawlings', because the owner's name was Rawlings. It was *not* the Rawlings who owned the cycle shop. This nickname made clear which of the Rawlings you were referring to. You will understand how the nickname came about in a moment. The shop in question was a double-fronted one where sweets were sold on one side, and a cup of tea or coffee on the other – a mini cafe! (Well, have you spotted the connection?).

The dentist room was rented for the school purpose; he did not live on the premises. Each child had to take sixpence; if no treatment or extractions were made you retained the money, otherwise it was handed over to the dentist.

A nurse would come occasionally for looking over the hair – boys and girls.

If she found head-lice or nits, parents would be asked to treat the hair by washing it in a special lotion, and then using a very fine steel-toothed comb afterwards.

Medical examinations were also carried out. Checks made on weight, height and general health. Once again, parents would be informed if any thing other than normal came to light. Any case of a parent being informed about the child, for whatever reason, would be followed up at a later date.

Another modern-day occupation is school photographs. Rarely were any taken in my time.

Exercises of the keep-fit style were done in the playground, supervised and instructed by a teacher. As previously stated in another article, field games were played on the Recreation Ground (now The Hawthorns Estate).

Chapter 9

A boy's view of school life in Keynsham
by Mr B. J. Robe

The new tenants from Bristol moved into 17 Avon Mill Lane (now Avon Road) in 1914, accompanied by their four-year-old son Bert Robe. The house, perched sideways on the top of the 'sidelands' above the Chew, had a magnificent view. Sadly, today the house is no more, having been in the path of the new bypass, but the octogenarian boy is still very much alive.

He confirmed the accuracy of Mrs Harrison's narrative and went on to write, 'The Standard III teacher's name was Miss Garrad, a Dorset lady. The teacher of Standard V was Mrs Reed, who lived in Temple Street in a house near the Ship Inn. These were in the Bath Hill school, the 'Big School'. Teachers in the newer Temple Street school, the 'Little School', in the pre-1920s were Miss Plattin and Mrs Bartholomew. Under the latter, at the age of seven, we learned 'joined up' writing from copy books in the copper plate style, copying such extracts as 'Charge of the Light Brigade', ('Charge for the guns, he said') and 'Come the three corners of the world and we in arms shall shock them'.

Miss Fussell, who taught six year olds, was a rather fearsome lady who reprimanded misdemeanours by holding a pupil's chin in her thumb and forefinger and giving it a hard squeeze and shake – quite painful – but it instilled the point she wished to make.

Mrs Harvey, the headmistress, was my teacher as an eight year old in 1918. She was then nearing retirement. On one occasion she caned the whole back row of the class, some eight pupils, for inattention, one stroke on the palm of the hand. I was the last in the row, and only knew half the answer. It was the only occasion that I was caned yet I still remember her with admiration and affection.

At the mid-day break at the 'Big School', the whole school sang an appropriate grace before dashing home for our dinners, and again on return we sang, 'We thank thee Lord for this our food, our life, our gifts, our power to give; may manna to our souls be given, the Bread of Life sent down from Heaven'.

At painting classes the subjects featured were mostly common garden flowers and vegetables, enabling each pair of children to share a 'model'. Dried small onion bulbs featured regularly, the best efforts being mounted and displayed on the classroom walls.

For heating, these high-ceiling classrooms depended upon a single 'Tortoise' coke-burning stove which at best took a long while to heat up. On frosty mornings the rooms were very cold so classes started with children standing,

The original Avon Mill Lane, now Avon Road, in February 1964, facing towards the GWR. On the right, the Ollis's field with Sunnymead just visible. Later, the bypass cut the road in half, necessitating the destruction of number 17, the second house on the left. The first house still survives, though much altered. (B J Robe's)

The view of 17 Avon Mill Lane in 1964, facing the opposite way, with the Fox and Hounds row of shops just visible. Houses still had gates then, to keep out the many passing cattle. Mr B J Robe recalled the havoc caused by a cow in this garden, when once the gate was left open.

Another piece of Keynsham yesterday. A close-up of 17 Avon Mill Lane in 1964, with an indication of the fine view it commanded. Mr B J Robe who lived there in World War One, recalled that in the stillness of a Sunday morning he could hear the chickens cackling behind the Temple Street houses.

The rear of the same house, viewed from the railway's Goods Station, at the far side of Avon Mill Lane, again in February 1964. (B J Robe's)

clapping their hands and beating arms across their bodies in unison with the teacher's lead, to generate blood circulation and warmth. Incredibly, most of us survived.

The playground for boys (probably matched for girls adjoining) was quite large, one third sloping upwards away from the school buildings, being tarmacadamed. The other two thirds was black soil, trodden down by many feet over many years, but creating dust in summer and mud in winter, especially in thawing frost. At the latter time marbles were in season, thrown or flicked with fingers towards holes scraped out at the base of the school boundary wall, calls being, 'Three-a-piece pecks' (throws) or 'Three a piece niggs'. Nigging, or flicking, was done with fingers in the mud. There were no washing facilities so we cleaned our hands presumably by wiping them down our pants (short ones of course), or down our jerseys. Yet somehow we kept the pages of our exercise books clean.

The boys' toilets were appalling, highly malodorous, especially in summer; there was no flushing in the boys' urinals, and only holes in boards for a range of toilets, these presumably being earth closets. I cannot say for certain because they were rarely if ever used, except in emergencies.

Very occasional dental treatment was given by a travelling dentist at 'Coffee Rawlings' shop at the top of Bath Hill, in a bare room with a minimum of equipment. Injections were given for extractions but were still very painful. The dentist's drill for stoppings was powered by a foot treadle, pressed on by the dentist. It was a grim and painful experience. There was no attendant nurse of course, but no payment was demanded. The children's names were on a list in school, from which individuals went in fear and trembling at the appointed time.

As a small boy I had read of a new boys' magazine being published at the price of two old pence, so I went into Miss Gibb's shop, and with head just above the array of comics and periodicals on the counter, I asked the rather forbidding looking lady behind it, 'Do you keep The Wizard?' She replied, 'No, and I don't think I'd like to either.' But there was a twinkle in Miss Gibb's eyes which did nothing to soothe my embarrassed blushes.

At the time when the cinema was operating in the High Street, the fire station was in Charlton Road opposite the Wesleyan Sunday School. It was moved later to the High Street, roughly where Curry's shop now is, and was never on the cinema site. I remember going to Saturday matinees about 1918/1919 when I am sure the entrance charge for me was one old penny. Among others, we watched one serial called 'The Clutching Hand' – very gruesome. The film was black and white and of course, silent.

Mr Sweet the chimney sweep had a sign in his garden at the bottom of Bath Hill East for many years which read, 'Orders PROMPLY attended to'. The 'T' was missing. Chimney fires were a frequent occurrence when house holders neglected to have their chimneys swept. Mostly they were dowsed by table salt being sprinkled on them, but some brought out the fire brigade's hand appliance. Mr Hine, the other sweep, was known locally as 'Sooty Hine'.

On the back of this photo are written the words, 'Keynsham Big School 1920'. The board on the ground repeats the words, 'Keynsham School 1920' with the added note that they were 'Group No. 5'. Mr B J Robe, the owner of the photograph, said that it was not taken on any special occasion. He added that though the children were mainly from Miss Garrad's Standard III class, which he was in, a few related brothers and sisters from other classes were also present in this Group 5 photo. Their ages were from 9 to 11.

Remarkably, 64 years later, Mr Robe can identify and name every child present, whose names he gives below.

Back Row
Ted Fowler, Charlie Gurnsey, Jack Rayson, Tom McMahon, Tom Chard and Fred Nixon.
3rd Row
Nellie Bray, Ivor Robertson, 'Heckon' Davies, Geoffrey Fear, 'Kelly' Godfrey, Roy Burchill, Henry Bratt, 'Ledger' Harvey, Arthur Olds, Walter Northcott and Madge Cantle.
2nd Row
Jack Cook, Joyce Belsten, Barbara Symes, Kathleen Davies, Gladys Nash, Rose Clapp, Phyllis Turner, Rose Burchill, Gladys Olds, Ethel Chard, ? Crew, Barbara Prescott.
Front Row
Clifford Taylor, Jim Taylor, Norman Robertson, Gordon Reed, Bert Robe, Fred Jeffries, Jack McMahon, Alec Grimes and George Bray.

Memories of the First World War

'My father was away on active service in the Royal Artillery. I remember seeing the wounded soldiers arriving at Temple Meads railway station, in their light blue uniforms and red ties. This made a big impression on me. One gave me a French penny. I was even more moved when I heard that Mr Ernie Waters, who lived down the road at 33 Avon Mill Lane, had been killed in France. This made the reality of war come alive. I remember Armistice Day vividly; our dog 'Rusty' bit me in the excitement.

With father away and food in short supply, we grew vegetables in the garden beside our house, where we also had chickens, mainly White Wyandots with a few Rhode Island Reds. There was a hole in the wall, through which the chickens were allowed to escape, giving us, in effect, free range eggs.

We had also an allotment off Manor Road, which was run as a communal affair. Mother would follow the farmer with his horse-drawn plough, down the one furrow allocated to her, planting potatoes as she went. These were then covered by the following furrow ploughed, for the next lady. There weren't many men about then.

Opposite our house was Ollis's field, which stretched from Dragons Hill to Sunnymead, in which they grew hay for the horses of their carrier business. It was also used for football and rugby matches. At hay-making time, my elder brother Frederick, as part of the war effort, would help turn the hay that had been cut by a horse-drawn mower. Mr Ollis would provide tea and buttered buns from his bakery.

In the early 1920s the Keynsham Cricket Club played on a field near Broadlands Farm off Charlton Road, before moving to 'Rockhill' at Chewton Road, or Wellsway as it is now called.

Below our house, across the Chew was the Colour Works, where about twenty men worked, including Mr Exon and Mr Anstey. There rocks were crushed to produce mainly red but some yellow pigment, to colour paint. There was no smell from the works but the turning water wheels produced a musical sound which was not obtrusive. One was aware of it but the sound fitted in with the local atmosphere.

As boys we would cross the river on the many irregularly placed stones when the sluices were down for the water to drive the wheels, but at four o'clock the sluices were raised. This caused the level of water to rise several inches, resulting in a small sudden bore of fast-running water that made it impossible to cross back for some two hours until the flow went down if you were on the wrong side.

Actually the Chew at this point was a very smelly river, which is not surprising as all the local sewage flowed into it until the 1930s and the arrival of the Council's treatment plant. Higher up the Chew at Chewton Keynsham it was cleaner, and provided a pool near Uplands Bridge, where local boys swam. We swam in the Avon too until we discovered how much disease was carried in the water.

A view of the East bank of the River Chew that we will not see again, as the new Avon Mill Lane sweeps across the sidelands between the two buildings, the house having been demolished. 1964. (B J Robe's)

A fine close-up of a typically constructed early Keynsham cottage. Note the style of the stone door jambs and lintels of this probably Georgian house at 17 Avon Mill Lane, in 1964. Notice how straight the stones have been cut and the evenness of the layers. (B J Robe's)

The aromatic smells of the local shops

Many shops had pleasant distinctive smells, far more than today. The bakeries provided a great yeasty aroma; the grocers an admixture of tea, coffee, spices and cheeses; the corn merchant a special 'grainy' odour; the ironmongers, like R D Hickling and Sons, a mélange of paint, paraffin, candles and many other intricate odours which were special to ironmongers; sweet shops had sweety and chocolate aromas varying from one shop to another, Exon's dairy being different from 'Figgy' Miltons and different again from Mrs Wood's shop next to Hickling's which couldn't escape having a fishy taint from the adjacent fish section; greengroceries had a special fragrance in which celery predominated and fruits, in season, added their distinctive flavours; Anstey's the saddlers in the High Street close to what is now Church's, the newsagent, had a very special aroma of newly-worked leather.

The pungent smell of burning hoof-horn from the farrier's smithy was not generally evident unless you sought it out in the blacksmith's building next to the New Inn at Bath Hill East. The blacksmith was Bill Trott, inevitably a brawny man with a large paunch which made it a mystery as to how he kept his trousers up with a solitary leather belt. A shed behind the New Inn was the local mortuary and here, also, was the 'pound' to which stray animals were taken.

When Avon Mill Lane led only to the mill

When I first went to live in Keynsham in 1914, our address was 17 Avon Mill Lane, one of the Glenavon Cottages, but very shortly afterwards it became 17 Avon Road. I never knew the reason for the change. The character of Keynsham in those days was derived from its lias limestone buildings and walls, mostly ruthlessly destroyed by modern 'developers'. The cottages in Avon Road were all lias limestone and pantiled, the stone quarried in the area, and the road boundary of Ollis's field for some 200 yards from Dragonshill to 'Sunnymead House', was a solid 5 foot high lias wall topped with 'header' stones.

Before the building of the G W Railway, I believe Avon Mill Lane led only to the Brass Mill and had no link with the Bitton Road at the County Bridge. The link from the Brass Mills over the Chew must have been built by the railway company to give better access to their goods station in Avon Road, because certainly in the 1920s and 1930s, it was the railway's private road, having at first wooden gates, and later iron gates which were closed and locked at about 5 o'clcok in the evening, though pedestrians were allowed through a sidegate.

On every Good Friday, railway workers were stationed at the railway arch to challenge the passage of anyone, including pedestrians, along the railway roads and paths. This was to preserve the railway's private rights, a process later dispensed with under the provisions of a Rights of Way Act in the 1930s which achieved the same result with a permanent notice board. I wonder if British Rail still exercises its rights.

One wonders how the local people reacted when the GWR bisected the Hams in the 1830s? Well, here is a view of one side of the Hams from the old Poolbarton Lane across to the Humpty Dumps taken in February 1964. Now the Hams have been further reduced by the new bypass built on the left of the railway. (B J Robe's)

The road leading from the Poolbarton to Station Road, with the Pioneer on the far right, in February 1964. The wall and the buildings on the left were demolished in the construction of the bypass. (B J Robe's)

A photo of Dr Gerrish's former house and the fine houses in 'The Park' (as opposed to 'Abbey Park') taken from Station Road, in February 1964. They were pulled down to make way for the bypass (B J Robe's)

1964, 'The Old School' and Major Tennant's fine Georgian house, Station Road, both sacrificed when the bypass was constructed. Far left, a wall of the Pioneer is just visible. (B J Robe's)

Chapter 10

Anecdotes from old Keynsham families

When horse-drawn coaches passed through the town

I discussed with Mr Ron Headington how Leslie Harding could remember the horse-drawn Royal Mail coach stopping in Keynsham. The mail was taken by train, so why the need of coaches? Ron explained that the railway needed coaches to bring the mail to them from the country villages, and before the advent of cars, this was done by coach. Mr Harding had remembered correctly!

Ron went on to say that his father remembered that at the turn of the century, horse-drawn coaches full of passengers would gallop up Bath Hill East. As they went by, he, with other boys, would run beside the coaches and call out to the passengers on the top of the coaches who were about to alight at the Talbot, 'Carry your bag?' and a passenger would throw them a farthing, or a ha'penny, to seal the contract while the coach was still moving. But boys made sure that only their mates would be allowed to do business on this site; lads from other parts of the town would be told to 'push off' and find their own pitch in another part of the town. It sounds like Dickensian London.

Ron's paternal grandfather did not approve of his son's activities, for he was a business man with his own garden nursery. Ron wasn't sure if his father did it for fun or for the money. 'Possibly grandfather was rather parsimonious'. Ron mentioned that the garage at the bottom of Saltford Hill was originally stables, which supplied trace horses to help those pulling coaches up the long winding hill.

At least up to the time of World War I, Bath Hill was much steeper than it is today, and the school wall much higher, being 10–15 ft high and much nearer the school door. Therefore the downhill road there turned more sharply, and many of the fine horse-drawn brewer's drays, coke waggons and others, had high springs. 'If one was not careful, the vehicle would turn over if travelling too quickly. On approaching the bend, the coachman used to pull on his brakes, while his mate would jump off and pour water on to the wooden brakes to lessen the friction and prevent them burning. I hate to tell you what they used if there was not water about!'

'Bath Hill road was simply earth. It was first tarmacked about 1920. I remember it well as I went out and fell flat in it. My imprint was in the road. The men picked me up. Mother wasn't very pleased but the men said, 'Leave him to us, Misses. We'll get it off. Just get a large lump of lard.' So they stripped and washed me and got the tar off. Mother said the clothes were not much good after that. To make the road, the men just poured tar on the road, then threw loose gravel on it, and rolled it.'

The chimney sweep

Ron said that at the rear of Flanders House, now the entrance to Bath Hill car park, was a field owned by his Ollis grandparents. There his mother would go with her pail and stool, and there milk their cows. Keynsham was another world in those days.

He recalled that near Flanders House, facing the old Fox and Hounds public house, was a cottage, then down several steps, but which like Flanders House, had once been level with the earlier road that led to the ford. In the cottage lived Mr Sweet the chimney sweep, and in his yard he had two handcarts loaded with brushes. In those days people cooked on an open fire, even in the summer, and therefore chimneys needed to be cleaned every few months. The use of wet logs made even more soot, so the chimney sweep was a very busy man.

Mr Sweet, who had two brothers, told Ron's father that as a boy he climbed up inside to sweep the local chimneys. 'It was terrible, it was awful. You wore pads on your knees and arms and something over your head. Bits were knocked off your hands nearly every day. Most boys wore light long trousers (the exception in those days). In some of the larger houses there were steps inside the chimneys.'

When young Sweet grew older, he took over the business. Later he married

BATH HILL WEST, early 1920s. Three Ollis girls face Miss Devenish's small sweet shop, with the Fry's advertisement, used by all the school children. The midwife, Granny Ware, with the white apron, is talking to Mrs L Headington in front of her home in the low-roofed Spring Cottage. The original Bridges' built gates, similar to today's, were then still there. Left is a KELPC street lamp, c. 1880, on a wooden post with overhead wiring.

and his daughter Annie married Mr Beale the baker who lived on 'the Skiddy Path', near today's town centre, a wide area of paving stones where children played with their hoops, roller skates and wheel carts.

Another chimney sweep

When I was discussing the subject of sweeps with Miss Fairclough, she recalled another one who was always referred to as 'Mr Hine'. 'He lived in Temple Street and later moved to Handel Road when it was built. He never rose to having a horse and cart like Mr Sweet. He went everywhere on foot, even as far as Chew Magna, with his bag of brushes over his shoulder.

'He would sweep his first chimney at 6.0 am, even if it was at Upton Cheyney, going all the way on foot, and would be home by sunset. He charged about 5/- early in the 1920s, which went up to 10/- in the 1930s. He always did a good job. It was a big occasion whenever he came, as one had to take up the carpets and clear the room as soot went everywhere. Having the sweep was a ritual.'

The Chew loses a victim

The river, prior to the alterations to the weirs after the Great Flood of 1968, used to flow more swiftly and was deeper. Locally the Chew has claimed a number of deaths in living memory, and how many more died in earlier times probably we will never know.

Mrs Doreen Gyles' father, Mr Tom Price, was in charge of the lower floor at the Albert Mill, and as such lived in the one house on the site which backed onto the river. There Doreen and her brothers grew up. She knew the experience of crossing there on foot the ancient ford, where one had to be particularly careful when the river was in full spate.

The Chapman family lived across the river at River View. One day, young Eldred, some five years old, fell in the river and was carried along until he became wedged in some bushes by the bank. Doreen's mother, Philippa, saw the accident and heard the cries of anguish of the boy's grandparents. Quickly she called for the help of a workman at the mill, who jumped over the high wall and rescued the boy. Dr Harrison was called and fortunately the boy survived, though at a cost.

Old Temple Street

Miss Fairclough said that in the Temple Street houses backing on to the Chew, their upstair windows were even lower than they seemed, as the road level had been raised. Quite a few of them had steps down to them from the road. When Mary was walking down Old Temple Street with a particularly tall American guest, the visitor was embarrassed at being able to look almost straight into the upstairs bedrooms.

No 17 Bath Hill West in 1911 where Miss Louisa Ollis poses as she returned from the funeral of William, her younger brother. A new storey had been added to this house, which was originally only as high as Spring Cottage, just visible. The lower part of 17 is under the bridge. (R Headington's)

A Temple Street boy remembers

Mr 'Jim' Ollis was born in 1912 at 75 Temple Street, two doors down from the London Inn, towards the Ship Inn, where the Gas Board HQ is now. He recalls the time when Farmer Fowler owned the farm on 'the bank' near the Dappifer's House, where one could buy butter and milk. Today it houses chemicals. The farmer owned the land between Bath Hill bridge and Dapps Hill bridge. 'There was plenty of good fishing in the Chew then, with roach, pike and perch. I was a boy then, when one night I heard the sound of a rifle shot that killed the last otter on the river, for they ate the fish. That was about 1920.

'The Chew was a deeper, faster-flowing and cleaner river in those days. I used to swim in it. One day when I was swimming I heard a commotion nearby. A boy named Pople, aged 12 to 13, who lived below the Pines on Dapps Hill in the short row of houses that face the river, had dived into the Chew, hit his head on the bottom, and didn't surface, so he drowned.

'Where the telephone exchange is at the bottom of Charlton Road was a pond, where Tom Chard, who lived in Temple Street opposite the Trout, kept ducks and few fowls to sell. Water still rises there, so every month the exchange has to have it pumped out.' Watery Keynsham indeed! 'Tom used to be a steam roller driver for Hembers of Queen Charlton, who supplied the K.U.D.C. with a steam roller when they needed one, between the wars.'

Jim lives in Cranmore Avenue. 'Where I live used to be fields earlier. At the back of my houe, behind the Charlton Road houses, was the public right of way footpath that led from the town along the edge of the fields, beside the quarry by St. Ladoc Road, across Pittsville and Lockingwell Road which was not there then, to the top of Charlton Bottom and on to Queen Charlton.'

Before you played a straight bat

A Keynsham Chronicle article of June 25, 1982, refers to the Keynsham Cricket Club in the 1920s. 'In the early days of the KCC, Dr Charles Harrison, father of Claude, was the only member who had a motor car, a 12 HP two seater Austin, and for the away matches the captain, Mr Frank Taylor, hired a taxi from Mr Reg Bailey, who kept the Railway Inn with his parents. (The Inn is now the electricity showroom near the parish church.)

Preparing the Saturday pitch was always a chore, but it was faithfully carried out on Thursday evenings after Dr Harrison's surgery closed. He and other members of the club would put a 100 gallon tank in the boot of his Austin and go down to Steel Mills Chew Bridge to fill the tank with buckets of water drawn from the Chew. Once the tank was full, the team members returned to the pitch to pour the water all over it. If the weather was exceptionally dry at least two more river trips were made to the river.

The wicket was finally covered with a tarpaulin to keep in the moisture. On Saturday the home team had to arrive early to take down the surrounding oak poles and steel hawsers and remove them to the boundary. These were used to keep Mr Bowering's [who owned all the land around there] flock of sheep which grazed on the ground during the week from trampling on the vital wicket.

In the early days all the players were local men and they changed at home because the hut accommodation was extremely cramped. It was not until Mr Spering became president that the present pavilion was built.'

Mr Leslie Whittock, a keen sportsman, said that Carpenters had the contract to roll the cricket field, and used to put big shoes over the horse's hooves so as not to damage the valuable 'square'.

That's not a football'

An interesting insight into the town's general tightness of money earlier this century is shown in Leslie's keenness in football. 'When I was about 11 or 12, the Veal's butcher's shop in Temple Street backed on to the fields by today's Carpenter's Lane. We used to wait until Veal's threw out a pig's bladder. We would take it, blood and all, wash it, then pump it up and use it as our football. It was all that we could afford.'

The prize winning animal

Les continued, 'Fred and Les Clothier farmed the Hams, which was some of the best land in the West because of the frequent flooding. Sometimes my Dad used to work for them. They bred prize-winning Devon beef cattle for the

Keynsham Fatstock Show and Sale held next to the Talbot, which was quite a big show. Mr David Fray, a High Street butcher, would display meat from the dead carcase in his window, with the Prize Winning Certificate below it, giving the details of the beast and who had bred it.'

Ice skating in Keynsham

Ron Headington recalled hearing of skating on the 'water pond' at Stockwood Vale, mentioned elsewhere. More interesting still is his account of his mother Louisa's activities in this connection.

Her father, William Ollis, owned a field that lies at Stidham, through the Brunel bridge just beyond Leo's new store, turning right beside the railway line. Opposite was the large flat low-lying field that had a stream flowing through it. As Ron said, 'Years ago, the winters were much colder. At the first sign of frost, the water was dammed lower down, and flooded the land to a depth of several inches, which then froze over. All rushes and such like were cut down earlier because if they stuck up, they would adversely affect the ice. Mother would hire ice skates from Bristol, and then hire them out to the wealthier people of Keynsham, with hot chestnuts and such for them to eat. This went on until the First World War.'

Miss Fairclough mentioned that her father had a photograph of the Hams of one particularly bad winter during the 1890s, when they were severely flooded and frozen over.

Bridge-building Brunel style

As a lad Ron had worked for a while on the local railway, where he was told the following story:

At the bottom of the park, over the Chew, beside the railway station, is a tall bridge. This was built under the very close supervision of Brunel himself, who instructed the men as to just how he wanted each brick laid in the overall design. When it was finished to his satisfaction, he then said that that was how he wanted all the bridges built from here to London.

Serving the dead and the living

At the turn of the century, 61 The High Street, now Fads, was then The Undertakers, owned by Mr John Carter. A photo taken around 1920 shows his two sons Charles and Walter outside the business, standing by a wooden handcart. Charles, fighting Parkinson's disease, carried on the family business, and is shown wearing his carpenter's apron. Walter, diagnosed as suffering from TB, left the business and married Bertha, the daughter of Charles and Naomi Hayman, who owned the china and hardware shop across the road at number 50.

When the Haymans retired in 1912, their business-like efficient daughter bought from her parents the shop and home in which she had been brought up. From then until their retirement in 1938, Bertha and Walter Carter ran a very successful business. A photo of the building taken prior to 1912 shows

Keynsham High Street looking towards Temple Street circa 1910. On the left, the Carter brothers Charles and Walter stand outside their father's Undertaker's business. Beyond them is the pointed Weighbridge. On the right, next to Hayman's shop, and outside Beake's the butcher at 52, is one of Keynsham's own early electric light poles. (P Clayfield)

Naomi and Charles Hayman's shop, 50 High Street, circa 1910, with jugs galore and mantel clocks. Today it is Lunn Poly. Just visible is 48, the home of Ed Wiggins. 46 was Loxton's and 44 Dr Harrison's. (P Clayfield)

the windows on both sides of the front door with rows of jugs, tureens, vases, wooden mantel clocks, carpets, mats and brushes. Later, under Bertha's management, she introduced a payment by instalments system, enabling the less affluent to purchase beautiful tea sets. On her retirement, the accountant found that there were no bad debts owing.

Walter owned about two acres of grassland behind Rock Road and Westview Road, now named Mayfields, where a bomb dropped harmlessly in World War II. There he had stables and grazing for his two horses and a shed for his carts. Because of his poor health, the doctor said he would never earn a penny, so to improve his condition, with his horse and cart, Walter started selling soap, paraffin and china tea services if required, in the local villages. He was so successful that he employed another young man to take the second horse and cart and sell at other villages. As his daughter Phyllis (Mrs Clayfield) said, when he came home in the winter his moustache would be covered with ice. In spite of that, he continued his rounds from 1912 to 1936, prior to retirement in 1938. He lived to be seventy-seven!

Phyl explained that he sold two grades of paraffin, each in a separate container. The better quality was more expensive, and was used by chicken breeders. However, another merchant in the town also sold the two grades of paraffin, but they both came from the one tank! On one occasion when Walter's horse was unwell, the other trader lent him his horse. This was fine,

Walter Carter circa 1920 off on his rounds to the villages with Dolly his lovely ginger mare who he had until his retirement in 1936. The lad on the left was Arthur, 'Art', Brookman and young Jim Macey. At the rear of the cart the paraffin taps are just visible. (Mrs P Clayfield's photo)

except that the new horse was used to stopping at all the public houses in the villages, and refused to go on for some time. Consequently Walter was very late home, and received an undeserved roasting for it.

Milward Lodge, Bristol Road

'Milward Lodge was owned by Mr Tom Davies, a Welshman. Today the boundary wall outside it fronting Bristol Road is capped by non-local stone. I believe these were brought by horse and cart from Keynsham railway station and came from the Prescelly Mountains in Wales,' wrote Mr Edward Cannock. Mr Davies wanted a little bit of his native Wales before his eyes, and could afford to have it brought to him.

Mr Davies used Milward Lodge with its farm buildings as an abattoir from the late 1920s to at least 1940. Edward recalled that the site of Milward Road was originally a field behind the house, where the owner grazed cattle, presumably prior to their slaughter. Also many pigs were kept in the farm buildings where he could hear them squealing, though exactly why he was not sure. There was an even larger trade in sheep, and large lorry loads of skins would be carried away, possibly to Morlands, Glastonbury.

In the overgrown walled garden above Cannock's garage, there was a caravan in which Mr and Mrs Harry Crease used to live, with a well, now capped, against the inside of the wall. Edward wrote, 'In the 1930s there was a paddock behind our garage marked by a circular path, trodden by horses being 'broken in' by Mr Crease, the horse dealer. The next field, 'Hawkswell', was the site of the pre-war Keynsham Amateur Cricket Club.'

Edward added that as his garden was higher than next door's, as a boy he could see over the wall and watch Harry at work. 'I do not remember him having a whip but just a long rope and the horses going round and round and being instructed to go quicker or slower or to stop. I did not find it particularly enjoyable or cruel, just interesting. It was an ongoing process, with many horses being involved. He was there from about the late 1920s until the end of the 1930s.

The Leslie Crowther link

Mrs Phyllis Robinson, née Glover, born in 1911, was the youngest of the five Glover children. When she left school she would go from her crowded home in 9 Fairfield Terrace along Wellsway to 13 Manor Road, and there would help Mr and Mrs Stone with their seven children. With the charm that the Glover family possess, she was soon asked to live in and so started a long and happy friendship between Phyllis and the Stone girls. Mrs Stone lived at number 13 until 1984.

Mr Walter J O Stone worked in Bristol for the tobacco firm of Edward Ringer and Biggs, while Mrs Winifred Stone was a keen photographer. All their children went to dancing classes, and moved into the world of ballet, where one of the girls, Jean, met a young man named Leslie Crowther.

Edward Cannock wrote, 'Mr Stone was an accomplished photographer favouring the 35 mm format with the early Leica camera. Mrs Stone used quarter plate equipment, mainly for portrait work. Mr Stone was President or Chairman of the local photographic club.'

There was a definite connection between Winifred Stone and the production of the Fry's famous advertisement of the five faces of a boy from Desperation to Realization, according to Edward. The child featured was Lindsay Poulton, whose grandfather Samuel Poulton was the photographer. Lindsay was born in 1882 and was only four when his picture was taken. Aged 80 in 1962 and living in Rhode Island, USA, he could still recall the pain which made him cry just when the camera was ready. This was produced by Samuel placing on the boy's neck a cloth impregnated with ammonia. That was in 1886. Obviously the advertisement was first produced in Bristol, where Fry's started in 1728, prior to their removal to Keynsham in 1924. Despite a number of enquiries, I have been unable to establish the link between the two photographers, other than that of the use of the camera, Edward concluded.

Mrs Stone's daughter, Pat, was a bridesmaid to Phyllis when she married Mr Frank Robinson in 1934. The happy couple moved to Stroud, where two babies were born to them, who sadly both died. After that, the Robinsons returned to Keynsham, where the friendship between Phyllis and the Stone girls has continued over the years. Mrs Robinson has now been a widow for 26 years.

Her friend Mrs Winifred Stone died in 1992, shortly after Leslie's accident. After a service at Corston Church, she was cremated at Haycombe Cemetery on October 6, 1992, the anniversary of Phyllis's wedding.

The Polysulphin Works and Mr Ivo Peters

According to Mr Jim Ollis, the offices of the Polysulphin works were originally in the Matthew's building near the marina. Born in 1912, Jim remembers that as a teenager, he saw large barges, painted green, being pulled by big heavy horses along the towpath from Bristol to the Polysulphin. They contained alkali and were left to be unloaded. The material was carried across the Avon from the Gloucester side by a boat pulled by a hand chain. He never saw the horses towing the barges back. He presumed they were carried back down stream by the tide. Mr Head of Bristol owned the fleet of Bristol barges.

Bert Robe wrote that, 'The Polysulphin Company, which manufactured bulk washing powder for laundries, was founded by a German named Bartelt. His son Fritz was in the British Army in World War I and was killed. When Mr Bartelt died, he was succeeded in the business by Ivo Peters senior who had married the owner's daughter, and the business prospered. The Peters owned and lived in Corston Lodge (now St Teresa's Nursing Home) there being a number of daughters and a son, Ivo Peters junior. The latter was an authority on the Somerset and Dorset Railway and published a number of books and photographs about it.

'Before the days of the railways and good roads, the Avon provided a trade link with Bristol, Bath and elsewhere. Barges were used to convey goods in bulk and for their passage, bypass canals with locks were built where weirs were constructed to provide power for mills such as the Brass Mill. Before the days of motor power, horses pulled the goods-laden barges along the waterway, hauling ropes being attached to the barges and the harness of the horses. Clearly that necessitated pathways alongside the river as towpaths, and these have existed for many years.

'At Keynsham, the towpath was on the North bank of the river, actually in Gloucestershire, although in some places it changed sides. Here, a chain-operated flat-bottomed ferry boat with sloping ends was kept available to transport horse and driver across the river to the fresh towpath. One such ferry existed at Saltford in the 1920s on the straight reach where regattas are now held. At points where a towpath crossed a road as at The White Hart [The Lock Keeper] on the Bitton Road, stout self-closing black and white gates were provided by the river authority, with similar gates where field boundaries extended to the river bank.

'The horses' job of pulling a heavily loaded barge from a floating start must have been tough, though becoming easier as they got under way. Nevertheless, they must have preferred pulling with the current rather than against it and in summer rather than winter, when the currents ran faster. The bargees and drivers must have refreshed themselves and their horses at the various locks they passed through, hence the siting of the inns, The Lock Keeper at Bitton Road, The Chequers at Hanham Abbots and The Jolly Sailor at Saltford.'

Gwen Newman recalled that the barges had been a common sight to her.

Chapter 11

Memoirs of a poacher's daughter

This biography of Mr Glover is based on an account given to me by his daughter, Mrs Gwendoline Newman.

Charles Edward Glover, 1876–1926

Charles was the eldest of the thirteen children of Edward Glover (born 1848) and his wife Sarah (1858). He was born at Lilac Cottage at the top of Aller Hill, near Langport, Somerset.

The Glovers lived in a thatched cottage. Grandfather bought it for £25, with no rates to pay. Oil lamps and candles were used for lighting. There was not a proper roof, and the stars could be seen pointing at you as you lay in bed. The floor was of flagstones, with stone stairs and bare boards in the one bedroom over a large living room. Part of the house was built of mud.

On the one side of the living room was a large bread oven, heated by wood and thorns collected from the fields. There were seats on both sides of the fire place, where one could sit and look up a large chimney to the sky. Sides of bacon, onions and such were always to be found hanging there, and a large three legged crook (an iron cooking pot) hung suspended by a chain, in which the food was cooked. This nearly always consisted of rabbit, vegetables, or a hare, which was always shot or trapped by the family.

All the guns were hung from large ceiling beams. Trees were felled to keep the fires going. With a growing family, grandfather had to do something about enlarging the house; as it was going to be difficult to find the money to do this, he sold a piece of land.

All thirteen children were christened in the famous font of Aller church, where the font is now in an alcove with railings around it, and a new one is used by the villagers. My father told me it cost 'tuppence a week' to send a child to school, but they all seemed to have had a good education in spite of this, though not many parents could afford to pay.

The only form of transport for the family was the donkey, which always took the pigs and other goods to market. As a child I remember having a pig behind the seat when I travelled with grandfather. The lavatory was a long way from the cottage. It was a dirt toilet with a round wooden seat, with one large and one small hole, with round lids, which all had to be removed from time to time for cleaning out with a bucket and spade. Clean earth was thrown in. There were no drains in those days.

Being the eldest of thirteen children, father, and the other children, all had to work hard in the fields. At harvest time they used a four-foot-six-inch flail to beat the corn. The straw was put aside for thatching. The corn was sifted, then taken some two miles to a place called Paradise to be ground. It was then used for bread, cooked with barm and yeast, in grandmother's oven.

Water was fetched from a well half way down the hill and carried to the cottage. The well was level with the ground and covered over with boards. It was built of stone and around the inside a number of frogs could be seen. And, of course, gran boiled everything. All un-needed water was put into barrels placed either side of the entrance. One was for drinking, the other for the pigs, and the donkey chose to eat the pigs' swill.

Father and his four brothers and eight sisters all had hobnail boots. A shoemaker used to walk from High Ham through the woods to collect boot repairs, for which they paid him a shilling a week.

Father told me that they were never idle, as there was always so much to do. All the children had jobs allocated to them. Blackberries had to be picked by the bucket, and primroses also had to be picked and sold. Ivy leaves were picked, pressed and put into bundles of from twenty-one to thirty. These were placed on top of each other, and sold for dyes. Peat was cut from the moors. Willows also were cut and stripped for use in making chairs and all kinds of basket work, made nearby at Curry Rivel. Though my aunt had tough hands, the willow-stripping cut into them. It was most painful.

Working in the fields was hard work. Teasels were collected for cloth. Mud and sand was collected from the River Parrot to make Bath Brick, a powder for cleaning steel and knives. Much time was spent crow scaring, gleaning the barley, singling the sugar-beet and hedging and ditching. A horse was attached to a rod and driven round in a circle to pulp mangolds and swedes, and for chaff cutting. Timber felling took time and I know that my grandfather was still doing this at the age of eighty.

The family lived by the gun and most poaching was done at night. When as a child I stopped there on holiday and they thought that I was asleep, I would look through the knot-holes in the bare floor boards. I had to walk carefully as the window came down to the floor boards and I might put my foot through it. There on the floor downstairs I could see rows of rabbits, hares, partridges and pheasants.

The children's play was limited. Sometimes a farm waggon took them to Burnham, starting at eight in the morning and returning at night. They played bat and ball, marbles, skipping, hopscotch and conkers. In the winter the children used to skate on a pond rented by grandfather George Wheedon. They had a great time at night when the moon shone down. At Christmas they sang carols at Farmer Whit's house. He gave them a penny, and promised to set the dog on them if they came again. Clothes were made from 'hand-me-downs' which seemed to be renewed about once a year.

The Glover family of Aller were well-known and liked as a hard-working family, though they were a mischievous family who were always getting into trouble. When father's brothers Frank and Ernest lived at home, they used a stile to get to Digger's Hill. The farmer who lived at Chantry Farm got his men to stop the stile with thorns, which the brothers pulled down. When the farmer again blocked the style, Frank burnt the thorns. As the boys were under-age, the irate farmer took Mrs Glover to court. On the day of the trial, she drove there all dressed up, in their donkey and cart, with a friend. Maps were produced, and the judgement was given that the stiles were to be left open as it was a public thoroughfare after all. When they came out of court, the people of the village clapped and hurrahed grandmother, and pinned red rosettes on the ladies.

At home it was business as usual, with moles being trapped and sold for 4d, and rabbit skins, with their heads on, being sold for 6d. For the defendant, it was back to making elver pies and cakes.

It was on March 26, 1876, that Charles Glover was born at Lilac Cottage. Elsie, the 13th child, was born there on Dec 29, 1902. The house still stands at the top of the hill, very much enlarged and modernised. When my grandparents died, my uncle Frank lived there. He later sold it, with the two fields attached to it, for £100 to a Mr Adams.'

Was it the birth of Elsie into a home already bursting at the seams that finally thrust Charles out from his loving parents? It would have been the normal thing. Elder girls would usually go into service. Charles went north. The year, 1903.

To pastures new

'My father then moved to Keynsham. He was a strong man, short and stocky, with a red face and auburn hair parted in the middle and forming two curls over his forehead. He could turn his hand to any kind of work because of his upbringing. On the local farms it was hedging and ditching, ploughing and sowing, reaping and thatching. No job was too hard for him.'

Ploughing would remind him of his Aller home and past competitions. 'The Glover boys entered ploughing matches, three horses in plough, competing in the Open Championship for the county. They spent the whole of the night before cleaning about a hundred horse-brasses. Each horse had to be well-groomed and its tail plated. There were twenty ploughs to each quarter of an acre, with measured pegs. The brothers won the first prize of £10 and a new plough.'

In 1903 Charles Glover was 27. In his subsequent marriage, he found again the home life that he had lost at Aller. He rented a stone house in the picturesque area of Steel Mills, where five children were born to him. The middle child was Gwendoline, author of the above narrative.

He was aware of the income that could be derived from farm animals, so he obtained a small-holding at the top of Workhouse Lane, as it was called in his day, opposite the entrance to Conygre Farm. There he kept goats, pigs, chickens and geese. Behind his small-holding was a large tipping quarry. At one time he had an agreement with Farmer Gifford to buy the produce of Gifford's apple and walnut orchard at Chewton Keynsham. By this time, Charles had moved to 9 Fairfield Terrace, from where he sold the crop. The vegetables for his family were grown on one of the allotments at the rear of the Workhouse, where the plots were let out annually.

A neighbour of his at 15 Fairfield Terrace sought his help because she had rats under the passage of her house. Charles fetched his ferret from its cage on the wall in the back yard, and placed it in the front of the neighbour's house.

Moments later mother rat appeared running away at the back of her house, followed by her litter. The ferret overtook and killed them all.

Charles always held the ferrets by their necks, and kept two or three,. He fed them on raw meat. As was the custom in those days, he used traps. These were wire snares which were pegged into the ground. When the head of a small animal entered the open wire circle, the loop tightened and the creature died. As his daughter said, 'He didn't use them a lot.'

More frightening still was the use of the gin trap. Wired to the ground, it had metal jaws which snapped shut when trodden on. The feet of animals small and large would be held as in a vice, until 'released' by death. When these were finally outlawed, Charles then turned to the greater use of nets and of the double-barrelled shotgun. Even then, just occasionally . . .

The Great War of 1914–1918

'Father was 38 when the war started, and he joined the Royal Army Service Corps.'

During the war, mules were of great use in carrying ammunition, food and supplies up to the front-line. The military powers in their wisdom decided that Keynsham, well known for its fine pasture, would be an ideal staging post at which to collect mules prior to their journey from Avonmouth to France. Accordingly, thousands of the animals were brought here by train, and were herded by troops up Park Road to the fields at the end of the road.

Unfortunately, anthrax broke out among the mules and those infected were killed, burned and buried in lime in the area between Conygre Farm and the allotments. Many mules survived the outbreak, and Charles Glover was among the RASC soldiers from Keynsham who herded the animals on to trains at Keynsham goods station, and went with them to France. Gwen, aged seven, was one of the many local children who saw their fathers off. A moving experience indeed.

Charles reached France safely, but there, the hernia that he had sustained as a lad of eighteen was discovered. At that time, only really fit soldiers were required, so Charles was discharged on medical grounds, and was soon back again in Keynsham.

The last days of well-water

The seven houses at the end of Steel Mills Lane boasted three wells. By early this century, one well at least had a pump inserted in it. In the morning, Gwen would come out of her home, wash her face under the pump, and allow it to dry as she ran off to school. The girls were allowed to use the outside toilet at Chew Bridge Cottage if necessary on their way to school.

'My father sank several wells in Keynsham in the period 1910–1925. My elder brother Ernest helped him. They dug two wells in the Breeches Lane area, another for Mr Hedges in Hurn Lane, and yet another in the Queen Charlton fields. He dug one at Lays Farm, but as there was seepage of manure from the cows in a higher field, he had to fill the well in again.'

In constructing wells, Charles used a bucket extensively to take up the soil

CHARLES HENRY GLOVER, 1876–1926.

He was a warm hearted countryman who could turn his hand to almost any task on a farm, and his services were in demand by the local farmers. Yet he could also dig wells, and with his ferret, was an accomplished poacher. His eldest daughter, Mrs Phyl Robinson, said of this photo, 'He is wearing his Army Discharge (Disabled) Badge which he was so proud of and wore wherever he went. His tie was never straight. The photo was taken at the wedding of his grandson Ian, the elder son of his daughter, Mrs Gwen Newman.' (Mrs Robinson's photograph)

that he had dug out, and to bring down stone for making the walls. His daughter, Mrs Phyllis Robinson, recently confessed that all that she could now remember about well-making was having lovely rides up and down in the bucket, while her brother Ernest turned the windlass.

Charles came from a religious family, and was always singing or quoting verse. However, when he had no work and no money, he revealed other interests. As Gwen penned,

> 'He poached and he gambled,
> His gun was his best friend.'

'My father was known as one of the local poachers, together with his friend, Butty Watts. When not working, my father could be seen with his gun under his arm, or folded in his inside pocket, with a spaniel at his heels. He wore a peaked cap and at most times a muffler round his neck. Breeches, leggings and a large poaching jacket would complete the picture. It was amazing what the pockets of that coat could carry, as they were made to go all round the back. It carried birds, rabbits, sometimes a hare, and always a ferret in a small hesian bag. It fell to my lot to make these bags on the hand sewing machine, and I know I lost the nails of my fingers as the material was so tough. In later years I made the bags for my brother.'

Charles worked on a number of farms in this area. Was this just chance? How this ties up with poaching is admirably explained by Oby [Obadiah], 'the most determined poacher', in Richard Jefferies' 'The Amateur Poacher', 1879, p 260.

'You see by going out piece-work, I visits every farm in the parish. The other men they works for one farmer, for two or three or maybe twenty years: but I goes very nigh all round the place, a fortnight here and a week there, and then a month somewhere else. So I knows every hare in the parish, and all his runs and all the double mounds and copses, and the little covers in the corner of the fields. When I work on one place, I sets my wires about half a mile away on a farm as I ain't been working for a month, and where the keeper don't keep no special look out now I've gone. As I goes all round, I knows the ways of all the farmers, and them as bides out late at night at their friends and they as goes to bed early; and so I know what paths to follow and what fields I can walk about in and never meet nobody. The dodge is to be always in the fields and to know everybody's ways. Then you may do just as you be a mind. All of them knows I be a-poaching; but that don't make no difference for work.'

In that late Edwardian period fashionable ladies wore fox furs and capes. There was a large demand for fox skins and poacher Charles obliged. 'He would track a fox or hare through a field and would always shoot it. I understand that he was a good shot. Father would help with the dogs in beating the hedges. He shot a number of foxes, most of which he would send to Yeovil for curing. He killed badgers too. His chief joy was his gun, though he never went shooting without his faithful dog Shamat, who never barked on such occasions as he was fully gun-trained.

'He shot a fox on Stidham's farmland, and had it made into a stole for my mother, who always wore it in the village. He shot another fox and pheasant which were stuffed and put into a glass case for the landlord of the London Inn in Temple Street, [now pulled down] and it was on show in the bar for years.

> The badgers and foxes he had killed by the score,
> With game, hare and rabbits there are hundreds I'm sure.'

Jefferies wrote that many farmers were happy to have the poachers shooting the rabbits, hares and pheasants as they ate their corn and clover. Gwen wrote, 'Father shot all the foxes and badgers as they were a menace on the farms.'

Some farmers called him in, others just agreed to him shooting on their land, while others banned him. Obviously he was only poaching on banned land. Keynsham's earlier fine stone Police Station embraced a total force of Sergeant Salmon, Constable Hale and another constable. A suspicious PC Hale said, 'I'll catch you one of these days, Glover', who replied, 'I'll be up at Long Wood [Saltford] tonight. Come up and catch me.' Against a loaded gun, Hale concluded that 'discretion was the better part of valour.'

When I asked Gwen if her father was hindered very much by game-keepers I received the surprising reply that he had been a keeper himself at Chewton House, where he had helped in organising shoots.

> The night was his best time, it was never too dark;
> To the woods he would venture seeking game in the park.'

At home Mrs Glover really did worry about his nocturnal activities. Gwen would sleep at the foot of her mother's bed until in her Fairfield Terrace home she heard the sound of his hobnail boots on the Dapps Hill bridge. Then it was 'You can go now, Gwen'.

But, of course, Charles could look after himself. If there was a thunderstorm when he was out at night, as a precaution against lightning, he would hide his gun under a hedge and collect it next day. If he was out in the daytime and was tired, and was possibly waiting for a fox to come along, he would unroll a newspaper and sleep on it.

He did have a gun licence. He kept two or three guns in the corner of the kitchen, pointing upwards. When Gwen was told by her father, 'Don't touch the gun, girl', she obeyed. She then knew that it was loaded. Sometimes she was sent into 'the village' to buy a box of cartridges. She had to go via Back Lane to reach Hickling's shop in the High Street to ask for 'Kinyax 5'. 'Be sure you go back down Back Lane,' Hickling would remind her. She certainly must avoid PC Hale, who would be in the High Street.

'Because he could turn his hand to anything, farmers would call at the house for his help,' Gwen said. Sometimes his assistance had nothing to do with farming. Early one morning he was walking beside the Avon by the Polysulphin works, looking for a fox, when he saw a bundle of clothing caught up on a branch of a tree jutting out over the river. He waded across and found that they were the clothes of a dead fourteen-year-old girl. He carried her to the village mortuary at the stable complex beside the New Inn, next to Trott's the blacksmith. From his home nearby, Charles collected a comb, washed it, and returned to the mortuary to wash and comb the girl's hair. He even polished her brown shoes. Apparently she came from Twerton, Bath, and had been pushed into the river by her brother.

'Father was full of fun and would do anything for a dare. One day, after catching a sack-ful of rabbits, he informed Mr Whiting, proprietor of the Lamb and Lark hotel, that he was going to let the rabbits loose in the smoke room, which was full of women. He did. After much noise and screaming, he caught them again and took them down to the Crown Fields for dog coursing.'

'With his breeches he wore brown shining leggings with string tied round his breeches below the knees. He never killed spiders. He sheared sheep with hand clippers, dipped pigs and put rings in their noses. He would bring home mushrooms the size of a dinner plate. At harvest time it was his job to scythe round the outside of the corn field, to clear a path for the horse-drawn reaper and binder. It was hard skilled work.

'I used to help him poaching. He would show me crumpled grass in a field where a rabbit had recently gone through. We used to put our nets over one side of the rabbit burrow, round at the tip of the Scrambles. Dad then put the ferret in the other end and out the rabbits would come. Though you could buy the nets, I made our own out of strong string, about three feet square. We usually took four or five nets. When caught, Dad would pull the rabbit's neck and shoulders, which killed it instantly. It was called "wristing their necks".'

Jefferies explained that, 'The ferreting season commences when the frosts have caused the leaves to drop and the rabbits grow fat from feeding on bark . . . Those who go poaching with ferrets choose a moonlight night; if it is dark it is difficult to find the holes. Small burrows are best because they are so much more easily managed.' He added that a person had to be particular how he fed his ferrets, for they must be eager for prey and yet they must not be starved else they would gorge on the blood of the first rabbit and become useless for hunting. Again, a ferret could be muzzled with string behind his teeth, or have the end of a long length of string tied round his neck before putting him into the burrows.

Gwen said, 'Father would spend a lot of time digging out a ferret of his that had gone underground and, content with his meal of rabbits, refused to come up. You could buy another ferret, but they were expensive and we were hard up . . . On the way home from a night's poaching, he would put a pair of glow-worms in the front of his cap for fun.'

He had a number of private customers for his fresh-killed game and rabbits. We have seen that fox furs were sent for curing and making up. Gwen commented, 'My sister and I helped dispose of the game. Of the three families that lived in the Pines on Dapps Hill (demolished) one family used to sell a lot of poultry, and we supplied them with many rabbits, for cash. Another customer and his wife lived opposite the Talbot, and would occasionally have a pheasant. There were many other customers. I don't think we supplied any of the butcher's shops.'

It was fortunate that this was nearer 1916 than a century earlier. G M Trevelyan's 'English Social History' [1942, p 507] records that, 'By a new law of 1816, the starving cottager who went out to take a hare or rabbit for the family pot, could be transported for seven years if caught with his nets upon him at night.'!

'Father was once summoned for trespassing and shooting at a place where he had not been authorized. He went to the Keynsham Court with a rabbit in his poaching coat. He was fined five shillings, and came out with a big smile, and showed the rabbit to Mr Willcox, the nearby builder, who really enjoyed the joke.'

'Legging rabbits' was the method by which a number of dead ones could be carried on a stick. Gwen explained the process. 'Get hold of the back legs of the dead rabbit, and with a knife cut a hole through the fur and sinews of both legs just above the paws, large enough to thread the legs on to a pole carried over the shoulder, with up to a dozen rabbits in front and a dozen behind.'

Charles shot a vixen and offered it to Gwen as a present. She rejected it as it had a slightly damaged skin, and he could easily shoot her another. The skin was cured and made into the finished fox fur, and was sold to a lady who still lives in Bath Road. The year was 1926.

That fox was the last animal he ever shot. The next night he was in great pain from his hernia. He was operated on in hospital next day, but sadly he died a few hours later, aged just fifty.

He had earlier bought two horses at the Bridgwater Fair. One now had to be sold for funeral expenses. 'When my grandfather Edward Glover came to Keynsham for my father's funeral, he had never left Aller before, and had never seen nor travelled on a bus nor a train.'

Charles had indeed died young for a Glover. Eight of his brothers and sisters averaged eighty-one years. Now even Fairfield Terrace has gone and not a trace of that remains either.

Chapter 12

'Sights and sounds of smoky old Keynsham,' recalled by Mrs Gwen Newman

The Keynsham Chronicle of March 3 1989 recorded the passing of 'Mrs Gwen Newman, née Glover', who would have been 81 next month. She was a resourceful, cheerful and hardworking person all her life, being one of five children in an age when young labour was mercilessly exploited.'

On 18 March 1987 I spent another of my many happy visits to her home, researching my initial interest in wells. On this particular occasion I took my tape recorder, and though that was now nearly four years ago, she, like Abel of old, 'being dead, yet speaketh.' Already she had given me permission to use her article, 'Money comes slowly', while together we had produced the biography of her father, Charles Glover. Now in her absence I will try to complete the recording for posterity of her memories and observations, expressed 'in ipsissimis verbis.'

The Workhouse, its tramps and its children

'The population of Keynsham in 1911 was 3,720. At the Workhouse there were 11 officers and 128 inmates. From Steel Mills, where I lived with my husband and our two sons, we could see the building . . . Dapps Hill is one of the best unspoiled parts left of Keynsham.

'The bell at the Workhouse rang three times a day, which was a great help to the surrounding workers. It also told us when we were late for school when it rang at 9.00 [also at 12 and 5?] . . . There were some local children at 'the spike', who were orphans or whose parents could not look after them. They were all dressed in drab clothes, and wore knickerbockers below their knees. When they came to school their hair was cut very short and looked as if it had had a pudding basin put on it. I can see them now coming to school, and it was a very sad sight.

'They came to the Dapps Hill Infants School [note the terminology] and Bath Hill School. I used to visit the children at the Workhouse. We would go and sit down and talk to them. With the women, they were just sitting about all over the yard. One woman sitting beside me had a stroke and no one took any notice of her. She just had to get on with it, until she got up. It was a terrible place, a terrible place!

'At the back of the Workhouse, there are steps going up. My mother had twin boys there, who died. We three girls used to go there, and she'd come to the top of the steps and wave and throw sweets down to us. That was in 1920.

'In 1897 they spent an additional £18,000 on the Workhouse. At one time Mr Dorey was the manager there.

'At the Workhouse they cracked stones and chopped wood, near the men's washing rooms by the rear entrance. My husband's father was a stone cracker on the roads in Keynsham. I remember him sitting down on the Wellsway, at the side of the road, cracking stones. He would sit there all day, with some bread and cheese. He had a heap of stones in front of him. They had a number of stone crackers in Keynsham – it was an everlasting job.'

'Tramps or hobos galore'

'The tramps were dirty and hungry, and were just always there, wherever you looked. They just seemed to belong. We took no notice of them. Though there were no street lights [where Gwen lived at Steel Mills], there were no rapes or robberies with them; they were harmless. Every day they would obtain a ticket from the police station for food, which they would spend at the shop in the front room of the house next to the New Inn at 4 Wellsway, where there was a lamp on the counter.' [There was a large range for baking in the spacious kitchen inside. I am sure that Gwen told me how the local sharp-eyed children watched as the old lady who ran the shop rested her thumb on the scales when weighing out food!].

'The ticket would provide them with 2 oz of tea, 2 oz of sugar, and some bread and some cheese. They would bring an old tin up to mother's, who would always give them hot water to make tea, but forbade us giving them milk or sugar, though I always gave them some food. Then you would see them asleep under a hedge or in a doorway. Later they would go up to the spike, as we called it, for the night and sleep on a straw bed.

'We always knew when there was a funeral in the village because the toll bell was rung as the cortege was due to pass St John's and could be heard until the mourners reached the cemetery. It was known as "the death knell".

'It was a sad day when Ruben Cox, of Prospect Place, Temple Street, was crushed and killed when working on the big wheel at the log mill and it moved. The path through the mill towards Chewton leads to the deeper water of the Chew, by the mill ground, where I've watched people being pulled out who have drowned themselves. There was old Mr Carpenter, then another man and later 'a lovely girl of Dapps Hill', who shall both remain nameless.

'In holiday times, people were always swimming and paddling in the river. We have actually walked on the frozen Chew towards Chewton under the bridge. The winters now are nothing compared with what we were used to. Horse and carts used to clear snow from the two Bath Hills and drop it into the river from a slope besides Flanders House . . . At one time the river was covered right over with flowers.'

Horse power of old

'Dad had a smallholding near the old quarry on the slope above Workhouse Lane towards Conygre Farm, where he kept pigs, chickens, ducks and geese. Before school my sisters and I used to feed them with small boiled potatoes and chopped-up barley meal. Then we would climb the hill again at night, and on the way back we had to dig potatoes and collect vegetables from father's allotment.

'The Logwood Mill at Crox Bottom was owned by Mr William Thomas, who lived at St Augustine's in Station Road. It was a common sight to see large waggons carrying heavy trees and Tom Carpenter trying to hold the waggon and make extra brakes for the horses on the steep hill down. There was Mr Crew and Mr Forest and others who worked on the chopper and lived in Steel Mills. It was a lovely old mill and we could see and hear it from our garden across the river at Steel Mills.

'Stan Clark used to work with Tom Carpenter, who used to live in Carpenters Lane and kept his horses there, which he used for carrying the trees for the mill.

'The well-known Bowering family, who lived up The Hollow, through Steel Mills and up Wellsway, kept lovely horses. They would drive to church in their top hats, driven in an open or closed coach. Dr Fox at Brislington had seven victorias where his wealthy patients could sit facing each other. It was a common sight to see them driving through Keynsham. He died in the Grange Nursing Home, where I used to work.

'Captain Kinnersley lived at the Homestead toward the top of Wellsway, a lovely big house that overlooked Chewton. His brother, who was a dentist, lived in Durley Hill. They were a well-known family. The Captain was a very tough man and was not liked very much. I used to work there in the 1930s. He grew oranges in Spain. He kept his dogs locked up. It was said that he treated his workmen and his dogs like he treated his niggers in Spain! He married Dr Taylor's sister. Captain Kinnersley always used to ride on horseback through the town.'

Life on the farm

'As a girl of 14 I worked with my brother Christopher at Conygre Farm. On one occasion I had to collect some young pigs from Marksbury with Austin the farmer's son. At this time all animals were driven by road and there were not many cars to be seen; it was mainly horse and carts. We managed them very well down Burnett Lane, which was a narrow road then. But at the bottom of Crox Bottom the children from Dapps Hill Infant School saw the pigs and started shouting and the pigs went all ways and one got stuck in a gate in Gooseberry Lane. But between us we got them to the farm.

'Some of my happiest times where when harvesting and stooking sheaves of corn. Then during a break I would share the bread and cheese passed round, and drink from the jar with a handle, good old rough Somerset cider. Sometimes I would sit and watch the horse walk round and round which helped to work the elevator to take hay up to the stack. There were no tractors in those days. Everything was collected by carts and waggons and most things were horse-drawn.'

Pollarding the willows for basket making at White's Mead, below Temple Street, probably between the Great Wars. The exposed River Chew meanders by.

'Making silage on Somerdale estate' is Fry's caption to this wartime photo. The name 'Clothier', who farmed the Hams, is on the headboard.

Brick town

'Oh, Prospect Place was a lovely place! It used to look straight down on the Chew. Fairfield Terrace was parallel with the river and was known as the "Brick Houses". Woodbine Cottages were the "Stone Houses". They were lovely cottages. There was a place in Temple Street where you could go under a tunnel to get to Prospect Place, and that was the original Labbott. Further along Temple Street was another entrance to Prospect Place. There were neither toilets nor electricity there, just candle light.

'At the cross-roads at the top of Bath Hill East was the Queen Victoria Fountain. It had steps all around the bottom of it, where we children sat and waved to the troops in the First World War. We drank from a heavy brass bowl there. When it was finally removed, it was laid in a builder's yard for years. I don't know what happened to it.'

The Fever Hospital

'This was where the Elim Church is now. It was just an old converted corrugated iron building, painted a khaki colour. It was divided into a scarlet fever section and a diphtheria part. I spent my 21st birthday there with diphtheria. I caught it from a workman's well that they used when building the Pits' houses. They treated it very severely then. Dr Willet was in charge of the hospital. They used to burn your infected clothes but I bribed the man to fumigate my birthday cards, which I was then able to keep for many years,' concluded Mrs Gwen Newman.

Mr William Sherer wrote that 'The old Keynsham fever hospital was situated near to where the Elim Chapel now stands. A driveway led to the hospital, and at the entrance stood a lodge, where presumably the matron lived. Visitors had to look through the windows to speak to the patients; there would probably be few of the former on wet days!' [as the hospital was in the middle of fields in those days before the estate was built.]

'I understand the interior was comfortably furnished, but the exterior of the building was most unattractive; it had a galvanised iron roof painted red.

'At the age of 15 I contracted scarlet fever. Our family doctor, the late Claude Harrison, told my mother it would be necessary for me to go into the hospital. My mother indignantly told him that no child of hers was going into that 'tin shed.' The doctor was most incensed at this remark, and told her it would be necessary for my sister Muriel and my brother Courtney to remain home from school for three weeks and have no contact with other children.

'When I recovered, Mr Watts, the then sanitary inspector, called and took away the bedding in a horse-drawn van for fumigation.'

He added that he thought that the fever hospital was seldom full, though people used to have a horror of fever years ago, and a number of local children died of diphtheria. The building was a single storey high and the entrance was in what is now Park Road. Though bedding and even one's pyjamas were removed for fumigation, they were duly returned next day.

'I remember an elderly widow named Mrs Williams who lived in Temple Street in the thirties. She used to supplement her meagre pension by selling sticks of firewood and jars of pickled onions and fruit from her parlour window. Would present-day planners approve of such pensioner enterprise?' asked Mr Sherer.

The late Mr Leonard Ellis, explaining that the fever hospital was in the wilds surrounded by fields, added, 'At the lodge at the top of the drive lived the matron, Mrs Botting. There was a lot of diphtheria about in those days, and my sister went there with scarlet fever. The horse-drawn ambulance was beautifully made, of real quality like a horsebox, and was not drawn by a heavy shire horse, but by a tradesman's lighter horse.

'As the ambulance went by, we always held our noses so that we didn't get the germs. Charlie Webb was the last driver of the horse ambulance. He would take you to the hospital, then return the same day to collect your blankets for sterilisation.'

PART TWO

WORLD WAR I
and the years before
WORLD WAR II

Chapter 13

Happenings in the Keynsham area in the 1914–1918 War

The well-known Keynsham personality, Mrs Susan James, kindly contributed the following account.

'Although I was only four years old, I remember clearly the outbreak of war in 1914. We were due to go to Switzerland to stay with the family of our much-loved Swiss nurse. I had been so excited at the thought of crossing 21 miles of water in a boat. To me a boat was propelled with oars, and anything with an engine was a ship. Its cancellation was a great disappointment.

'In the summer of 1914 my brother Guy was taken ill with appendicitis. He was too ill to remove to hospital, so the dining room was covered with sheets and sprayed with carbolic, and the kitchen table well scrubbed as an operating table. Fortunately the operation was a success.

'My brother was really very ill and my mother, Mrs Beatrice Parker, had to attend to him at night. We lived at that time at Woodman's Cottage, on Lansdown, above Bath, and during my mother's night time vigils, she became aware of a flashing light in the direction of North Stoke. She made notes of the long and short flashes, and reported it to the 'powers that were'. She was asked to continue to keep watch and make notes of the flashes. This she did and duly reported the results. In a short while the flashing light ceased. We were never told what happened. It would have been very interesting to know!

'One year we had a glut of plums at our fruit farm. The starlings had descended on the trees and pecked the fruit, making it unfit for sale. So my mother wrote to the 'powers that were' and offered to make jam if they would supply the sugar. This was successfully accomplished, the jam being made in the chaff house that was usually used for boiling pig food. My sister Mary and I were set to work to crack the plum stones and remove the kernels, which were put into the jam.'

'One of our great sorrows was the requisitioning of Jolly, our beautiful chestnut cart-horse, who no doubt came to a sad and terrifying end in Flanders. We were not the only ones to part with a valuable horse. All the farmers in the neighbourhood had to lose one.

'In 1916 my father, John Scott Parker, went to France. He was too old for active service, but he went to start the task of making war cemeteries into peaceful gardens.

'The winter of 1916 was very cold. On Lansdown the snow was so deep that you could walk from end to end of the down and not see a wall. The Bath bakers named Plenty delivered bread with a horse and cart, and one day the delivery man became so cold that he collapsed and was found dead seated in a snow drift.

'Our house, being just below the brow of the hill, was properly snowed in.

But Mother, ever resourceful, got in touch with the Commanding Officer of the troops billeted in Bath, and asked to be dug out. Two hundred men were sent out, 100 worked on the road across Lansdown, 50 on our drive and round the house, and 50 dug Bannerdown End out. Though rationing was strict, milk could be had with no restriction, so large quantities of cocoa were made for the men working on our drive.

'We used to have a gallon of milk a day, which was scalded, and we had large bowls of Devonshire cream, the skim milk being used for puddings. Rude remarks were made to the effect that we were 'profiteering'. But of course the cream helped out the butter which was strictly rationed. So was margarine.

'Mother used to drive into Bath on Fridays, in a pony and trap of course, to do the shopping. She would take my sister and me with her so that we could queue for margarine. No one could buy more than ½ lb at a time, so it helped if there were three of us. Otherwise Mother would have to spend ages rejoining the queue after each purchase.

'After my father went to France, Mother took over the management of our fruit farm, which was down in Pipley Bottom. She wore breeches in the winter and gingham bloomers and tunic to match in the summer. She was considered 'very modern'. She worked very hard. I remember one summer when the raspberry crop was heavy, she stayed down at Pipley weighing and packing the fruit for market, arriving home at about midnight.

'In 1919 the family went to France to join Father. The country was still very unsettled, with German prisoners clearing up the battle fields, and the Chinese Labour Corps doing the manual work for the army behind the devastated area. My father took us to see the Ypres battle field. He wanted us to realise what war meant.

'I remember standing on the Ypres ramparts looking over a ravaged country-side. No building was more than 2 or 3 feet high. The woods were shattered and covered with brambles. There were no land marks. Everything was a dull-coloured sameness. The roads were sleepers laid on the mud and the trenches still in being. That is where we saw the German prisoners clearing up. So we learned the results of war, not only in the devastation, but in the senseless loss of life, and the misery of the country people who lost so much.'

'Just a boy of six

The much respected Mr Leonard Ellis, for many years a member of the Keynsham Urban District Council, told me that his father, Mr William Finlay Ellis, came to Keynsham at the turn of this century from Hamilton, Strathclyde, Scotland. He was a representative for the printing company, Edward Everard, and for a whisky company. One evening in 1913, after a day's business in London, he alighted from the train and made his way to his home at 31 Avon Mill Lane, Keynsham. As he walked, he saw a man in the River Chew struggling in great distress. Bravely William entered the strongly-flowing river and safely rescued the drowning man. Unfortunately for Mr Ellis, he caught a chill, which turned to pneumonia, then to tuberculosis, from which he died a year later.

Many years later, Leonard wrote that 'I was six years old when the First World War started, and I remember well the talk about the wicked 'Kaiser Bill', and we children were very often 'frightened' to bed by being told that he would get us. At school (Keynsham High – up three steps!) we had prayers every morning taken by the Head (Gaffer Wheeler), especially for those men from Keynsham.

'Coal being short, we were told to 'put the poker to bed' for the rest of the war, and to sieve all the ashes to take out the cinders for burning again. The electric street-lamps were blacked out, leaving a small circle of light at the bottom, which was not much help for walking at night.

'One day early in the war, there was a gathering of local soldiers, in uniform, outside the old Lamb and Lark Hotel, (where Ronto's is now), who marched behind a local band to Keynsham railway station and to an unknown destination, possibly Salisbury Plain. I think they were part of the Somerset Light Infantry.

'As the men were called up, the ladies took over sweeping the untarmacked roads, and working in the "munition factories". One was in the High Street where the Halifax Building Society now is, and another was in Bath Road at the Tangent Tool Company, now Somerdale Motors.

'My father died in 1914 in the week that war was declared, leaving mother with five children. Times were very hard and food was short and dear. I remember my mother walking to Bristol and back to get some dripping. When I was older, I often used to walk to Bristol and back.

'I attended services at St John's, the parish church, which was lit by gas lamps. When the vicar came to his sermon, the gas was turned down to half, as a black-out precaution.

'A very vivid memory is of the mules who were kept at the end of Park Road, where the allotments now are. There seemed to be hundreds of them and they kept breaking out, especially at night and then we would hear the soldiers on their mules galloping all round Keynsham to round them up, and driving them out of people's gardens. Towards the end of the war, there was an outbreak of anthrax (I think the disease was) and many were killed and thrown into lime pits. They burnt hundreds of them. Soon after that, they closed the whole operation down.

'Armistice Day, 1918, I remember, was a day of joy and sorrow. There were crowds in the streets and a service in the Parish Church, where scaffolding was pulled up to the church tower because there was no flagpole there at the time on which to hoist up and fly the Union Jack.'

I would not want anyone to think that men were chauvinists, but Mr Ellis said to me later that 'The first Armistice service in the parish church in Keynsham was for men only. The parish council was invited, which at that time included a lady, a Mrs Crease, who insisted on attending and she did.' A case of more war-time courage, eh?

'Some of the soldiers married Keynsham girls and stayed in the district. One of the soldiers named Hooper lived in Rock Road, having married a Keynsham girl,' concluded Mr Ellis.

Large posters showed General Haig with his finger pointing outwards, and the caption declaring, 'Your country needs you.' So many men responded to the call to arms that women undertook men's work. Mrs Gwen Newman said, 'My mother was one of a group of women who helped the war effort by sweeping the streets of Keynsham to Hallatrow. Sometimes the sweeping was followed by a mounted horse-drawn barrel of tar, which was sprayed on the road.'

Mrs Newman recalled that during the war the buildings on the far South side of Keynsham's workhouse in the Conygre Farm direction were used for training nurses to help at 'the Front'.

Conditions on the 'Home Front' in Keynsham in World War

I am indebted, for the following information, to a man above reproach, the tall respected figure of Mr Jessie Stickler, who has distinguished himself both in the banking profession and as a Methodist local preacher. Born in Chipping Sodbury in October 1902, he was only six months old when he came with his parents to live at Number One, Station Road, Keynsham. Next door to them was the vicarage, which Mr Stickler declared to have a garden of almost two acres, which encompassed most of today's Vicarage Green.

His father, in the leather business, wanted young Jessie to mix with the local children without 'any snobbery', and accordingly sent him to the neighbouring school at Temple Street. 'From there I went to St George's School, then I took a degree at London University, where I got an Honour's degree, a First, in Bachelor of Commerce. The University does not offer it now as the banks would not support it, so it died out.'

Mr Stickler continued, 'And of course, before the buses took all the trade, crowds of people would go down for the morning train. In those days, before the War, you could tell the time by the people who caught the trains. Joe Bloggs always caught the 7.19 and Miss So-and-So the 8.37. The road was full of people catching trains. You would get hundreds between 7.30 and 9.30 in the morning.

'On some Saturdays, an even bigger crowd would come up the road off the 1.00 train for rabbit-coursing, down the lane beside the Pioneer public house, and before the police could stop it, it would be over. Hundreds of people came to that. Of course we didn't see it. It was all 'hush hush' and our parents didn't approve of it. But we knew what was going on. They were such a rough crowd and I was only a boy then.' One imagines that in one of the fields at the end of the lane, one group had rabbits in boxes, while another group held dogs. Presumably bets had been placed earlier, and at a given signal, one conjectures that both groups of animals were released, with betting on which dog killed first, or on which dog killed most rabbits. Whatever actually happened, it was obviously a pretty bestial affair.

Jessie continued, 'If a car came, we all ran to the door to see it. You could hear it coming, as there were no silencers much in those days. It was quite an event, and all the children stopped what they were doing and went out to look, from the triangle outside the church. Opposite St John's was the vicarage, which had most of the land where Vicarage Green now is. It had a wacking great garden of almost two acres, I think it was.

'I recall the buses coming too. It was nine pence a return to Bristol, which was a lot of money in those days. Then the Pioneer started a bus which would come a minute before the other one. They didn't publish a timetable, but the people supported it against the big concern, the Bristol Omnibus Company. There was quite a performance about this.

'I believe the houses in Station Road did have wells, but we had a tap. We lived at Number One, but things are completely different now. There was a path on only one side of Station Road, when I was a boy. There was no path on the church side. There was no need for one. The railway bridge is the same as it used to be, and I used to arrange to be on the bridge at eleven o'clock in the morning to see 'The Great Bear' go through. It ran from down south somewhere right up to Carlisle.'

[Bert Robe wrote 'I travelled on a train pulled by 'The Great Bear' several times about 1918–19 when it was under test as a stopping train from Swindon to Bristol. But it proved to be too heavy for the 'Express Train' work for which it had been designed.']

'There was a well up Charlton Road on the left hand side just before you came to Charlton Park Road, and you could turn the handle of it until quite recently when some hooligans knocked the rollers off it. I remember Mr Coles, of a leading Methodist family, who had to go there and draw water when West View Road ran short, which they did every now and again. And he found tiny minnows in it,' laughed Mr Stickler.

He continued, 'In 1914, Victoria Chapel had decided to start a Scout troop and we youngsters persuaded our parents to let us join. We turned up for the first enrolment and lined up in two ranks in the old church hall at the rear of Victoria, and a chap, one of the Jenkinses I believe, agreed to be the Scout Master. It so happened that he was also in the local yeomanry, I think, and he went off and got killed in the war so we never saw him again. We had all turned up and been told what to do and how to get a uniform, which was the big draw.

'Most of our men went into the North Somerset Yeomanry. It was the correct thing, if you belonged to a sufficiently high social family, to borrow a horse or own one if you could, and join the NS Yeomanry. You used to go off for a fortnight and have a good time. I believe Tubby Loxton was in that. It was a form of the Territorials.'

[Bert Robe wrote that 'A number of Keynsham young men were in the NSY. In addition to Tubby Loxton there were, to my knowledge, the Stokes brothers, Cyril and Eric, and Mitchell Bond, who was in France in 1914 and served in the Home Guard in World War II.']

I asked Jessie about food rationing. 'I lived with my Mother then, and we had half a pint of milk twice a week. Things got a bit bad towards the end of the First War . . . I well remember when the grocer's boy, who was delivering the groceries, kicked over our half pint of milk. There was consternation in the camp!

'I was called up at the end of the Second War, but it was so near the end that before I could do so we were told not to.' I recalled that the young men were called up first, and that only slowly was the call-up age raised. Mr Stickler agreed, and explained why. 'You see, I was 37 in 1939 and if I was reasonably intelligent, I could be of some use [to the country, not conscripted] whereas a boy of 17 could be dispensed with.'

He thought there were no Zeppelin raids over Keynsham in the war, though my Mother recalled them being picked out by the searchlights over Streatham, London, and how she and her family had all gone to the windows to look at them. Jessie said, 'They were about but we didn't get any.'

'There were a number of air-raid shelters built in the village, but we did not have one. I lived with my mother then, and we decided that we would die in our beds if we were to die at all. A right decision I think,' commented Mr Stickler. 'I think that most of the bombing that we got was in the Second War, when Bath and Bristol were both bombed.

'There were trams in Bristol and trams in Bath, and when the bus service started, it ran from Brislington, which was the end of the Bristol tram lines, to Newton St Loe, which was the end of the Bath tram way. But they soon found that the buses, which were run by a Methodist or a churchman of some sort, from Brislington, did not go out on Sundays, and nor would the Bristol Tramways, who only did so when they were bound to. That is, they did not have the moral courage not to when the Greyhound came along and ran theirs on Sundays, so the Bristol Tramways decided to run on Sundays as well. As it was 9d to go to Bristol, you thought twice before getting on.'

['The owner of the Pioneer buses was a Mr William Russett, a well-known Baptist who was often at the Ebenezer Baptist Chapel in the High Street. The buses were based at Barton Hill in Bristol,' recalled Bert Robe.]

'I suppose there was some poverty in Keynsham in the First War, but nothing desperate, nobody starved or anything like that. In those days Temple Street was the down-town area of Keynsham.'

['Jessie Stickler is being unduly critical of the inhabitants of Temple Street. Poor many of them may have been, though not all, but there were many worthy people among them. They had a strong sense of "community",' wrote Bert.]

Jessie did not remember the houses in Albert Road being built, but recalled that Martin Gibbon's mother remembered there being gates across the top of the road when it was still a farm track.

Mr Stickler continued, 'There used to be more horse transport than cars in those days, and I remember a horse falling down and breaking the shafts of the cart outside our house. This caused consternation in the camp, too. You see, outside the church, where the pavement at that time was so wide, was the meeting place for people. That was the centre of Keynsham. It is the Council that has forced the centre of Keynsham down to the top of Bath Hill. In those days you used to get quite a few travelling cheap-jacks, who made their living by doing funny things, and by buying and selling. I remember one Doctor selling quack things but he said he must not call himself a Dr. Then I did not know what he meant but later I realised that he had been a Dr who had done something naughty and had been struck off. Some people would do a bit of conjuring, and then pass the hat around.

'I can just remember the two upright stone pillars with hooks in them, just outside the church wall, where worshippers would tie their horses. The pillars were some six foot tall, and the Council later took them away. The Loxtons used to come down from Queen Charlton to Victoria Methodist church by horse, and used to put their horses near the hut at the back of the church, at 'Stoke's Stables', which used to sell hay.

'In those days the roads had not been tarmacked and when they were, people did not understand it. I remember a chap with a motor bike and side car coming along the High Street, turning into Station Road, which had just been done half an hour earlier, and his bike went one way and he went another, and sat himself on the tarred road.

'Before that, they used to have men sat at the side of the roads with a pile of stones, smashing them up. They used to have a thick pair of trousers, with string tied round their legs just below the knee. Someone else would come along to fill up the pot holes and level the road with the stones. That was more skilled work. I remember that.

'Whenever I walk by Ronto's, even now, I can't help feeling dust in my eyes. There were clouds of dust from Bath Road and the High Street and Temple Street. There was no tar on the roads. I still get the sensation now and then. I came out from the car park the other day, near where the Lamb and Lark used to be, and I found myself half closing my eyes and blinking. I remember also the water carts spraying the roads in the hot weather, to keep the dust down.'

Young Jessie Stickler did have a bicycle, but not until the roads had been properly tarmacked. 'Then you could ride a bike alright. We did have a carrier in the village, a Mr Short, of Albert Road I think it was, who would take parcels and things into Bristol for you for about 3d in his van. He didn't take letters. Then one day he went off to America, and I never heard of him again. Rather a pity because I used to play with his son.

'Keynsham was a quiet town, with not much excitement in it that I knew of. It wasn't a village of heavy drinking. The Wingrove was near us, but it was not one of your ordinary Keynsham pubs, but a better-class one. The gentry went there. I remember the village's one bobby, but I kept on the right side of him.'

Billeting

Mr Stickler recalled that during the First World War, soldiers would from time to time march through Keynsham on their way to the coast. 'They would usually stay in the village one night, and a Lieutenant or a Captain would knock at your door and look at your house to see what room you had and would then tell you, not ask you, that you would take one or two men for that night.'

He knew that mules had been assembled on the Conygre Farm fields, adding that 'Some were there for quite a time. Mules and horses were used a fair bit in the war to start with, together with some London buses, and probably some Bristol buses too.'

Jessie gave me the following photo, sited in Keynsham, of some of the wives and mothers of the village, just after the war. Taken by 'Fredk. M Orchard, Photographer, K'm, Som.' it also had written across the back, in ink, 'Keynsham W. Methodist Women's Bible Class circa 1919.' Mr Stickler had received it in a letter from Mrs Madge Dorey, who wrote, 'Leslie's [her husband] mother is the one nearest to the wall on the right hand side, without a hat.' Jessie could pick out Mrs Coates, Mrs Gibbons and Mrs Upton.

Mr Stickler recalled that in Station Road was the Pioneer Inn, John Harvey's newspaper shop and Hobb's plumber's shop. Unlike today, then, most of the street was of private houses. In one of them lived Mr Taylor, who was the plebeian doctor. Dr Willett lived across the road in Milward House, and in the High Street lived the physician of the élite of the village, Dr Harrison.'

In 1914 the village was unbelievably rural, for as Jessie said, 'I used to go up Charlton Road gathering armfuls of cowslips, while today they are rare enough to be a protected plant.'

Mrs Hettie Wilson, who was Hettie Sears in 1914, recalled that the family had just moved into Dragon's Hill House. She remembered the arrival of the celebrated mules, at the hands of a very rough bunch of soldiers. At that time she was going to school in Bristol by train, and at Temple Meads station saw a great number of equally rough Australian soldiers hanging about for their trains. A defenceless young girl, she kept well out of their way.

She could not recall seeing in Keynsham any wounded soldiers in their blue uniforms, or men suffering from shell shock, or hearing of local people sending white feathers to those men who did not volunteer. But Hettie commented, 'It was hard for the fellows who had to stay behind to keep things going. The food situation became pretty awful, but we were lucky as we kept chickens and I did not have to declare them, but I had to in the Second War, and to agree to other people having eggs.'

On a lighter note, Hettie's father had married a Miss Priest from London, and as both were from active Methodist families, they were fittingly daubed, presumably by their witty London friends, 'the Priests and Seers.'

Convoys through Keynsham and a Flying Corps connection

More seriously, Mr & Mrs Seymour Smith, who ran a paper mill in Bristol, lived at 'The Elms' in Bath Road, Keynsham, just beyond the Grange Hotel and across the road. Their daughter, Hilda, later Mrs Charles Gibbons, went to school with Hettie and they became firm friends. Hettie recalled that, 'In the first three days of the 1914 war, an almost continuous convoy of soldiers passed through Keynsham, mainly in lorries [commandeered?], with a few cars and some buses, for Avonmouth and embarkation. A group of lads, including the Smith children, sat on the wall outside the Elms cheering the soldiers and throwing apples to them.'

Meanwhile, at the end of the summer term at the Skipton Grammar School in Yorkshire, a Mr Wilson asked his 16-year-old son, Lionel, if we wanted to stay on at school or join the Royal Flying Corps. He opted for the latter. So after a period of training, Lionel was able to join 'those daring young men in their flying machines.' Possibly he flew a Henri or Maurice Farman biplane. Both were of flimsy construction in the extreme, with only bars joining the top and bottom wings, and merely more bars joining the tail flaps to the small cockpit. Daniel David in 'The 1914 Campaign' [Spellmount Ltd. 1987], wrote that 'The Henri Farman biplanes were used for observation by both the British and French early in the war', adding that 'Aircraft were not armed at this point and were more feared for the artillery they could bring down.'

Mr Smith of Bath Road, Keynsham, was Lionel's uncle and was greatly surprised when his nephew just 'dropped in' by plane on to the field at the rear of the Elms for a brief visit. At the Front he had flown solo, but on this occasion he was in a cockpit for two, for, though it was strictly forbidden as Hettie said, 'Lionel gave a number of the boys a ride in his plane as he taxied round the Elms field'. Among those was a local lad named Ronald Headington, whose mother helped out at the Elms, and who remembers to this day the thrill of his ride in the plane. Ronald recalled that, 'The event was after the war, around 1920, and the biplane had struts between the wings and it was all bits of string and canvas.'

In the war his father, William George Headington, served in the Somerset Light Infantry and survived being blown up and half buried. He returned home in 1918 and managed, with difficulty, to resume his work for six years, until he was too ill with his head and legs shaking all the time from shell-shock, when his wife and son had to do everything for him. In the last year of his life, he seemed to have suddenly recovered, but the doctor warned them that this was just the lull before the end. He died a year later.

Perhaps it is pertinent to ask at this juncture how much the British Tommy was paid for his service to his king and country. Well, Mary Waugh in her book, 'Smuggling in Kent & Sussex' [Countryside Books, 1985 p 13] wrote that in 1720 on the Weald, 'a farm labourer could earn no more than 7/- or 8/- for a full week's work . . . whereas for a successful night's effort carrying contraband he could expect about 10/- if everything went well.' Yet of a soldier's pay nearly 200 years later, Daniel David [op cit] quoted the 1914 slogan, 'A shilling a day, blooming good pay.' I wonder what William Headington thought about that?

A few years before the outbreak of war, William had married Louise Mary Ollis, whose mother had had sixteen children, and who looked rather askance when Louise had but one child, Ronald, born Jan 6 1915. However, while her husband was away at the Front, Louise's war effort was to work at a lathe at the Tangent Tool Company.

It was a very exciting day for the four-year-old Ronald when, toward the end of the war, he saw an English airship, with ropes hanging down from it, pass over Keynsham. At first his story was not believed, until the news was released that an airship had broken away from its Bristol moorings and had crashed in Wiltshire.

In the early 1900s Keynsham was still a small tightly-knit community in which everybody knew each other. Not only that, but many families were related to each other. Ronald was related not only to the Headingtons but to the extensive Ollis family, the Gibbons and the Smiths of Stockwood Vale. He declared that, 'At one time I had 64 cousins and could hardly walk a few yards down the High Street without meeting a relative.'

John Harvey and his wife started their well-known newspaper shop in the old Home Farm premises of Keynsham Abbey's Pool Barton, by the Pioneer in Station Road, in 1899. The family business passed down to their son Russell

Harvey, then to his niece, Pamela Harvey, who ran the shop from 1962 to 1979. Meanwhile, Pamela had married Ronald Headington, who described their trade as 'a stationery and confectionery business.'

Miss Fairclough remembers

When I recently visited Mary at her home and asked her if she could remember World War I, she replied, 'I have a feel I can remember when war broke out. I was at Grandmother's house [Mrs William Thomas], St Augustine's in Station Road, now the Doctor's house, sitting on the lawn with a lot of the family there, including my parents and grandparents, when uncle came out and told them something that upset them all appallingly, and I think that that was the announcement that we were at war.

'After that I do remember from the bedroom window at 16 Avon Mill Lane [now Avon Road] being lifted up to see the droves of mules being brought in from the goods yard where they had been unloaded from the cattle trucks and were being driven past our house. I think they took them up past the police station and down Pogham's Lane, past Brick Town, over the bridge and up Workhouse Lane to Conygre Farm, which was the most direct route and would cause least disturbance to any traffic, though there was very little in those days.

'As they passed us I can remember seeing the lanterns and hearing much shouting. It must have been evening, and the noise woke me up. My impression was of the moving creatures, shouting, and the lights at the front and the back and of small boys blocking garden paths.' Mary thought the light was from hurricane lamps, though she believed she saw flames in one of them. The year was probably 1914 or 1915, as 'Father was called up in 1916, so Mother and I left Number 16 and went to live with Grandma at St Augustine's.

'Father was in the Royal Garrison Artillery and stationed at Pendennis Castle, Falmouth, though we never could work out why he was sent to Cornwall. So in 1917/18 we were in lodgings there in the town.'

An officer and a gentleman

A large vegetable garden recently dug and free of weeds, at the rear of his bungalow in Keynsham, is of particular credit to its gardener because he is a nonagenarian. Mr Edward Loxton was born at Queen Charlton on May 2 1894, the youngest of the three sons of Mr James Loxton and his wife Charlotte. His eldest brother is now a mere 98! They lived at Charlton Farm, opposite the present village hall, where James had been a tenant farmer since 1887 of nearly 300 acres, with a herd of some 60 milking cows.

The Loxton family were active Christians and attended Keynsham Methodist Church. The commencement of James' tenancy coincided with the opening of the Victoria Chapel in 1887. Prior to that, the congregation had worshipped for some 80 years in the original Wesleyan Chapel across the road in what is today the Halifax Building Society, with its third storey added after the departure of the Methodists. Edward Loxton thought that his eldest brother was the first baby to be christened at Victoria. Edward said that the family used to drive to Keynsham in their horse and trap, which he believed they left at the Lamb and Lark Hotel, where a hostler would put their animal in stables used for guests and local farmers. The brothers would return in the afternoon for Sunday School, led by Philip Gibbons the superintendent. Farmer Loxton would be back again for the evening service.

'In my joyful school days . . .'

Mr Edward Loxton, echoing the words of Charles Lamb, recalled that, 'At first I went to the village school opposite our farm in Queen Charlton, for the village hall used to be the village school. The teacher then was named Mrs Butt and her salary was £60 a year and free fuel and light. She lived there. I went there from being four until I was eight. There was a private school started in Keynsham in rooms above Herbert's fruit shop, where the National Westminster Bank is today, with eight pupils, my brother being one of them. It was run by a lady from Bristol. Now there are two plaques in the Victoria Chapel, one to Philip Frome Gibbons [J P 1856–1927] and the other to his brother Augustus F Gibbons ['Called from among us June 14, 1929']. It was through Augustus Gibbons' wife that the school started, and I think I am right in saying that the lady who took on the school was a Miss Jones, but as she had to come out from Bristol, Mrs Gibbons started the school in the morning. Later Miss Jones lived in Keynsham.

'Of course the school increased until there were about thirty pupils, so it moved to 59 Charlton Road, two houses up beyond the Methodist Manse. I was there from eight to twelve, when boys had to leave, but girls were allowed to stay to any age.

'In those days people were accustomed to walking much further distances than they are today. Edward recalled that when he attended Eglon House School from 1902 to 1906, he used to walk back to his home at Queen Charlton for lunch each day, then return to school. This was no mean feat, even though he used the bridle path across the fields.

'In 1906 I started at Redland Park School as a weekly boarder. On a Monday morning I used to walk from home to the top of the Red Lion Hill, where I had to be by 8.0 am to catch the electric tram car as there were no buses in those days and there was nothing to beat them either. It was two pence to the Morley statue by St Nicholas Church.'

The North Somerset Yeomanry

Despite not enjoying very good health in those days, Edward recalled that finally he was accepted by the NSY for active service. 'I joined the all horse mounted Yeomanry at Bath at the end of Feb 1915 [aged 21] and was billeted at Walcot for two months, and then the whole regiment went to Lord Lansdowne's at Bowood House Park. We were 'The Second Line'. The 'First' went to France in 1914. Then we were drafted to Canterbury, and having left our horses behind, we took over the West Kent's horses. Then we went to Maresfield Park in East Sussex, where we eventually had our horses taken away and we were given bicycles at Kelvington for the defence of the East Coast in Essex.

'In September 1916 we were drafted to France, where some of us were attached to the 5th Dorset Infantry Regiment, and were sent to Rouen for more training as foot soldiers as this was different from that of cavalry drill. Finally, until Christmas 1916, we were in the trenches North of Arras. Then we were moved back into billets, where some of us were asked if we were interested in becoming officers and a group of us said 'Yes.'

'We were trained in Scotland and commissioned as sub-lieutenants in 1917. I was gazetted to the East Lancs Regiment and drafted to the Punjab in India. There three or four of us were attached to the 9th Hampshires and received further training south of Delhi. The Colonel of the 9th asked us to go back to him, but as the East Lancs, which we had initially joined, was at Bangalore, India, we rejoined them there, where the weather was not too bad in winter, and far better than the sticky heat of Bombay.

Later Lieutenant Loxton, with three other officers, was drafted to Mesopotamia, 30 miles north of Baghdad, to join the 6th Regiment of the East Lancs just after the fighting against the Turkish army at Kirkuk had finished. 'We moved camp to the River Diyala where we were when in 1918 the Armistice was signed. I never fired a shot in the whole war and never received any of the medals to which I was entitled,' he said.

Chapter 14

The Parkers of Upton Cheyney and the letters of Captain John Parker of the War Graves Commission

Mrs Susan James, née Parker, gave me the fascinating information that her ancestor, the Rev Edward Parker, was 'admitted to Holy Orders, 1 Aug 1675, became Curate of the Parish of Bitton in August 1687 and Vicar of Bitton in 1691'.

In 1657 Edward married Miss Alice Seede of Seede's Manor House (now Seede's Farm, Upton Cheyney), where they lived. Their son Edward bought 'Upton House', Upton Cheyney, in 1702. At one time the Parker family there owned most of the village and four farms, together with the fruit farm at Pipley Valley on the edge of their estate.

During the eighteenth and nineteenth century, a number of successive Parker sons entered the Anglican ministry, some with distinguished service in the missionary field in India, as bishops. Plaques in Bitton Church record their names, dates and positions, while Susan has large impressive oil paintings of some of her clerical ancestors.

When some twenty years ago the wooden floor at Bitton Church was renewed, an underground vault was discovered, and was found to be the forgotten vault of the local Parker family. But the workmen simply covered it over and rearranged the pews to form choir stalls at the East End of the Nave, covering the vault, and completed their work, long before Mrs James was informed. Naturally she was far from pleased, and with her keen interest in her family history, was greatly disappointed.

In the following pages, we shall learn something of the unique World War I service of Susan's father Mr John Scott Parker. She explained that, 'Though his was a civilian job, one had to be in uniform to work in France during the war. So he was given the rank of Lieutenant and was later promoted Captain. He wore the General Service Badge. In 1924 he was awarded the OBE. He was also awarded the Vietchian Medal, which was quite a high award in the horticultural world.'

Mrs James wrote of her father that, 'His most cherished possession was a silver cigarette case, a personal present from King George V which he received after the Royal visit to the cemeteries in 1924.'

Though prior to the war John ran the fruit farm at Pipley Valley, their daughter Susan was born at Upton House, and has precious and happy memories of it. However, by 1912 the House had been let and the Parker family never really lived there again. Mr Parker did not return to England from living in Europe with his family until 1935, and he died in 1938. His wife and daughter then bought a house near Glastonbury.

John Parker's son, Charles Guy Wyndham Parker, inherited Upton House, but was an officer in the Regular Army, serving in the Royal Engineers. After a brief period in civilian life during the 1930s, he rejoined the Army at the outbreak of war, and served in the RASC in the Middle East. He left the army with the rank of Lieutenant Colonel, and worked in the Foreign Office until his retirement. He was also awarded the OBE.

During his long period of service, the family home was let, until the late Colonel Parker sold it in 1946.

We now come to Mrs Susan James' introduction to her father's unique war service, from which so many fallen servicemen, from both World Wars, have benefited.

* * *

AN OUTLINE OF HOW THE IMPERIAL WAR GRAVES COMMISSION CAME INTO BEING, AND THE WORK DONE BY MY FATHER, THE LATE JOHN SCOTT PARKER OF UPTON CHEYNEY

* * *

In 1916, a man named Fabian Ware went out to France to work for the Red Cross. He found that his work was almost all with people enquiring about missing relatives and those who had lost their lives.

He realised that though the various regiments kept their own records, there was no organisation that was collating those records. Through the hard work put in by Fabian Ware, the authorities agreed to the formation of the Directorate of Graves Registration and Enquiries.

(This became a branch of the Civil Service, known as the Imperial War Graves Commission, and is now the Commonwealth WGC.)

At that time in 1916, my father was looking for a job that would suit him as he was over-age for active service, and he felt that running a fruit farm and market gardens was not the best way of serving his country.

On hearing of the formation of the DGR&E, he wrote to a friend in the horticultural world, Mr Charles Hill (later Sir Charles Hill, Director of Kew Gardens), and asked if there was a job for him – the cemeteries would need to be maintained in good order.

Mr Hill had been looking for someone to take on the job of Chief Horticultural Officer for the War Graves, so very shortly afterwards my father set off to France with the rank of lieutenant.

All that could be done then was to clear the cemeteries of weeds and sow them with mixed annuals, which were broadcast.

Many of the seeds were given by friends and relatives of the fallen who saved them from their gardens.

The graves were marked by a wooden cross treated with creosote. The name, rank, number and regiment of the fallen were stamped on a metal strip and affixed to the cross.

The next stage was to decide on a plan for the permanent planting of the graves.

It was finally agreed that there should be a flower border 18″ wide in front of the crosses. In this would be planted perennials suitable to the local soil conditions, polyantha roses of a single colour in each row of graves, giving bright strips of different colours, and much lavender. No plant was to obscure the inscription on the crosses.

The rest of the land was to be laid down to grass. The effect was to be as near as possible to that of an English garden.

This plan was approved by the Authorities.

Nursery gardens were started and work went ahead.

* * *

We now come to the remarkable World War I letters of Captain John Parker ('Jack') to his wife Beatrice at their Pipley Valley Farm, near Bath. He narrates in detail his work behind the front line, the terrible conditions in which the British troops fought, and the enormity of the loss of life there.

The letters are edited by Dr C J Fitter.

* * *

> G.H.Q. D.G.R.& E.
> 2nd Echelon
> B.E.F.
> July 10 [1916]

My dear B.

Thanks for many things. Shirts – just the very things, I sent you back the other one – have you got it? Pens – I wanted them badly, they cannot give me a decent pen here.

Since I last wrote I have been racketing about all over the place. Up to Aire, Hazebrouck, Lilles and all round that neighbourhood. Twice to Etaples and Le Touquet. The latter is a lovely spot. Twice to Boulogne and Wimereux and once via the coast road to Calais. The day of the latter run was perfectly gorgeous, and from the tops of the high lands we could see the Chalk Cliffs for miles and miles. Only then did I realise what a tiny strip of sea divides us from the Continent. No wonder Napoleon strolled round the cliffs at Boulogne biting his nails waiting for an opportunity to cross. The country was looking beautiful on that day and at Wimereux and Ambleteuse the people were all out in their many-coloured frocks, hats, parasols and bathing suits. The places looked all alive with colour and war seemed beyond the moon except for the wounded men. The French are most resigned to the war. I went to a watchmakers just now to get a repair done. I said 'It does not wind up properly, it goes on for ever'. She said with a beautiful shrug 'Mais oui, monsieur, comme la guerre'.

Hill came out the other day for a month to look round the cemeteries – he is very good at seeing things and seeing the best way of arrangement of borders and planting. He and I went out together to some of my cemeteries yesterday and coming home we came through the place which is H.Q. Tanks. You never saw such a sight, rows and rows of them parked together like the cars along Pulteney Street, hundreds of them. One was out for a walk and was standing skew-ways across the road and we had to pull up. Somebody in the road shouted something and the tank made a sudden lurch and twisted itself longways up the road; the jerk was so sudden and the noisy clank so disturbing that our driver thought it was blindly blundering and got scared, jammed his clutch in and fairly made the car skip, much to the amusement of the onlookers, particularly of two who were lying full length on the top of the tank.

The business of the Cemeteries is becoming a most tremendous one, and the General, in course of a speech made the other night when three of our men got the D.S.O and were entertained to dinner at G.H.Q., said that the most important business just now was the beating of the Germans and the next was the proper management of the Cemeteries and the records of the DGR&E. So important do the people at home consider it that the sum of £50 a week is allotted to photography and gardening only, of which gardening takes £20. A small commission of three men have been sent out and arrived here yesterday – Lutyens the greatest British Architect of the day, Baker another architect of a different pattern, a man who will build you a house and pleasure grounds park and landscape all at once and Aidkin, who is director and custodian of the Tate Gallery. These men are being taken round to various cemeteries and they are going to formulate some general idea which has to be followed in the making of new and the development of old Cemeteries. The General is here and the conversation at Mess is something too delightful for words. They will be here for a week or so.

H.Q.   July 16 [1917]

Dear B,

I have only 3 sheets left in my block and I have a lot to tell about so don't mind small writing. I'll make it as legible as possible.

Yesterday I had orders to get an early move on and go out with two other men and make a report on some cemeteries in the South. So we got away early and ran down through Doullens to Albert. You remember that when the Germans first attacked Albert they as usual made a dead set at the Church. Albert Church is about the most hideous church ever built and so the Huns did not do the real damage they might have done had it been a place like Chartres. The main feature of Albert Church was a colossal statue of the virgin holding aloft at arms length the figure of the Child. It was a hollow figure supported on one long iron girder running its whole length. It was standing on the top of a dome which was a framework of iron, covered with brickwork. The whole statue and dome were highly gilded and the standing figure must have been most impressive. Now the most extraordinary thing has happened. We read about it in the papers at the time, but nobody thought much about it, no one realised the utter strangeness of it. A shell struck the dome and scattered all the brickwork; the top of the dome, collapsing, removed the upper support from the iron girder, which toppled over; the butt end was firmly fixed however and held fast. The falling statue bent the girder until it assumed rather less than a right angle and there it stuck. As you pass along the street beneath the tower and look up, you look straight into the faces of the Virgin and Child. The latter's arms are spread wide – he is held high above the Mother's head and both are gazing straight down at you as you look up. The whole colossal statue leans right over the street, and a traffic policeman stands beneath and tells you the way if you've lost it. The Church itself is an awful ruin; there is enough of it left to show that it is a ruin, nearly half the tower is still standing although it is pierced in ½ dozen places and has had great chips taken out here and there. The walls are cracked in places with cracks so wide that you can see through to the other side where iron clamps have been used. One end of the clamps has held fast and the end hangs loose, but attached to it is the stone into which it had been sunk. In one case a huge block hangs to the end of its clamp 3 parts of the way up the tower. The whole of the circular staircase is revealed to the open air, some of the steps still remain. Some of the bells were blown out; one is visible, still in the belfry, lying unhung amid the wreck of the rolling stock.

Albert itself is pretty badly knocked about, but the place is alive with troops and the shopkeepers do a roaring trade. I got a small picture book for you which shows fairly well the position of the figures on the tower.

We picked up another man at the office here and under his guidance ran on up the Valley of the Ancre. When the Germans blew up the big dam North of Albert the whole of the reservoir came roaring down and converted the valley into a primeval swamp, behind which they ran their trenches on the high land opposite Thiepval. The whole valley was three years ago a thriving agricultural and timber growing region properly watered by the Ancre – now it is just what it might have been in the time when coal was growing. As we went on the desolation grew. Woods at first had trees with branches on them – now they had no branches and no bark even. Finally there were whole acres where perhaps only 20 trees stood, these being reduced to perhaps 10 feet in height. One tall tree stood alone near the road which attracted attention thereby, quite 60 feet high it was – not a shred of bark remained on it and not a branch and right up at the top hanging round the severed end of the main stem was a twisted coil of barbed wire. The whole trunk was marked with holes and seams; a shell had entered a little wide of the centre, had burst and had ripped nearly half the tree off and hurled it away. All the stumps of the trees looked like gigantic shaving brushes. When a tree is knocked down by a shell it means that a shell has burst close by and has just torn the trunk in two, every fibre of the tree has sprung away from its neighbour and stands up separately so that the effect is that of a huge brush.

We continued along a side valley running up to the left of the Ancre valley. All along one side were enormous dugouts, along the other were every conceivable sort of debris you can think of bar dead men. And yet they were there too, cemeteries, little groups of graves – single graves, the crosses standing alone among the grass, were dotted up and down this valley in extraordinary numbers – and what wonder? I was looking right up the valley where the Naval Division raged among the Boche dugouts. Here was the famous Y ravine where our fellows died in thousands and every yard of ground held a Boche machine gun. The whole ground was honey-combed with tunnels with concreted entrances now blown in - they contain absolutely un-numbered dead, mostly German. Our fellows were got out, the Germans left and the tunnels blown in. Further on, the ground was more broken, tree stumps could be seen here and there again, and the guide made some mention of Beaumont Hamel. I said 'Whereabouts is Beaumont Hamel?' He waved his hand round and said 'Here.' I looked about and saw nothing but heaving mounds of earth all grass-grown and wild. If you looked carefully you could see a brick. In one place there is a piece of wall still whole, standing up perhaps 10 feet high; it must have had a charmed life.

Now I had heard of the desolation of the Somme country. I had heard it so often and from men who were fresh from it and I had heard of it in so minute a detail that I thought I realised what it was like. But when I saw the shattered forests, standing in lagoons and swamps, when I saw the little graves and cemeteries scattered about everywhere, when I saw the litter ranging from rifle cartridges to an overturned engine, the Y ravine, the dugouts and the place where Beaumont Hamel was, and more than all when I realised that this ocean of waving grass was not beautiful fertile prairie where you could gallop for miles, but was really a place where it was almost impossible to walk, where shell hole ran into shell hole, where you literally fell out of one into another, a place where men who know the country carry compasses, a place strewn with iron splinters of burst shells and, worse than all, hundreds of unburst shells which may explode when you tread on them – when I saw it all, I realised that nothing I had ever heard, anything I had ever read ever has or ever could describe a battlefield of the Somme.

The vegetation was simply outstanding, over scores and scores of miles long and far beyond the furthest horizon that we saw this desolation stretches; and yet it is not desolation quite. The land has been turned up 4 feet deep, a regular 4 feet all over. Here and there of course a heavy shell hole would be 12 feet deep, but the average depth of disturbance over all would be about 4 feet. This has been turned many times and has had a winter on it. Yet the vegetation has begun. Every hollow contains water – near the water are water plants – dragon flies are hovering over the pools and mosquitos breed. Here and there you can see what the crop of 1914 was in a particular bit of ground where you see an ear of corn or oats standing above the muck.

Weeds and grasses predominate, but there are clovers, sanfoins, vetches amongst them. And it shows really how much seed – what an enormous amount of seed there is about only waiting for man to leave it alone in order to come up and simply establish dominion over the earth.

There is a cemetery on top of a high ridge of land – the cemetery is called Redan Ridge No. 5. It stands away some 400 yds off the road. The path is merely a foot path made across the broken ground – no 10 feet of it is straight as it winds along the lips of the craters. Down among the grass you can see the litter of battle – bits of leather belts, cartridges, cartridge clips, punches, dixies, spades, picks, helmets, all manner of things. And yet the salvage corps has been over the ground. Just in front of the cemetery we could see a place where the Boche had defended himself pretty thoroughly. There were long lines of trenches, the white-ish grey and brown soil making curious patterns away and away till you couldn't distinguish them, in front of them were masses of red rusty barbed wire hung on iron cork-screw posts flung up into high weird heaps, and along the immediate foreground were three lovely prairie sloughs, lying all blue and beautiful in the grass. They were mine craters, the largest was 100 yards across at least; it may have been two together, but the effect of these tarns, blue as the sea, set as it were in a world of green – the green running down the slopes to the water's edge – was too lovely for anything, I cannot describe it.

And then our guide, the officer of the district, began to talk and that put the giddy summit on. He showed us where the Hun lines ran and where ours were. The masses of wire were heaped up just as our guns had left them. Such a regiment attacked there and such a one over there. Here was a place infested with machine guns and hundreds were lost while taking them. The mines did the final work and we went forward after the Hun until that hill over there was surrounded on three sides – our men could not get round fast enough and many thousand Huns who defended the hill got away when we thought we had them.

Then he waved his hand towards the opposite slope about as far away as Dundry is from you and ——. 'There are 35000 men buried in that bit of country.' He said he had buried 4000 odd. Thomas had buried nearly 6000, Ramsden another 5000 and so on – each officer with his party had been carefully over the ground working it in squares scientifically and had cleaned it all up. Besides these were the countless numbers of men both English and German who had been blown up, buried, lost in dug-outs that nobody can ever see again. The whole land is one vast cemetery.

The effect of standing on that ridge overlooking that gigantic battlefield was almost stupefying, one could not talk about it, one could only look in amazement. . . . Nothing I have ever seen or thought of comes up to what I saw and did today.

FRANCE

[1916–17?]

My area is steadily increasing. I simply cannot do it all. I hope when they see the cemeteries looking dirty and untidy they won't come down on me, because the number of corporals is limited, the number of men is quite insufficient to do the places properly and the area is one which is almost too big for one man to hope to manage properly.

I am going east of Albert now, and although I know the country well between Maricourt and Miroumont and have become quite accustomed to the awful desolation of the country yet I think the further east you go the more awful the desolation becomes. The actual destruction wrought

Captain John Scott Parker, OBE, of Upton House, Upton Cheyney

His daughter, Mrs S James, wrote, 'This photo was taken in 1922 when he was awarded the OBE. He was also awarded the Viechian Medal. His most cherished possession was an inscribed silver cigarette case, a personal present from King George V, which he received after the Royal visit to the cemeteries in 1922.

by shells, trenches and mines is not greater than at Beaumont Hamel and Beaucourt-sur-Ancre, but what makes the difference is the presence of the crosses.

During the early part of the fighting when men and material could be got up along a number of good roads, the dead were brought together into cemeteries and very few were left about. Further on when we had to get everything up over wastes of mud the work of burying was very perfunctory. Cemeteries abound all over the area of the Somme fighting, but far more were hastily buried by burial parties just where they lay. Many were thrown into shell-holes and a few shovelfuls of earth were thrown over them, but the majority of them were buried in shallow graves a foot or two under the surface and not a few were left out unburied – never found by the burial parties.

The order went out last June that this ground was to be searched, all bodies found were to be buried after being identified and where possible a roughly buried body was to be exhumed, identified and reburied in a proper grave. All new graves were to have a white cross placed upon them, and all bodies to be buried exactly where found.

The consequence is you can see exactly where and how the fighting went. You can see the Boche trench and our trench – you can see our men swarming up the slope in ones and twos and, where they were coming on in close order, in tens and dozens, where the machine gun caught them. The crosses as they stand in their thousands all over the country, few on the long slopes behind our trenches but in hundreds in front of Boche trenches give you a tremendously vivid idea of it all; every cross shows just how far each man got in the awful race with the bullets. If he could reach the Boche trench all right of course he had shelter, but then he had to take to the bayonet. If he cleared them out he had a chance of life till the next attack. The most amazing thing is how any man ever came through alive. We know now that seventy-five thousand men did not, and of this number no less than fifty-five thousand are marked with the solitary white cross just where each one of them fell.

It is simply stupefying to stand on some of the Boche positions and see the men, our men, swarming out of our trenches and rushing up the hill – the whole country seems populated, the whole scene is reconstructed and you can almost see the battle. I had heard it described before, but until the other day I had never seen it.

Where the Boche had a machine gun the crosses stand for hundreds of yards in a V-shaped front – the machine gun being on a swivel acted like a fan and swept the ground on its own front, the further the spray of bullets ranged the wider spread the fan became – at extreme range the crosses are few, the closer the range the denser the crosses stand until they cluster thickly where the gun emplacement was. Thomas's men became extraordinarily expert in finding bodies. They searched for these emplacements and if they found fragments of the gun lying about, the probabilities were that it was knocked out by a shell. If no fragments are found, it may be that it was removed by the Boche before our men got near, or that they did get up to it and captured it. They had means of finding out somehow which of these things happened and they carried out their search accordingly.

Your map will probably show a long thin rectangular patch of woodland called the Bois de Bouleaux. In front of this wood the crosses are frightfully thick and I stood the other day and watched them swarming up the hill; I moved to get another view and saw close by me in the bottom of a shell hole full of water the whole of a Frenchman's equipment bar the rifle; he himself was just below the surface of the ground. I fished up the helmet by the chin strap with my stick and now have it among my souvenirs on the shelves in my room. He had got up a long way from our position and had nearly reached the first German lines when he was hit.

I walked through Combles and joined the car further on. Then we ran on out to Raucourt on the Bapaume-Peronne road, and home through Bapaume. I was spending two nights at Courcellete last week and went over some of the new ground with Thomas.

Mametz, Montauban, Frones Wood, Bernafay Wood, all names that were famous in 1916. No one told us one five-hundredth part of what was going on, and unless someone was writing it all as it happened for people to read when the war is over no one will ever know the true history of the Somme Battles . . . Of course men who came through it know, but they cannot tell you, some because they don't know how to, some because it simply cannot be talked about. But now when the crosses are new and standing upright it is possible with imagination to gather something of it . . . but only something.

Then, the whole country was a wilderness of mud – now it is clothed with a dull dead carpet of weeds. Last summer it was clothed in sheets of colour – this summer the colouring will be deeper because the poppies, cornflowers and charlock have sown themselves.

H.Q.   July 29th. 17

My dear B,

I have had a pretty strenuous week and have covered something like 500 miles. Most of it down in the country between Arras and Albert. The first trip I took down on to the battlefields was somewhat of a hurried one and was made in company with men who did not want to see what I wanted to.

Well, on Monday I got away early with a small 4 seater Ford car and the best driver in the unit and went down to Doullans where I purchased newspapers and bread. I had put up a large hamper full of lettuces for the man I was going to because I knew he would not have eaten green food for weeks and was also short of bread. I looked in on several cemeteries on the way down and finally got into Auchenvillers where the mighty crop of currants was. The cemetery here lies just behind a C.C.S. (Casualty Clearing Station) which is now a mighty ruin. A farm house, barns and cowsheds had been used for the C.C.S. and from there the cemetery was filled. A beautiful spot right in the centre of a biggish village surrounded by orchards and gardens or what is left of them. From here we ran on to the top end of the Beaumont Hamel valley where the utter destruction begins. Auchouvillers is not destroyed, it is only ruined; there are degrees of comparison. Mailly is knocked about, Colincamps has walls standing, at other places roofs are frequent, but Beaumont Hamel simply is not.

I told you about B. Hamel in my last and I thought I had described it, but I hadn't. I couldn't, nobody could. I have heard the General say that he has to go down to the Somme once every fortnight in order to keep the memory of it fully in his mind. You may know it all and live in it all, but the impressiveness of it never goes. You wonder all the time. It is I suppose because each heavy shell has done something just a little unlike any other one did.

After 2 hours, we ran south along the Ancre and I took more notice of the trees than I had been able to do before. It was curious to see how different were the effects of shells upon tree trunks. Some had struck at a glance and had thrown out a crop of splinters above and below – others had struck at the same angle and had just gouged out a passage and left no splinters round a clean hole. If a big shell struck it seems to have either blown the top of the tree right off or to have split the whole trunk from top to bottom. Every tree was dead, every one was scored and rent and stuck full of bits of shells and bullets and shrapnel. Now and then a whole shell stuck fast unexploded in a tree.

The dug-outs where Wilson and his party were quartered were made by R.E. for themselves and they are really good comfy ones with well hung doors and windows (only some brutes have pinched the windows). Wilson had made up a good substitute by means of tracing paper.

We stripped off coats and collars, yelled to the batman for supper and had a good swill down. Then coatless, hatless and collarless as in the old days on the prairie we sat down in a typical North Western shack and ate a typical North Western meal amid surroundings so nearly resembling the prairies as to be almost identical. The open spaces, waving grass, treeless, bushless and houseless, the great sweeps of distance. The sky and wind, the flowers and everything you could see from the shack brought it all back. But what reminded one more vividly than anything was the silence. Not a sound. Think – what was there there to make a sound? – Men? They had fought for the ground, won it and had gone on leaving it empty. Birds? One, the Golden Oriole, I heard but not till next morning – I think he had come up from below as he likes woods. No birds live there, there is no tree or bush to build in, there are no birds that sing on the prairie. Beasts? All gone, no horse or cow could walk over that country without breaking his legs in the bottom of a shell hole. There is no life and no sound.

When you see a tree lying at the stump shattered and riven – you think poor thing it got in the way of a shell that was meant for quite another job, but the feeling towards that tree is quite different to the feeling for a tree that has been neatly cut off with a saw – cut on both sides and left lying. Most of the roads in France are bordered by avenues of trees. Here we went for miles through lines of prostrate trees.

Between Puisieux and Bucquoy we came across huge breadths of rye cut and stooked. This was a Hun crop, the ground was reclaimed and ploughed by the Huns and sown to rye. The Hun had to leave it however and had no time to destroy it, it was about the only things that he had not destroyed.

The two places mentioned are biggish places especially Bucquoy, they had been entirely blown up.

Bucquoy must be quite a mile each way in diameter and yet house by house and street by street the Huns had blown it all to bits. When a shell hits a house it will do funny things, it may blow out the back and leave the front intact, it may blow the roof off or it may turn the whole house inside out and leave the fabric standing. But when you deliberately set about to blow a house up you get a different result. In a very great number of cases the results will always be the walls will be blown outwards, all the floors will come down and the roof will come down on top. I saw loads of cases where the house has just been removed from under the roof and the roof has quietly sat down on the ground. Bucquoy and Courcelles Hannes camps, Bienvillers, Fonquevillers were all alike. But I think the most impressive was Fonquevillers. Here were some fine big houses standing in spacious jungles out of which rise splinters of cedars and pines showing where large gardens and grounds formerly existed.

One fine big Chateau was built in an L shape. A shell had pitched right on to the roof at the joint between the two wings. It had torn out the whole of the end of each wing exposing the interior of what now looked like two houses. I think that Chateau is the most dreadful looking thing I have seen in France.

At Hannescamps the cemetery lies behind the Church; by the by, I did not know it had been a church till Wilson told me and I looked more carefully and found evidences.

The whole place is seamed with trenches old and crumbling, running under walls and houses, through gardens, under roads, turning twisting everywhere; so narrow that the grass has almost joined together at the top and nearly screened it from sight. Round the corner of one of the massive walls of the church we came across scribblings on the walls. It was a safe-ish place the walls were so thick and must have been a forward observation post or something of the kind. All over the walls were names and Regiments of men, the usual thing – two hearts entwined and two names, the man's and the girl's written thereon.

You somehow got an idea of what was going on. The man would be there who could not be knocked out of his cheery old frame of mind and when the shells were yelling overhead he'd get out his pocket knife and laboriously scrawl 'What'll win the Derby'. Another man of a different temperament comes along deadly sick and tired of it all, probably shell-shocked and trembling. He gets out his knife and writes 'God end this awful war'. Another thinks of his girl at home and writes her name up, begins an illuminated surround and before he can finish he is recalled or perhaps a bit of questing shrapnel finds him out.

Wilson and I stayed there quite 5 minutes in that little corner looking at these records; and I realised one thing very certainly and that is that I have never yet seen the war. All these ruins are 8–9–10–12 months old, they are grass grown and beautiful. What they must have been in the making I simply cannot imagine. We saw the writings on the wall written by the men who did it all, but what they went through no one will know, because no one could describe it. But if you can stand as we did in that ruined church in absolute silence and read the pictures on the wall you can, with an effort of imagination, arrive at perhaps a faint idea of what it must have been.

In another place there is a Hun mistake. They were trying to mine a road and had evidently taken measurements wrong with the result that the mine was laid underneath a church yard. The explosion had no effect on the road, but had considerable effect in undoing the work of the village sexton for the past century.

In some places the Huns have left the fruit trees alone and there are some good crops of plums, greengages and apples.

H.Q. 28.9.17

Dear B,

Four days hard going has landed me back here in a perfectly limp state of utter fatigue. My driver too is worn out and we both must have several days rest. We covered 667 kilometres.

On Monday I did an uninteresting round in the neighbourhood of Aire. I got back very hot and very dusty and had a splendid wallow in the baths there. I turned out early next morning and had another.

From Aire I went right down to Acheux without a stop and after looking in at the office there turned northwards and ran up to some cemeteries just South of Arras. Being within 10 miles of Arras I thought I would run in and try and find the cemetery at Rouville. I had never been in Arras before, and for the first time saw what a big town can look like when it has been shelled.

The Germans had held the Southern end and we had the Northern. Street fighting went on incessantly, many of the streets were barricaded with barbed wire some of which is still lying about tossed up in heaps out of the way.

Fools rush in where Angels fear to tread. Many of the streets and squares are out of bounds to every one, inhabitants and troops; and being entirely ignorant of the rule we pushed the impertinent presence of our despised little Ford car into absolutely deserted & silent streets, into old squares where every house is decorated according to some general plan. Ancient old places in every conceivable stage of ruin and destruction. Some houses lacked roofs, some had not a vestige of front wall left and every room was exposed to view. Some were beautifully carved and decorated. Where a whole row of houses spanned the pavement, the outer walls resting on beautiful stone pillars the different effects of the shells was extraordinary. Here and there a pillar or two would be shot away and the house deprived of support on that side has made a stately bow to the opposite side of the street. So solidly built, it has refused to break up and just leans over. Then a shell has burst in the upper parts of a house bringing it down with a run in a jumbled heap of timbers & bricks through which you can see the capitals of the pillars sticking up, the only things which have remained.

A good sized house, one of a row in a biggish street had been entirely destroyed, there was nothing left of it but a chaotic heap;' but through the heap there still stood the iron pipe with the tap still on it which supplied a basin or bath room upstairs. It stood at least 20 feet high and slowly swayed about in the wind. I'm quite sure it is the most idiotic thing of its kind I have yet seen.

And then the old Cathedral, the palace and the beautiful buildings of the Hotel de Ville. Oh dear, oh dear, it simply makes one sick. Walls, gables, fragments, bits of beautiful doorways, a single mullion of a window with a piece of the leading hanging to it; all manner of things suggest more than indicate what the beauty of the place must have been.

And what do the stay-at-home English people know of it – I tell you it is impossible to realize it. You have photographs – you have films – you have wordy descriptions and newspaper articles, you get an idea what the place looks like but you can never know what it feels like and that is what counts the most.

When away from the car peering in through a hole in the wall, wandering down the cloistered pavements where on the one hand you had glassless windows piled with sandbags and on the other hand in the street were huge ramps of stones torn from the street pavé; standing in the absolutely silent Square, trying to reconstruct some shattered piece of decorative work the spirit of the deserted place got hold of one, and as I have tried to explain you cannot realise what such a place is until you have been there. And if possible go alone.

You feel sort of sorry for the people who have been turned out – you feel a sense of irreparable loss at the destruction of the beautiful old work but then you feel also a perfectly insane desire to get after a Hun, and this feeling comes uppermost – to get after a Hun with a pickaxe and chop at him till he is mincemeat.

We got back fairly tired about 6 that night and getting quite cold.

Next day we had a long round from Albert to Corbie and visited 18 cemeteries, tired again.

On Thursday an officer from H.Q. came down and joined me together with the Officer Commanding Lines of Communication Area. We all went off with supplies of food & drink to hunt for a number of battlefield cemeteries which are not awfully easy to find. We had some old maps on which they were marked and we trusted to a pair of excellent glasses and a long tramp to find them. We first ran down the Station Road at Beaumont Hamel and went on from there to Bailescourt Farm. This Farm I have described before. It lies on the north bank of the Ancre Valley almost opposite Grandecourt. I have seen a whole lot of places but always come back to the Ancre with the fixed notion that nothing is quite so impressive as the wide valley, dotted everywhere with shattered stumps standing in still lagoons where the reeds and grass have by this time grown to a tremendous size. Standing at the cemetery at Bailescourt you look up and down the valley for several miles. Opposite is the high ground culminating in the huge ridge of Thiepval all seamed and streaked with trenches. All around are the heaving mounds and deep pits formed by the bombardment, a bombardment so heavy that even now all round the ruined farm house there is nothing growing; the chalk has been churned up so deeply and so thoroughly that even the flower seeds have been killed.

We walked for miles, I should think about 6 or 7 altogether that day, it took us the whole day to do it; but at hardly any place were we quite free from an odd, old, musty smell – the whole country is simply sown with dead. We were out hunting for cemeteries however and looked about for an observation post.

About ¼ mile ahead was a 'Pemple' or Strong-point which the Germans had built on the highest point of the ridge. We clambered over to it and from its top saw two cemeteries. All the cemeteries in this area are distinguishable for miles by a tall white cross on which is painted the name and number of it. The first we found was River Trench and further on River Trench German, a small group of German graves. Then on ½ mile to Swan trench. Near here was a strange collection of all manner of things. Every sort of bits of equipment both British and German were lying about in an extraordinary litter. No salvage had been done and things were just as they were left lying when our men went out.

This was the last in this direction and we made a line for where we had left the car. The travelling is simply awful over country such as this. The long grass covers everything, hiding pickets and barbed wire, masking the smaller holes, almost meeting across the narrow trenches and you have to walk in a sort of crouching attitude with bent knees testing the ground at every step; now and then, notwithstanding every care, your foot goes down a hole and brings you up with a crash that jolts you all up. A piece of wire holds up a leg and pulls you up short and you wonder how long boots and gaiters are going to hold out. However we found the car and went back up Beaumont Hamel Valley and stopped opposite the mouth of the Y Ravine.

We left the car again and went up the Ravine. I now understand why it was we found it such an awful place to take. The Ravine winds and at every corner there was a fortress of machine guns. No fortress actually visible, but guns let into crafty holes cut in the bank that would simply scrape everything living off the bed of and banks of the Ravine. But our fellows took it – how they did, nobody knows and now on the high ground on the top are the cemeteries.

Hunters Cemetery contains the bodies of about 80 or 90 Gordon Highlanders who fell when they took the ravine. In shape it is circular, heads outwards, feet inwards; a deep moat runs round the circle and a mound has been formed over it. My notion of decorating and planting is to raise a gigantic tumulus over the Circle, plant it all over with heather, and embed in the summit a vast block of Grampian Granite. This and nothing else.

On our way from here to the car which had been sent on we had to pass near some curious looking country. I couldn't make out what it was. The ground was a curious rusty red colour streaked with white and I made a detour to see what it was. I clambered over some bare mud heaps where nothing grew and suddenly found the cause.

Do you remember – I had forgotten – when R.N.D. took B. Hamel that they sent up a most successful mine, it was considered one of the best things done up to that time and was certainly the biggest.

I was looking into a hole quite 50 perhaps 60ft. deep. From rim to rim it was over 100 yards, its colour was a light rusty red from the subsoil and it was wrinkled and seamed by hundreds of little water courses. The curious thing was there was no water in it. The Great Sap by which our men worked up and laid the mine now acts as a drain and takes away all water that flows down the sides. I called to the others and they came over and we stood and gazed down at this great pit in amazement. Only one thing did we see that gave any indication of the fighting – an old cigarette case with a ragged hole clean through it. Lying a little way from the rim, further back we found a boot still occupied, but did not connect it with anything in particular till we saw the crater. The garrison of the trenches immediately over the mine must have taken two days to come down and were probably spread over the space of an English county.

It was hot – very hot, we carried our coats, there was wind fortunately. Not much sun except at intervals – distances were beautifully blue and fairly clear. The colour of the Prairie has changed to a dull brown, all the weeds have seeded and are fading, the water plants are flagging and lie untidily in the water; no butterflies are there but an occasional peacock or tortoise-shell, the colours have gone and things are not as they were in July.

We at length after what seemed an interminable time got back to the car, had a drink from the remains of my lunch tea, lit a big pipe and got into the car with a sigh of relief.

We arrived at H.Q. just in time to change and have a tremendous dinner. I was not tired – then, but I have been tired almost ever since. I have two more days easy and then I shall be out again.

H.Q.   13/10/17

We went via Mountainvillers & Patay and ran through a huge open arable country quite treeless. Large farms miles apart were the only houses visible. Five km out of Orleans we had a puncture and mended it in pouring rain and driving wind.

We had not gone more than 3 km when another wheel went flat; this was mended under like conditions. As we got in the driver said in a cheery tone – 'Now for the third!' Before we had gone more than a few hundred yards the same wheel punctured again. It was by this time getting dark and the dirt, rain, wind, mud and general confusion caused by being unable to see anything made us about the most uncomfortable trio you ever saw. One thing we were thankful for, and here one never forgets it, we were not living, walking, eating and sleeping in three feet of liquid mud as our fellows are doing, this minute in Flanders . . .

VERDUN   Sept. 14th. [1918]

My dear B,

Anything more disgusting than this awful weather I have never come across.

I awoke this morning to the sound of splattering rain. However, it had rained at intervals during yesterday. Heavy storms were travelling about and I sheltered from the worst one in Fort Douaumont. So I thought I would set out and get to the famous Hill known as Le Mort Homme, and see the quarries of Haudremont. So I got some lunch and packed my old pack with that, some beers and a camera, and started.

It rained and blew, the wind was behind and I travelled on, through Charug and Bras both entirely smashed and almost rebuilt. From Bras I struck right into the Mountains, for indeed such they are. The road grew worse and worse and the surroundings were of the most awful description. I was in a gorge or ravine as these valleys are all termed, and on either side rose enormous hills of ruin. Before the war they were covered with thick forest, of biggish trees. Now, every tree is gone and the young undergrowth is springing. The whole height from road to summit is one mass of shell holes and splintered trees.

Up on the north side of the Ravine I found the quarries. The Boche had got in fairly early on in the Battle of Verdun and had mined under the whole hill. I had no torch and so could not go far, because when they were turned out they soaked the place with petrol and burnt out the shoring timbers. There was enough left to see how well installed they were, with chambers cut from the solid rock with electric light, remains of furniture and even picture frames.

The rain stopped and the clouds began to break and I thought I was in for a fine day. Took a couple of photos and went on. The road divides just hereabouts, one fork going up the main ravine to Douaumont and the other – passage interdit – up a smaller and more fearful looking place. Of course I took the passage interdit.

What these ravines looked like during the bombardments when the Boche thought nothing of putting 50,000 shells a day into a single ravine I can hardly imagine. Down the bottom percolated a small stream. I say percolated because it couldn't run. It was dammed by a shell hole every yard, and it spread out across the narrow floor of the ravine in the most dismal morass where reeds and bullrushes throve.

The Ravine got narrower and the hills on either side became steeper, till I came to a sort of amphitheatre where two other smaller ravines came in. Here was chaos complete. It was fought over for two whole years, this point, and here they had collected mountains of shells and were blowing them up. It was an off day today and no one was about. I quite understood why the passage was interdit and was glad it was an off day. The road became impossible beyond this point, you could not see whether there had ever been a road. So I turned and came back against the gale and the driving rain which had begun again.

I struggled back to Bras and in an estaminet full of workmen ate my lunch with hot coffee and cognac. It rained ten thousand streams and blew great guns; I thought of coming back by train, but railway luck was out. No train till 4.21, so I buttoned my soaking mac up again and started. I got wetter and wetter but only below the mac. The old thing kept everything out. But I arrived at the hotel dripping from the knee down. Got a change and had a sleep. Am quite alright now.

In spite of the filthy weather I am glad I came, I have got quite another idea of proportion. The British did fairly well during the war. The French admit that – they would. But unless you have seen something outside the British Zone you have no idea what France did. I have seen the Chemin des Damen and have always said that the devastation there was worse than anything in the British Line. But Verdun beats the Chemin des Damen all hollow. For pure ruin Verdun is the last word.

The Boche wanted it in the worst way. They lost 700,000 killed in front of it, and the French lost 400,000 defending it. We have our Ypres, our Vimy, our

Somme, but no nation under heaven ever had a Verdun, and you will never realise it till you see it.

H.Q

3.11.18

My dear B.

My fountain pen holds two full squeezes of the filler. I filled up when I began to write my report and only just finished before the pen ran dry.

Only in this way I can make you realise (a) the amount I had to write and (b) the amount of country I saw and cemeteries I visited during the time Hill and I were out (we saw 95). We were away from H.Q. for fourteen consecutive days rushing about in a car, sometimes over old country full of familiar landmarks, visiting old spots where I had been at work and which

Press photo of Captain J S Parker, at Etaples in 1922, during the Royal visit. The Captain later wrote, 'We looked down on to five acres of white headstones marking 11,000 graves dotted all over with the thousands of flowers in full bloom.' The photographer commented that his photo in the London papers would make the Captain famous overnight.

had been derelict for 6 months, and sometimes over quite new ground where all details were the same – only the broad landscape and names of villages were different.

A titled gentleman in a brazen hat came out from Whitehall to look for the grave of his son. He was sent up to the D.A.D. of the Area in which the grave was and was taken through the town of Baillene.

Now Baillene is marked on the map, and so it is, you would think, marked on the face of the earth. To say that it now is not so marked would be an exaggeration, for there is an area of rounded heaps of rubbish, much of the same formation as the humpy dumpies, which has a general consistency of bricky fragments . . . but that is all.

But the brazen-hatted gentleman who sits at home and makes war for a living gazed upon the ruin and turned to the D.A.D. and said, 'Well, I've never seen anything like it'. The D.A.D. who is 6 ft 4, 17 stone, boxer & county cricketer, turned a withering eye upon him and replied 'No, I don't suppose you have'.

Of course he never saw anything like it, nobody ever has. Nobody ever saw a town of 5000 people (P.S. Baillene was more than that), rendered down to a heap of rubbish in five weeks. And it is just this that makes me quite despair of ever putting down on paper that which will enable you to grasp what this thing means to France and what it might have meant to England.

Next day Hill and I went out alone and went over a lot of ground newly ploughed with shells.

It is an extraordinary thing, the change that is coming over the Somme country. In '16 it was ploughed to an even depth of about 4 ft, a ploughing which cast up millions of dormant seeds and left them lying on the top. In '17 these germinated and painted the whole face of the earth with the colour of their flowers. Meanwhile the seeds of the grass were germinating too and now the weeds are giving place to the grass and the whole country is becoming green.

At Roisel there was another big cemetery and we sat on a German tombstone and ate sandwiches. After that we got into the country which had been Boche for years. Hargecourt is right on the great Hindenburg line and the whole country for miles and miles in depth is seamed and scored with their trenches. The Hindenburg line is not a vast ditch running across the face of the earth, if it were only that we could have blown it all to blazes ages ago, but it consists of line after line of trenches not necessarily running parallel to each other or even facing the enemy, they face any old way; each trench is designed to outflank an attack on the next one and all are protected by miles of dense banks of wire. How anything could have remained alive on the top of the ground with the Hun trenches filled with machine guns is one of the wonders of the war. The idea of anything short of an Archangel being able not only to live but to over-run the whole depth of the system and turn the Huns out of it never dawned upon Hindenburg; what he must have thought when the whole of his precious line was in our back areas, I don't know. If he had seen four British Sisters in their pretty blue and white standing fluttering in the breeze on the top of one of the high places of his impregnable line I think his knees would have doubled under him.

We drove on straight down to St. Quentin through country utterly blasted, littered with debris, passing mile after mile of trenches. Every slowly-rising curve of country is scored at its foot and summit with trenches, each coupled up with the other with narrow alleys through which reinforcements could be rushed. It is not to be wondered at that Hindenburg pronounced it impregnable. It is miles deep. When one system is taken it only reveals other systems beyond. Yet our men went over them and through them in a manner that no one except the few officers who could look on could ever describe.

At every cross road and in deep cuttings where the banks came down to the roadside were the craters made by the mines the Germans fired. In some cases we passed round them on improvised corduroy road and in others a fine trestle bridge had been erected spanning the great chasm. The road runs quite straight taking valley and hill just as they come and from the top of the ridges you get the wonderful views of this wonderful country, treeless, houseless and lifeless.

And as you gaze at what you can see and try and imagine all that you know of the country that you *cannot* see, you begin slowly to realize the awful nature of the Hun. Here is a strip of France 300 miles long varying from 5 to 50 miles wide where no habitable house remains, no cultivation is done, where nature is coming back as mistress over the beautifully tended fields of the French, where not a church nor a calvary exists and where countless thousands of men are lying, men who were the bravest in the world, some in cemeteries where their graves are known and named, but others – thousands of others – in unnamed, unknown shell holes which no one will ever know.

Then we had two days running around Doulleus and Arras. When I was in Arras before, I saw the big square, now called Barbed Wire Square, and the remains of the Hotel de Ville. This time I saw the Cathedral. It is in the most awful state of destruction but like all the big Cathedral-like churches it was built so solidly and well that much of it remains standing although shot through and through.

Bethune was in the first place shelled very badly by the Boche and then he sent over incendiary shells and burnt it clean out. As we ran in along the familiar roads we were stopped time after time by fallen houses; only one road has been cleared through the town and it took us a long way round. We left the car at the market place and intended to walk to the Grand Place. We were soon walking over 6 ft of rubble that was lying on the cobble-stones and as the way became more difficult we turned down the small street leading to the Little Place in front of the Cathedral. Here the fallen houses lay a good ten feet deep over the road but by scrambling on we arrived at the Place. The surface of it was completely covered with bricks and stones. The great red brick tower of the Church which dominated the whole country for miles was lying spread out over the ground and every house in the neighbourhood was reduced to a rounded hillock through which a few stumps of walls projected.

We clambered up to the top of the heap of bricks which was the tower and looked around. The spectacle as seen from this height was simply awful. Actually as far as one could see not one house remained. Some of course were heaps of rubble, others stood in a tottery state without roofs and floors – mere empty shells.

Merville is without exception the worst of the big towns I have seen. The suburbs are standing in patches – shells of houses – but the centre of the town is one immense rubbish heap. I have never seen Bailleul since we shelled the Boche out. I hear from men who have that it is the worst instance of destruction in France – I mean among the big towns. But if it beats Merville I shall be surprised. There is nothing more to do to Merville except to beat the stones into sand and even that has begun.

The big church is almost gone. The western front is completely skinned, all the clear face stones and every bit of decoration has been blown away, all that is left is the massive wall, built of brick and dented all over with direct hits from the shells. One huge tooth of masonry sticks up from the ruin in a fantastic style and is visible from some way off because all the houses are flat.

The bridge over the canal on the north side is gone and you run the car over a temporary bridge built a little way off. The locks have been demolished and the water has been reduced to about 2 feet deep. The bed of the canal is littered with all manner of hideous rubbish. The big trees along the tow path are lying in every direction, most of them in the canal bed.

The cemetery no longer exists. The shells fell into the soft ground and bursting scattered everything broadcast. Nearly every one penetrated to below the bodies and the resulting debris is too abominable for words.

We can reconstruct of course, but what will be the good? We know that no cross we put up will cover the body, for shell hole lips shell hole. The only thing we can do is to put up a big memorial and write on it 'Near this spot is buried ....'. Of my nursery only a few plants remain, the trees have all gone. Two sacks of grass seed I had left in the hut were still lying among the ruins, and the sacks were covered with a healthy sprouting of green. There was nothing to do, and so we cleared out for our next stopping place.

I have always thought of Ypres as having been entirely demolished during the four years of shelling to which it has been subjected, but really there is more left of it than there is of Merville.

The curious part is the evidences of the huge population that Ypres still contained up to a very few weeks ago: every hole and corner was roofed with a few beams and stones and covered with a thick layer of earth. Inside were a few makeshift bed places, a fireplace and something of a table. The cellars of the houses opened through the heaps of rubbish overlaying them and a makeshift doorway gave upon the open air. Dugouts were everywhere in all manner of unexpected places, the place was honeycombed. It is only by walking through the streets and over the piles of rubbish that one realises what was meant by Ypres being in the occupation of the British. (Which is the right way? I can't remember). There is one terrible feature in Ypres, it is the number of cemeteries, they are everywhere. We know up to a certain point but we can never know the full total.

I think of all the places I have seen Ypres has more fascination about it than any other place but St Eloi. Ypres has seen four years of modern fighting and its name brings all sorts of associations with it. From the early days when we had few guns and few men and ammunition enough for one shell per gun per week; when our fellows lived and ate and drank and slept in three feet of water for weeks on end without relief through the whole of a winter; right through two Boche attacks which were meant to break through to the coast and were driven with the utmost of their power only to pile their men in heaps in front of our trenches; through the first gas attack which the Canadians have never yet forgiven; through a thousand days and a thousand nights of ceaseless harassings from shells and bombs from three sides at once, hardly a day among them all without some toll being taken in British lives; to the last attack of all when we thought it would have to be given up and finally when the baffled Boche at last drew out of range leaving its ruins telling a tale that no other ruins in France can tell.

Since then I have been very busy unable to write more than a scribble to you. I heard on my return that we had decided to move and on Thursday 6th Nov. we said goodbye to the sea, the dunes and the wonderful beach and came back here where we had come from and have settled down in the town in offices that don't suit us a bit. I am pretty certain that we shall move, especially if the Boche decides to come in.

By Jove, what times we live in! Fancy three whole armies going over the top in one moment, what can the Boche think of us?

He would have been surprised to see the leave boats unloading the other day – thousands of men coming back from home to fight – singing and calling to each other and marching off full to the neck with pure beans.

Yours, Jack.

[4 YEARS LATER: PEACETIME]

The Visit of King George V.

Headquarters, I.W.G.C.,
Longuenesse,
St. Omer,
FRANCE.

May 15th, 1922.

> The tumult and the shouting dies,
> The Captains and the Kings depart

And we who have been at fever heat for four delirious nights and days are left behind to pick up the threads of every-day routine as best we can.
So many things had to be taken into consideration – French Secret Service, British Secret Service, French and Belgian Railways and their time-tables, conditions of roads (a loaded Rolls Royce weighs three tons), the wishes of the French and Belgian Governments, the personal wishes and comfort of the King and most important of all the provision of as many opportunities as possible of visiting cemeteries.

I was on duty six times in as many different places en route and in not one instance was the programme departed from for more than fifteen minutes all round. It was so arranged that the King was enabled to go through the elaborate state functions at the Belgian Court and then spend three days knocking round by car and train without being affected in any way. He got his meals punctually and regularly, his interest was kept up, he was not allowed to become tired, he was never bored and was as full of fun and beans at Meerut on the last day, when he pulled Clive Wigram's leg for being unable to read the Arabic inscription on an Indian headstone, as he was when at Hopstore Cemetery on the first day he turned to Haig and said he didn't think much of the German shooting when they could not hit a huge barn which existed right through the war alongside the cemetery and was used as a casualty clearing station.

It was at Hopstore that I first came into the picture.

I got there nearly an hour before the cortège was due. By and by some French troops came along and I explained to them where they were to stand. We pushed a few people back out of the way when the King's car came in sight and fell in. As the King and General Ware got out of the car I could not help contrasting them, Ware, huge and overpowering, the King, small and very dapper, dressed in Field Marshal's uniform.

At ten paces we came up to the salute and remained there till he acknowledged it. Then General Ware presented me and I presented the gardener in charge. This man was a D.C.M. and Croix de Guerre. The King spoke to him some time and he and I went all round the cemetery with him.

Immediately after being presented, Haig walked up to me and shook hands and said in a tone which it is quite impossible to reproduce because it was quite inimitable, 'How do you do? I am so pleased to see you.'

When the Cortège had gone I jumped into my car again, pulled out my brushes and polishing rags and started on my boots and gaiters, which had got dusty on the road. We boosted along to Poperinghe where I emerged from the car as from a band-box and began the work of staging the show. The folk had to be herded back: the Maire shown where to stand, the gardener fallen in and fully instructed. I had not more than completed everything when he came along. He shook hands again with me and I presented the gardeners; I had forgotten two of their names and had to make them up on the spot!! However it didn't matter: all went well.

We went all round again repeating the first performance, I answering all sorts of questions regarding the general treatment, and finding him a most delightful talker, a good listener, keen as mustard, very observant and full of fun and humour.

At Longpré, when the King alighted and looked round he said it was the most beautiful he had yet seen. And as he said, it the village brass band struck up 'God Save the King'. They had got the music the afternoon before and had been practising all night. They gave us five whole verses with elaborate variations. A small girl came forward with a bunch of lilac and presented it to the King who put his hand on her shoulder as he thanked her. It was very splendid and all so beautiful, the rain had stopped and the sun was beginning to push through the clouds. We were up on a hill overlooking the great valley

The visit of King George V and Queen Mary to the Allied Cemetery at Terlincthun, in May 1922. Captain Parker recorded, 'It was a brilliant gathering. The soldiers with their red hats and ribbons up; the naval men in blue; French troops, French Generals, French civil dignitaries and all the commission in full dress with medals and swords.'

of the Somme, bursting with all the green things of the earth. The flowers, the green turf, white headstones topped by the beautiful Cross of Remembrance with its Crusader's Sword.

We came on through Abbeville to Etaples and arrived there as the sun was setting amid an amazing bank of clouds. The photographer went plumb off his head. The long low light was streaming across the sand bars exposed by the tide and gleamed in all the pools among the sand. The distant sea was indigo except for the path of light. The dunes were shining a warm pink and the long ridges of pines stood out against the further sand ridges as if cut in steel. From the great platform we looked down on to the five acres of white headstones marking 11,000 graves dotted all over with the thousands of flowers in full bloom.

Next morning I went up to Meerut, the Indian cemetery, and was once more at the helm. He came strolling along and gave me such a cheery good morning. Behind him came Rudyard Kipling among the suite.

He highly approved of all we had done and wanted Colonel Clive Wigram to translate the Arabic inscription of the headstones.

I pointed out to Rudyard Kipling the grave of Gunga Din (you remember him in the Barrack Room Ballads) and he stood musing for a moment. Then he said: 'Of course we'll have to suppose that this was my man. No it couldn't be, Gunga Din was written thirty years ago. Ah! I have it, it's his son – it must be his son.' He was awfully bucked.

When we had seen him off we walked down to Terlincthun, the ceremony there has doubtless been described in every paper. It was wonderful. The sun was just blazing and the flowers were at their best. The Queen had joined the King the evening before and they both came in together. It was a brilliant gathering. The soldiers with their red hats and ribbons up; the naval men in blue; French troops, French Generals, French civic dignitaries and all the Commission in full dress with medals and swords.

The ceremony itself was just superb, it fairly thrilled. The King remained at the salute in front of the cross for nearly a minute and everyone almost held their breath. The Queen laid her wreath and there was some hand-shaking among the French. Then the King stood right out in the middle and read his speech; you have read it, it was splendid. His delivery was simply excellent, every syllable of every word was audible. General Catelnau replied.

Then he came wandering round the fringe of the crowd speaking to one and another and said goodbye to our crowd. They walked on towards the War Stone and had just got there when there was a high scream from a distant bugle. At the end of the first phrase every soldier and sailor froze stiff and came up to the salute. The crowd, mixed up now with the men in uniform, caught the attitude and likewise froze. And so we stood, not a movement in the whole assembly, while the two crack buglers from the Grenadier Guards blew the Last Post from the slopes of the opposite hill.

That put the crowning touch to the most wonderful thing I have ever seen.

The pomp, the dignity, the reverence and the inner meaning of the whole thing was simply overpoweringly grand. And then the lovely picture broke up and soon from the top of the Cliffs we saw the Royal Yacht steam past the French Destroyers who fired their salutes as she passed, while away at sea,

The 1922 Royal visit to Hopstore Allied Cemetery. Left to right: General Sir F Ware, HM King George V and Captain J S Parker. Photo courtesy of The Graphic Photo Union, Tallis St. London EC4.

outside the three mile limit, lay the dim shapes of our own Destroyers waiting to take her home.

Never shall I see anything like it again.

HOTEL DE PARIS

Verdun, le Sept 13 1922

My dear B.

Today I have done so much that I shall have to wait until I see the photographs in order to realise quite how much.

For I have seen Fort Vaux, Fort de Souville and Fort Douaumont. And when you have done that you have had a full day. That is, if you go with eyes that see and an understanding which is based upon experience. I saw some parties in cars and charabanc who rushed to the place, rushed in, rushed out again, and got back into their cars. They thought they had seen the place, the owls; perhaps they had cast eyes upon it and *had* seen it but as to imagining the thing, as to trying to get the spirit of it . . . they couldn't if they tried.

To the West it is fairly free of devastation, there are a few villages about, but to all other points of the compass you look over vast trails – leagues long – of purest devastation. Not a house, not a tree exists, it is all wilderness, where shell hole lips shell hole, where remains of dug outs and trenches and concrete pill boxes seam and dot the greenery. Everything has been hammered away by the guns until the whole of it has been returned to primeval conditions.

I could hardly get away from Douaumont, but I was warned by twinges of hunger and so came down to the road again. Here I entered a long Army hut, and saw a wonderful sight. Heaped on either side of a main aisle were scores and scores of coffins and all the walls were covered thick with photographs.

Photographs of men who were lost at Douaumont and in the trenches around and were never heard of. The remains are those of unknowns, and people come from all France and pay the Curé who lives there a few francs for the burning of a candle and the saying of a prayer for the soul of their man who was never found.

It is an ossuary of inconnus and on the coffins are hundreds and hundreds of cards, visiting cards left by families who have lost someone at Douaumont and who fondly hope that one of the coffins contains the man they love.

It is a weird idea and a most impressive one. I saw an old woman of the poorest peasant type, fumble in her bag and extract 10 francs, hand it to the Curé, begging him to say a prayer on October the 1st, and then blunder outside, blind with tears. She stumbled down the road and subsided on a heap of stones and just rocked to and fro.

Beyond Douaumont is another interesting spot.

A trench had to be held at all costs. The order went out and the French ——— manned the trench with bayonets fixed. They remained there under the bombardment until every man was buried, and buried standing.

And today you may see the outline of the trench marked out by a line of bayonets standing upright from the ground, and you know that the butt of every rifle is still held by the men who manned the trench, and they are still there doing their job.

Albergo Paradiso,
Asiago,
Prov di Vencenza,
Italy

Sept. 1925

My dear Guy,

Once more I am down in this delectable country. It is a country of extremes. A beautiful day is more lovely here than any where I have been. A beautiful night is just the same. A bad day is just about the worst thing you care to hit against. Wind is something solid. A thing to lean against. Rain flays the skin off the ground. Fortunately of cold I have not tasted, I can imagine it to be utterly relentless.

I have been at work on 3 of the lower lying cemeteries for four or five days and am now busy with the last two, the higher ones, at Granezza. One of these lies rather higher than I thought, it is just about 4,800 ft.

The way the trenches have been quarried over these mountains regardless of all obstacles fills me with amazement. They go for miles and miles, all along the old Front line – Front and Reserve lines just as we had in France. Dug outs here and there. Gun emplacements, Machine gun emplacements, Red Cross Stations, Ammunitions Stores all the whole paraphernalia in perfect order, and every single thing carved or blasted out of a solid mountain of rock. Tommies needed to be skilled dry wall masons, for as the trench was blown in by a burst it had to be put up again. There was no shovelling, there was nothing much to shovel, it was all building and dry building at that – same as the Woodmans buttresses.

The dugouts of course will last till the heavens depart as a scroll, no shoring is wanted, the men just blew away the particular rock in front of them and took it out. All or much of this rock is curiously divided into strata up and down. You follow along the level of one stratum, and the fissures between horizontal strata and your guiding hills; having got out one block you are roofed and shored by adjoining strata.

To go out at night in front of a trench, among rocks quite four feet high standing about a foot apart all round, each rock of some 20 tons weight and worn smooth by weather, must have been some job. Take with you slung on a pole 1 cwt of wire, also pickets and then begin to think how you are to drive them. You just cannot drive them. So you have certain of your party carrying stones. You set up your picket in a narrow crack and wedge it up with stones. But how the devil they slung the wire over such country beats me altogether.

Some of the wire is the very fiercest stuff I have ever seen. Each piece of the two-stranded is as thick as an ordinary lead pencil. I suppose it resisted H.E. more effectively.

The effect of a shell burst in this sort of country was multiplied ten million fold. Not only did the shell itself break up pretty completely but it distributed about two tons of rock, finely divided, each fragment a potential wound. Blindness was caused more frequently in these mountains than in any other theatre of the war.

I should like to have heard – heard only – a bombardment in these mountains. I know the sound of a shell in the waste spaces of Flanders, where all is open plain. The bump of the gun is a single bump. A howitzer, however, says bl-ump. But here the echoes must have been marvellous.

The discharge of a gun so many times, the volume of the sound of a voice must have awakened echoes that had slept since the mountains were first blown out of the flat. . . .

There was an Alpine barracks on a summit near Asiago about 6000 ft. The Austrians hammered it prodigiously and finally took it The Italians recovered it after fearsome slaughter and never lost it back again. Its gaunt ruined walls still stand, and morning after morning I have seen them glow in the rising sun as if the fires of those fearsome days were still smouldering.

Upton House,
Bitton,
Bristol.

Feb. 25. 1935

My dear Everybody,

Grace has suggested that I should write a general letter telling you how I got home.

The excitement began on about January 25th when a deputation of Horticultural Officers came to my office and after many words presented me with a beautiful silver salver inscribed as being presented to me by the H.O.S. of the Commission on my retirement from the Service. It is a real beauty about 15″ in diameter and stands on 3 low legs.

Then came a dinner on 26th at the Hotel Univers, at which all other heads of Departments, senior clerks and what nots – plus their wives, turned up. We were able to rope in the Padre and his wife too, as they were visiting various sick folk in the neighbourhood. We sat down 19. After dinner the Col. got up and told stories about me and made a sort of farewell speech. I replied by saying that I didn't think much of his originality in the story telling line because he had told the same yarns about me at least four dozen times.

Then another man got up and after another speech gave me a very lovely cigarette case inscribed 'As a token of esteem from friends at Arras'.

We drank large quantities of wine and ate very largely of a most delicious dinner. The Col. had told the Patron that it was up to him to send Capt. Parker away with the firm conviction that the French really could cook. And right well he kept his end up. We tried to dance afterwards, but there was nothing to be had but a very inadequate gramophone which wasn't loud enough. So we gathered round a tin-pot piano and sang songs and told stories until one o'clock.

That was on the Saturday (Jan. 26th). On Sunday afternoon – the following day – the H.O. from Bethune came for me in his car. He drove me over to Bethune in a blinding snow-storm. I had some tea at his house and went to Church. Church is held in the Office. Desks and chairs are chucked out, one of the office tables is used as an altar and they have a really beautiful altar frontal. The Padre had come down from Ypres.

We had a very nice service. The gardeners had come in from some distance, because they heard I was coming, and the office was crammed. I read the first lesson and a head gardener the second.

After service they came round to say goodbye and I was amazed how they remembered something I had said – something I had done – 10, 12 & 14 years ago and called my remembrance to it – things that I had completely forgotten – but had somehow stuck in their memories. One chap came up and shook hands, and tried to say goodbye. He could only close on my hand like a vice, and make noises in his throat, and went off. In a few moments he was back and had another shot . . . no good. . . . I had just got the fingers of my right hand undone, when back he came again, and this time said Goodbye. I thought the goodbyes those fellows said – in broad Cockney, broad Wessex and broad Lancashire – were some of the most lump-in-the-throat speeches I ever heard.

Then we cleared off and dined at the house of the H.O. after which we drank the fag end of the last bottle of old Canteen whisky he had left. The Padre then started for Ypres and I went off to my hotel.

I had four days in London. Three were on duty, during which I cleared everything up and saw a good deal of my successor. With the usual perversity of Government Departments, who invariably put a square man into a round hole, they have appointed a man who knows nothing whatever of the job, having spent the whole of his life at sea . . . a naval officer. I have had several nasty knocks from the Commission from time to time, but this is the unkindest cut of all. There are six of us who run the Department, myself and my five officers, all of whom have had anything up to 40 years experience in gardening, and to have a man put over them who doesn't know a berberis from a bull rush has created a perfect fury of indignation.

Next day I left for Bath where B met me with Anstey's car.

On arrival at Upton I was greeted by a small gathering of villagers outside the gate, headed by George Watts. They came to welcome me home, and if it were not for the fact that I should have had to kiss them all, I should like to have kissed Lizzie Mortimer – but I draw the line at Mrs. Hawking!!

I shook hands all round and thanked them for coming to see me arrive.

It was very nice of them.

Now I must finish up.

We had a very jolly Christmas, Grace and Brice, Guy and Phyllis with their daughter Marion. We did the proper things at their proper times. Goose, plum pudding, absent members of family, goodies and then into the drawing room. 'See amid the Winter Snow.' Carols, cake, Scrooge and then replete and staggering – to bed.

 Cheerio.

  Best of luck for 1936.

   Yours

    Jack

1922, Captain J Parker, right, looking up at the Cross that dominates the cemetery at Etaples, France. Trains from nearby Bologne to Paris would slow down as they passed the cemetery. Stubbins, left, was one of the pool of drivers who also worked for the War Graves Commission, and whom the Captain always choose as he was a 'good reliable chap'. Beyond the sand dunes the Straight of Dover is just visible.

Chapter 15

The Wood family and the Red Cross Society

In the 19th Century the Wood family were farmers in Keynsham. According to Mrs Diana Carbery, née Wood, her bachelor uncle lived at Chandos Lodge at Durley Hill with his sister Eliza, from where he farmed the Hams from the Avon River up to Station Road, long before the bypass was built, though the railway already split his land. At the same time, according to Mrs Corena Wood, his brother Charles Harris Wood, or their father, owned the land from Bath Road to Saltford, and up to Burnett Point, which he rented out to tenant farmers. Mrs Wood has a photo of the Wood sisters, and their parents, in their garden at Rockhill Farm, and she mentions how the locals referred to going down 'Urn Lane'.

Evidence from The Kelly's Directory of Somerset

The Hunt's Directory of 1848, under 'Keynsham', includes the neighbouring villages as far away as Westbury, Downend and Long Ashton. However, under its heading 'Gentry, Clergy, etc.' it records only one Wood entry, that is 'Wood, Mrs Esther, Keynsham' with no precise address given.

The Kelly's Directory of Somerset for 1861, in the section on Keynsham, listed under the title 'Commercial' only records,
'Wood, Henry, farmer'.
The KDS for 1866, under 'Keynsham', records,
'Wood, Charles Harris, farmer, Rock Hill Farm,' and below it,
'Wood, Henry, farmer.
The KDS for 1875 is slightly different. Under 'Commercial', is,
'Wood, Alfred, grazier and landowner', the entry followed by,
'Wood, Charles Harris, farmer and landowner, Rock Hill House'.
The 1889 edition of KDS twelve years later, again records,
'Wood, Alfred, grazier and landowner'.
'Wood, Charles Harris, grazier and landowner'.
The KDS for 1894 is a more informative issue. Under 'Private Residents' as opposed to 'Commercial', it lists,
Wood, Alfred, 'Chandos Lodge'.
Wood, Charles Harris, Rockhill House.
Wood, Edward, Bath Road.

But it also has a surprising entry, that is, 'Fry, Francis R. Rockhill House'. This identical entry also appears in the KDS for 1897, but not in the 1902 edition. So obviously, just for those few years, Charles Wood and Francis

Fry shared the Rockhill House complex. This supports Mr Ron Headington's story of the Fry family being domiciled there for a while.

The KDS for 1897 has more Wood entries under, 'Private Residents',

Wood – Miss, Ladbroke
Wood – Miss, Newton House, the High Street
Wood – Alfred, The Lodge
Wood – Charles H, Rock Hill House
Wood – Edward, Bath Road, and
Wood – Samuel, Ashington House

Gunner Charles Henry Wood, 1881–1917.

In 1987 there was a 'Wood, Joseph Henry, The Lamb and Lark Hotel', where presumably he was the landlord, but there were no Wood farmers. Presumably around this time the male Woods died, for in 1902 the only Woods mentioned are the two Miss Woods, at Ladbroke and at Newton House.

He left a wife Hilda and two children, John and Diana.

Charles Harris Wood

As a man of some standing in the community, the farmer/landowner was a devout Anglican. An interesting incident was recalled in the Keynsham Chronicle concerning him when he still lived at Rockhill Farm. He was the Vicar's Warden at St. John's which in those days was a powerful position, and was in charge of distributing the Poor Law money. He was very upset one day when he discovered that the then vicar had already given the money out. Things were never the same again, and consequently the Wood family attended St John's in the morning and the Methodist church in the evening.

Notwithstanding, there is a memorial to him high up on the south wall of St John's church, near the vestry. Vertically shaped, it is of white marble on a black base. It reads, 'Sacred to the memory of Mary, wife of Charles Harris Wood, of this parish who departed this life Nov. 11, 1867, aged 60. Also of the above named Charles Harris Wood, who died March 15, 1894 aged 69. Also of Charlotte Elizabeth Wood, wife of the above, who died June 23, 1894 aged 51. Also of their son, Charles Henry Wood, R.G.A., killed in action at Ypres, July 25, 1917, aged 36 years.'

Apparently the family was armigerous, for at the foot of the memorial was the family crest. On the top was a Father Neptune type figure with something on his left shoulder, seated on an embattled coronet. On the first of the four quarters of the shield is a tree (representing a Wood,?), while the second quarter was of the head and shoulders of a two-horned deer or antelope. The lower part of the shield repeated the above, with first the deer, then the tree. The motto below was indecipherable. Charles Harris's phaeton had the crest on it, and today his family still use the crest.

Charles Henry Wood, 1881–1917

Henry, the son of Charles and his second wife Charlotte, was born in 1881 at Rockhill Farm, on what is today called Wellsway, but was then named Burnett Hill. He was the son of Charles Wood, the grazier and landowner. Young Harry had four sisters, Bessie, Helen, Celia and Lottie. Bessie and Helen attended St John's, while Celia and Lottie worshipped at the Wesleyan Methodists.

Henry married Miss Hilda Maud Skidmore of Penn Lea Road, Bath. Their marriage was blessed with two children, John Skidmore in 1913 and Diana Wood in 1916. Henry went into business in Bristol, possibly in the ink business. Diana thought he was in the dyeing trade, and was about to move to London.

In 1914 when the First World War started, Henry was already 33 and as such was not called on to enlist. However, he did so and joined the Royal Artillery, and was sadly killed three years later in Ypres. His tombstone in France reads, '1007222, Gunner Charles Henry Wood, Royal Garrison Artillery, 25 July 1917, aged 36. Beloved husband of Hilda Wood, Keynsham, Somerset. Love is strong as death.' He left behind a daughter he may never have seen, and a young son of four: it was all very sad.

Diana mentioned that her father had been a tall man at over six feet one

BRITISH RED CROSS SOCIETY.
Incorporated by Royal Charter, 1908.

V. A. D., SOM./24.

KEYNSHAM.

Red Cross Comforts Depôt.
Reg. No. 1396.
1915-1919.

To Miss C A Wood.

We wish to thank you most heartily and sincerely for the valuable work you have done as :—

Secretary of Keynsham Wesleyan Working Party

The supply of Comforts sent to our wounded in the Bath Hospitals, increased every year, owing to the untiring efforts of each worker.

Vice President. Maud Stephen Fox

Commandant. Mary F. Hollier

Quartermaster. Bessie Wood.

A Certificate of Appreciation to Miss C A Wood, for Red Cross parcels.

inch. A very popular person, he was a sporting type of man who played a number of games including cricket, hockey and tennis.

Miss Bessie Wood

Henry's sister Bessie possessed the family trait of being tall. This slim lady knew the meaning of 'noblesse oblige' and accordingly worked unceasingly for the British Red Cross Society in Keynsham. An undated certificate presented to her, possibly in 1920, referred to her 'untiring work for the detachment from the year 1910, and especially as quartermaster during the years of the Great War, 1914–1919.' Its 33 signatures, all female apart from Dr W Peach Taylor, are of local ladies, many being spinsters, representing many well-known families and reads like a list of local people of some standing. One presumes they were all members of the Keynsham branch of the Red Cross.

Apart from the Doctor, no men are mentioned. But of course, most of Keynsham's men had volunteered or were conscripted into the army, tragically many to become just more canon-fodder for the dreadful war machine.

'The History of Methodism in Keynsham' records that when the foundation stone for the new 'Victoria' Methodist Church was laid on the 15 December 1886, 'in addition to the foundation stone, sixteen memorial stones were laid' [page 23]. Mrs Carbery said that her grandmother, Mrs Charles Harris Wood laid one stone and her aunt Miss Eliza Wood laid another, and recalls seeing one of the engraved silver-plated trowels, with a carved ivory handle, later used regularly on family occasions.

As we have seen, her nephew Charles was a keen sportman and when the Keynsham Cricket Club was formed, he was a member of the thriving club and of the men's hockey team. They played at the Frank Taylor Memorial Ground, Frank being a friend of Charles. So each Saturday Eliza's young nieces, the Wood sisters, were called upon to provide tea and cakes for the teams in the small hut which was all they had in those days.

Miss Celia Wood

Celia must have worried dreadfully about her brother's welfare in the trenches of France and Belgium. Increasingly, buses of wounded soldiers passed through Keynsham from Bristol for the Bath Hospitals. She could not help her brother but she could aid the needy soldiers suffering in hospital nearby. Another certificate, possibly of 1920, records:-

'The British Red Cross Society, VAD Som 24, Keynsham, Red Cross Comforts Depot, 1915–19, To Miss C A Wood. We wish to thank you most heartily and sincerely for the valuable work you have done as Secretary of Keynsham Wesleyan Working Party. The supply of Comforts sent to our wounded in the Bath Hospitals increased every year, owing to the untiring efforts of each worker.' It was signed by the Vice-President, M S Fox [presumably from the Brislington Home?], the commandant Mary Hollier and the QM Bessie Wood.

A copy of the well-known photo of the Peace March through Keynsham exists with the caption on the back, 'Peace Day, Saturday July 19, 1919,

BRITISH RED CROSS SOCIETY
KEYNSHAM

We wish to ask your acceptance of the accompanying gift, in token of our appreciation of all your untiring work for the Detatchment from the year 1910, and especially as Quarter-master during the years of the Great War, 1914-1919.

Mrs Stephen Fox, Vice President.

Dr W. Peach Taylor, Medical Officer	Miss Hollier, Commandant
Miss Fryer, Lady Superintendent	Mrs Tennant, Assis.nt Quarter-master
Miss Bowring	Mrs Loxton
Miss Callender	Mrs Newport
Miss D. Callender	Miss Newell
Miss Carwardine	Miss Nurse
Miss M. Carwardine	Miss Parnell
Mrs Cooksley	Miss Z. Parnell
Miss Gore	Miss Parsons
Miss Gibbons	Mrs Harold Smith
Miss P. Gibbons	Miss C. Smith
Miss Harrison	Miss Stokes
Miss M. Harrison	Mrs Frank Taylor
Mrs Hunt	Miss Tennant
Miss Jeffreys	Miss Tipney
Miss Knowles	Mrs Vowles

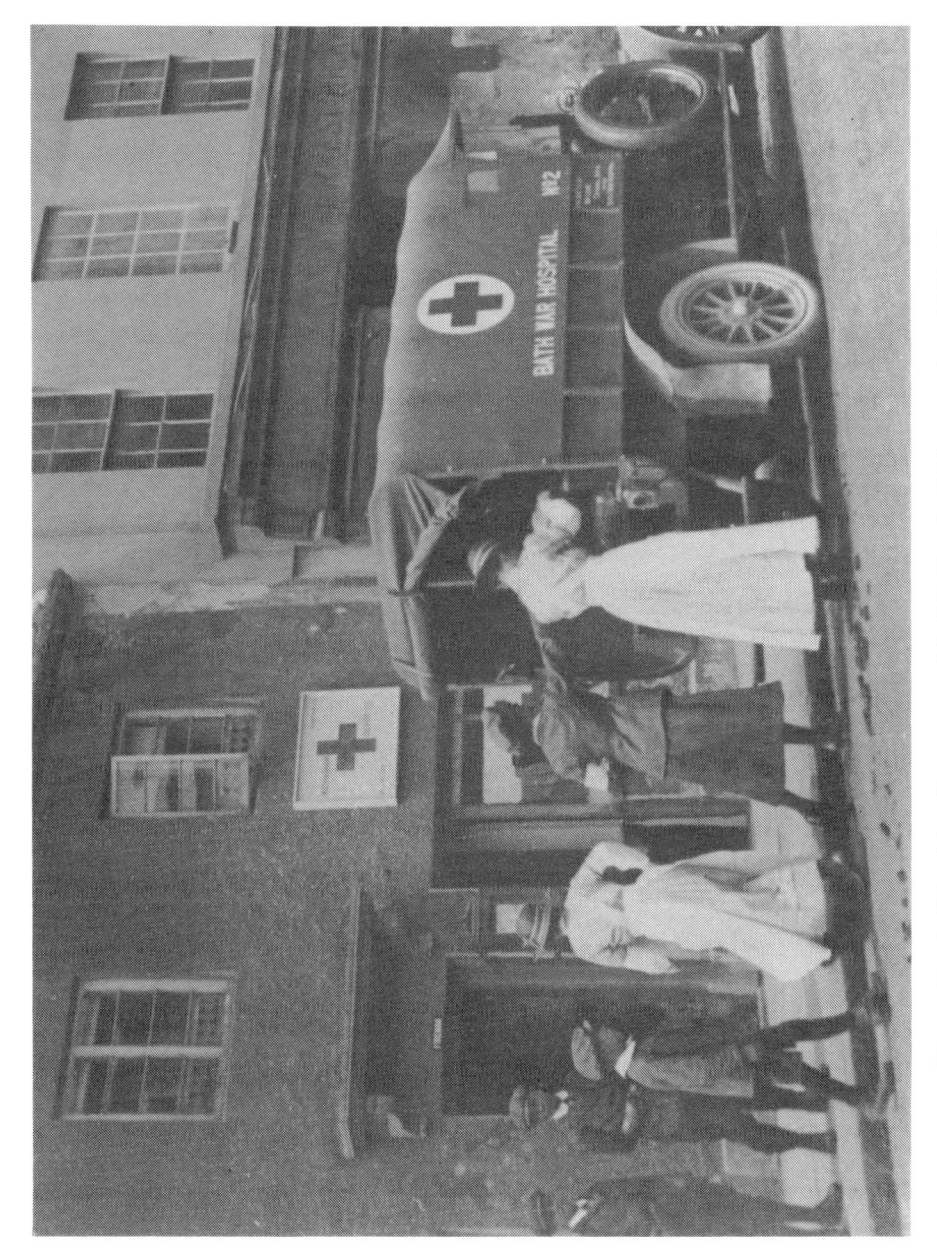

Nurse Bessie Wood loading up outside Mr Fear's old home, circa 1914–18.

Keynsham Temple Street. From Mrs Wood, Westbourne Avenue'. This photo shows the local nurses in full uniform in the procession. Another photo in this book shows what is surely the same nurses seated on the grass in a Keynsham garden. A number of octogenarians have said the faces look familiar, but hesitate to add names. These must be members of the Red Cross Society, including the Wood sisters.

Another photo depicts an early Red Cross Hospital lorry parked in the High Street outside what is today the Fear Institute, next to Ernest Hickman's shop. Mrs Carbery thinks that the house shown, Number 30, belonged to the philanthropist Mr Fear, and 'being a small cottage, probably the whole house was used for storing Red Cross supplies [comforts]. The tall nurse was probably Miss Bessie Wood, and the date around 1915'.

Mrs Carbery explained that another photo is of the FANYS, that is, The First Aid Nursing Yeomany Service. 'This group of ladies drove the ambulances. They felt that they were a cut above the ordinary nurses, who wore blue and white uniforms. The FANYS were mainly wealthy ladies who had their own cars in 1914, and whose service was unpaid'.

They had khaki uniforms, with white shirts and black ties, heavy great-coats and goggles over an assortment of peaked hats, and knee length boots. How many were Keynsham ladies we will never know, though all these ladies were FANYS. Yet if none were, why is it among the Wood collection of momentos? Mrs Carbery said there were no ATS girls in the First World War.

Not St Keyna but Westbourne Avenue!

Mrs Carbery said that after the war, in the late 1920s, the Wilcox firm built the six houses in a row by the telephone box, on land that was still part of the open fields. Much to the annoyance of the local people, he then changed the name of the road from St Keyna to Westbourne Avenue, the name it still bears today.

At the top of Westbourne Avenue is 'Ladbroke', the fine six bedroomed stone house which today is part of the Abbeyfields Home. From at least 1897 until about 1987 Ladbroke was the name of the home of many of the Miss Woods. But as Mrs Carbery explained, the first Ladbroke was the bay windowed house in Avon Road [No 8 or 12?]. When around 1910 Mr A Coles built a short row of houses at the then St Keyna Road and the two very large semi-detached houses round the corner, the Wood family bought one and brought the name of their former home with them, as people today take their telephone numbers with them. One wonders how widespread the practice was?

'Aunt Eliza' Wood lived in several houses in Keynsham, starting with Rockhill Farm, Chandos Lodge, Brislington House on the Bristol Road, which lies well back from the main road before one comes to the Hospital, and at the Conservative Club in the High Street, when it was a private house. 'According to Mrs Carbery, 'She put the fear of God into the maiden aunts.'

A party of presumably local Red Cross nurses, in a Keynsham garden.

The First Aid Nursing Yeomanry Service of lady drivers on active service.

Chapter 16

The Willcox family
by Mrs Isabel Andrews

Mrs Isabel Andrews, née Ollis, with a little prompting, has kindly written the following history of her family and its connection with Keynsham.

She wrote, 'My grandmother, Deborah Jane Selby, was the daughter of a mine-owner who came from the North Country to open up mines in the Midsomer Norton/Radstock area in the late 18th century. Deborah ran away from home to marry a mason, John Willcox, who worked on her father's estate. She was promptly disowned and rejected by her family.

'The young couple came to Keynsham where they lived at 86, Bath Hill for the rest of their lives. John Willcox set up work as a builder and decorator, and over the years built up quite a substantial family concern. He built a number of houses and main drainage systems in the area. The name 'John Willcox' can still be seen on some of the manhole covers in Keynsham. Westbourne Avenue houses were some of his construction.

'My grandfather joined the local Somerset Light Infantry Territorials, where he excelled as a marksman, taking part in International Shooting Contests at Bisley. He was also known for his interest in bee-keeping and honey production. He had hives at home and on Exmoor. Eventually he became a judge of honey in the Bristol area horticultural shows. When he died, the first duty of his eldest son was to inform the bees.

'Their family increased to four sons and four daughters. The sons joined the family business and at the outbreak of the First World War, enlisted in the SL Infantry.

'My grandmother had a hard life bringing up her large family under difficult circumstances. I shall always remember her for her lively spirit and generous smile. She had the most glorious Titian hair reaching her waist.'

Brief notes on each of her children

1. Frank Willcox

He became an Officer in the SLI at the outbreak of World War One. Unfortunately he had his leg shot off during the campaign, and was left unconscious at the side of the road. A passing German patrol thought he was dead and pushed him into the roadside ditch. He was found later and taken to a Military Hospital. He returned home and eventually married and then moved from Keynsham to Brighton, where he joined the local Council as a Surveyor and Building Administrator.

His hobby was also bee-keeping. He carried out research into the history of bees and journeyed to Egypt, where he investigated the ancient tombs to find traces and records of the origin of bees as we know them in this country.

He had two sons. Anthony was a pilot officer in the Fleet Air Arm during the Second World War, and was shot down over the sea.

Peter was an officer in the Burma Campaign. He was captured and imprisoned by the Japanese. He was released at the end of hostilities and nursed back to some semblance of his normal self in a hospital in India. He married his nurse and they returned to her home in New Zealand, where he lived a very quiet life until he died in 1987. At no time would he tell of his experiences at Japanese hands.

Having an 'English Public School' voice, Peter became a News Reader on the NZ radio.

2. Henry Willcox

He was the eldest and weakest child of the family. He was invalided out of

A photo taken in 1902 of the pupils at Bath Hill School, Keynsham

Attached to the rear of the photo is the following list of names of the children;
Standing
'Phylis Harvey, Flo Davis *, Herbert Davis, Edna Parker, Jos Davis, Mabel Harvey, George Harvey, Flo Harvey, R Tuckwell, another Tuckwell, H Ollis, another Ollis, P Ollis.'
Second Row
'Russell Harvey, Clarence Harvey, Golding, another Golding*, two more Goldings, J Wilcox [with only one l], D Wilcox, G Wilcox, J Wilcox, J Ollis, S Ollis, T Ollis.'
On the grass
'H Brookman, A Brookman, R Tyler, W Tyler, B Tyler, F Ollis, J Ollis*, R Singleton, R Harvey, F Singleton.'

Footnotes on the list
'The Tylers lived in Albert Road and went abroad'. The * [really a cross] indicates 'Passed on.' 'R Tuckwell is a BBC singer. The photo was taken in 1902.'
When I asked Mrs Andrews why Wilcox was spelt with only one L in the above school list, she replied that it was said to be because the Headmaster could not spell.

the army and returned to the family business, dealing with all the paper work and accountancy matters. He married, with no children.

3. Jennie Willcox
   She died of diphtheria in early infancy.

4. Eleanor Willcox
   She remained unmarried. She joined the then Bristol Electricity Company, and wearing a smart uniform became one of the first 'meter readers'.

5. Jack Willcox
   He was a member of the local Territorials and was also a good marksman. When he enlisted at the outbreak of World War I, he was immediately given the suicidal job of a sniper. After numerous sorties into enemy lines, he was eventually killed by a German bullet.

A Family Group

This is the family of John and Deborah Willcox, taken outside their home at 86, Bath Hill, Keynsham, around the year 1895 or 1896.

From left to right is:
John Willcox holding baby Dorothy, standing is Jessie, Jack is on the horse, Henry (eldest, born c. 1885), Nellie, Frank and Deborah holding baby George.

Mrs Andrews explained that though her grandmother Deborah was cut off by her parents, gifts, usually clothes, did arrive at Christmas, so possibly this is where the rocking horse came from. Isabel added that, 'Considering their circumstances, the children were well dressed. Jack has a fur hat and buttoned-up gaiters. Jessie had a velvet hat and yolk to her dress. Grandmother has a lace collar. It is Grandfather who is in his work-a-day clothes, possibly all that he had at that stage, and was last in the queue'.

The room on the right of the photo was a carpenters/builders shop. It was John who inserted an inside door to it, linking it with the house, and made it the dining room. The stable to his left was a carpenter's shop, with store rooms upstairs, and the wooden ladder, which is still there, was the only means of access. Eventually John employed his own carpenter.

At the rear of the house was an underground tank, near the toilet, for collecting rain water, which was brought up with a hand pump attached to the wall and was working some five years ago. Mrs Andrews said that she used to wash in the water when she visited there, and that her grandmother only ever used their rain water for washing her hair. They used it for everything apart from drinking, which was supplied from the water mains.

Isabel added that, 'Grandfather built the bathroom upstairs in the former nursery. He had to work very hard in those days building. There were no lorries and he had a fleet of handcarts to push to supply building material. Later he owned Lichfield Lodge next door as well'.

6. Jessie Willcox

She joined the nursing service during the war. She served her apprenticeship at Dr Fox's Hospital, Brislington. This was a hospital for severe mental patients. She received no pay for the first few years and was, in fact, charged for her tutorials and keep. The nursing staff worked on a one-to-one basis with the patients, and as they were often very violent, Jessie soon learned to exit backwards through doors at all times!

She married Bill Barnicot at Exeter, and together they moved to Northern Rhodesia, where Bill, who was an X-ray technician, set up equipment in the hospitals in the district and Jessie opened local medical units and stores.

7. Dorothy Willcox

The youngest daughter of the family, she was the one who stayed at home and worked extremely hard without holidays or pay for many years. She married Benjamin John Ollis, who lived with his parents at 'Felixstowe', Avon Road, Keynsham. This family of Ollis were tenant farmers at Sheldon Farm, now Sheldon Manor, where Benjamin was born. Later they lived for a short time in the Saltford and Keynsham areas. They lived at 41 and 76 Bath Hill for approximately thirty-five years.

Benjamin Ollis played lacrosse when he first married. The Keynsham team played on a field now known as the Frank Taylor Memorial (cricket) Ground,

Captain Peter Willcox, born at 86, Bath Hill, Keynsham, shaking hands in front of his men with Sir Winston Churchill, prior to leaving for the Far East to fight in the tragic but ultimately victorious Burma campaign against the Japanese.

Nurse Jessie Willcox, of the well-known Keynsham family, early in the 1914–18 World War, as a student nurse at Dr Fox's Home at Brislington.

Wellsway. During the Second World War he became an active member of the ARP service and was the Area Supplies Officer. He also organised the local Savings Campaigns, and an office opened in the High street, where National Savings stamps and certificates were sold to raise money for a 'Spitfire', and other campaigns. Office and street groups were also arranged for the sale of NS stamps.

Benjamin and Dorothy had one daughter, Isabel. She joined the local Police Force during World War II. She had many various services to perform including sounding the Air Raid Warning Sirens, certifying unexploded bombs, issuing certificates for cattle movements during an outbreak of Foot and Mouth Disease, etc, etc. Her account of her work follows:

The Keynsham Police Force during World War Two

The Keynsham Police area was part of the Long Ashton Divisional HQ and included the Whitchurch, Woolard, Pensford, Marksbury and Saltford areas. The regular staff consisted of an Inspector, Sergeant, two Motor Patrol Officers, one detective constable, and two PCs. The remaining war time staff consisted of one auxiliary motor-cycle patrol, and six constables. The regular staff of Inspector, Sergeant and one PC were all accommodated in quarters in the old Police Station on Bath Hill.

The 'Specials' were a volunteer force who trained to assist in any emergency conditions. Their Officer Commanding was Mr Charles Gibbons of The Glen, Saltford.

My own duties, as 'Auxiliary Police Constable 45', were carried out in eight hour shifts, six days per week. Most of my work entailed manning the 'phone and the Air Raid Warning system, attending to all Petty Session's correspondence and agendas and keeping records of daily incidents.

As I spent many hours alone at the station, I was issued with a revolver with very brief instructions on its use. The weapon was so heavy it had to be kept in a table drawer. One time during an 'invasion scare', two foreign combat soldiers walked into the station and of course I was at one end of the room and my revolver was at the other. They were two parachutists – deserters from the Free French Army – and had dropped into a field at the rear of the station. They were returned to the Free French Army, but it was a tricky moment for me while it lasted.

Auxiliary Police Constable 45, Isabel Ollis, later Mrs Andrews, of the Long Ashton constabulary, stationed in her home town of Keynsham at the Old Police Station in Bath Hill, during the early years of the 1939–45 war.

This is Keynsham's Victoria Police Station where, during World War II, Miss Isabel Ollis, APC 45, ably fulfilled her many responsibilities.

During an air raid, a huge bomb fell right down through the middle of Fry's Factory, but did not explode. The Bomb Disposal Squad brought it to the Police Station on a trailer and it was my job to examine it and sign for it in the Army register. The Fry's employees made a collection of a shilling a head for the men who defused the bomb.

The American Army had a camp in Keynsham, causing quite a stir among the local female population. One Court case involved a young mother who claimed maintenance for her child from a 'darkie GI'. The American policy was to imprison all darkie GIs who associated with British women, and their pay was discontinued. So the young mother was unable to claim any maintenance whatsoever!!

The Old Police Station

Before the Second War we only had a sergeant in charge of the station. He was Sergeant Bowditch. He was one of the old school, and was very strict with his men. He was very tough and would take no nonsense from hooligans, and would just take the law into his own hands. He was the law in Keynsham between the wars.

Facing the Station from Bath Hill, the sergeant's quarters were in the centre of the building, downstairs. On the projecting left wing was the constable's quarters. When our first inspector took over during the 1939–45 war, Inspector A Allen lived on the right of the station.

To the right of the Inspector's quarters, is the gate marked 'Entrance to Court', through which the accused went, then up the external stairs, to the Court Room, which was above the sergeant's quarters. As children we would stand around to see the accused being led up and down the stairs.

My actual office was in the new courtroom at the rear of the station, the one-storey building which is still there. The cells were along the corridor. My shift was 6.00 am to 2.00 pm, or 2.00 pm to 10.00 pm. Walter Millard, a retired constable, came along to do the 10.00 pm to 6.00 am shift. The phones had to be manned at all times. I was the first woman constable there. Two more came later but did not stick it.

The force was seriously depleted of men. We had one constable stationed at Whitchurch, whose wife answered the phone when he was on his beat. I felt quite sorry for her because of the number of times I had to phone. There was another constable stationed at Saltford. There were three Auxillaries attached to us at Keynsham. Detective Constable Campbell lived in Wellsway.

There was very little crime in the town. There were a few matrimonial cases, but mainly the Petty Sessions were concerned with motoring offences, such as speeding. There was very little burglary. In fact, my grandmother, Mrs J Willcox at Bath Hill, never knew what it was to lock her front door all her life.

After the war was over, I married Mr Charles Andrews and continued to live in Keynsham.

8. George Willcox
'He was the youngest child of the family, and survived the First World War, but he received severe 'trench-foot' or frost bite, while serving in the trenches.

A fountain was erected at the top of Bath Hill to celebrate Queen Victoria's Golden Jubilee in 1887. Mrs Andrews remembered it being there in 1928, with a plaque on it. Though it was called a fountain, she could never remember any water in it. Later it was removed to widen the road junction there. Two parts of the pillar are to be seen today as edging to the garden bed of 86, Bath Hill, John Willcox's old home.

He married Mercia Gill, also of a Keynsham family, and had one daughter, Monica, and one son Michael. Michael married in due course and has six daughters, but sadly, no sons.

Due mostly to the advent of two World Wars, it will be seen that the male line of the Willcox family is now extinct,' concluded Mrs Isabel Andrews.

Charles Willcox

According to Mrs Andrews, Charles was John's younger brother, and came to Keynsham a little after his brother. Charles had his own building firm, but as he had no children, it was not as large as John's. According to Mr E G Wiltshire, Charles built the houses on the right hand side of Rock Road and Mr Thomas built those on the left.

Mr R Headington said that Charles married a Miss Jarrett. About 1890 he built at the bottom of Bath Hill West the Jarrett bakery, a commercial building, well back from the road. There the Jarrett daughters all worked. Then Charles built the large private house for Mr Jarrett, number 44. On the strength of this, Mr Jarrett gave his son-in-law the vacant site nearly next door, where Charles built number 46, Collenso House, and lived there himself, with his builder's yard behind it. A glance at the facade of both houses shows their overall similarity. It has been said that with an eye to the future, Charles so placed and designed his home that it could be extended on both sides into a terrace, but it was not to be.

Mr Headington mentioned that Charles and John, working together, built the houses in Westbourne Avenue and the two bungalows there. He described Charles as 'quite an important builder'.

Mrs Andrews recalled that he built 76, Bath Hill, which was also to have been a pair, but the top wall was too wet. At one time she lived there with her parents.

I was thrilled to find this lovely old Georgian stable, with its stone floor, within a short distance of the High Street. The wooden stairs used to be the only access to storage rooms above. Notice the roughness of the white-washed wall. From upstairs one could look out on the later cattle pound by the New Inn. The stable is to the left of the long drive at 86, Bath Hill, and in 1890 John Willcox used it as his carpenter's shop. The white object is a refrigerator. The photo was taken in 1990.

Chapter 17

The Somerset Light Infantry

'By 1689, the year of Killiekrankie, the regiment had been in existence for four years, and had already served two masters. Theophilus, 7th Earl of Huntingdon, had raised it at the request of James II . . . and its first task was to guard prisoners taken during Monmouth's defeat at Sedgemoor;' so writes Hugh Popham in his book, 'The Somerset Light Infantry', published in 1968 by Hamish Hamilton (page 14).

He continues, 'The Regiment served in Scotland, Ireland (1689), and in Holland (1701), Portugal (1704), and Spain (1705) in the Hundred Years War against France. The 3rd Earl of Peterborough 'summoned the 13th to Vinaros, where they arrived, according to Fortesque, 'with red coats ragged and rusty, yellow facings in tatters, yellow breeches faded and torn, shoes and stockings in holes and more often altogether wanting.' Peterborough inspected them, and then, after complimenting them on their gallant services, said, 'I wish that I had horses and accoutrements for you to try if you could keep up your good reputation as Dragoons.' Whereupon, from behind a handy hill, were produced 800 horses, ready accoutred, and Barrymore's Foot, the 13th, were transformed into Pearce's Dragoons.' History does not relate how 27 Officers and 660 weary and tatterdemalion infantrymen took to horseback riding . . .'

Although in its early years the Regiment occasionally had its name changed, as when an officer bought the colonelcy of the Regiment, it still retained its designation as 'the 13th'.

In 1751 'a Royal Warrant established uniformity in clothing, standards, colours and regimental numbers. Pultney's Foot [since 1743] became, officially, the 13th Regiment of Foot, and so would remain for almost a century, although, by Royal Command in 1782, they were directed to 'take the County Name of 1st Somerset Regiment, and be considered attached to that county.'

Earlier, they had fought against the Highlanders of Scotland. 'The 13th, who had withstood them at Killiekrankie in 1689, and fled before them in 1746, faced them for the last time on 'Bare Culloden's heath', with its English victory and its terrible aftermath.

'The army trailed its shadow of wives, mistresses, children, contractors and miscellaneous camp-followers round with it, and they were all legislated for. 'Disorderly women' were given up to 200 lashes and packed off, though recognised wives were permitted and were a great solace to their menfolk.'

Later in 1746 the 13th were tramping the Kent coastline for smugglers. After a period in Gibraltar, in 1801 they overcame Bonaparte's troops in Alexandria and Egypt. 1824–26 saw the 13th in India and in the Burmese War. By 1838

A group of young Keynsham Territorials, 'at ease', in a summer training camp at Salisbury, under canvas, in 1913.

The NCOs of 'C' Company of the 4th Somerset Light Infantry, en route for India 1914. The ½d stamp is franked, 'Salisbury 11.15. 30 Oct'.

Men of the 'C' Company of the 4th Somerset Light Infantry, camped on the South coast, prior to embarking for India in 1914.

The Officers and NCO of the 4th Battalion of the Somerset Light Infantry, at Peshawar, on the North West frontier, India, c. 1915.

they were part of the Army of the Indus on the savage NW Frontier. In 1842 they were honoured for their bravery, for, 'Her Majesty had been graciously pleased to approve of that regiment assuming the title of the 13th or Prince Albert's Regiment of Light Infantry; and its facings being changed from yellow to royal blue'.

'The Prince Albert's' missed the Crimean War but were in India in 1857 to put down the mutiny. 1879 saw the Regiment in Natal on Kambula Hill defeat a large attacking Zulu army.

'The 13th pattern of service, which had been developing fairly consistently over a century and three-quarters, had, by 1858 when the 2nd Battalion was formed, achieved an almost formal routine. Of its first 173 years, the regiment spent no less than 111 out of England; and of the last 36, from 1822 when it first went to India, 25 were spent either in India or Africa, the majority in the former. And from 1858 to the end of the Second World War, one or other of its battalions was invariably stationed in India'. (Page 80)

'In 1782, . . . the 13th became the 1st Somerset Regiment; in 1822 it became a 'Corps of Light Infantry'; and in 1842 the 13th or Prince Albert's Regiment of Light Infantry. In 1881, the '13th' was finally dropped – to the regiment's chagrin – and they became Prince Albert's (Somerset Light Infantry). In the following year, the two militia battalions became the 3rd and 4th of the Regiment.

'For their part in the involved and unhappy war (against the Boers), the Somersets were awarded two new Battle Honours; the 2nd Battalion, 'The Relief of Ladysmith' and 'South Africa 1899–1902', the 4th 'South Africa 1900–1902'. (Page 97)

Of the tragic loss of life in World War One, 'The Golden Book of Remembrance, which was placed in Wells Cathedral in 1922 contains the names of 4,756 officers and men of the Somersets who were killed in the war'.

'Already by then the Regiment was down to a mere five battalions; the 1st and 2nd (Regular), the 3rd (Reserve) and the 4th and 5th (TF) The rest had already become a memory, revived for a few years by annual reunions, and by reminiscences that gradually lost their edge, and finally, their meaning. It is, perhaps, the saving grace – as it is one of the desperate ironies – of war that the sense of comradeship is more enduring that the sense of futility which is its concomitant.' (Page 116)

There are a number of photos of Sergeant Williams of Keynsham and his fellow NCOs at camp in England prior to the 1914–18 war, and their departure for India. In 1915 he saw service in India on the North West Frontier. There his company for a while apparently augmented the 2nd Battalion of the SLI, who, much to their bitter disappointment, were to remain in India throughout the war and were unable to join the other Battalions of the Regiment fighting in Europe. Later, from February to April 1916, with the 1st and 4th Battalions of the SLI, he was in the battle for the relief of the besieged city of Kut-el-Amara in Mesopotamia, the scene of a great battle fought between the British and the Turks in 1915/16, when the Allied forces in Kut were forced to surrender. The last entry in the Battalion Diary for April is as follows, 'April 29. General Townsend, owing to total exhaustion of food supplies, compelled to surrender Kut-el-Amarah'. Here the Diary ends. [History of the SLI, 1914–19. Wyrall,

Presumably the 2nd Bat. of the SLI on parade at Peshawar, NW Frontier, India c. 1915. Its strength in 1917 was 23 Officers and 884 other ranks.

p 103.] 'The strength of the 1/4 Battalion on leaving Sheikh Sa'ad was down to 14 Officers and 590 NCOs and men.' [p 104].

A handsome man, Sergeant Williams, complete with his baton, wore a thick moustache which he waxed at the pointed ends. Not long after the war, he was invalided out of the regular army suffering from malaria, and returned to his Rock Road home and family.

There he supplemented his military pension with work as the caretaker of the army's Drill Hall in Bath Hill, which in addition to its military usages, was in demand for concerts and Gilbert and Sullivan light operas. Naturally Harry

The photo above is from the front of a postcard addressed to 'TL Bowden, The Pharmacy, High Street, Keynsham'. The pharmacist's son William was a Territorial in the First World War, and the caption at the bottom of the card states, 'NCO's, C Coy, 4th Som LI'. Franked over the 'Half Penny' green stamp on the back, is, 'West Down Soldier's Camp. BO, Devizes, Aug 4 [1914?], 10 [am?].'

The NCO wrote, 'West Down, South, Wednesday. Tonight at 10.15 pm we leave camp, march to Amesbury and entrain there for Dorchester. In that neighbourhood we shall bivouac till Saturday, fighting the regulars. Our kit bags, packed, will remain here and some men will remain to take charge of them and strike camp. We shall bring them home on Saturday, but I don't know at what time. From WB.'

These Territorials comprised four sergeants, three corporals and four lance corporals. Of the eleven men, six wore moustaches, which included all the sergeants. You can see that the five on their knees were all wearing putties. Behind the group, parts of several tents are just visible.

Now 76 years later, Mrs Jean Williams, with her own connections with the Som LI, believed that happily William survived the war. He had two maiden sisters, the Miss Bowdens, who 'were very much to the fore at St Johns Church, and lived together in a house below St Dunstan's Church,' she said.

Recruiting Colour Sergeant Henry (Harry) Williams, 1883-1926

Harry was born in Bow, London, and lived at Pimlico where his father, who married twice, was a carpenter. In the army, Harry's attitude to discipline, his good conduct and sense of responsibility, resulted in promotion to Recruiting Colour Sergeant in the 4th Battalion of the Somerset Light Infantry.

He married Miss Edith Newman at St John's Parish Church, Keynsham, and bought a house at No 1, Rock Road, which has been in the family ever since. Their marriage was blessed with four children. Dorothy was the eldest. Her husband was a radio engineer, and drowned at his post when his ship went down off Cardiff. Dorothy then trained locally as a nurse and worked in Oxford, where she remarried.

John was the eldest son and married Florie, while the next son, Percival, married Phyllis, and the third son William, born in 1915, married Jean, and in the course of time all three boys became grandfathers.

recruited his sons to help with his duties at the hall, and the story is told of how one day when the boys were handling the rifles stored there, young Percival pointed a rifle at a lamp shade, pulled the trigger, and the gun went off, with a scar the building bears to this day. As William's grand-daughter Vera said, 'Percy got much more than a telling off'.

Though she added 'He was a Tartar with the boys', an aunt said, 'He had a heart of gold, but a brusque manner.' As a senior NCO, he had been used to giving orders for many years and expected to be obeyed and to have life properly organised. Shoes should be kept clean. Appearance mattered. Though his word was law in the family, it was a case of kind but firm.

Sadly, he died of a heart attack in 1926 at the young age of 43. A popular man, there was a great turn-out for his funeral. He was buried with full military honours and Mrs Winnie Allen, just a girl then, declared 'It was one of the biggest military funerals I could ever remember seeing in Keynsham'. Today he lies in peace in Durley Cemetery.

The Drill Hall in earlier times

Kelly's Directory of Somerset, 1875, under Keynsham, just mentions it,
'Volunteer Rifle Corps (7th Somerset), Headquarters, Keynsham, Thomas Murdock, Sergeant-Major.'
Kelly's 1906 Directory equally succinctly records,
'1st Volunteer Battalion Prince Albert's (Somerset Light Infantry), Bath Hill. ('C' Coy Captain J H Evans, Sergeant William Codrington, drill instructor.)

Chapter 18

The Chairman of the Keynsham UD Council, Leonard Ellis, 1908–1990.

At my request, Mr L Ellis, when he was nearly an octogenarian, kindly wrote out some of his pedagogic memories. Upright in character and stature, with a dry wit and a sharp mind, he permitted me to record some of his other recollections of the town he so much loved and for which he worked so faithfully to the end of his days.

The chapter is divided into two sections; his earliest memories of school; and then, life as he saw it in Keynsham in his later years.

A Keynsham Dame School in 1911

I think I must have been about 3½ years old, when with my two sisters, I went to my first school, a 'Dame School'. It was in a three storied house over a baker's shop on Bath Hill, somewhere near where the Handyman's shop now stands. I think the shop was run by a Mr Parsons, who lived over the shop. The lady who had the school had the next floor. I think that she may have been a lady in what they called in those days, 'reduced circumstances'.

She was a gentle old lady (or she seemed old to me) but was very firm and strict. We had to go up a rickety flight of stairs to reach her room, and I remember I had to be lifted over a missing tread in the stairs. I seem to remember that there were about eight pupils. There was Mervyn Jarrett, a baker's son, and Jack Taylor and his sister, whose father kept a public house in Station Road called the Pioneer Inn. I also think that a girl called Bees attended.

The fee was sixpence a week. We all had slates with slate pencils. We were taught our letters and numbers; we drew 'pot hooks' but above all, we were taught good manners which I for one have never forgotten. Mrs Boston disappeared about ten to twelve every day, with her little wicker basket, returning later with a chink of bottles.

How long I stayed there I am not certain, but I later went to the infants school in Temple Street. This was a big shock to me, coming from a comfortable Victorian room to a huge class room with tall windows too high to see out of. There was gas lighting and the room was heated by a large coke-burning stove, surrounded by a large fireguard.

Mrs Harvey was the head teacher, whose husband sang in the parish church choir. He had lovely 'mutton chops' whiskers, and as a young member of the choir, I was fascinated to hear a high tenor voice coming from the whiskers. One thing that stays with me still from those school days, is the awful smell

'Temple Street at the top of Bath Hill, where Kwik Save now is', pencilled in Len Ellis. 'Daniel Gilbert had an industrial archaeologist to look at his premises, who described the beams of the shoe shop as 16th century, and those of the tall shops beside it as 15th century,' recalled Miss Fairclough.

'Temple Street opposite Bethesda Chapel, now Cashmans ['Carpets']' wrote Mr Ellis. The height of the lorry reveals just how low some of the cottages were, due to raising the road level. A solitary anti-cart-wheel stone bollard is on the pavement. There are more on Dapps Hill outside the former 'Pines'.

of the toilets. There were no flushes, and they were only swilled once a day by the cleaners.

I well remember one teacher, a Miss Fussell, a rather large lady who had a rather nasty habit of pinching your chin between her finger and thumb, which was not very pleasant for a five year old child. As far as I remember, she rode her bicycle from Warmley, where her parents kept a coal business.

We were taught the three Rs and on Friday afternoons in the summer, we went to 'the Rec', for games. In the winter, those who sat by the large coke stove were roasted, while those at the back of the class shivered.

The large iron fire guard around the stove was handy for drying clothes in the winter.

Then came the great day when we were to go up to the 'big school'. We had been told the previous term that we should be leaving for the new school. We would have been about 7 years old. This proved to be a very strange experience, being with boys and girls up to 14 and 15 years of age. The girls had their own play ground, separated by a high stone wall. We learned up to the 12 times table, parrot fashion. We started to do long division, fractions and other branches of arithmetic.

It was called a Parochial School, and it seemed dominated by the Parish Church. The Governors, Miss Gwen Wills, Mr Sam Knight, Mr Joe Gerrish and Mr Edward Wiggins, would call in about once a week to check the register, have a look at our books, and ask questions. At the end of the month they would call and pay the teachers their salaries.

The head was called Gaffer Wheeler, and his wife Janice took the girls for needlework. Every dinner time Frank Hoddinot, whose people kept the Ship Inn in Temple Street, was sent home and returned with a clinking of bottles, and Gaffer was rarely to be seen during the afternoon.

Other teachers I remember were Mr Griffiths, Miss Davis, Miss Gunstone, Miss Garrad, Mrs Frank Reed and the sadistic Mrs Jones. Gaffer was followed by Mr A M Mansey.

Keynsham through the eyes of Councillor Leonard F Ellis

Leonard Finlay Ellis was born in Fishponds, Bristol, the third of a family of five and moved to Keynsham at the age of two. 'My father was a gentleman and came to Bristol from Scotland to open up the West to Johnny Walker whisky. We lived at 31 Bath Hill, the large middle house. My mother's parents lived in the cottage next to us at 29. Grandfather had a huge garden there and was a keen gardener and kept all that area beautifully', Leonard told me four years ago in a taped conversation.

'Just across the road from the bottom of the garden was the Fox and Hounds Inn. When I was very young before the First World War, a German Band would come and play on the forecourt there.' Then Leonard recalled something else that had made an impression on him years ago.

'From the corner of our garden I saw a man with a bear on a chain dancing there. It was a big black bear and the man had a sort of whistle. The bear had on, not a muzzle, but a leather strap round its mouth. When he played the whistle, the bear shifted from one leg to another, then the man would

A Godfrey team of three horses passing the Old Vicarage in Station Road, early this century, pulling, according to Miss M Fairclough, 'an old local type of Somerset waggon.'

Mr L Ellis wrote on the rear of this photo, 'Godfrey haymaking in Manor Road, Keynsham. Elsie Orchard, Elsie Godfrey, Grannie Godfrey, Mary Godfrey and Jim Godfrey', circa 1910. A jolly good hay harvest, all the work being done by horse or hand.

Note the two flagons of cider, of which Miss Fairclough said they were the recognised 'arvest 'llowance jugs,' used locally, while 'the long stacks were a common sight in sheltered positions, as opposed to the circular ones on the exposed land at the top of Wellsway and at the end of Park Road. The Westons of 'donkey farm' at the top of Charlton Road, were the only farmers still using hay rakes in 1920. Those whose families emigrated to Canada before World War One, like the Stokes, returned with ideas of mechanisation, but it was not until World War Two that mechanisation on the farm really got going,' she concluded.

go round with the hat. It was pitiful really. We children had a grandstand view. There were only a few passers-by watching; it was hardly worth his while. Then he would go up to the Lamb and Lark car park, for another 10–15 minutes' performance. The bear didn't really dance, he just lifted his feet as quickly as he could. There was no whip or cruelty that we could see. He came every year.'

Local Elections

'The election times were very exciting. My father was a Tory and many times we had our windows broken, as 'Bricktown' or 'Piddletown' was just behind the New Inn. That was the roughest part of Keynsham and we weren't allowed to go down there. The results of the elections were given out from the balcony of the old Liberal Club. I was a Liberal all my life and I used to go canvassing with George E Chappell and Mr Hopkins. We were part of the Frome division.

'I remember a gentleman from Durley Park who changed from Liberal to Conservative. To let it be known, he led a cow, painted blue with a dead rat tied to its tail, through the High Street, with his coat turned inside out. Politics were very important then.'

Changing the subject, Len said, 'I remember the cattle pound behind the New Inn. I saw many horses and donkeys there. It had an ordinary five bar gate, and the entrance was from the lane side. The wall was about 4–5 feet high.'

He recalled that, 'Barney May was a local milkman who carried his milk in two pails suspended from an old-fashioned yoke around his shoulders. He would knock at customer's doors and give them milk from a pint, half pint or a gill measure. One day he was walking down the High Street when he saw in the distance Mr George Watts, the sanitary and weight and measures inspector, coming towards him. Knowing that he had just 'watered' his milk from Pump Court, Barney conveniently fell down and split all his milk. . . He didn't have a shop, just a shed on Dapps Hill and kept a couple of cows.'

Poverty and the Poor House

'There was much poverty caused by drink, particularly in Brick Town. On a Saturday night there would be a fair bit of drunkenness. . . .The Workhouse was a very strict place. It was a great fear of the elderly people that they would die there, for they still regarded it as the Workhouse, although the 7ft 6in walls had been lowered when it was made into a hospital. . . .The fear was in the minds of the older people. Though the inmates had sufficient starchy food such as potatoes and swedes, the regime was just repressive. You were a pauper. You had no rights at all. There were two large gates there that locked at night. My late father-in-law's father, Jonas Godfrey, was one of the Guardians of the Workhouse.

'I first went there when I was three or four. When we lived in Avon Road we had a servant, a Miss Harriet Britain. Later when she was there, mother used to take us over on a Sunday afternoon to see her. It was a terrible place,' Len said.

'Women with small children would not go into the Workhouse if they could help it. If they did, the women would then have to scrub the stone flagged corridors. The inmates were mainly young or old, but mainly the elderly. When the children reached fourteen the girls would be sent into service and the boys went farming.

'The tea tokens that the tramps received were given by the Union for extra chopping done...[not from the police]. There were only two policemen in the town and they, the sergeant and his constable, both lived at the station on Bath Hill. Later the force swelled to three, the third man living in Albert Road.'

The Doctor Harrisons

'I remember Percy from the Union, who used to take a large wicker basket to the surgery at night to collect the inmates' medicines from the Doctor's. When you went into the waiting room from the High Street, there was a long wooden partition on the left, with a hole in it part way along. There were seats on the other side, and Dr Charles would shout through the hole, 'What's the matter with you?' or, 'What do you want?'

'One night Percy had a bad finger and was told to poke it through the hole, which of course he did. The Doctor looked at it, then after a moment without a word, he just got out a scalpel and lanced it. My, Percy did let out a shout . . . He was a bit simple but was not the worst.

'There was no privacy at the Doctor's until his son Dr Claude Harrison took over. He would come out from his surgery and send his patients into one of three rooms to wait for him to see them individually. On one occasion I had back trouble, and I had to strip while he fixed me up with some heat treatment and went out. I waited and waited but he did not return. Then in came Miss Bowden, who lived opposite at the lovely old fashioned chemist's, (now Menzies) who exclaimed agitatedly, 'Oh, oh. Does the doctor know you are here?' 'I hope so.' 'Well he's on his way to Compton Dando now,' she said, so I dressed myself and left.

'I remember even now 5 or 6 children from the Workhouse arriving in a crocodile formation at Bath Hill School, with their heavy boots and shabby-looking clothes . . . I remember the first Roman Catholic girl to attend Bath Hill. Everyone shunned her. No one spoke to her. I believe she went to Victoria Chapel. It was her parents who were Catholics. Her name was Ivy Lewis. I never spoke to her. It was not done in those days. The Catholics were hated then. There was a great local outcry when it was suggested that a Catholic church should be built here; there wasn't half! It's amazing how we have got together in fifty years.

'I was in the same class as Miss Gertie Cox at Bath Hill School and I remember the afternoon when she was called out of the class by the headmaster, to be told that her father had been killed at the mill. Sadly he had been working on the wheel when it was still moving, which he should not have done.'

Changing the subject, Len remembered that behind the old Fox and

A delightful scene of Keynsham High Street around the turn of the century. What a lovely old pram! Is it a load of coal, wood or manure that the lad is pulling across the earthen road?

Bath Hill after the removal of Spring Cottage but before the destruction of Flanders House, seen on the left below the 'Ten Houses', around 1960.

Hounds was a stable block used by a man who made ice cream there which he sold locally from his cart. One day something went wrong with his product, and many people became unwell. 'It was terrible, that was. I was terribly ill. Two people died, one in Corston and one in Keynsham. Nearly half of Keynsham and the surrounding district were ill. He had sold ice cream for years.'

Reduced circumstances

'After father died, life was very difficult. We were given two loaves of bread a day from Jarrett's on Bath Hill which I collected, and we had one pint of milk, which wasn't much for five growing children. Mother had ten shillings [50p] a week to keep five of us. We left Avon Road and lived in Park Road . . . I remember a boy who lived near us and is still alive, whose mother made him a suit from sacking. I remember his calling out, 'Don't hit I, Mum'.'

Horse training

'My brother Charlie worked for Mr Grimes, and at night would gallop bareback on his horse up Park Road, where there would be no one about, to put the horse out to grass for the night further along the road.

'Nearly opposite the Park Cottages was a field where a man trained horses. He had a large ring of tall galvanised iron, so you couldn't see what was going on. Later he would take one along Park Road in a trap, with what we boys called a kicking strap tied to one of the horse's front legs and through the harness up to the driver. If as they went along the horse became temperamental, he'd pull the straps and lift the horse's foot off the ground. That stopped him.

'At the end of Albert Road, when you turn left, was a shed which stood back a bit. That's where I saw my first car. I was about 7 or 8.

On the subject of the thousands of mules kept by the army at the end of Park Road during the First World War, Len said, 'They came from abroad, possibly Spain, and were partly trained here. They left for the 'Front' via Avonmouth. Thousands died of foot and mouth disease, [anthrax?] and were buried in the fields in lime pits. The soldiers would not let you go along there.'

The local ramifications of Church division

Though Len was for many years a very active Anglican and was even married at St Johns, he recalled that when he first attended as a youngster, 'I was turfed out of a seat in the middle of the church by the verger by the scruff of the neck to 'How dare you sit there!' Yet in all truth, as Len himself said, 'People paid pew rents. We used to at Victoria too . . . I also remember St Johns having all gas-lit chandeliers.

'Keynsham was a divided place in those days', Len said, 'The churches had their own special shops, supported by those of their persuasion. In my younger days Chappell Brothers were the main Church of England grocers and Stokes was the coal merchants. Chappell Brothers had a wine and spirits licence which was handy for Anglicans who drank while Methodists did not.

The Church of England undertaker was Charles Carter in the High Street, and their chimney sweep was 'Pranny' Hine.

'The main Non-Conformist grocer was George E Chappell: Herbert Belsten in Charlton Road, now Guyans, was their undertaker. Also theirs was 'Bert Sweet, Chimney Sweep, 69 Temple Street.' Ernest White and Jim Godfrey supplied most of the Non-Conformist coal (there were no vacuum cleaners in those days).

'Gordon Reed was the Baptist grocer, with Horace Veale where Dr Barnardo's shop is. Sidney Grimes was their chimney sweep.'

The Red Mill in the Memorial Park

Len recalled that there was a row of cottages by the river, in addition to the three or four buildings that comprised the Red Mill. It ground the red ochre that came by train, and the pigment was then sent away in sacks to be used in paint making. 'Quite a few people worked there, possibly fourteen or fifteen. The owner, a chemist, was a health fanatic, and so he cycled in from Bristol every day.

'His manager was Mr Hickling (brother of the shop owner) who lived across the road from the ironmonger's shop, in what is now the sports shop. Jack Exon, who lives down Rock Road, was the wheelwright and in charge of the machinery. As with other things today, they make paint with other ingredients, so the business closed down. When the Council bought the park, the buildings were in a poor state, so we pulled them down, but preserved one of the wheels.'

Going on to other matters, Len wrote,' I remember the water cart spraying the roads to keep the dust down in the summer, as the roads were not tarmacked years ago . . . The town band would play outside the old weighbridge near the Lamb and Lark, usually followed by the Salvation Army band. The town band also played at the football matches and toured the roads at Christmas week. On Boxing Day all the tradesmen including the postmen, the dustmen and the bell ringers, called on householders to collect Christmas boxes.

'Washing days were an all-day job and the coal-fired boiler had to be lit and filled with water', he wrote in his notes on old Keynsham.

The Keynsham Chronicle in its obituary on him on May 5 1990, recorded that 'He was apprenticed to the electricity supply industry with whom he spent 44 years. He married in 1937 and had three daughters. . . . During the war he became responsible for the supply of electricity to RAF Fairford.' When I asked him what he did in the war, he did not wish to discuss the subject at all. It seemed to be of no importance to him.

The Chronicle continued, 'Len's wife was a Methodist and the family became very committed members . . . He was interested in every aspect of Keynsham. He was a founder member of the League of Friends of Keynsham Hospital, a Governor of Broadlands School and a member of the Library Committee. Until quite recently he was an usher at Keynsham's Magistrates' Court.'

[Actually he said to me that, 'I was an usher for sixteen years and worked in

Councillor Leonard Ellis receives a helping hand from his wife Mary as he inspects his chain of office as the new Chairman of the Keynsham Urban District Council, circa 1963.

'Charlton Road corner opposite the Victoria Methodist Church, now the Midland Bank,' wrote Len Ellis. The top of the Fear Institute just peeps out at the right hand corner, and Fred Dorey's Labour Exchange.

three courts after I left the Electricity Board. This was at Keynsham, Temple Cloud and Radstock.']

'Leonard Ellis, known to everyone as 'Len', had been Chairman of the former Keynsham Urban District Council in 1961/64. At this time he had been a councillor for 14 years, having successfully fought five elections. At his appointment it was said he was a man 'who was not afraid to say no when he meant no'. He had served on every committee in the council during his term of office.

'Len's wife died 11 years ago. He is survived by his three daughters, six grandchildren and one great-grandson, and his sister Violet, the eldest and last survivor of her generation', concludes the Chronicle.

Having had the pleasure of knowing Len, and having received so much help from him in researching old Keynsham, I have no difficulty at all in fully believing him when he said, 'My father was a wonderful Scottish gentleman . . .' Like father, like son.

Chapter 19

'My school days in Keynsham'
by Miss J Cannam

I was born in 1912. I started kindergarten school rather older than I should have been, because my mother waited until my younger sister was old enough to go, at the age of 5. Therefore I was about just under 8 years old.

I had been formerly to another school nearby where I was extremely unhappy because the school was run on very strict, harsh lines. I was a nervy, sensitive child, never having mixed with other children. It was a living nightmare to me. So my mother let me leave.

Then later I went, with my sister, to Mrs Jollyman's school, at 37 Charlton Road, which was a private school. I could read at a very early age. The teachers at the school were Mrs Jollyman herself, who taught French, being, I think, of French extraction, Miss Taylor, who was the chief teacher, and Miss Newell, who taught needlework and hand work, chiefly cross-stitch.

The schoolroom was in the front room of the house, and a smaller room at the side was also used. We learnt a small amount of French, arithmetic, adding, subtraction, short and long division, and the adding of a double column of money figures. We learnt reading and spelling phonetically by the use of the Red Reader, Blue Reader and the Yellow Reader books. Miss Taylor taught us composition. I remember that once she stopped me in the High Street, by Mrs Gibbs' stationers shop, to tell me how well I had written an essay on Autumn. I was about 8–9 years old then.

Miss Margery, 'Newell' as we called her, taught us sewing – the various stitches. I well remember having a dreadful struggle with threading needles, my sight was so poor.

On Friday afternoons we attended dancing classes, held in the front room. Miss Helen Jollyman, called 'Pug,' was an accomplished pianist and played the piano for us. Chiefly, we were given squares of coloured chiffon, which we had to wave around with our arms and hands. We also danced Scotch Reels, which I loved, and an Irish Jig.

By this time a neighbour's two children went to the school. In winter time after dark (no fear in those days before motor traffic and child molesters), we used to run home, we four girls, with dresses tucked in knickers, which children used to do. As we passed over the Old County Bridge with the stone niche in the centre, we could see the funnel-shaped chimney of the Brass Mills. The chimney belched flames in the air. We imagined these were connected with witches.

We had a play-time in the middle of the morning. In the summer we went in the back garden. My sister and I had a 1d (penny) bar of chocolate each.

Mrs Jollyman provided dinners, but the four of us always used to run home and back, dresses tucked in knickers.

I remember quite well various young members of the school, some who are well-known names in Keynsham. These included John Reynolds who came from the States, Jackie Strudwick, the Higgs boys and one daughter, Phylis Neate and Ruth Pole. There was Alison and Ian McPherson, and from Rookhill House Cicely and Gordon Camm. Sadly Gordon was killed in World War Two. The Hamblin family, of whom Emily became a doctor, lived with her brothers Bert and Edward, in the large stone house next to Cannock's garage. There was Margery Shepperd, Jackie Webb of the Avenue, Mary Hawker of Hawkswell House, and Nadine Guest, whose father was a cattle dealer. From Park Road came my friends Joyce Kemp and Kathleen Rich. Jeffrey Whittington lived in the very old stone house in Charlton Road. Other pupils were John Hughes of Priory Road, and Boysey Southall, whose father was the Chapel minister and lived in Charlton Road. There was also Evelyn Ansell of the Homestead, Wellsway, and Nancy Ashton from Saltford.

One of my favourite games was playing horses. A length of rope was tied round the upper arm of the participant, the other took the rope to guide the 'horse'. We skipped also, had hoops and tops. The indoor game was draughts.

Miss Pug kept a pony in her stables, which she used to drive round in a trap, to deliver bread for Pearce the baker. The chief pastime of us young people, boys and girls, was to go into Charlton Park, after school.

Charlton Park was then, on each side, green fields. A few hundred yards away from Mrs Jom's as we called it, was a pond overhung by a willow tree. It was only a small drinking-pond with stone walls, in the field from which a footpath led down to Park Road. It was on the left hand side, at the very beginning of Charlton Park Road, which ended, in those days, in fields and bramble thickets. We used to climb this tree and fish in the pond with nets. The pond was full of newts and tadpoles. At most times, a few newts were taken home in a 2 lb jam jar, and placed with weed in a large zinc wash tub at home. They were continually fished out and the water changed.

Much more of my early schooldays I cannot remember.

At the age of 14, far too old, I left Mrs Jom's and was sent to Redland Collegiate School, to which we travelled every day by train, via Temple Meads.

* * *

Miss Mary Fairclough, who lived just up the road at number 43, also went to the same school. She recalled that, 'I was there in 1920 and 1921, but due to constant asthma and bronchitis, I never managed to attend more than three weeks in any one term, but at least I learnt to read there.'

'Mrs Jollyman started the school before the 1914–18 war, and continued probably up to about 1940. It was a Montessori school for children who needed extra care.

'It was for their daughter Pug, who was not very strong, that Mr Jollyman built a stable at the end of the garden. The pony, named Dolly, only arrived after I left, though I can remember her frequently riding it. There were no stables in the other Charlton Road gardens.'

The old-fashioned shops in Keynsham

The author of the following fascinating description of the local shops concludes her article by revealing herself to be, 'Miss Joy Cannam, born 1912 at Crane Lodge, Bitton Road, Keynsham. These memories date mainly to the pre-1926 years.'

I was born in the early 1900's so I remember a world quite different from how it is today – how different Keynsham High Street was in comparison with the street today.

Old-fashioned shopkeeping makes me think of early memories of the shops, 50 years ago. There was a very different atmosphere in Keynsham. From my childhood memories, it must be said, it was a snobbish place. There was a sharp division in the population. On the one hand, the genuine villagers (and there was a lot of poverty amongst them in those days) and on the other hand the polite, middle-class society of people who had settled in Keynsham.

As a child one was looked down upon if your parents were seen shopping in certain shops. To belong to the best people, one had to buy one's groceries at Chappell Bros., not George E Chappell's (which later became the International Stores). There was a bakers and a drapers which were also in the same class. One had to be a customer of William Pearce for bread and cakes and buy from Loxton's the drapers.

There was no such thing as pre-packed goods. Everything was weighed in lbs. and ozs. and wrapped by the shopkeeper in paper bags or for larger parcels in brown paper and string. Farthings were in circulation. Nearly everything bought at the drapers cost an odd $\frac{3}{4}$d (3 farthings) such as 3/11$\frac{3}{4}$ or 2/11$\frac{3}{4}$. It sounded so much cheaper than 4/- (four shillings) or 3/- (three shillings). For the farthing change from even money a packet of pins or hair pins was given. What a strange old custom!

Station Road

One of my first memories is of Harvey's paper shop (newsagents) in Station Road, housed in the original low windowed, low doored Tudor stone cottage, Mrs Harvey, the mother of a long family of boys, very often stood at the door (there was a step down from this onto a stone-tiled passage way). She was a plump woman who wore a large white apron and a man's cap on her head, turned back to front. Stickler's cobblers shop was also in Station Road opposite the church. George Stickler was a north country man, as was his pretty little wife, with her lovely freckled skin and red-gold hair.

The High Street

Going down the High Street on the left-hand side from the church was the first shop I remember. It was a toy shop. As a very young child, many a time I pressed my nose against the window with a farthing clutched firmly in my hand, gazing at the Japanese dolls (then common) and the wooden jointed Dutch dolls as we used to call them – really Deutsche – German.

After that, I recall Milton's sweet shop. It was the rendezvous of all the children who used to go to Mrs Jollyman's school at 37 Charlton Road. The most popular sweets were 1d and 2d bars of chocolate (one was rich indeed if one could afford a 2d bar). There were dolly mixtures, dew-drops (tiny boiled sweets), acid drops, rose buds, raspberry drops, pineapple rock, satin cushions, sherbet bon-bons, toasted teacakes (dipped in icing-sugar or coconut) and flat sweets, covered on top with white hundreds and thousands. All these sweets were weighed by the 1/2oz. or oz. on the swinging brass scales and put into small pointed bags. Nearby was Chappel Bros. shop. It was stocked high with all the best groceries, wines, and cheeses, which were cut at the customer's request.

After the old Royal Oak public house came Köhler's the barbers and umbrella shop. I remember Mrs Köhler, a fair haired lady. She used to gaze over the top of the window fixture at the goings-on in the High Street and the horses and carts that passed up and down.

Quite a few of the trades people were owners of horses and small carts, used for delivery. Then came the Co-op grocery shop. It was a low ceilinged shop, packed with goods. Overhead wires and cups were used for carrying the money, which was the usual practice in those days. However, it was not the thing to be seen shopping there as this might be connected with voting Labour, which was a terrible stigma. My parents shopped there, because they were devout believers in Socialism and profit sharing.

Next to the Co-op shop was a photographers's place kept by a Mr Orchard, who had a large family. I remember him as being Edwardian in appearance, with full mutton-chop whiskers.

After this was Longton House, at one time, but not in my memory, a private school.

Top of High Street

The Post Office

Next was the Post Office, privately owned by Mrs Gray. I remember buying here those glass pen holders with a moving bubble with coloured liquid inside and with a nib, of course. Bottles of ink and stationery and all these kinds of things were sold. There was usually a telegram messenger boy standing outside. He was dressed in navy blue uniform with a wide leather belt containing pouches for the telegram. By the side was a heavy, high bicycle, so that he would be all ready to go.

Further down, I can remember the cinema, where Charlie Chaplin films were shown. I think a fire station was here too, and later, the St Keyna garage.

Then came Mr Downs' old-fashioned newsagents, toy and 'all sorts' shop, as we used to call it. I think a cobbler's shop was further down, kept by a Mr Jarrett.

Miss Withers kept a drapers shop on the brow of Bath Hill. Then came one of the most well-known shops, a newsagents shop kept by the Miss Gibbs, Kittie and sister – ladies of great character. Edwardian in appearance, they wore black velvet bands around their necks and had 'Chinon' hairstyles. They had very forbidding manners, assumed for young people.

The Slaughter House

Mr Brownsey's high class butchers came about here. There was a slaughter house attached to this, and the poor creatures who entered under the archway on the path to their doom are best not recalled.

In my young days, the round weighbridge building stood opposite, in the middle of the road. On the other side, at the top of Bath Hill was Parson's the Bakers, which after became Beales'. On the corner was a depressingly big slaughter house, which served Keynsham and district.

The Cycle shop

Crossing over the road to the top of Temple Street was Rawlings' cycle shop, which has been run by three generations. Grandfather Rawlings sold new and second-hand bicycles, mended punctures, did repairs. He sold all the equipment needed, including the old oil burning head-lamps, which were so dirty and fitful in burning.

Just about where Jane's flower shop stands was a rather poor greengrocer's shop. ['I think Miss Cannam must be astray. The greengrocery shop was a very good one run by Mrs Rawlings who moved there from the shop later occupied by baker Ollis now as a café. Miss Garradd, the Bath Hill school teacher lodged with Mrs Rawlings for many years. Mrs Rawlings also operated the public weighbridge standing where the mini-roundabout at the top of Bath Hill now operates,' wrote Mr B Robe.]

Then came Ollis the bakers. The famous Ollis family of twenty children ran this and a carrying business. How well I remember the batch loaves and the miniature cottage loaves Mr Ollis baked. My mother used to buy me these little loaves, to cut up and butter myself. Mr Ollis had a small pony cart for his bread delivery, which later on, his younger daughters drove. Then came Freeth's a well-stocked, well-patronised grocer's shop.

Where Mr Church's shop stands was Stroud's sweet and fruit shop. I remember muddled, neglected windows here. Then came Miss Roger's wool shop and Mr Roger's watch and clock makers shop. He was a clever old man at his trade. I remember him as a dark-eyed, heavily-bearded man. Then came Anstey's low fronted saddler's shop. It was hung close with harness and all equipment. He must have done a good trade in those days.

'The only means of light'

Further along was Carter's oil and hardware shop. There were two paraffin oil businesses in Keynsham, the other one belonging to a Mr Skuse of Rock Road. They supplied the country places outside with oil for their lamps, burnt during the long winter evenings. The lamps were the only means of light. Mr Skuse sold paraffin and assorted chandler's goods, which he carried by horse and cart.

Further along was a fish and sweet shop kept by the Fry family. The owner was called 'Fishy' Fry. It was a very old-fashioned, low windowed little shop. Mrs Fishy Fry sold the sweets. They were the common variety – Gob Stoppers, Fairy Whispers, Liquorice Bootlaces, etc. She wore dark clothes and a knitted wool cap on her head and a blue and white striped linsey apron. Linsey was a wool material – dark blue and white striped used for butchers' and fishmongers' aprons.

The shop floors were nearly all flagstoned in those days. The counters were massive heavy wooden ones, over which one leant for a bit of very confidential local tittle-tattle. [Mr B Robe wrote, 'I think Miss Cannam's memory is astray in assuming that the lady in the fish and sweet shop (a strange combination) was Mrs 'Fishy' Fry. She was Miss Woods, probably a relative of 'Fishy' Fry, who later acquired two 'girl' friends with whom he used to walk around Keynsham with one on each arm. Some time later he married one of them.']

Retracing steps back a little way was Loxton's drapers shop. If one was of the superior society, one had to buy one's combinations from Loxton's not Shellabear's. Loxton's shop was a big one with big double windows, approached by a flight of steep steps. I was told by an old Keynsham lady – Mrs Atkins – that here stood a mansion at which she worked as a servant when young. She 'lived in' and had to be indoors by 7 pm. If any of the servants were late, they were locked outside the big gates and could not get in. Somewhere near this was Dr Harrison's surgery.

The Ironmongers

Hickling's, the iron mongers, was near here. It was the most comprehensive iron mongers I have ever seen. Then came Stokes', corn chandlers. It was an old established business. I remember my mother saying that at one time, grain was ground at the back and made into bread.

Right, the first shop is Mr E Jolls. The railings front the Wesleyan Methodist church, later the Eyelet factory, then Strudwicks and now the Halifax. Left, Wiggins, Loxton's Drapery, then Dr Harrison's tall house.

On the corner of Charlton Road was the Milward Dairy. Milk was delivered to the door, put into jugs with a dipper from the milk can. Further down Mr Bass had his toy and stationery shop – a delight to children. We bought note books, pencils, chalks, marbles and wooden pen holders, which were fashioned into a nib-shaped point on which there was a dab of some purple indelible ink. One wetted this with water and proceeded to write. They made a terrible mess. Next door was Mr Boseley's shop – a man's outfitters.

Somewhere near here was Pearce's wonderful bakers shop. Grandfather William Pearce baked delicious crispy bread and mouthwatering cakes – meringues in the shape of mushrooms, iced cakes with marzipan, cream slices and cream horns and bigger cakes in the shape of tortoises.

'Administer very strong poison'

There was a chemist shop at 18 High Street (now Starzec's shoe shop). It was kept by a Mr Robertson. My chief memory I now recall of this was of my mother saying he would administer very strong poison to an animal to destroy it. There was no veterinary in those days or any other means, other than drowning in the river, of disposing of an animal. So we have progressed a little in the right direction!

Lastly came Wilkins' bakers, Shellabear's drapery, George E Chappell's (brother of Chappell Bros.) large grocery shop, a branch of Lennard's, kept by a Miss Patch, and lastly Mrs Dorey's greengrocers shop, which was the premier greengrocers in the town. [Mr Robe wrote, 'It has been mentioned several times that George E Chappell, the grocer, was related to the 'Chappell Brothers', the grocers, quite separate establishments. I have always understood that this was not the case. Certainly to my knowledge there was no facial resemblance between George and the Chappell Brothers, who were strikingly alike. The report I had was that George was of quite humble origins who 'made good' with his grocery business, was a prominent Liberal in politics and stood for Parliament in a Dorset constituency]

Wilkins' bakery was a large double-fronted shop, managed by a Miss Barnes. The windows always seemed rather bare, but it was nothing to see a large cat curled up asleep in one of them. Shellabear's Drapery Emporium, I remember so well, as if it were yesterday. The Shellabears came from Helston in Cornwall. They had a son Graham and a daughter Winnie, who was musical. She had a loud booming voice, sang in the church choir and taught music. Diminutive Mrs Shellabear, her hair in Chinon style in a hair net, stood behind the counter. When the doorbell tinkled and if she did not happen to be present, Winnie interviewed the customer and shouted to her mother 'Ribbons forward'. There was an enormous stock of old-fashioned drapery – vests, combinations, bloomers, elastic and ribbon by the yard, cottons, buttons, needles – everything you could think of. Overhead hung racks with the goods displayed. The wire and cup method was used to send the money and change flying across the shop, from one side to the other. ['Two other shops worthy of mention were grocers shops next door to each other, Cridlands, later taken over by Mr Grimes, and Willoughby Brothers, a well-respected family business, one of whose members was a county councillor,' recorded Mr Robe].

'A Toady'

Miss Patch of Lennard's shop I remember very well. She was a lady with a bad stutter, but as a child, the thing that struck me the most was the very red and blue veined appearance of her face. She was what was known as a 'toady', but all the shopkeepers were in those days. That is, she very obviously laid down the red carpet for the better-off customers.

Now Mrs Dorey at the greengrocer's was indeed a character. According to this lady, Mr Dorey would not work; she was the man of the establishment and a moaner. She sold-high class goods. In particular, I remember the great hands of pale yellow bananas. People in those days expected constant delivery of goods, even to two or three lbs. of potatoes. It was not lady-like to be seen carrying a heavy basket of shopping. Even up until the last war, milk was delivered twice a day.

One day, there arrived in Keynsham from Bristol two or three young men, by the name of Pople. They sold bananas from baskets, which they carried over their arms. Mrs Dorey's nose was put out of joint very much. She called them in a vitriolic manner 'the Po-Po Boys'.

[Mr Robe commented that 'The "Poples" referred to were a Keynsham family who lived in Steel Mills. They were poor but very respectable and well-behaved and the episode of their selling bananas (which I remember) was one of their efforts to "keep the wolf from the door". They were regular church-goers and a story is told of the eldest son putting a shilling in the collection plate and taking some change. Commendable I think. He might so easily have let the plate pass and given nothing'.]

There were probably other shops, which I do not remember, particularly the butchers. I was brought up as a vegetarian, so my mother did not patronize these.

['Understandably then, Miss Cannam has omitted the pork butcher's shop (next to Chappell Bros) run by Mr Mountie, the butcher's shop next to Carter's oil shop and run, unusually, by a lady, Mrs Connett, of small stature but highly efficient. She had two daughters and one presumes her husband died and she carried on the business. It was taken over by Dave Fray, a noted 'Miler' at local sports meetings. Another butcher's shop (with slaughterhouse) was at the bottom of Bath Hill East, next to the Fox and Hounds Inn, and run by Mr Linham,' wrote Mr B Robe.]

Times have changed. No doubt there are other people who have longer memories than I, and could tell them in much more detail. So much for the alteration of the High Street as we know it today and our way of life and all connected with it.

The Great Houses of Keynsham

Notes on where the rich people lived

The High Street

Opposite the church is a house where George E Chappell and his family lived and ran their grocer's shop.

Further down, on the same side is the house that was formerly a bank and is now an eating house.

Next to Victoria Methodist Church is the house that was Stokes' shop latterly, with grounds that ran back into Charlton Road. Recently it was Whiting's furniture shop.

Further along was Loxton's drapers shop, as mentioned previously. It was fronted by big iron gates that were locked at 7 pm. Sadly it was swept away by developers.

It may be mentioned here, that the Lamb and Lark public house, now demolished, was probably an old inn, incorporated with farm outbuildings, as the landlord was often a jack of all trades at these country inns. Before it was demolished, one could see at the back very old-looking stonework. It was a coaching inn. The Trout Tavern was a mansion house at one time.

The Dapifer's House

Going down into Temple Street at the top of Dapps Hill, on the right, there is a very old stone house, believed to be the oldest farm in Keynsham. More or less opposite it was a fine old house – 'The Pines', now demolished.

Bristol Road

On Bristol Hill is Milward House, which belonged to Dr Willett and is now the Labour Exchange. Dr Willet had his surgery here and attended the upper-class people of Keynsham.

[Mrs Susan James, née Parker, wrote that 'The family had no connection with Keynsham until about 1840, when Joseph Parker Junior came courting Miss Louisa Jane Milward, who lived at Milward House. Married in 1842, they lived at Upton House, Upton Cheyney. They had four children. Edward Milward Seede Parker, the second son, married Mary, daughter of Dr Thomas Dowling of Chew Magna.

'Edward served for some years in the Merchant Navy and on his retirement, came with his family to live in Welford House, on the Bristol Hill in Keynsham. He also acquired Milward Farm (now Milward Lodge). The farm lands extended up Stockwood Vale. That is when he assumed the soubriquet 'Squire Parker'. The family moved to Weston-Super-Mare in the early 1900s.']

Next comes the old manor house, the home of the Bush family in past generations. Today it is an hotel.

At the bottom of the hill is Milward Lodge. Dated 1600, it has been sold for development as housing units.

Lastly, beyond Durley Cemetery is Chandos Lodge. The Chandos family were aristocrats and land owners. They are connected with Sudeley Castle near Cheltenham. Happily, this building still stands.

[Chandos Lodge appears to have been built by Sir Thomas Bridges around 1663 as his hunting lodge. According to an undated newspaper cutting, 'It is recorded that he (Charles I) hid in what is popularly known as 'the stud farm' but which was originally a hunting box on the estate of the Chandos family'.

On the death of George Bridges in 1750 'without issue' and of his wife in 1758, the property, with all its land, passed to his cousin James, Duke of Chandos.

In 1854 when Richard, Marquis of Chandos was declared bankrupt, the property was sold to 'Edward Newman, yeoman, in the occupation of S Parker, yeo, tenant.' [98 acres]. Mrs S James commented, 'He was not one of us'. In 1867 Alfred Wood, yeo, stationer at Bath, purchased the whole estate for £2,300. On the death of this bachelor, his sister Eliza Wood of Keynsham, inherited the estate. On her passing, the estate was sold in 1904, by auction, for £2,485 to Mr James Millard.]

Coming back on the other side of the road, it may be noted that the beautiful old gabled house by Cannock's Garage, fast falling into disrepair, was a very old farm. Coming to the top of the hill was the 'Uplands', demolished now to make way for the Vicarage greenhouses.

Then came the Vicarage itself, also demolished.

Station Road

In Station Road was probably the most spectacular of all the great mansions. The Bridges family built it, so they say, from the stones of the dissolved Abbey. The only part that remains of it is the stone archway.

Coming back into the High Street on the church side about half way down is Lloyd's Bank. Looking at the back of it, it seems obviously to have been a very handsome house at one time.

Bath Hill

Then on the brow of Bath Hill was the Court House. At one time the grounds extended in front of it. It was here that Judge Jeffries' men tried the Keynsham men who took part in the Monmouth Rebellion. It has now, sadly, been pulled down.

At the bottom of Bath Hill, on the other side, was Flanders House, now demolished. This house was said to be haunted. Near the top of Bath Hill East is Hill House, where Mr Gibbett, a fine sculptor, lived.

At the top of the hill is the New Inn, said to be the oldest one in Keynsham.

Further along, on the way to the Wellsway, is Rock Hill House. It was the home of a Miss Bowring in my young days (before the 1920s).

[Mr Robe recalled that 'Rock Hill House was the home of the Bowrings. Miss Bowring, a pillar of local society, was the sister of Mr Bowring, who had several sons and a daughter Faith. He let a part of the land adjoining his house to the Keynsham Cricket Club at a modest rent but maintained the right to pasture his sheep on it. Eventually he sold the present ground to the Club, but with a restrictive covenant that it should not be developed with buildings. The price paid reflected this restriction. Frank Taylor, to whom the ground was dedicated as a memorial, was the captain of the club in the 1920s and died of cancer during his term of captaincy. He was a very popular Keynsham man and was with the Imperial Tobacco Company.']

Bath Road

Coming back and onto the Bath Road is firstly Keynsham House. Painted white, it is now flats. In the 1920s it was occupied by the Rogers family.

Then comes 'The Grange,' on the right hand side, which at one time must have been a noble old house. For many years it was occupied as a nursing home by Nurse Wells and her husband. Much enlarged, today it is an hotel.

['The Grange' was occupied as a dwelling the 1920s and like many 'Granges' was said to be haunted. An explanation for this was that goods trains passing through Fox's Wood tunnel caused a tremor in some rock fault which created a sympathetic tremor in the walls of a bedroom in 'The Grange', 'it being only heard in the dead quiet of the night,' recalled Mr Robe.

Mr 'Chris' Wiggins wrote, 'The House was owned by Mr Charles Shaw Stuart, a direct descendant of Charles I, and was run by two lady housekeepers, the Miss Densleys. The County Council took it over during the 1939–45 War. Later it was used to house young Saltford children, until the new school was built in Claverton Road.']

Longreach House

Coming nearly into Saltford is the big house where Miss Gwendoline Wills lived. The house is not so old, but big. After she died, it was bought by Horace Bachelor. Today it is a Retirement Home.

Early memories of rural Keynsham

Miss Joy Cannam wrote the following delightful account of her early life in Keynsham for a local paper, but it merits a more permanent place in local history:

I hardly remember the time when I did not ride a bicycle and, in my teens, I explored nearly every inch of the lanes and by-ways for miles around Keynsham.

I recall the summer evenings. The after glow of sunset seemed to last until nearly eleven o'clock. The lovely soft half-light and the balmy summer air were magical. The hedge banks were full of flowers – night scented campion in profusion, with feathery angel-white moths fluttering amongst the flowers.

One evening in the lane above Tucking Mill the bank was spangled with fairy lights – those intriguing little creatures, the glow worms. It all seemed so exciting, so wonderful, so full of an unknown something that the future might reveal. The glow worms have gone. I never see a glow worm. Petrol fumes have driven the fairies away.

When I was a child the children from Mrs Jollyman's school, which was at 37, Charlton Road, used to run down the road at full speed – home for dinner, about four miles there and back. We, the girls that is, often tucked our dresses inside our elastic waisted and legged knickers. This was most comfortable and it was with rebellion and great regret that we had to stop this custom as we grew too old.

There were no houses above the Milward alms houses in Charlton Road, just a hedge and fields that stretched down to the Bristol Road, before the estate which was at first called Pittsville was built.

I well remember clinging to the hedge in my efforts to learn to ride a bicycle. The monkey puzzle trees in the almshouse's gardens were always a source of talk. They were supposed to be unclimbable. There was nothing of Charlton Park – just scrub and fields and willow trees. Quite a deep pond on the footpath down to Park Road was a constant rendezvous for the catching of tadpoles and newts.

On occasions as we were running home, we used to catch up with a galloping horse and cart and half scramble on to it for the thrill of a forbidden ride, with the shouting driver gesticulating with his whip!

The winter evenings seemed very dark and, coming home along the Bitton Road, I remember rustling calf-deep among the dry golden leaves on the pavement.

As we passed over the old-niched county bridge (scene of many a skirmish between Somerset lads and Gloucester lads, in living memory) the black outline of the brass mill's furnace chimney could be seen standing out against the sky. It belched sheets of red flame that burst suddenly upwards and lit the old buildings, the dark and gleaming river, and the rough stonework of the bridge.

We thought that the witches were adrift on their broomsticks calling forth brimstone and casting spells on any who were in their path.

We very rarely walked on the pavement by the enormous wooden advertisement hoardings as we were coming down Station Hill. Instead, we used to enter the farm gate at the top and chase down over the grass on the Hams side of the wall. In the spring, the most beautiful violets flourished there. They were highly scented and a shade of pale pinky mauve.

There were so many lanes that must have been just as they were in medieval times. They were very narrow, they dug into the high banks and trees and bushes overhung them. Unmetalled – dusty in summer, rutted and muddy in winter, and in spring – primroses all the way.

When I grew older I felt very sad as so many of these lanes were altered, widened and surfaced to make way for increasing motor traffic.

My father acquired a motor cycle and sidecar in my teens. Many of the more important roads were still stone-surfaced instead of the tarmac of today. I remember going up Tog Hill literally in a covering cloud of dust. The 'combination', as it was called, jibbed halfway up and the pillion passenger, usually me, had to hop off quickly to stop it from running back, amidst rather panicky shouts of instruction from my father!

We used to get absolutely filthy, shabby and dishevelled on this combination, and I hated it. It was cold too riding on the back – four up, driver, pillion-rider, and mother and sister in the sidecar.

Very often the combination's engine went as dead as a doornail, but after copious flooding of the carburettor and all three pushing from behind, father at the handlebars manipulating the gears and the carburettor, it usually started up.

My father looked rather wild with a brown leather helmet fur-fringed round the face, riding to the top of his head, and the straps flying behind. This must have been a most funny sight by present-day standards, but nobody seemed to think anything of it at the time. A hoot, in other words.

I said, 'hoot'. Yes. The bike had a hooter with the usual rubber ball that one pressed. This was used profusely and always at every corner, and everyone else did the same.

I do not remember the type of lights which we had on the motor bike, but I do recall using oil lamps on my own push-bike. The oil had a smell peculiar to it and the lamps used to smoke up and get very dirty. If you were the possessor of a carbide lamp – which gave a very white light – you were a very superior person. The carbide was sold in tins. It looked like bits of whitish chalky material and reminded me of the granite chippings used for covering graves. The carbide was placed in the lower container of the lamp and, according to my memory, was dampened with water, when it gave off a gas which was ignited.

A car on the roads was a novelty when I was young. One was either a commercial traveller or a 'somebody' if one possessed such a thing. Horses were the chief means of transport.

In tears

Many a time, as a little girl nearly in tears, I shouted at a driver who was whipping an overloaded horse up Station Hill.

I recall, very clearly, the lovely carthorses which pulled great burdens – particularly in the city. I remember watching them with my heart in my mouth as they backed into a warehouse over a narrow cobbled runway. If one fell, it was a tragedy to me. They often did fall on the road and sometimes the poor creatures could not rise again. Sometimes during the dark sparkling, slippery weather, just prior to Christmas, when horses were overloaded at this very busy season of plenty, do I recall the hush and distress of my mother when it was said a horse was down.

I am so glad those bad days are over. I almost feel it is worth putting up with all the noise and ugliness of modern roads so that this can no longer happen.

* * *

It seems appropriate to follow the sensitivity of 'in tears', with one of its writer's poems. As Miss Cannam wrote, 'The poem was written to express the emotions felt, on seeing a beautiful French picture of an old peasant woman, hand in hand with a young child and followed closely by two dogs. The road they are walking is rough, steep and stony. They are receding into the distance, up the hill, towards the open skyline at the top. On one side is a low bank, on the other the edge of a precipice.'

The poem was entered in the City of Bristol Eisteddfod in 1976, and was awarded a First Class Certificate for Reading One's Own Original Poem.

The Road to Heaven

The precipice of time! Over the edge
Does silver-fringed winter turn to spring?
Do we hear the sky-lark sing?
Or do we sink upon a mossy bank
And fall asleep in deep tranquillity?
But do we wake again?

Age and youth, hand in hand,
Faith close to heel and Hope behind.
The Scythe has mown the sheaves to bind,
Green stalks with the brown.
The road's trodden once and once alone.
Maker of man calls beast, bird and child.

Not 'til we get to the top of the hill
Shall we see the view at the end of the road.
Over stumbling stones with a weary load.

At last on the edge, eyes blinded with Light,
They are taken from sight –
The old one, the dogs and the child.

* * *

From Miss Cannam's many other poems, I have chosen her 'On finding a dead hedgehog in the old ruins of Keynsham Abbey.' In deference to the artistic form in which it was written, I have reproduced it in its original form, rather than just typing it out mechanically.

On finding a young dead hedgehog in the old ruins of Keynsham Abbey.

Look on the sleep of the great.
  Laced stonework, stain-drenched glass,
Wide green cloisters,
High vaulted roofs;
Ambitions for a mighty House.
Where are these things?
The rich tombs of Abbots
And greater men
Are hewn to dust.
The ornaments and gold
Pillaged out of lust.
Only a grassy hillock
Marks the place
Wherein lay the breath
Of Prelates and black robéd lesser men.
The silver plate
And jewelled goblets gone,
The noble fabric to create
A house for those
Who have faded too.

Look for these things
In dew and mud.
Conjure before the eye
A picture of deep sleeping vaults
Men lying richly robed,
Their golden baubles by their sides.
Find not these things
Amongst the weeds ~
Only fragments of tiles,
A bone, a clasp.

But what lies here?
None the less in God's sanctity,
Amongst the broken shells
Of snails.
Little creature
How did you die?
So much the less
And yet in beauty
Just as great.
Your tender spines do not curl,
Your helpless body
Into defence.
Your soft pink hands
Lie out-stretched.
Your little eyes are closed,
They no longer speak
Of pain or fear.
There you lie,
A baby thing.
How did you die
Amongst your snails?

                        Joy Garnam.

Chapter 20

Keynsham Town Silver Band

Mrs Lily Harrison recorded that, 'Keynsham Band was originally a Brass Band, and its history goes back many years. From playing at Keynsham Flower Show, they would attend other shows and fetes in the district. On Armistice Sunday the band would head the procession to the Parish Church for the Remembrance Service.

'Prior to Christmas the band could be heard playing carols around the various streets. Then on Boxing Day morning they would move through the main street playing carols, and there would be an exchange of seasonal greetings with householders.

'Success was gained through entering Band Contests. In about the year 1921 they visited Laycock with eighteen bandsmen on that occasion. Often more than one member of a family played in the band.'

'Invitations were sometimes extended for them to visit some of the large private houses in the area, and one of these was the home of Captain Wills at Corston. He took a tremendous interest in their activities, so much so, that he provided silver instruments for the band. Afterwards they became known as the Keynsham Town Silver Prize Band.

'It was disbanded prior to the Second World War. When hostilities ceased, two of the former bandsmen, Mr C Webb of Avon Road, and Mr Harry Keeling, went about the district gathering together all the instruments it was possible to find. Many hours were spent by these two men cleaning, polishing and putting them in good order.

'Today these instruments are being used by the Broadlands Youth Band.'

'There is an amusing TRUE story my uncle often told of the time when the band was marching along playing, came up to a fork in the road, and the band went one way, and the drummer went the other,' concluded Mrs Harrison.

Mrs Jean Williams wrote, 'I know very little of the original band, although my husband William always said that his father, 'Cockney' Williams of 1, Rock Road, helped to start it in the very beginning, and played the double bass.

'When Bill and I met in 1934 it was a Silver Band, with the leader, Melbourne Close of Albert Road, taking them for miles around the countryside, walking, to play at the Big Houses at Newton St Loe, Farmborough, Saltford and Brislington House amongst them. They played and had a collection to raise money for the instruments and the uniforms. They played by ear or with the light of lanterns in the dark.

'Many tales have my family heard about these jaunts, especially of the patient at Dr Fox's Brislington House, who they thought was trying to kill

This lovely old photo of the Town Band was found among the late Mr L Ellis's possessions by his daughter Mrs Alvis. 'That's the school room at the top of Bath Hill,' declared Mrs I Andrews, who dated it after World War I. Mr B Robe thought the photo was pre-World War I.

The Town Band

Mr Harding's photo of the 19 members of the band comprises Fred Davis, Charlie Webb, Melbourne Close, Fred Harding, Charlie Harvey, Joe Wiltshire, Arthur Harding [his uncle], Charlie Jones, another Harvey, Jack Exon, Fred Harding [another uncle], Harry Keeling, Jack Cook, another Harvey, an un-named bandsman and the Bandmaster, cum-treasurer/secretary, Ralph Harding [yet another uncle!]. I remember well the band in the lower picture which, I think, was taken in the 1920s.'

them. When he did eventually catch them, he just said, "Touch. Now you touch me!"

'I think they all had new navy blue uniforms, with the tunics trimmed with red braid, when they played on the old football field in Charlton Road, opposite the large houses with balconies, for the coronation of King George VI and Queen Elizabeth in 1936. Very proud they were too, and smart!

'My husband Bill played the cornet and his brother Percy the euphonium. When Keynsham Picture House, in the High Street, was opened, they played on the stage there, and even my husband's mother, Edith Williams, went to hear them: it was the only time she ever went there. Bill played a cornet solo and very proud we were of him.'

[Toby Robe wrote, 'I think the Keynsham Picture House referred to by Mrs Williams must have been the 'new' one in Charlton Road, not in the High Street. The High Street cinema did not have a stage and closed at the end of World War One.']

'Music was their lives and it was a crime to miss Band Practice! It was always taken by Melbourne Close but my memory eludes me now as to where they practised.

'They always played at Keynsham Flower Show in Avon Road on the first Monday and Tuesday in August.

'In 1937 Bill went to Oxford to work for Morris Motors and sadly his band days were over, except for the life-long love of all band music, especially military music. So soon after that, war came, and I think there were no young men to keep things going, and indeed we had other things on our minds in those dark days of 1939 to 1945.'

Mr Leslie Harding has a photo of the band with 19 members. He said, 'The

Mrs I Andrews thought this might be the travelling German Band that her mother spoke of that came round before World War I and played at the top of Bath Hill. Their type of uniform went out after that war because it was too German.

bandmasters changed from time to time and sometimes came from outside the town. They practised at the Lamb and Lark Hotel for a long while, probably without any charge because the landlord welcomed them as they all drank beer! Possibly they used the coffee room downstairs. My father Herbert was in the band for many years, but is not in the photo as he was a kettle-side drummer, and they were going out of fashion in town bands. My brother Clifford went to the practices for a short time only.

'The band was probably at its peak before the war. They used to play for the yearly Remembrance Day services, held at the War Memorial, which was in the church in those days. At Christmas we used to go carolling and do all the big houses in Keynsham, and I used to hold one of the lamps for them to read their music. Then we used to go to the home of Captain Ronald Wills (now the home of L Crowther), to play for money, with our brass instruments. They were all old, bashed about and dented, and were really a disgrace, so he presented us with a new set of silver instruments. So we became 'Keynsham Silver Band',' Leslie chuckled.

Mrs J Williams explained that the football field was on the right hand side of Charlton Road heading for Queen Charlton, opposite the large three storied houses with balconies. 'Before the Second War, the football field (between about 1930 and 1939), was on the far edge of the town then, as there were no houses at all on the right hand side of the road. The pitch was just off the road, and parallel with it. The photo was taken in front of a row of small

Three of 'Cockney' Williams' children. From the left, William, in his town band uniform, Joan, and Percy with the baby, during the celebrations on the coronation of King George VI at Keynsham's earlier Football Field off Charlton Road.

'When the (old town) band was on parade',
Weekly Chronicle, Thursday, April 30, 1970

Under 'Notes of the week', the paper comments, 'As Keynsham prepares for the Festival 700 Carnival procession on May 9, this old photograph will bring back memories for older residents of a similar event nearly half-a-century ago.

'The picture was taken on May 23, 1923, as the old town band headed a carnival procession towards the Crown Field. It must have been a great thrill for local children, both those taking part and watching, in an age when entertainment was chiefly of the home-spun variety.

'Judging from the numbers lining the route, the carnival must have attracted' people from miles around, remembering that Keynsham 47 years ago had nothing like its present day population.

'Fashions of the roaring 20's can be seen on the right of the photograph, and there is a notable absence of transport with the many gaily decorated floats expected on May 9 this year.

'Alas, the old band is no more, but its modern counterpart, the recently formed British Legion Band, will be in the May 9 procession but not in uniforms like those of yesterday.

'Neither will the May 9 procession be making its way to the Crown Field, the centre of most of Keynsham's outdoor events of the day, and instead the venue will be Fry's sports ground.

'Mr Harry Keeling, of Wellsway, Keynsham, who played in the band for 30 years, can identify most of his former colleagues shown in the photograph, belonging to Mr Brookman, and reproduced for us by Mr John Hucklebridge.

'Mr Keeling said the bandmaster, at the rear in a trilby, was Edwin Pritchard. Others included Mr Keeling himself, Mr Jefferies, Jack Exon, Jacob Cook, Ernest Harvey, George Webb, Charlie Webb, John Parker, Edwin Tipney, Cliff and Arthur Harding. Also included were Mr Wiltshire, Ralph Harding, Ernest Hitchcock, Fred Davies and Ted Harvey on the big drum'.

poplar trees. They grew to be very tall before being cut down for building Park Close houses.

'Of course, Charlton Road in 1937 was only half its present width then. The short length of grass in the middle of the road used to have beautiful tall elm trees on it until the coming of Dutch Elm Disease. That patch of land used to be the hedge row of the total width of Charlton Road. It was fine for a horse and cart! Beyond the football pitch were just fields of corn and cows,' recalled Mrs Williams.

Mr Martin, who lived with his sister in one of the large houses mentioned above, and who always had a most beautiful front garden, mentioned to me years later that as children, they used to be able to hear from their balcony the cry of corn-crakes in the fields across the road!

Chapter 21

'Money comes slowly,'
by Mrs Gwen Newman

Mrs NEWMAN made a tape of her early memories of old Keynsham which she so loved, and which was broadcast in 1972 by Radio Bristol. Years later she presented me with this copy of her text to include in my book, which now follows, slightly edited:

> My father's a hedger and ditcher
> My mother does nothing but spin
> And I am a pretty young girl
> But the money comes slowly in

My father was born in Somerset, the eldest of thirteen children. He was a happy, round-faced man with lovely blue eyes and red cheeks – and very healthy. He died following an operation at the age of fifty, and this was the only illness I ever remember him having.

He led a very full life. Among the jobs he did were ploughing, hedging, thatching and tree-felling; and he also sank several wells here, in Keynsham, where we lived. But his real hobby was shooting; in fact, it was more than a hobby. He took two jobs as keeper to estates, and did a bit of poaching as well. I remember once he let a bagful of live rabbits loose in the smokeroom of the village pub, which at the time was full of women! He was once summoned to attend court for poaching, and had to pay a small fine. As he came out of court, all smiles, someone asked him how he'd got on, and from his pocket he took a rabbit which he'd taken to court with him – you can imagine how they enjoyed the joke.

I remember him coming into the house one day, when I was about eight or nine, and saying to me, 'Have you skinned a rabbit yet?' I said, 'No, Dad, not yet.' So he took a small rabbit and said, 'Here you are – skin this one,' and he stood over me and taught me how to do it. During my years of domestic service I was grateful for all I'd learnt at home about the picking and preparation of partridges, pheasants, hares and rabbits. And later, when my son, who was in the Squirrels Patrol of the Scouts, asked me to skin a squirrel, it came easy to me. I tanned it the same way as I had the rabbit and badger skins, which were stretched and nailed on a board, and rubbed with salt and alum until dry.

My father's funeral I will never forget. The coffin was placed on a bier on wheels and pushed all the way from the house to the cemetery, all the family walking behind. I think it was about a mile and a half, but it seemed very much longer.

I was born on a Thursday. It's said that Thursday's child has far to go, and although I didn't go far, I spent very little time in my own home. This was a lovely old cottage where we only had paraffin lamps, and always a candle at bedtime. On one occasion, when the five of us were going to bed, my brother caught the curtains alight, and I remember struggling upstairs with a bucket of water. We had a parrot, and a pump at the back door where we had to wash before going to school.

Our living-room consisted of a well-scrubbed table surrounded by six hard chairs, a large wooden settle, and one armchair which we all seemed to take in turns. My favourite seat was on the large fender, which was steel and kept polished with bath brick – it used to look lovely. Mother always covered it over if there was lightning. The floor was red tiles with a large home-made rag rug at the hearth.

The front and back doors were never locked day or night, but we were never nervous. We kept a spaniel dog which was usually very quiet, as it was gun-trained and would only bark if a stranger was about. One night my father bought a pair of heavy boots from a man he met at a pub. He brought them home and put them under the table, but the next morning they were gone. The dog must have known the thief, as he didn't bark.

I went to school when I was four, but I hadn't been there long when I was sent to stay with my grandmother, as Mother was having a baby – this was my youngest sister.

My first journey away from home was very exciting. It was in 1912. I was four. My father took me to the station, sitting on the handlebars of his bicycle. I was then put on the train at Keynsham in care of the guard, and I remember sharing his bread and cheese with him.

I was met at Bridgwater by one of my uncles with a pony and cart, and taken to my grandmother's house at Aller. It was a lovely old house at the top of a hill, with a thatched roof and a huge oven where the bread was baked. Inside was an open fireplace with long seats on either side, where I sat and looked up to the sky through the chimney. There was always a side of bacon or some onions hanging there, and a crock on a long chain which always seemed to have something cooking in it. Across the ceiling were large wooden beams on which hung guns of different kinds. Sometimes at night when I should have been in bed I was on my knees looking through the knot-holes in the floorboards to see what the family were doing below.

My grandfather bought this house for £28; it had a large garden, an orchard, a field, and some woods. Water was carried in buckets from the well, and sometimes I used to see frogs in the side of the well. I didn't think there was anything wrong with that – but I know I would now!

Once a week I looked forward to going to market with Grandma. She had a donkey which she harnessed to a little cart, and most weeks she took a pig to sell. Another visit I liked was to the little shop. Grandma would put on a large white starched waist apron and we'd walk to the bottom of the hill. She'd put all the groceries in her apron, holding them in safely by the corners, then when we got back she'd take them all out, take off her apron, smooth it out and fold it, and put it under a cushion ready to wear on the next visit.

I was very happy there, and fond of Grandma, with her round face, wavy hair and lovely blue eyes. No one had much money to buy me toys, but my uncle made me a wooden doll cut from a round block of wood. I can still remember watching him make the eyes, nose and mouth with a red-hot poker.

When it was convenient for me to come home I was fetched by one of the family. I then went back to school, but I don't remember learning much, except to write in a tray of sand with a wooden skewer, and not long after, I was sent to stay with my Aunt Caroline at another little country village called Priston. My cousin was cook-general at the rectory there, and sometimes my aunt and I would go and have supper in the rectory kitchen. One evening when I was there, the rector's son came in and asked me to hold out my hands. He filled them with coins, and said, 'Now you can say you have held a handful of sovereigns.'

My aunt later moved to Nailwell, and Mother sent me again to stay with her. This time I went to school. It was a long walk and I carried my lunch with me; often by the time I got there I'd eaten most of it. I was very hungry when I

Mrs Gwendoline Newman, 1908–1989

The daughter of Charles Glover, she was a direct, trusting and most warm-hearted soul. One of a large family, in her early years she was in service, and worked hard all her life, even helping her father in poaching rabbits. She married and had two sons, Ian and Ray. Ian was in the Royal Marines. Gwen had a great love for Keynsham and its history. Mrs P Robinson's photo above was taken at Ian's wedding.

got home at night, and after my meal I had to walk to the farm at Dunkerton to get a can of milk. Most days, walking home from school, I picked a bunch of wild asparagus, which looked very much like green wheat; Aunt cooked it in salt water and I was very fond of it.

I was next sent to my Aunt Ada at Wilmington. She had a baby called Kitty, and one day, when my aunt was in the outside wash-house, a woman came into the kitchen, took the baby and ran off with her down the road. I heard later that it was an adopted baby and the mother had taken it. I was then sent home once more.

I remember the 1914 war starting, and a lot of the men from our village went, including my father. We schoolchildren were allowed a day off to see our fathers depart; and hundreds of mules went by train the same morning from the goods station. All the mothers and some of the children cried. I remember walking home with Mother; when we got there I chopped some sticks, put them in the open grate, put the kettle on and soon made a cup of tea.

Hear the pennies dropping

I wasn't very old when I decided to try and earn some money, and a local lady agreed to give me some jobs between school hours. I used to go there at 8 in the morning; she would spread some newspapers on the kitchen windowsill (outside: I wasn't allowed inside) and I had to clean the steel knives with bath brick. Sometimes I cleaned shoes, and the downstairs windows, for which I got sixpence a week, and Mother used to give me a penny. You could get quite a lot for a penny then: some aniseed balls and a stick of licorice.

Some afternoons my 'Mistress', as I was told to call her, went to Bath, shopping, and I met her from the station and carried her parcels home. They were always heavy, but I felt very proud walking beside her because she looked lovely and always smelt nice. On one occasion she took me to Bath with her; it was my Christmas present, and we had tea and muffins from a silver dish at the Old Red House. I was able to tell all my friends how wonderful it was, and afterwards she let me choose three strings of beads for my sisters and myself.

Eventually I was allowed to do some inside cleaning. Some mornings when I arrived she'd cooked kippers or haddock, and would give me a piece of dry bread to use up the fat that was left in the enamel dish. When cleaning the hall floor one day, I found a shilling under the grandfather clock, and gave it to her. Again, I found a shilling under a chair, and the third time I found one under the doormat which I had to shake. When I told Mother, she told me to tell her that the next one I found I was going to put in my pocket, but I didn't find any more.

I think my most exciting day was once when my Mistress sent me shopping. As I was walking along the road I saw a large round thing fall from a lorry. It looked like a hat box, but was so heavy I couldn't move it. Just then a milkman came along and I asked him to take it to the police station for me. I forgot all about the shopping and ran home to tell my parents. My father took me to the police station, where nothing had been handed in, so with the police and my father I walked to the milkman's shop. I wasn't very old, and I was small for my age, but I felt very proud going into that shop. The policeman was very annoyed that the milkman had taken it home; it was a huge cheese, and he gave orders that it was to stay in the shop, and if it wasn't claimed in three months it was mine. It was never claimed, and my father brought it home. I know he gave the policeman a few pounds of it, but not much to the milkman.

I didn't think sixpence a week was enough for my work at the old lady's so I decided to get another job between school. I went to the local greengrocer's and used to tidy the house Saturday mornings. I had my lunch with the family and afterwards spent an hour watering the tomatoes with a hose, and then delivered the vegetables.

Now that my father was in France, in the Army Service Corps, Mother took a job sweeping the roads with other women. She wore a khaki overall and a green arm band. She also worked in the fields, mangel-hoeing and mangel-pulling. She was taken to work and brought back with the other women in a horse and trap. I understand they had some quite good times.

My sisters and I had to have a hot meal ready for her when she got home, as well as for my two older brothers and ourselves. We took it in turn to do the washing, cooking, shopping and house cleaning.

At weekends we three girls had our hair washed and took our baths. This meant lighting a coal boiler or 'copper', filled with water from the yard tap. We used a galvanised bath in front of the kitchen fire. Mother always washed my sisters' hair first: I was last, as I was the eldest. She used soft green soap bought from the chemist in a three-pound tin. My sisters also had their baths before me, and hot water from the boiler was added between each bath. The water wasn't very nice by the time it got to my turn, but it was no use complaining.

My sisters and I spent a lot of time collecting firewood; we'd take an old truck which my brothers had made, walk miles collecting dry wood from the hedges, and come back loaded – it was called 'sticking'. It could be exciting as there was always something to be found, such as flowers, mushrooms or blackberries. On one journey, we'd picked some blackberries and were looking for something to wrap them in, when I noticed a paper high in the hedge. When I got it down I found it to be a pound note in perfect condition. We were all very excited and took it home as fast as we could to Mother. We didn't worry any more about blackberries that day.

We worked very hard at home without much time for play. We were allowed to go to the Band of Hope once a week, and to the Girls' Friendly Society, where we made friends and practised singing and dancing. We also rehearsed plays which were put on at the Women's Institute. I remember how proud I felt when I sang alone on the stage:

> You are sailing, my sweet, to lullaby land
> Where the sunset colours glow,
> Your cradle of rest carries hues from the west
> All crimson, purple and gold.
> You are sailing, my sweet, to lullaby land,
> And hear as I softly say,
> I'll hold your dear hand 'til you reach the fair strand
> Where shadows, dear, melt away.

On Sunday evenings we went to a little mission at the bottom of Fairfield Terrace and Woodbine Cottages, beside the River Chew. The minister always spread his white handkerchief to kneel on when he prayed, and afterwards folded it very carefully and put it in his pocket. I often wondered if he used the same one each time.

We all went to Sunday School and took their pennies for the collection. At the end of the service the teacher played a hymn and the whole class marched to a chair at the front of the room and put our coins on a plate. Then we walked back to our seats singing these lovely words:

> Hear the pennies dropping, listen how they fall,
> Every one for Jesus, He shall have them all.
> Now while we are little, pennies are our store
> But when we are older God will give us more.

My first Sunday School prize was a book called *Come Home Mother*, the story of a drunken home. I won three First Class certificates for Bible study and always hoped to frame them, but they got so damaged that they had to be destroyed. I was very upset at the time, and wish I could show them to my two sons today.

I wouldn't say that school days were happy days for me. I wasn't very good in my lessons, but I was popular with one teacher, who gave me a muff and a pair of brown high-legged boots. During some lessons I used to sit on the headmaster's knee in front of the class while he taught them. When I left I was given my School Character. I didn't get many top points, but it stated that I was one of the most cheerful in the school.

One day, a schoolfriend and I were arguing over a game of hopscotch and she threatened to throw me in the river; of course I dared her, and she did. There wasn't much water, but I split my forehead on a pointed stone. She ran away, and I was left with the blood pouring down my face. Mother wasn't at home, but a neighbour took me to the doctor and I was stiched. The doctor said I'd been so good that his little girl gave me a doll and white rabbit.

With my brothers and sisters I spent very happy times at Bill Trott the blacksmith's, opposite the New Inn. We took it in turns to blow the bellows to keep the fire red, and, like the poem we learnt at school, we watched the sparks that flew 'like chaff from a threshing floor'. It was somewhere to go in the cold evenings when we got tired of playing 'touch'.

Once a week I went to cookery class. The teacher was very strict and if a girl's hair wasn't 'braided back' she'd tie it back with a piece of string; of course we always felt very ashamed. The cooking was done on an old open range, and a gas stove, and we were each supplied with a pastry bowl, roller and board; I often remember the teacher's words when I'm washing my pastry roller: 'Scrub well the way of the grain' and 'Do not dry in the sun as it turns the wood yellow'.

Our local flower show was something to look forward to, as there might be a chance of winning some money in the exhibitions. I was very fond of knitting lace, and darning, and was nearly always lucky enough to win something. I also entered steamed and boiled potatoes, and spent a lot of time collecting every wild flower I could find to make an arrangement.

Christmas was a very exciting time for us. We went out and cut the tree from a wood and dragged it all the way home. It was my brothers' job to get the holly and mistletoe. I must confess I really did believe in Father Christmas, and tried hard to be good, as we were told he wouldn't bring us anything if we weren't. I was always rather nervous on Christmas Eve, though I wouldn't say so. Mother would call up the stairs, 'Now, you girls, say your prayers and go to sleep, or he won't come.' We always sang when we went to bed – everything we could think of: hymns, songs and carols. Our black woollen stockings were hung in a row over the fireplace on Christmas Eve, but they were always hanging at the foot of the bed when we woke. They had more or less the same contents every year: nuts, oranges, apples, sweets, and a doll or a toy.

Faggots and fire-engines

When I read today of people starving, my mind goes back to the days when, on the shortest day of each year, the poor of this village were given free bread. The money was left by a wealthy inhabitant. I was nearly always given the job of queuing to collect it. As we were seven in our family we were entitled to three loaves. There was also an occasion once a year when we could collect soup in large jugs from a public house. After they had a special dinner there for some important people we were allowed to have it free.

Sometimes life was very hard at home and my parents had to apply for 'parish relief'. We were allowed a special ticket to take to a grocer and butcher, where we were given plain food to the value of five shillings or seven and sixpence. I remember asking once if we could have some sweets or biscuits, only to be told this wasn't allowed, as they were luxuries.

We had a small oven at home with an open fire where there hung from a hook a large iron crock. The contents varied from stewing beef to breasts of lamb, rabbits, and sometimes a hare with 'doughboys' as we called them. There were always plenty of vegetables, from the garden and from an allotment at the top of the hill, which we called 'Workhouse Hill'. My sisters and I had to go up there, dig potatoes, and bring home enough vegetables for a few days. Father also kept poultry, geese and pigs there. We had plenty of large jugs in the house which the milkman filled, using the metal measure which hung on a hook inside his can.

The River Chew was at the bottom of our garden and I spent a lot of time fishing for eels with a stick and a pin on it. We washed and skinned them in one of the two outdoor sinks shared between the nineteen houses in the terrace, and I must admit we were all very healthy. Maybe it was because each Sunday morning we all went to Mother's room and took one large teaspoonful of brimstone and treacle from a basin. We didn't mind – we got used to it and even liked it – and we never had bad skin and were seldom ill.

There was lovely fresh spring water near the bakehouse. Sometimes I took a bottleful home to bathe my sister's eyes, which were very weak following an attack of measles. There was also a good supply of watercress at the spring, which we were told was good for us.

Saturday nights could be exciting: if Mother could manage it we were allowed to buy fish and chips. For sixpence we'd get a piece of cod and chips, which we ate with a large piece of bread to help fill us up. Often we'd take a china basin to an old lady who cooked faggots and peas for a few coppers; these we took home hot and ate with more bread.

We always seemed to be hungry and longing for the next meal. I think Sunday dinner was the favourite: it was nearly always roast rabbit stuffed with sage and onion and sewn up with double white cotton. Alternatives were belly of pork, stuffed, or breast of mutton. There was always a batter pudding whatever the joint – not like the Yorkshire pudding we eat today, but a large solid one swimming in fat. This was followed by a large rice pudding with raisins in, which was put in the oven early and cooked all the morning.

At Christmas, Mother always sent us to the baker to have our Christmas cake cooked, for which we paid sixpence, and often we had a goose cooked at the same time. On Shrove Tuesday a bell was rung at the church at 11 o'clock, as we were coming out of school. It seemed to say, 'Pan on, pan on', and we dashed home to pancakes for lunch.

Another treat was rook pie; I remember once Mother gave me the choice of going to a social at the mission or staying at home and having rook pie. I'd helped to skin and pick the rooks, so I stayed home. That was the night I had my hair bobbed – it was a craze at the time. My sisters both had nice fair hair but mine was dark and scraggy. Everyone thought the bobbing was an improvement, but I cried after it was done.

Getting back to food, it was quite common to see tramps wandering about, men and women. They'd go to the police station [surely to The Workhouse] where they were given a food ticket to take to a little shop [being the front room of Rockwell House, Wellsway]. I went there many times and watched them being served with 2 oz of tea, ¼ lb of butter, a little cheese and some bread. They carried a tea can, usually made from an old tin with a piece of wire for a handle. They'd go to a side lane and boil some water on a stick fire, or knock on any door and ask for some boiling water to be poured on the tea. I know that many a time, unknown to Mother, I put a bit more tea and sugar in the can, and sometimes some milk. I think there was a rule that they called at the workhouse for a bath, and unless they were moving on they'd sleep there.

There were never many callers at our house. Sometimes gypsies came to sell lace, and clothes-pegs which they made from withy trees. Mother was a bit superstitious and would never send them away without buying something. The last purchase I remember was two tiny pictures which she bought for my two sisters. I was very upset because I was told she couldn't afford one for me; but the gypsy gave me a picture of a lovely lady wearing a large hat with a feather on. I thought it was beautiful, and treasured it as long as I can remember. The gypsy told me, 'Your beauty is hidden'. I've never understood this, but it's been a family joke ever since.

Another caller was the fish lady. She would open the front door and call out, 'Any haddock today, or kippers?' She was always dressed in a large floppy hat, white apron, and carrying a large basket; and she used to keep her horse in her back garden: to get there it went in her front door and through a passage to the back. [This was, of course, a reference to 'Fishy Fry's' in the High Street.]

The oil man was a weekly caller, as we always needed paraffin and sometimes a wick or a lamp-glass for our table lamps. He also sold candles, which we used about the house and in the outside toilet. Sometimes I helped him deliver his goods, and he'd give me a penny or a halfpenny. He also had a horse and cart; people in the village said it stopped at every public house – and there were fourteen at the time!

We had a lot of fun when there was a fire in the village. The Fire Brigade used a horse and cart with all the hoses and equipment hung on the side, and the firemen sat in the cart wearing caps with spikes on. The horse was loaned by Mr F Ollis, local baker, and if the fire got too big another horse was hired from another baker. Sometimes a horse was unobtainable, and then the firemen ran the cart themselves. We children always followed the fire contraption in great excitement, hoping it would be a fire worth watching.

A common sight in summer was the dust cart, which was drawn round the roads by a horse, to lay the dust. It was fun to follow behind and jump into the spray of water coming from the back of the cart. The driver filled the cart from the village pumps. (We always called it 'the village', as the population was only just over 3,000. Everyone knew each other, and if we saw a stranger around we soon found out who he or she was, and what they were doing here).

The town cryer could be heard ringing his bell whenever there was any important news or a meeting. He always appeared looking very smart in blue with gold braid; he wore a three-cornered hat, long coat, breeches, white socks and black court shoes with shining buckles. He would ring his bell three times, deliver his message, then move on and repeat it several times. There was always a crowd, mostly children, to listen.

In the centre of the village at the top of Bath Hill West, was a weighbridge with a little round house, where coal and coke brought from the goods yard were weighed and checked. It was a familiar sight to see the heavy horses and wagons waiting their turn for attention.

One morning, when I was about twelve, Mother informed me that my aunt (she who had the adopted baby stolen) was ill in hospital. I was to go and stay with my uncle and three adopted children. My uncle went to work and I had to cook, clean the house, keep the children clean and send them to school. It meant scrubbing a large table and the flagstoned floor, and blackleading the open grate on which I cooked. In the evening when my uncle returned we all had the hot meal which I'd prepared. He often complained that I hadn't cleaned the house properly, but I felt I'd done my best and could do no more. I was always very tired at night. I asked my uncle one night if I could go to bed, and he replied that I could have gone before if I'd said "please". The children were difficult and unruly, and my health soon began to suffer; I was also undernourished, as the main diet was vegetables and bread.

Another aunt, who was living not far away, contacted my mother, and I was sent home at once. I then went back to school again, and stayed there until I left at the age of fourteen.

Service with a song

On leaving school I was sent as a 'daily' to Conygre farm where my brother was also working. I was very happy there although the work was hard. A kitchen range had to be cleaned and lit early in the morning; also an open grate in the sitting-room, where huge logs were burnt. The large table and flagstoned floor was scrubbed each day. Everything had to be scrupulously clean, as butter was made in the kitchen, all food was cooked there, and the family dined there. I enjoyed making the butter and was always glad to hear it flop flop; then I knew it had turned and was ready for 'patting', which I did with two wooden pats and a little salt.

The pigs were killed on the farm, and sometimes I helped with cleaning the chitterlings. The cream was scalded in a white enamel bucket suspended over a 'copper' of boiling water kept hot by a coal fire. One day the bucket slipped and all the cream was wasted; there was a terrible row, but the lady herself was responsible as we weren't allowed to touch it.

At mealtimes my brother and I sat in a corner at a little table on our own. We always had good food, all farm produce, and were both strong and healthy. For my 'lunch' during the morning I had a glass of raw cream straight from the dairy, and often a mug of milk from the cows before it went to the cooler.

The son of the house was still at school. One afternoon he and I were sent to a distant farm to collect some young pigs. We were bringing them down Steel Mills Lane when suddenly the children came running home from school; the pigs got very excited and ran in all directions, one getting his nose stuck in a gate. We were both very upset, but managed to get them home safely.

Occasionally the farmer would come home noisy and bad-tempered after drinking too much. We disappeared when this happened and sometimes hid behind the hay mow until he was asleep.

My job at the farm only lasted a few months as Mother decided I wasn't earning enough money. She thought it was time I went into 'service' and slept in. So a big black box was packed and I was sent to work in a local nursing home (The Grange, Bath Road) for aged and mental people.

It seemed a very large house, and as a child I'd heard that it was supposed to be haunted. The only happy thing about my going there was that a schoolfriend of mine went too. We shared the same bed in a room on the fourth floor. We were not to be addressed by our first Christian names but by our second – mine was Sarah and my friend's Nelly.

The cooking was done on a four-chimney oil stove with an oven on the top. The week's ration of food for the two of us was kept in the kitchen cupboard: tea, sugar, jam, margarine, and anything else Matron wished to put there. Our wages were five shillings a week.

Our favourite patient was a very dear man in a wheelchair, called Mr Cavell. I used to put his feeder on and feed him, as he was paralysed. After every meal he liked to read his Bible, which I propped up for him; and I would pop in and out to turn a page. One old lady had been put there when her home was sold up; unknown to Matron we used to try and cheer her up. Another lady was very ill and we knew she was going to die. I used to comb her long hair and powder her nose; she liked to have her hand mirror and look nice.

She used to ask me for her Bible and liked to hear me sing the 'Army' hymns while I cleaned her room. She died while I was there. The lady in the bedroom next to ours walked about her room at night, talking to herself, but we took no notice of her: we said our prayers, blew out the candle and went to sleep, as we had to be first up every morning.

Nelly and I found it hard work making the food go round and were often hungry, but on our afternoons off we always brought some food back with us and hid it in our bedroom. One night Nelly's aunt gave her an apple tart to take back and my mother gave me half a roast rabbit; although we tried not to let Matron know she found some remains in our bedroom, and then we were really in trouble!

We used six gallons of paraffin a week to cook all the food, and Matron said she'd give us a sixpence rise if we could cut it down to five. We tried, but we couldn't. Anything that was broken or lost had to be paid for from our wages. Nelly once broke a small china cruet, and we got a ladder and hit it on top of the dresser. I don't think it was ever found.

Nelly and I used to go to the Salvation Army meetings and we were always singing when Matron wasn't around; it used to cheer the patients. One night Matron asked if we'd be all right alone with the patients if she and her husband went out for the evening. We agreed and asked if we could have Mr Cavell downstairs with us. Matron said 'yes', and he was brought down in his chair. We knew he liked the Army tunes, so we got our books and had a lovely evening with him. On our birthdays he always gave Matron the money to buy us a new apron each: he knew we couldn't afford them.

During the winter months the kitchen was very cold. There was a large range, but we weren't allowed to drop the front down or have a big fire. I couldn't put up with this, so one day I dropped the front, making an awful noise as I did so, and made up a good fire. When Matron found out she was furious and told me to pack my box the next morning and go. I told her that we always had good fires at home and I would be pleased to go, and I left the next morning.

My next two jobs both involved child-minding – first for a young couple with a baby son and then for a vet and his wife with a three-year-old daughter. But both families moved from the area, and I found work with a middle-aged couple. Madam was German and played the violin very often; she was a really nice lady. I had to open the front gate every morning for master to go out in his three-wheeled car, and close if after him. They'd just bought the house and I used to help them with the decorating. I also worked hard in the garden, digging and carrying large stones to build a rockery. In fact, I seemed to spend more time working in the garden than in the house – which gave me a good appetite. One day Madam informed me she thought I ate too much, and as the house was costing a lot more than she'd realised, she couldn't afford to keep me. So I had to leave. It was while I was working here that a boyfriend started to take me out. Later he was to become my husband.

I now went to work for a lady of about sixty-five; she was a Greek widow and a great sufferer from arthritis. She had a bachelor son whom she called 'Manno' for short. I became very attached to them both. I had a half-day a week off, and Sunday afternoons. Most evenings I helped to get Madam to bed: this was difficult if her son was out, as I had to push very hard to get her up the stairs; but she was always grateful and kind. I made sure the bed was warmed with bottles before she got into it, and I also warmed it with the flat iron heated at the fire. I tucked her into bed for the night, not forgetting her little Cairn dog, who slept on a blanket at the foot of her bed.

She liked to have flowers near her husband's photograph, and I gathered fresh ones every morning before she came down to breakfast. She told me it gave her great joy, as she never knew what kind of flowers she'd see there. I enjoyed doing it as I loved flowers and gardening – and still do. Madam taught me quite a lot about cooking and life in general – manners and appearance being the most necessary. She was cross with me if I left a jug of milk uncovered in the pantry, as there were mice there who would dip their tails in and suck them.

While working there I developed diphtheria and was sent to the local fever hospital (by the Elim Church); but after some weeks I went back to her again. I had my twenty-first birthday in hospital, and she gave me an ebony hand mirror. To celebrate the birthday I had a photograph taken, and she said she'd like a copy; but after a few days she returned it to me saying it wasn't like me: 'The smile is not there so it is not the face I know.'

She was considerate in every way, and if she were going for a drive with her son she allowed me to have my fiancé to tea. But again I was getting restless, and I needed more money if I was to save to get married. So I left, and not long after that she went to live in the north. I heard that her son had married and I was very pleased.

And in my lady's chamber

After leaving my nice Greek lady I went to a local family as kitchen maid and 'general'. It was a four-storey house and I slept alone in the attic. I was up at six or six-thirty and had to make up the fires, clean the breakfast room and prepare breakfast before the family came down. The stairs were brushed once a week with a stiff brush, and every flat brass stair rod cleaned. Cook used to help me with some of the best carpets. We used a vacuum which worked like a pair of bellows: cook would work the handle backwards and forwards and I would clean the carpets with a nozzle. For the older carpets I used a large pump, similar to a bicycle pump, but not before I'd covered the floor with tea leaves, which were saved in the sink strainer every day.

Washing day was quite an occasion. The water was heated in a coal boiler and the clothes worked in a dolly tub – this was like a long-handled stool with three legs, which was rotated in the same way as some of our washing-machines are today. The very stained clothes were laid on the lawn if there was hot sun, and kept wet by continual watering with a can.

Madam was French, and often asked me into the drawing room to listen to her playing the piano. I didn't know much about her kind of music, but it was a rest for me to sit down, and I think I learnt every note of 'Alice, Where Art Thou?' The two younger ladies of the house took part in plays which were held in the local Drill Hall: *HMS Pinafore, A Little Child Shall Lead them, Pirates of Penzance* and others. I always enjoyed helping to dress them, and it was my job every fortnight to dye the daughters' hair.

In the little spare time I had I helped Madam in the garden, and I was always allowed to arrange the flowers in the drawing room. Sometimes I took the grandson for walks with the Airedale dog; he got into fights, or would roll in manure in the field, and I nearly always seemed to have to bath him.

I found the work very hard and soon left to move on again.

My mother still expected me to hand over quite a bit of my wages to her, often sending for money even before I was paid – and even after I was gone twenty-one. I remember how annoyed she was when my fiancé said it was time I put some money in the Post Office or we should never be able to get married. It wasn't easy to save: my uniform used to cost a fair amount.

The next situation was with a local family who had been very kind to me during the poorer days of my childhood, buying me and my sisters black dresses for our father's funeral. Again there was the usual hard routine of early rising, grates, cleaning, breakfast for six and helping to get the children off to school. I had to iron damask tablecloths over six feet long, and white honeycomb quilts. But I got used to it.

The youngest of the four children was just a baby; the next one, a little boy, often seemed at a loose end. He liked to ride on my back when I was polishing floors and I was very fond of him. In the evenings when I cleaned brass or silver the children would sit with me in the kitchen and we'd sing songs and hymns together. I was then going regularly to the Salvation Army, and they liked to hear the choruses.

When it was my half day off my fiancé would come and wait for me at a field gate near the house, and the children almost always asked to come for a walk with us, and sometimes we picnicked together in the fields.

One day when I was alone in the house four men came to the door and asked for food. They looked very dirty and tired, and told me they were miners from South Wales. They were walking to London and were on strike. As there was always plenty of food I gave them some bread, sausages and eggs. The ducks used to lay their eggs at a stream near the house and there were always more than we needed. The men took the food and were most grateful. They lit a fire in a corner of the field opposite the house to cook it. Some years later – after I'd left – they returned to thank me for my kindness. They explained that they now had work and were in better circumstances, and wished to repay me. But the mistress told them I'd gone.

I left this family to go to another situation, as there were times when I felt I couldn't cope. But during my years of service I returned to them three times – between other situations. Each time, of course, the children were older and things seemed a little easier. Looking back over forty years I realise I earned every penny of the wages I got there, but I remember the happy times too.

I now decided to get a better-paid job in the city, which was about six miles away. I entered a doctor's house as a parlour maid – though as there was only a cook general there besides me, I knew my work would be pretty general. The house was large; in fact it was two houses together, which meant lots of stairs. One half was used as surgery, waiting and consulting rooms, and above these were the family's bedrooms and bathrooms. Cook and I shared the same bedroom in an attic on the 'house side'. She used to drink gin at night and I didn't find her very good company. We had to use the same washstand, jug and basin, and were only allowed one bath a week. We were told when to have it, and we also had to wash our hair in the bedroom, with water carried up from the bathroom.

Cook and I took it in turns to have a half-day off a week, and alternate Sunday mornings and afternoons. When we got in at night there were always the tea and supper dishes which had been left to wash. Sometimes the family had entertained, and then there was quite a lot of clearing up to do before we could go to bed. When I had Sunday mornings off my fiance would cycle into town and we'd go to the Salvation Army Citadel together; and when I had Sunday afternoons we'd walk to the Downs, or sometimes I'd ride on the back step of his bicycle – I must have ridden many miles with him like that.

The first Sunday morning I was there cook had the morning off. I was rather nervous about cooking the lunch – it was the contraption I had to cook on that was the problem: it was called a multi-cooker, with two gas jets under an oven and two other jets for vegetables. As they were going through the hall on their way out to church I heard the daughter ask her mother if she thought I could manage, and I heard the reply: 'If she's got any gumption she can.' I decided I'd jolly well let them see that I had! The lunch was roast beef, Yorkshire pudding, vegetables, and rice pudding with prunes, and after it was served they told me it was a wonderful meal.

Once the house bell rang at two o'clock in the morning, and as it wasn't the surgery bell the doctor didn't hear it. Cook wouldn't come down with me, and I was very nervous; but I thought it might be urgent, so I went down alone and got the message. I then woke the doctor. He was pleased with me and said I was very brave. It had been a serious case and one of his private patients; he gave me two shillings, which of course meant a lot to me.

I was very fond of the doctor, and later he trusted me with house and surgery telephone calls; sometimes I was answering them both night and day. I got to know his regular patients, and sometimes to deliver their medicine to them. When he visited patients he rode in a phaeton, driven by a coachman who sat up high in the front and wore a smart uniform and a top hat.

Once a week a dear middle-aged man came to the house to help with the cleaning. He was a tinker by trade and lived in a very shabby little dwelling at the bottom of a flight of steps in an old part of the town. I had to take a message to him once and I felt so sorry that he had to live alone in such a hovel. He was a good-living man and a Christian. He always came to the house on his three-wheeled bike, upright and tall, and he had a long white beard. His job was mostly cleaning brass and silver, getting in coal, chopping sticks and scrubbing the basement steps. He always enjoyed his lunch in the kitchen with cook, the coachman and myself.

My wages now were nine shillings a week, and after keeping myself in clothes and uniform I didn't have much left over. If I was ever to start saving properly to get married I would have to try for a new situation and higher wages.

Pray let us be married

Like myself, my fiancé was trying to save all he could so that we could get married. He was a jobbing gardener working on his own, and when he'd paid his mother for his keep there wasn't much left to save, especially as he was a rather heavy smoker. When it was wet or too frosty for gardening he was sometimes given indoor jobs; failing this, he couldn't work and there were no wages. He worked very long hours when he had the chance; among other things he made two tennis courts, and always kept them neatly cut. Once – after we were married – he was home ill with pneumonia in the winter, and he remembered an employer owed him some money. There was no dole or sick pay then, and we had no other income, so he suggested that I should go and ask for it. I did so, only to be told, 'Your husband should be able to save sufficient in the summer to keep you in the winter'.

After leaving the doctor's house where I'd been working, I went to some Jews not far away. Madam was an aged widow with a middle-aged son and daughter. There was also another gentleman living with them as a paying guest. They were very kind, and paid me ten and sixpence – one and sixpence more than the previous job.

My bedroom was in the attic with just a skylight little more than a foot square. It was cold and damp, but I was quite prepared to put up with this as the rise in pay meant a lot to me. The washing was done in the cellar, and coal buckets had to be carried up long flights of stairs. Once a week I took Madam to the shops, and I sometimes used to find it very embarrassing as she wanted to sample most of the goods she bought. She helped herself to grapes and so on, and ate them in the shops, and she spent a long time deciding and arguing over an article before she purchased it. One day she discovered she'd bought a bad grapefruit, and as she was too frail to go out alone I had to return to the shop and change it.

The food they ate was most interesting. Always keen to find new ways of dealing with food, I soon learnt some new dishes. Their chief food was chicken, but it was never roasted, always boiled with a special macaroni which I made. This was made like pastry rolled very thin, hung up to dry and then cut into long strips. Fish was also popular. Fresh herring was prepared with spices and eaten raw. Fresh salmon, cut thin, was also treated and eaten raw. Bream were stuffed and steamed: nothing was ever roasted. The bread was black and contained caraway seeds: I liked it very much myself. Bacon, ham and pork were never eaten, and other meat only when the animal had been killed in a certain way. Nothing was ever made with lard, but I was allowed to have a frying-pan of my own to cook anything I wished.

While I was there a relative died and the corpse was brought to the house. The coffin was placed on a long table and covered with a white cloth. The pictures and mirrors in the room were also covered. A young local lad was hired to sit all night with the coffin. It was winter and dark mornings, and when I came downstairs at 6.30 the young man would always be there standing in the hall smoking a cigarette, with his cap on! He wasn't allowed to speak to me. This went on every morning until the day of the funeral, and you can imagine it was a very uncomfortable feeling.

On the day of the funeral other mourners arrived – all men, in silk top hats. Everything was very quiet and strange, but when they all returned from the service they left their hats in the cars, and the noise they made was like bedlam. They ate a large meal, and nothing good could be said about the deceased relative. I had prepared the meal, and waited on them, but no one spoke to me. If they didn't wish me to hear their conversation they would immediately start to talk in Hebrew.

The self-denial fast day was quite an occasion for the Jews. All the family went to the synagogue early in the morning and stayed there for the whole day, having nothing to eat or drink until they arrived home in the evening. They always looked ill and tired when they came in, and I understand that some people at the service fainted from being too long without nourishment. It was a mad rush to the dining room where I had prepared a special meal for them. It was like feeding starving children.

I was puzzled by the metal attachments nailed over the door of every room. They contained a tiny scroll of writing which could be taken out by releasing a sliding catch. I never did find out what was written on them as it was all in Hebrew.

On the Saturday, the Jewish Sabbath, I was 'lent out' to help, as it was against their religion to do most of the necessary jobs. I would wash the dishes which had been collected from all the meals on that day, and light the gas stoves and fires. I remember one Saturday I was asked to strike a match to light a cigarette for the daughter, who was ill in bed and alone in the house.

As I've said, my bedroom was damp and cold; probably because of this, I became ill, and the doctor I'd previously worked for was called in. He said it was muscular rheumatism and I was to be taken home at once. It wasn't easy to get an ambulance in those days, so my brother fetched me with a motor cycle and side-car. Wrapped in blankets, I was driven the six miles home, through snow and icy roads. I never returned to the Jews' house again.

I now decided to get work nearer home and save money on bus fares. This family were Scots, a young couple with a baby son. They were both very fond of gold. I was trusted and left quite a lot with the child, and became very fond of him. He really was a most lovable and intelligent child. I seemed to walk miles with him and his little dog called Bobs. I didn't know then that one day I should have a son of my own and would call him by the same name –Ian.

I fitted in the housework and walks to suit myself, and was allowed to have my own front door key. My fiancé and I used to cycle to my home and back twice a week. I remember one night in particular. The General Election was on, and in those days the result was given out on a loudspeaker from a shop in the village, as not many people had wireless. We were anxious to know which candidate had got in, but it was getting late and I had to be in by 10 o'clock. It was nearly 10.30 when I got in, but before I could apologise the family said they were very disappointed that we didn't know the result. They asked us to return to Keynsham and not to come back until we knew it. It was a good ride each way and we were both delighted to have more time together.

I shan't forget one holiday, when they went away and asked me to be sure to take very good care of a large silver golf cup which the master had won. They said it was very valuable and important. I couldn't sleep that first night as I thought so many people knew about it and where it was. So I got up in the night, wrapped the cup in a large towel, and took it to the house next door, waking the maid by throwing a stone at her window. I slept in her bed with her and we put the cup underneath. (She and I are still great friends after about forty years.) I heard the next morning that the local Post Office had been burgled, so I felt I'd done the right thing, but of course it was always a joke with the family and their friends.

I now come to the time when my fiancé and I learned that a cottage was vacant and was to be altered and then let. So at last we fixed a date to get married: November 1930, after courting for seven years and being officially engaged for six weeks.

From that day forth

We couldn't afford a grand wedding, but we were able to have a white one, as my mistress leant me her own wedding outfit. The reception was at my parents' home. We were then both teetotallers, so all drinks were served in a separate room.

When I look back on the conditions we lived in when we were first married they hardly seem possible. There were flagged stone floors, a range which stood out into the room with a chimney pipe let into the wall, and a square trap at the side where the soot was to be taken out. There was a brown sink standing on bricks, about two feet high; a coal boiler; and a dresser with cupboards which took up the whole of one side wall. The lavatory was at the end of a long garden; and the rent was eight shillings a week – a lot of money to us then. We wondered if we'd be able to manage. We had to get a cat, as there were always mice; and coming into the house in the evening, the walls would be covered with cockroaches, which we had to sweep down in shovels and dustpan and burn in the range.

Still, we thought we had a wonderful house; and we were able to pay cash for our furniture, although it was a struggle. Best of all, it was our own home, where I didn't have to curtsy and say 'Yes, sir' and 'Yes, madam', and it was lovely not to be changing caps, aprons and uniform twice a day.

After only a fortnight of marriage we realised we couldn't possibly live on my husband's wage alone. So I took charring jobs, and although I only earned sixpence an hour to start with, I was given lunch and sometimes dinner, as well as little things like a cup of dripping or the odd dress, and this helped more than the money.

I continued working until our first son, Ian, was born. I brought him home from hospital on the anniversary of our wedding. I can honestly say that was the most difficult year of our marriage. People were beginning to do their own gardens and it wasn't easy for my husband to earn enough as a jobbing gardener. He worked all hours and in all weathers, and then took ill with pneumonia. I had to apply for parish relief and was allowed fifteen-shillings worth of groceries; I paid the money back when I was able to work again. The landlord wasn't very understanding about the rent, and times were difficult.

As soon as Ian was able to walk I left him in the care of my sister-in-law and went to work at the Talbot Hotel. Although I was a teetotaller, the owner said I should drink an Oakhill Stout every morning as she thought I really needed it. This, and the breakfast I had there, was a great help. I usually had either kidneys and bacon, sausage and mushrooms or haddock and poached egg, and all beautifully served. After this, people got to know me and I was sent for to work at several places. One job was serving teas at the St Keyna Tennis Club on Saturday afternoons. Croquet was played there and I used to like watching our old local doctor [Dr Charles Harrison] playing with the elderly ladies; he used to swear and chew his handkerchief to shreds!

I soon found it difficult to clothe Ian. I knitted him jerseys from cheap wool, or from something I had unpicked, and I was lucky to know an elderly lady who was willing to make trousers for him from an old skirt or man's trousers, as long as I unpicked and pressed the material beforehand. She lined them, and made pockets, and charged me sixpence a pair; he used to look so nice in his first real trousers.

Ian started work at the age of fourteen, and after a year of waiting managed to get apprenticed to a letter-press printing firm; he still does this work. When Ray, my second son, was old enough to be left with a friend of mine, I started work again. As well as doing housework, I served as waitress at a café, helped with school lunches and waited at wedding receptions. I travelled about and got to know a lot of people, and the tips helped towards little luxuries for the family. Two of the ladies who employed me towards the end of my working days remain very good friends, and now that I'm a widow I know I can turn to them for help and advice.

My dear husband died nine years ago. I nursed him through a long illness, and after his death I knew I must do something. So I started to read the Bible, and I read it right through, every page. My sons are both happily married and I have grandchildren.

I know that to start with I was only a 'skivvy', perhaps looked down on by some of my schoolmates, but even now, forty-four years after my marriage, and having brought up two sons, I feel I can tackle almost anything. I've learnt to be thrifty and how to manage a home, sometimes on very little money.

I live in a small but comfortable Council house now. I have a garden where I enjoy growing enough vegetables and flowers for myself, with some over for friends. I think the truest words ever written are, 'One is nearer God's heart in a garden than anywhere else on earth.' When I'm there I forget everything else, even the house! I still like sewing, and I keep in touch with the Salvation Army, which I've loved ever since I was fifteen years old.

I feel I have learnt to live a full and happy life.

Sadly, Gwen died in 1989, aged 81. Her obituary in the Keynsham Chronicle of 31 March 1989 ran to almost a whole page. It commented, 'Mrs Gwen Newman whose death was announced last week was not a wealthy woman and yet the legacy she left Keynsham is beyond price'. This referred to her tape recordings, which we have just read. The Chronicle concluded that they gave 'an insight into life for ordinary people through those difficult years'. Her husband died in 1963 and her son Ian in September 1985. With her excellent memory, this octogenarian became an authority on old Keynsham for the period through which she had lived. Her letters on the subject frequently appeared in the Chronicle.

Chapter 22

Childhood memories of village life
by Mr Monty Veale

The Veales were one of the several emigrant families of skilled metal workers from Holland/Germany that were brought over around 1685 to help with the local brass-making industry, and have lived in the area for three hundred years. Mr Monty Veale is the youngest son of the five children of Gilbert Veale who took him and his mother to Toronto, Canada, where in World War One Gilbert joined the Canadian army. Later the family returned to their beloved Keynsham, where Gilbert's brother Harry was a butcher in Temple Street and Horace a grocer. Monty now takes up the story.

I was born in 1920 and my earliest memories were of care-free days as a child, probably of above seven, when we lived at Durley Hill. Unemployment was rife and my father found work as a tailor difficult to find. An important person in our life was our landlady, Mrs Fox, who was looked upon with awe and probably fear, because the rent was probably often in arrear. Her husband, Dr Fox, owned the huge Georgian Building on the Bristol Road at Brislington, which was at that time a mental institution, as it was when George III was a patient there.

Percy Baker lived at the end of our terrace of three. There were no drains, so that the toilet bucket was emptied daily or lime added to it. When it rained there was always a puddle of water on the flagstone floor at the back of the house, which was below the level of the field behind.

I clearly recall my brother and sisters playing with a ball in the middle of the main Bristol-Bath Road outside the cottage during the General Strike of 1927, when there was no traffic whatsoever on the road. We had become acclimatised to this and were completely taken by surprise when suddenly a bus appeared from the direction of Bristol. The driver shared our surprise on finding a whole family of youngsters in the middle of the road. He stopped, got out and helped us retrieve the ball from under the bus.

Some of my time was spent watching Mr Hanney the grave digger hard at work in the cemetery which was a few hundred yards down the road. He was a kindly elderly gentleman and often gave me some of his bread and cheese when he stopped for lunch.

My brothers and sisters attended the school in Bath Hill, which was a very considerable walk. It was always a matter of very great concern as to whether Mr Exon the milkman would turn up in time and would allow us to ride part of the way in the back of his horse-drawn dray amongst the large churns from which he would ladle pints and quarts into the jugs which were left on the doorsteps.

He was a very kindly man but there were the odd occasions when he lost patience at being used as an honorary school bus.

I remember father speaking of the arrival of the Royal Mail Stage-coach. Coming from Bath, the posthorn would be sounded at the bottom of Wellsway, and the coach would stop at the Lamb and Lark, where the horses were changed, before going on to Bristol.

We moved from Durley Hill to 50, Temple Street, which was owned by Uncle Horace Veale who ran the grocery store next door. I think the rent was five shillings weekly. Next door again was the Trout Tavern, and further up the street there were also The Foresters and The Lamb and Lark, while down the road was the London Inn and the Ship Inn. Friday and Saturday nights were often very noisy at closing time and there were often fights and noisy scenes as some of the drunkards arrived home to be harangued by their irate wives.

Most of the haulage in my early days was by horse and cart. Mr Carpenter had stables in 'Rec. Lane' [now Carpenter's Lane] and a number of huge shire horses, as similarly had the Godfrey Brothers in Temple Street, where Mr Beck had his blacksmith shop. The smell of burning hooves often filled the air as he fitted hot shoes to all kinds of horses. He sometimes let us work the bellows and we were fascinated to see the glow of the embers increase with our labours.

Our doctor was Dr Charles Harrison who lived and held his surgery in a large Georgian house in the middle of the High Street. In my father's day he used to carry out his visits on a three wheeled trimobile, built in Keynsham. I don't know whether he ever received any payment for his services. I have a strong suspicion that both he and his son Dr Claude were probably the town's major philanthropists.

Dr Charles Harrison was a keen sportsman and related to the famous cricketer, Dr W G Grace. Reports of any pheasants or game spotted around the village would be conveyed to Dr Charles who would pick up my father who would stand, precariously balanced on the axle of the trimobile and carry the twelve-bore shot-gun while the Doctor drove, until the quarry was sighted, stalked and occasionally bagged for dinner.

Diphtheria and Scarlet Fever were major illnesses with children in those days and patients were taken to the Isolation Hospital off Park Road in a horse-drawn coach. Entire families were often victims of TB and Typhoid. Outbreaks were common and a source of great concern in respect of water contamination.

My father was goalkeeper for the Town's football team and they used to walk very considerable distances to their away matches. The match with Radstock would always finish up with a running battle with the miners as the team left for home if they had won.

My interest in fishing started when my father worked an allotment at the Mead alongside the River Chew. The entrance to White's Mead, as the area was always called, was down the path beside Zion Chapel at the top of Dapps Hill. The allotments were on the left, and covered the whole area down to Bath Hill Bridge, and were used until 1946. Father would set up his rod with a bit of cheese or bread paste on the hook and leave me to watch the float whilst he dug the potatoes or cut the vegetables.

We often fished at daybreak and often landed some wonderful bags of roach. In later years my cousin Brian and my brother-in-law Ernest Wiltshire often fished at the Logwood Mill, the Park and at the Red Mill, and many large trout fell victims to their lures.

The Red Mill at Bath Hill used to produce a red dye and we spent many happy hours with Albert Parsons who occupied the cottage alongside the river. Monster eels used to migrate down the river at certain times of the year and rest in the mill pool where Albert would help us land them.

The huge iron mill wheel used to drive a series of cogs and grinders which would reduce rocks to fine powder. Albert managed the mill sluices. The water-level at the mead would drop very considerably, revealing all kinds of rubbish, bicycle frames, perambulators and even a horse-drawn cart complete with shafts. At times of flood Albert would liaise with his opposite number at the Logwood Mill at Dapps Hill and they would open the hatches to prevent undue flooding in the mead and mill grounds.

My school days from the age of eleven were spent in Bristol. There was a half day on Wednesdays which should have been spent indulging in sporting activities or detentions if one had been naughty, which I invariably was. Somehow I would cut these and find my way to Keynsham on the bus for six pence return and as often as not find my way to the river with my fishing rod.

Finally, another event that Father told us as children was connected with Mr Wansborough. He used to drive through Keynsham from Bath looking very smart in his top hat as he sat in his gig, drawn by two trotters. He was on his way to Bristol, where I think he founded the firm of solicitors bearing his name.

Chapter 23

The Harveys of Keynsham

On June 12 1954, Ronald Headington married Miss Pamela Faith Harvey, and thereby is able to supply details of the Harvey family.

The Harvey family's association with Keynsham goes back several generations. Pamela's great grandfather William Harvey was a carpenter and decorator by trade, and as a church warden, was an active member of St John's Church. There he collected fees for funeral services, paid out parish relief and even tolled 'the nell'.

Given his trade and there being no undertaker in the town, he made coffins. He also kept a long thin book, his Register of Burials, dating from May 9 1830 to May 26 1850. Obviously he was a very capable and literate man in the early nineteenth century when many were neither literate nor numerate. An extract from his Register is shown.

Due to the confusion caused over the generations by the presence in a small town of so many branches of the Harvey family, a simple but effective way of distinguishing between the branches was to prefix the surname with the name of a colour, such as 'Green Harvey' as in Pamela's family. A copy of Letters of Administration granted in February 1896 show the estate of Emma Bruce of West View, valued at £155, being executed by 'her lawful nephew Joseph Green Harvey'. This was Pamela's grandfather.

Another branch was the Grey Harveys. Yet the name 'Green' was not passed on to daughters, as they were likely to marry. And in reality, the old practice ceased with Joseph Green Harvey's generation.

Locally there are a number of lovely old photos of the Harvey's ancient shop in Station Road where papers were sold. Photostatted is a copy of their first order of the Bristol Evening News from the Baldwin Street Office. Ronald has written under it, 'First News Bill paid by Mr Joseph Green Harvey at his house, 7 Station Road, Keynsham. He opened his kitchen for the sale of Newspapers etc. October 1889. The present premises were opened as a shop and living accommodation in 1939, when the front wall was rebuilt and the original cottage turned into a bungalow. The old building is all that remains of Keynsham Abbey Farm House.'

To elaborate on that, Ronald pointed out that by 1939 one had to go down three stairs to the kitchen, with its bedroom above, as the road had become so high, as at the Cannock's old home. So a false ground floor was inserted part way up, and the two low rooms became one lofty room with the lower part of the roof being lifted, and the former upstair windows made longer. The original front wall was altered but the outline of the building was unchanged.

The main house at the side of it originally had a joining door, with a lovely walled garden at the rear.

Joseph G Harvey, with his fine mutton-chop side-whiskers based on a certain Duke, married Sarah Faith Flowers from Timsbury. She was descended from the earlier influential Flower family of Saltford Manor, which doubtless led her to bestow upon her 15 children high-sounding fancy names. One, Clarence Flower Harry was nicknamed, 'The Duke'. Another, Gilbert Seymour Thomas, became the father of Pamela Faith Harvey.

Joseph was a fine man, who was still delivering a few newspapers in his 80s. He died in 1938, in his 90s.

Ronald mentioned to me that, 'the railway was the making of them. The crowds that used to catch the morning trains to Bristol would pause to buy a

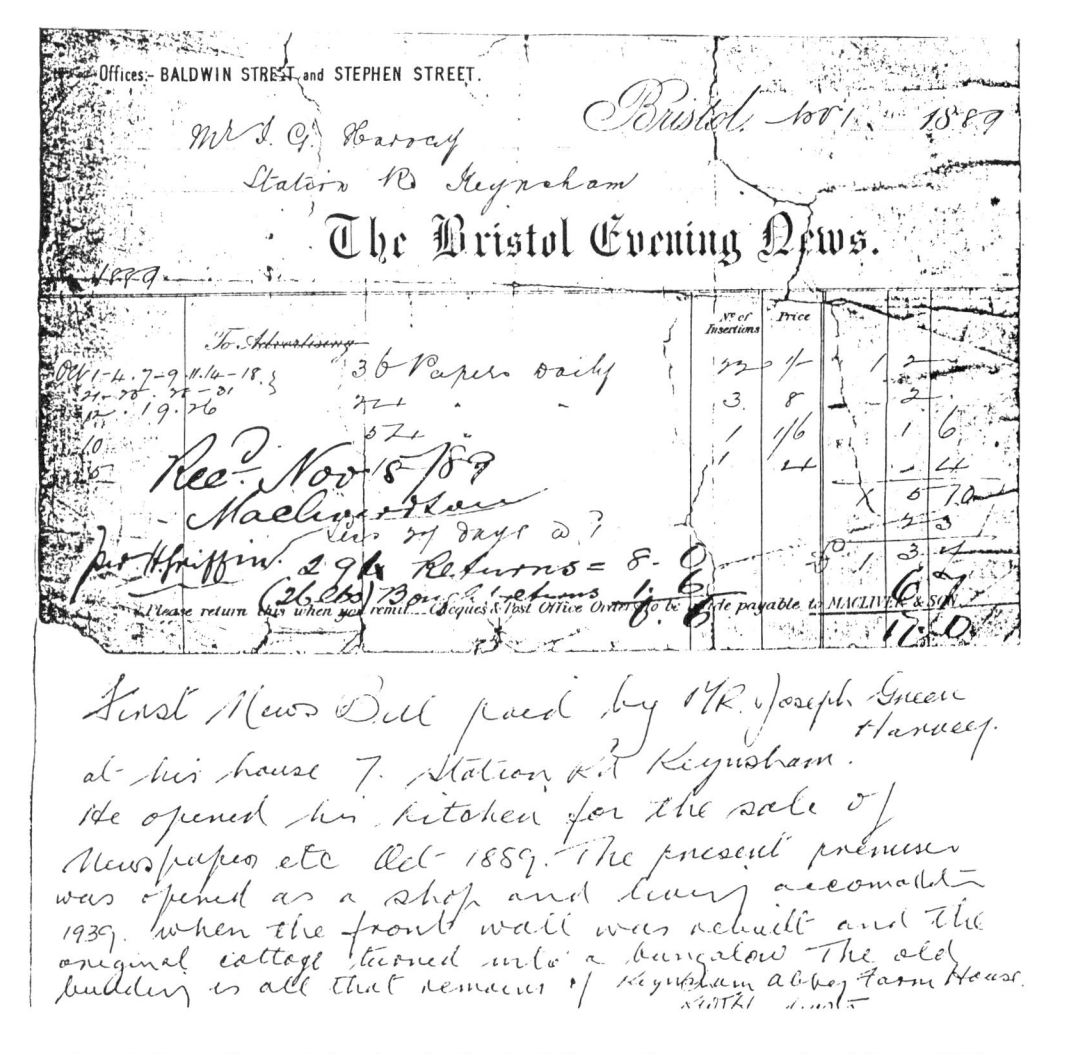

Joseph Green Harvey's first invoice for the delivery of newspapers, dated Nov 1 1889. For the 'Return' of unsold papers, he was allowed an initial 8/-.

The District Registry at Bristol

In Her Majesty's High Court of Justice.

BE IT KNOWN, that at the date hereunder written, Letters of Administration of the personal estate of Emma Bruce of West View in the Parish of Keynsham in the County of Somerset deceased, who died on the sixteenth day of January 1896, at West View Keynsham aforesaid a Widow without Child or Parent Brother or Sister ———————— intestate, and had at the time of her death a fixed place of abode at West View Keynsham aforesaid within the District of the Bristol and Bath present County Court Districts

were granted by Her Majesty's High Court of Justice at the District Probate Registry thereof at Bristol to Joseph Green Harvey the lawful Nephew and one of the next of kin of the said intestate, he having been first sworn well and faithfully to administer the same.

And it is hereby certified that an Affidavit for Inland Revenue has been delivered, wherein it is shewn that the gross value of the personal estate of the said deceased within the United Kingdom (exclusive of what the said deceased may have been possessed of or entitled to as a Trustee and not beneficially) amounts to £155-0-0 and that the said Affidavit bears a Stamp of £1-10-0

Dated the Eleventh day of February 1896

W. Poole Clarke
District Registrar

Extracted by Clifton & Co Solicitors Bristol

Letters of Administration granted to Joseph Green Harvey in 1896 as executor of his late aunt's estate.

paper. The building of Frys in 1922 was a further great help. Also Mr Harvey had a tremendous paper-round.'

Pamela and Ronald took over the family business in mid 1960 and ran it until January 1980. 'We sold the paper-round to Ogborns and sold confectionary, tobacco and papers. Then after being a thriving business for 90 years, it was killed by yellow lines being painted on the road outside the shop and the wardens strictly enforcing them. What a shame!'

Mr Ronald Headington, a scion of the well-known Ollis family

'My mother, Mrs Headington, was born in 1886 as Louise Ollis, at Spring Cottage on Bath Hill, the daughter of William Charles Ollis, who was the brother of Fred John Ollis the baker. In addition to the bakery business, they had a dairy at the rear of the cottage and made cream and washed the milk churns in the "spring" water from their dipping well in their sloping garden. There they also grew and sold watercress, at the turn of the century,' Mr Headington recalled.

Alas the lovely old Spring Cottage, built on the level of the ford, is no more. It was a victim of the building of the latest bridge. However, as Ronald said, 'The lower part of Spring Cottage was Elizabethan, that is, the kitchen and the lower rooms. The house was built on two elevations. One level faced the road while the older part with its stone mullion windows, the river. When the packhorse bridge was widened to accommodate the toll gate traffic, in the time of my great grandmother, Mr Ollis refused to move, so the bridge was built through the upper bedrooms, while the ancient stone toilet and the coal house remained under the bridge, where years later I could hear the traffic overhead. There was no compulsory purchase then. In compensation the family were excused paying rates.'

Who were these entrepreneurial, firm-minded Ollises? What was their origin, where did they come from, and when and why? Their scion Ronald already carried their genes and most eloquently answered the questions in the following manner.

'After the dissolution of the monasteries, the presence of the mills and water at hand led to the desire to establish a brass industry in the district. The difficulty was the absence of the necessary know-how, so skilled workers from the continent, from Holland, were brought over around 1680. They settled locally and started building the mill at the Shallows, Saltford, in the 1700s, as well as the Keynsham Brass mill. Their names were anglicised. Vory became Fray, Steger became Seager, Hollis became Ollis and Frankom remained unchanged. The Ollis family all descended from the original Nickolas Hollis, according to my grandfather, Joseph Ollis.

'Obviously there was much local opposition to the coming of the foreigners, and the parish council refused to be responsible for the poor of the foreigners, so it was decided that, 'The brass workers were not to become a charge on the local community. They were to care for their own old and bury their paupers.' Accordingly the brass workers built their own steep pitched roofed houses, following their Continental practice, which homes were then passed down through, and kept in, the brass working families.'

Due to their skill and Teutonic capacity for hardwork, they and their brass industry prospered, and over the years they won the respect of their neighbours who latterly referred to them as 'the gentleman brass workers' who always wore top hats to work. As time went on they diversified their trades, but prospered through industry.

Ronald, referring to the paternal side of his family, said, 'My grandfather, John Headington, had a market garden at Dapps Hill and another along Charlton Park where he grew tomatoes and flowers in the greenhouses, which was rather lovely. Then around 1930 he sold it for building land.'

Building Stone

'The Keynsham mills and the land around them had originally belonged to the abbey. The land below Avon Road that stretches along to the railway line was called the sidelands. This consisted of excellent building stone, and was cut into quarry-steps to provide material for the local houses. That is why even today the slope is so steep in places. I can remember climbing the rocky hillside and Dragon's Hill Quarry, as a boy. The sidelands on the abbey side of the Chew was not quarried as it contained so many springs, hence the monks built their 'fishpond', and we had Spring Cottage.'

'At the rear of the Fox and Hounds Inn, beyond their garden, were the Ollis stables and sheds, for 'Ollis Carriers' and the bread rounds; and the orchard, where some of the trees are still there on the slope.'

[Bert Robe recalled that 'The stables were a long, single-storied, black-painted, corrugated iron building along the riverside opposite Spring Cottage, with access off the Bath Hill East side of the Chew Bridge. Adjoining it was an orchard and a field extending up the hillside to Avon Road. Mann's Lane formed one boundary of this field, and adjoined the entrance to the stables.']

The Bakeries Old and New

Spring Cottage, being a long building, housed both the Jarrett and Ollis families, being mill property. There Jarrett started his business as a baker. Later across the road, on more mill land, Wilcox built him a new house and a separate bakery, in which he used modern steam heated ovens. Today it is a sign writer's.

When the Jarrett's vacated their part of Spring Cottage, the Ollises took over the whole house. Later some people said they were not keen on steam baked bread, so Frederick thought he might try the old oven himself, which he did with great success. Ronald described the process like this.

'My uncle Frederick Ollis baked bread in an old type baking oven, which was heated by large bundles of faggots, which burned fiercely for twenty minutes in a domed topped oven. The oven bricks became very hot, and the ashes were raked out and the cinders removed with a wet mop making the oven clean, and providing steam. Bread was placed in the oven at the end of a long wooden shovel, which was then sharply withdrawn, and the wooden door

Photograph]   At Longreach, Keynsham   [*C. H. Rayn*

Keynsham around 1930. On the road to Bath. Sadly the elms have gone but the houses remain.

hotograph]   Keynsham from the Bristol Road   [*C. H. Ray*

The Crown nestles into the hillside behind the second lamp-post. The pasture opposite is now the rugby field, with the willows gone and the stream out of sight.

quickly shut. Later the business transferred to what is now Antonio's in the High Street.'

Miss Mary Fairclough has interesting memories of one of these bakers. She recalled that in 1904 when her newly married parents lived in what is today 16, Avon Road, [in those days the houses there only had names] they always had their bread from Mr Jarrett, who owned the land around his bakery, known as Jarrettt's yard, and the orchard toward what is now the car park. 'Mr Jarrett was a terrific character. He had five children, known locally as 'our Aby, our Clar, our Eileen, our Ivy and our Merve', the only son. Mervyn used to take a lump of dough up to Mother, who would add in fruit and spices, then return it to Jarrett's, who would bake it into a delicious fruit cake.

'Mr Jarrett would go alone in his horse and trap to Jolly's of Bristol, where he would buy hats for his wife and daughters, which they all dutifully wore! ... One daughter married the landlord of the Lamb and Lark Hotel, and another married Jack Titley of Abbotsford House, whose chicken farm covered what is now the Memorial Park at the rear of his home . . . Mr Jarrett senior died in the 1920s and Mervyn some ten years ago.

'The Rev Mann married mother's aunt, Elisabeth Thomas, and they lived in the tall narrow house that faced Avon Road and backed on to the steep sidelands, where it stood out. The narrow footpath that led up beside the house was known as Mann's Alley. To the Baptist congregation, the house was known as 'Mann's mansion in the sky'.'

Changing the subject and returning to Ronald's memories, he said that in connection with the early fire brigade around 1900, it was Joseph Ollis who had the contract to supply a horse with all haste when the alarm bell went off, and to take it to the engine and put it in the shafts ready to go. If necessary, he was to provide a second horse. The first fireman to arrive was to light the boiler to provide the steam power to drive the water in the hoses.

Crab's Castle

Ronald quoted his grandfather William Charles Ollis as saying of one of the group of three former cottages on Avon Road, on the sidelands, of which only one remains, 'It was a pub, an ale house' where I used to drink. . . . The Bolwells used to live there, and one day Mrs Bolwell walked down the narrow side path and drowned herself in the Chew'. It was not a pub in Ronald's time, but it was already one before the Bolwells lived there. His mother described it as 'a cider house, not spirits.'

As Ronald pointed out, it was ideally situated to cater for thirsty men finishing a day's work at the Red Mill in the park, or farm workers or railway workers on their way home. He thought it was named after a 'crabby' landlord there. Miss Fairclough thought the appellation was attributable to someone of the older generation, possibly Charles Abbot, the town clerk and last clerk of the works at the Brassmill.

[Bert again. 'The public house in Avon Road formed part of a group of lias limestone buildings comprising two cottages and the inn, and was approached by a flight of stone steps from Avon Road. At one time, the pub was known as 'The Elm Tree Inn', doubtless taking its name from an enormous elm tree

A photo of Mr Francis Fry of Rockhill House, Wellsway, the son of Mr J S Fry, Keynsham's largest employer, which he gave to Miss Louise Ollis when he and his wife finally left the town.

which grew within about 20 feet of the inn, which faced the River Chew overlooking the Red Mill. The tree must have become a hazard, for it was cut down one fine summer's morning in about 1919/20, falling accurately towards the river and away from the Inn which by this time was occupied as a dwelling by the senior Mr Bolwell.

'I saw the tree felled. The trunk must have been 4–5 feet in diameter. The small branches were removed by the fellers and burned, and the trunk and large branches cut in large sections. There they lay for many years on the valley side and became a favourite play spot for local children and known as "The Logs". Just below the logs, a horse drink had been formed in the river by building two high stone walls so that the animals could approach the river safely from the field. At this point, too, there was a deep deposit of river sand, quite different from the local lias limestone and this was used as an outsize sandpit by local children.']

According to W G Ollis, there was a very early Right of Way up the sidelands on to Avon Road, from a ford sited below Crab's Cottage, opposite the former bandstand in the park. On the town side of the river, the old Packhorse Way linked up with Back Lane.

On the Avon Road side of the river, Ronald recalls there was a walled approach to the ford, wide enough for a cart, where as a boy he used to swim in the 1920s. The Right of Way went through the side courtyard of Crab's Castle, which still retained the open gate into the 1920s. It linked up a little way down Avon Road with the ancient 'Gaston's Lane' that led along Stidham Lane through Saltford to Bath. 'It was a more direct route than going over Dapps Hill Bridge, up Steel Mills Lane and along Manor Road,' he said.

'However,' as Bert wrote, 'I doubt the existence of a path on the sidelands between the River Chew and Avon Road; the slope was too steep at this point and there were no surface signs of a path. "Elm Tree Inn" or "Crab's Castle" certainly had an opening in its boundary wall facing the river and this was likely to have been to enable the customer (brass mill workers?) to take a short cut across the fields to the Chew Bridge and their houses in Temple Street, through "The Labbott".

The walled section described was a horse/cattle drink as mentioned above. The mill buildings and the leat would have blocked any passage over a ford which would have led into the park lands. This was not a public park as it is now, but was occupied as a large poultry farm in the early decade of the 20th century by Mr Jack Tetley. All the cottages on the river side of Avon Road, as well as long sections of the road, had lias limestone retaining walls which would have prevented a direct access to Dragon's Lane leading to Gaston's Field. This lane was about 100 yards long from Avon Road to Gaston's which had no direct link with Stidham Lane except field paths to Bath Road and to Stidham Lane under the railway arch.'

Mr Francis Fry of Rockhill House

Francis Fry, the son of the well known J S Fry, Keynsham's largest employer, [now Cadbury's] lived at Rockhill House as a gentleman farmer, and his well-kept stables housed many fine horses, both hunters and chasers.

Mr Headington now introduces his story.

'My mother, Miss Louise Ollis, was keen on riding horses. Early this century, around 1905, when she was a teenager, she was allowed on a Sunday to take one of her father's horses from his stables for a ride. In those days you could ride up across Avon Mill Lane, and over fields to Bath Road, and then straight on to fields the other side on what is now Chandag Road Estate, then belonging to Mr Fry.

'One Sunday morning she went riding there on the horse her brother used for delivering bread, with an old torn saddle, and gaily jumped a low-looking hedge on what is now the estate. Unfortunately on the other side there was a long drop. Louisa just managed to stay in the saddle, and narrowly missed a couple riding beside the hedge, but previously out of sight because of the low ground.

'Who the devil are you and what on earth do you think you're doing? You've nearly killed us! And where did you get that broken down looking nag?' asked an angry cultured voice. 'I'm sorry sir. I'm Louise Ollis and I was just out for a ride.' 'Oh, you're one of those, are you?' he said as he calmed down. 'Well Louise Ollis, if you can ride like that on a battered old horse, and get it to jump a hedge like that and almost kill us in the process, you had better come up to my stables next Sunday, and my groom will fix you up with a real horse and then we will see what you can do, and I will be on hand to see what sort of mess you make of it.

'So next Sunday an anxious village lass presented herself to Rockhill House stables, where Mr and Mrs Fry kindly took her under their wing. They taught her how to ride correctly, and took her with them to run in many cross country races, where she did very well.' Later they left the district, and presented her with photos of each of them, which Ronald has still.

Fording the Chew

He said that according to his grandfather, not only had there been a ford over the Chew above the old stone Dapps Hill bridge that Queen Elizabeth I reputedly went over, but there was yet another one beside the Bath Hill bridge, on the opposite side to the Fox and Hounds. 'It was used until the coming of the turnpike roads. Flanders House and two old cottages had been on the level of the ford, and you had to go down twelve steps from the road to the cottages. When I was a boy the original run down to the ford was still there and you could still take a horse and cart down.'

Both the late Mrs G Newman and Mr W Sherer recall seeing horses backing carts down to the river from Bath Hill East, beside the bridge, on the old ford pathway, depositing cleared snow in the Chew. Surely here we have verbal evidence not only for the presence of a mediaeval ford for carts and cattle, but for a packhorse bridge beside it, possibly similar to that at Allerford, Somerset. We know that when the Bath Hill bridge, damaged by the great flood, was demolished for the present one, the pillars of a yet earlier bridge were discernible. Presumably the track from the bridge led up the steep footpath that passes the lovely old stone cottage of 31 Bath Hill, which Miss Fairclough thinks was wider before the new Bath Road was dug out.

In excavating the foundations of the Clocktower House on Bath Hill, in Jarrett's yard, the stone wall immediately in front of the Clocktower was over 12 feet deep, though the top has been removed and railings erected. This very high wall, comparable with that in Back Lane, goes straight down to the river, beside the old bridge, at quite a steep angle, and marks the other side of the very ancient ford.

The Weighbridge, at the top of Bath Hill West

The Keynsham Gas Company, formed in 1857, had a weighbridge built in connection with the sale of coke from the gas works. After the company went into voluntary liquidation in 1928, the Council took over the building, and leased out the franchise of collecting tolls. In the 1930s the building was removed for the construction of underground toilets, a not very successful venture and only short lived.

The enterprising Mr Frederick Ollis lived at 68, High Street, almost opposite the weighbridge, and paid the Council for the right to operate the weighbridge and retain the income raised. He had sixteen children, eight boys and eight girls, among whom was Grace Ollis.

She commented, 'We had the key opposite and would run across the road to unlock it. We weighed coal, corn and building stone. Ernie Combs from Corston used to bring stone over from his quarry to be weighed. Once, for fun, he locked my sister Norah in, and she had to keep banging until we released her.

This private footpath on Bath Hill East is believed to be part of the medieval packhorse lane, made narrower by the new road. (M Fitter)

'I am 79 now but I was too young to have been allowed to take money or to know how much they charged. There was no chair inside the weighbridge building, just a table with an account book on it. My elder brothers and sisters used to go over to take the tolls. We all had jobs to do. I was on the bread round. Most of the vehicles using the 'bridge' were horse-drawn. We children used to jump on it to try and make it move but it only shivered slightly. It was of course very central and could be used any time of the day.

'Visiting salesmen would come round there to sell their wares, like vet's potions and embrocation. There was quite a lot of bartering. I recall my mother saying, 'A man's gone down the ladies'' and he came up a moment later looking very embarrassed. I did not see any wood being weighed for the Logwood Mill.'

Mr Ron Headington mentioned that C C Stokes, the coal merchant, had his own weighbridge by the Keynsham railway goods yard.

'This little pig went to market; This little pig stayed at home . . .

Between the two great wars, Keynsham was still very much a busy market town, with spaces between some of the shops and houses, particularly so in Temple Street, where some were used for farming purposes. Here and in neighbouring side roads were houses with parcels of land of varying size, with sheds for horse and carts, and an occasional cow or sheep and even pigs. One well-known local man, now in his advanced eighties, recalled that in the 1920s he had a pig at the bottom of his garden. Some people kept Large Whites, others had Wessex Saddlebacks.

He recalled that Washington Harvey in Temple Street had 4–6 pigs, and Mrs Ford in Albert Road also kept pigs, long before all the spare land there was built on. Number 16 Wellsway had a pig in their lower garden. These random cases show that he was quite correct when he said that most people who had some spare land had a pig or two. It was their hobby and the pig was almost a family pet. 'It was quite a common sight to see a person driving his pig down Temple Street,' he added.

As a lad he had worked in the 1920s for Willoughby the grocer in Temple Street. There the firm did its own killing of pigs in their back yard. 'The pigs were killed cold, that its, unstunned. A chain was fixed to a rear leg and the beast was hoisted up on a windlass, and its throat quickly cut. When it had been bled, the carcass was taken down, moved away, and had straw placed between its legs and round the body. The straw was then burned, first on one side, then the other, to remove all the hard hair.' Cridland, next door to Willoughby, had its slaughter house a little further behind Temple Street. Veales, further along Temple Street, poleaxed its animals before killing them.

Ron Headington, born in 1915, moved from 17, Bath Hill, to 17, Bristol Road, and lived in Devon House, opposite St Dunstan's. He said, 'During the period of 1922–1925, mother used to take in young lambs or pigs, the runts or daks as we called them, to bottle feed them for the farmers. When they were strong enough, they would take them back. We had some huts at the back of the house in which to keep them.

'As you were the only person the lamb or pig had ever known to feed it, it took you for its mother and would follow you around. One morning, having fed the pig I did not shut the door properly. As I walked up Bristol Road for school, there was a commotion behind me and the sound of a pig squealing. Our pig had got out, and had run up the road to catch me. Unfortunately, in trying to run round or between the legs of Mr Devonish who kept the sweet shop opposite, it had knocked him down.'

Ron added that during World War II, many local people kept one or two pigs to implement their food ration, as they also kept chickens, and fed them on potato peelings and other scraps. When fully grown, the pigs would be sold to the government slaughterhouse, who would give them back a proportion of the beast in place of their meat ration. Some people with two pigs would quietly get the first pig killed by the local butcher and only then declare the second! For those registered as pig keepers, food was provided by the local authorities in round metal tins containing food waste from hotels or other households. 'Waste not, want not' was the maxim in those dark days of food rationing.

The few apple trees at the side of Fox and Hounds Lane are part of the Ollis' orchard, where in the 1920s they had sheds for their horse and carts, for hay, and a yard for their pigs. On the other side of the Chew River was their home and the family bakery. Grace Ollis, who lived there, recalled how they had their own boat linked by a chain round a tree on either side of the river, so that food for the pigs could be pulled across the river by boat without having to go onto the road.

It was Grace's responsibility after school to cut hay for the animals. Later, she would follow her father in his horse and cart with two baskets of extra bread carefully balanced on either side of the handle bars of her ten shilling bicycle. She would deliver in Keynsham from Courtenay Road to Durley Hill and even up to Stockwood, sometimes returning home in the winter with frozen hair and eyebrows. When her father Frederick Ollis retired, she took over from him and used to drive his pony Jerry and the cart and do the bread round in the villages.

One winter the Chew was frozen over, and at Spring Cottage, her elder brother Ted with his friend Bert Taylor threw heavy stones on the ice without cracking it. Then, to his sister's consternation, they finished up by both walking across the frozen river. Grace added that in the summer she, with some of her brothers or sisters, would walk across the nearby Chew weir in their bare feet.

Mr William Sherer recalls that his father, who was a wholesale and retail butcher in Bedminster, kept a large herd of a hundred pigs on their land in Courtenay Road before World War I, when an outbreak of swine fever killed many, which were buried in a deep hole on their land. Between the wars, they had 60–70 pigs, being Large Whites, Wessex Saddlebacks and his father's favourites, Middle Whites. His father used to carry pigs in his horse and cart to his Bedminster shop.

Later he took his pigs to Fisher's, at the top of Bath Hill, with its slaughterhouse in Temple Street. On one occasion his father bought some lambs at Faringdon Gurney, which he took to Fisher's to be killed. Unfortunately, one lamb escaped and ran across the top of Bath Hill, and seeing a reflection of itself in a shop window where Nix's now is, jumped through the window. 'That cost father a bit,' William remembered.

In the 1920s as Fisher only slaughtered pigs and sheep, and before cattle vans became common, Mr Sherer, with his son and a helper, would drive some seven or eight cattle from Courtenay Road through Keynsham to Bedminster. 'It was a long walk', the son remembered, though he said, 'Professional drovers would drive cattle from Faringdon Gurney to Bath, or through Keynsham to Bristol. Before my time they even drove cattle from Bridgwater to Bristol market. But of course, it was quite common every Monday to see cattle being driven down Wellsway for Keynsham's own cattle market even after World War II. But by then we only had about 20 pigs.'

He recalled that during World War II, farm workers in Keynsham with the land had pigs in their sties or orchards, though already there were restrictions as to where they could be kept in relation to human habitation.

He said that up to 1939, it was still a common sight to see sheep and cattle being driven through Keynsham. Mr Fowler, whose farmstead was at the top of Dapps Hill, kept his cows in the Manor Road sports field, and twice a day used to drive them down Wellsway, and up through Dapps Hill to be milked.

Chapter 24

The arrival of the internal combustion engine

There have been many significant turning points in the history of Keynsham. The local men of the Dobunni tribe may have looked with scorn and possible jealousy when, possibly around the third century A.D., the Romans started to build a stone village on the Hams. Dr Robin Harley believes in the existence of such a village. The uncovering of a playing field at Cadbury's, which appears to reveal 'Roman Keynsham', would seem to confirm his belief. The construction of part or the whole of a Roman settlement was a turning point in the 2,000 years of the unbroken history of Keynsham.

The advent of conquering Saxons, and then the Danes, were momentous events. The building of the local Abbey, the arrival of the monks and the spread of their land, was a further major turning point in the town's history, as was the later demise of the Abbey. 'Begun Diggin the Rail Road June 11, 1836' and the building of the GWR was yet another major event of immediate importance. Succeeding the romantic age of horse-drawn coaches, toll roads and highwaymen, was the new age of steam. The existence of the Pioneer and the Railway Tavern testify to the impact of yet another turning point.

If the building of the railway changed the face of Keynsham, how much more has the arrival of the internal combustion engine, fitted in cars, buses, lorries, tractors and motor cycles. The emergence of small garages, then large car parks, wider roads and an even bigger bypass, has been the result. The age of the car would seem to have been the greatest turning point in changing the face and history of Keynsham.

One does not wish to stand in the way of undoubted progress, though it is not all gain and a high price has already been paid to accommodate the car. But the historical question to be asked is how did this all come about? As with the proverbial oak tree, it started like the acorn in a small unobtrusive way.

By the turn of the century, early trams and buses were in operation. From 1906 buses ran from Brislington through Keynsham to Saltford and on to the Globe Public House. On the Bath Road outside Keynsham, beyond Ellsbridge House and on the same side, was the Avon Motor Manufacturing Company, now the site of the Shell garage. It would appear that this firm is to be credited with the building of the three-wheeler Trimobile at the turn of this century. Dr Charles Harrison certainly owned one, according to Mr Monty Veale.

Mr Edward Cannock said that a photo of one used to stand outside the walls of the Crown, Saltford, which in March 1981 Mr John Norris copied, and reproduced as the focal point in his large painting. It was commissioned by the Post Office, and was some two feet by three feet. It was the third in a series of four that he painted to commemorate the Royal Mail Carriers from

TELEGRAPHIC ADDRESS:—
AVON MOTOR. SALTFORD, BRISTOL.
WORKS TELEPHONE Nº 21Y. KEYNSHAM.

Cars driven by any of our Staff at Customers' own risk solely
Bristol Representative — S. WORTHINGTON, TOWER HILL.

The Avon Motor Manufacturing Co.

ALL COMMUNICATIONS TO
. Works.
KEYNSHAM.

Bristol, 1st September 1910

Proprietor: GEO HENSHAW, C.E.

The AVON LIGHT CAR

1, 2 and 4 Cylinders
also LIGHT
DELIVERY VANS,
to carry up to
10 Cwt.
MANUFACTURERS
of the AVON
Motors
from 2 H.P. to 30 H.P.
mechanically
operated
valves.
for MOTOR-CARS,
RIVER BOATS,
LAUNCHES
and FARM WORK.
Gear Cutting
a Speciality.
REPAIRS OF EVERY
DESCRIPTION.
ACCUMULATORS
RE-CHARGED
& PETROL
SUPPLIED.
Motor Accessories
of every description.

Miss Cox,
 Home Downs Lodge,
  Ashchurch, Nr. Tewkesbury.

Dear Madam,
 We have made an examination of your Trimo and beg to quote you two alternative prices. We are afraid it is a more expensive job than was anticipated, but should you decide to have same done we think we shall be able to meet you as regards payment.

To making a sound job, putting in a new piston, new clutch flywheel, new pin in clutch fork and new leather, new gear box cover top, new sliding gear, sleeve pinion & bushes, bearings adjusted, new lugs and brakes relined in back axle, and a new silencer, re-assembling all above, the price would be £16.10.0.

OR

Patching cylinder, new bearings, new spindles, rebushing crank case, new throw pin, fitting contact, doing up the clutch, new flywheel, new arms and new leather, patching up gear box, new sliding gear, sleeve pinion, rebushing bearing relining brakes and keys fitted to back axle, repairing present silencer, the price would be £10.10.0.

to painting car green and lining in stripes £3.0.0.
to fitting one fixed door and one opening door 27/6d.

Should you entrust us with this work we would accept £5 on delivery of the car and the balance in easy equal instalments.
 Yours faithfully,
  The Avon Motor Manufacturing Co.
   Manager.

The priceless letter of Mr E Cannock that ties up Miss Cox's possession of a Trimobile with its construction at the Avon Motor Manufacturing Company, Bath Road, Keynsham, cira 1905.

Bristol. The other three were of the SS Great Britain, the Royal Mail Stage Coach and lastly the Concorde. Mr Cannock, representing Keynsham and the motor trade, was present at the special meeting in Bristol when the four paintings were formally handed over by Mr Norris to the GPO. He later presented a copy of the third one to Mr Cannock. The caption with it reads, 'The Avon Mercury Trimobile, built in Keynsham, leaves Small Street Post Office loaded with mail circa 1905.' It had pneumatic tyres, front suspension and sprung forks. Three cycle-looking cross-bars joined the front wheel to the back axle. Mr Cannock suggests that as each machine was handmade, they could all be slightly different. He hesitated to suggest the engine horse power, but added that the Trimo is understood to be the first vehicle used by the GPO with an internal combustion engine.

In 1906 motoring in the West Country was still in its infancy. Former modes of transport were still being advertised. The Kelly's Directory of Somerset 1906, contains the following notice. 'F Symes and Co. Carriage builders, wheelrights . . . wagonettes, phaetons, dog carts, rustic and business carts, vans, and every description of vehicle built to order on improved principles. Repairs and painting neatly and expeditiously executed. Back of St Mary's Church, Canon Street, Taunton'.

The same directory lists, for the whole of Somerset, just five 'motor agents', one being the Bath Motor Company. There were four 'motor engineers', three 'motor garages' and one 'Motor body builders', Fuller S and A, Kingsmead Street, Bath. Likewise, for the whole of Somerset, there were but four 'motor manufacturers', The Bridgwater Motor Company Ltd.; Hawkins, Walter, at Burnham; Richardson, John, of Wellington and Milverton, and lastly, 'The Avon Motor Manufacturing Company Ltd, Bath Road, Keynsham, Office Bristol.' That was 1906.

We have a copy of the priceless letter of Mr Cannock, dated 1 Sept 1910, which links the production of the Trimobile with Keynsham. In the reply of the Avon Motor Company to his great aunt, Miss Cox, they wrote, 'We have made an examination of your Trimo and beg to quote you two alternative prices. We are afraid it is a more expensive job than we anticipated . . .' That phrase has a horribly modern ring to it! The interesting thing is that this letter is not to a local Keynsham doctor, but to a lady living in Ashchurch near Tewskbury, some sixty miles away. Trimos being so rare, apparently she had come all the way to Keynsham to make her purchase.

Mr Edward Cannock, writing in the Keynsham Chronicle of March 10 1989, stated that, 'The Trimobile was a two seater, driven by a single cylinder water cooled engine. Ignition was by a low tension system which proved rather unreliable, as did the leather faced clutch. I believe the fuel consumption averaged 28 miles-per-gallon. The Trimo was employed as a postal delivery van, the first use of an internal combustion engine by the GPO. The proprietor was a friend of Mr Joe Barter, designer of the first Douglas motor cycle. A Mr Worthington represented the company from premises in Tower Hill, Bristol'.

The proprietor of the Avon Motor Company was Mr George Henshaw, a chartered engineer, who lived in a bungalow at the bottom of Saltford Hill. His manager was Mr A North. Not only did they produce The Avon Light

John Norris's picture carries the caption on its back 'The Avon Mercury Trimobile, built in Keynsham, leaves Small Street Post Office loaded with mail circa 1905.' His Corgi mark is far left, beside man in black.

In the ruins of the Old Saltford Steel Mills, by the Shallows, is the date stone for the construction of the Great Western Railway. It records, 'Begun Diggin The Rail Road, June 11, 1836.' (Author's photo.)

Car, but engines from 2–30 horse power. Possibly the Trimo was ten horse power. Another interesting item in their list of merchandise on offer was 'petrol supplied'. As Mr W Sherer commented, there were no petrol pumps in those days! He recalled hearing of an enterprising man and wife sitting either side of the Bristol–Weston road, with cans of petrol for sale.

Mr Raymond Parsons, born in 1897 and whose father had a baking business at the top of Bath Hill, in 1980 wrote in a letter to Edward Cannock, 'I remember Henshaw well, as my father arranged for me to become an engineer there when I left school, Redcliffe Boys, but I did not wish to take the job, and eventually I ran away and got a job with a cinema outfit, and the Police Sergeant's son also got out of it, and eventually went to Australia. His name was Eddie Salmon . . . Your dad always used to tune my Morgan three wheeler and we had great fun racing it in events on Brean Sands and similar places. Sometimes your dad would drive, being a great enthusiast.'

Mr B Robe wrote, 'I note that the owner of the Avon Motor Manufacturing Company was George Henshaw. He must have left the Bath Road works shortly after the letter dated 1 September 1910, because by 1914 the premises were occupied by the Tangent Tool Engineering Company owned by Eric Montague-Smith who lived at 'Sunnymead', Avon Road, now a nursing home. Henshaw may have been connected with the engineering company, Strachan Henshaw in St George, Bristol. The son of Mr Joe Barter mentioned by Edward Cannock was a young engineer on the management staff of the Tangent Works and made me a model steam engine and steam boat when I was a boy in the early 1920s.'

Mr Edward Arthur Cannock, 1896–1963

Kindly, his son Edward provided me with a photostat copy of the arrival in Keynsham of his father, Edward Arthur Cannock, in 1910 at the tender age of fourteen. He was driving his aunt, the same Miss Cox, in presumably the same Trimobile referred to above. His driving at that age was quite legitimate as a Trimobile was rated as a motor cycle.

Edward said that his grandfather came from the Forest of Dean, and that earlier his father had lived in Bristol and had been trained in engineering. Father returned to Keynsham when he was eighteen in 1914 and stayed with his aunt, Miss Cox, in her picturesque house, 'Homeleigh' at 36 Bristol Road. At the outbreak of war, he volunteered for the army as a despatch rider, but was turned down as 'unfit'. Consequently he worked in Bristol, possibly as an apprentice, for Brazil Straker, who had made the Straker car, and was then making more than fifty staff cars and four-ton lorries a month, and commenced the construction of the Aero engine under the guidance of A H 'Roy' Fedden.

During the war the firm employed over 2,000 people, but in 1918 it contracted, and E A Cannock, then eighteen, seized the opportunity to set up on his own at his aunt's house. Originally there was a stable attached to the house, which he used as his workshop. Soon after that, he was joined by Percy G Hawley as his mechanic, who stayed with him the whole of his working life. In 1922 Mr Cannock married Miss Elsie Dorothy Taylor, whose father

Mr E A Cannock as a lad of 14 in 1910, driving his aunt's Keynsham-built Trimobile, outside a pair of fine gates in Brislington on an earth road.

This lovely old photo brings a touch of nostalgia for rural Keynsham around 1910. The scene is of Miss Cox outside her front door at 'Homeleigh', 36 Bristol Road, facing the road. The photo is thought to have been taken by her nephew E A Cannock. Even at that time, the garden sloped up towards the road. His son Edward thinks that the three bedroomed house is about 400 years old, and so probably built in the days of the last Stuart monarch, Queen Anne.

was the time keeper at the Avon Brass Works. Perhaps she was the attraction that brought him to Keynsham? Three children were born to them, Edward 1923, Betty 1924 – now Mrs Kenneth R Baber of Queen Charlton, and David in 1933.

Miss Cox died at Homeleigh around 1925, but the Cannock family lived there until around 1933. Edward enjoyed living there and described the old house as 'being in good order and cosy with coal fires. There were three bedrooms, and a passage which stretched from the front of the house to the back, which divided the house into two sections. We used to play in the fields at the back, and occasionally the stone-flagged floors would get flooded. That does not happen now. We have deeds going back to 1748 but it has been dated as built around 1700, according to the style of the drip stones and the main beam. It was never a farm house. Keynsham was a small community when we lived there, and I was interested in the activity of the motoring business'.

The Tangent Tool Works

Edward was of the opinion that the Avon Motor Company closed around 1914. Possibly so many of his men were conscripted that he could not carry on building cars. However, Mr Ron Headington remembered that in 1914–18 the firm made parts required for the war, as his mother had worked there on a lathe.

Around 1920 we find the premises being used by the Tangent Tool Works. Mr W Sherer recalled the building, as his father kept sheep in the field opposite it. He described it as a large rectangular brick building. There was a shop window as the business was wholesale. He thought that later ATCO took over the business and both built and serviced their lawn mowers there. Edward referred to it as 'The Keynsham lawn mower, by all accounts a classy machine'.

'The Tangent Tool Works designed and manufactured 'The Keynsham Motor Mower' and 'The Keynsham Motor Roller', putting them on the market about 1921/22', wrote Mr Robe. 'They were a good product but the trade recession defeated them and the Company was forced to close down. To my knowledge, they were never linked to ATCO.'

'I worked for the Tangent Tool Company when I left school at fourteen in 1928', said Mr Jim Ollis. 'It was owned by Montgomery Smith of Bath, and we made motor mowers, motor rollers for the Council, and did general engineering. Joe Barter was the designer and Mr Robe the foreman. Joe Barter was a great friend of Bill Douglas, so that later Douglas's took over the design of our engines. There were about 25–30 men employed there. One man came from Hotwells, five from Bath, which included a man in the paint shop, two from Cadbury Heath, and two or three from Kingswood. Most of these came on bicycles: The other men came from Keynsham, such as Percy Phelps. In the office was the secretary, Miss Davies.

'The factory stood about thirty yards back from the road, and inside the large gates was the brick round house for worn castings/bearings. Behind that was the main factory, an old building of galvanised iron, with girder roofing. It contained the large machinery area and a blacksmith's department. To

Deposited Plan No 852

Keynsham Rural District Council.

July 20th 1926

APPROVAL OF PLANS.

Sirs,

I beg to inform you that the Plans deposited by you for the erection of a Petrol Installation in Bristol Road, Keynsham for Mr E U Cannock were laid before my Council on the twentieth day of July 1926, and approved, ~~subject to~~ for a temporary period of three years and thereafter at the option of the Council.

Yours faithfully,

H.W.Argyle
Building Surveyor.

To The Anglo American Oil Co Ltd
Baldwin Street
Bristol

NOTICE—Any deviation from the deposited Plans must be notified to the Building Surveyor before the work is proceeded with.

24 hours' notice to the Surveyor must be given before the work is commenced, and before any foundation, damp course or drain is covered up, and 7 days' notice of its completion before any building is occupied.

Mr E Cannock's letter of his father's, giving the Council's permission for him to erect one petrol pump, for a temporary period of three years.

HAWKINS BROS.,
Builders, Contractors, Plumbers, and Decorators.
45, BRISTOL ROAD, KEYNSHAM,
Nr. BRISTOL

PLANS AND ESTIMATES ON APPLICATION

MORTGAGES ARRANGED.

July 24th 1936

Mr E A Cannock

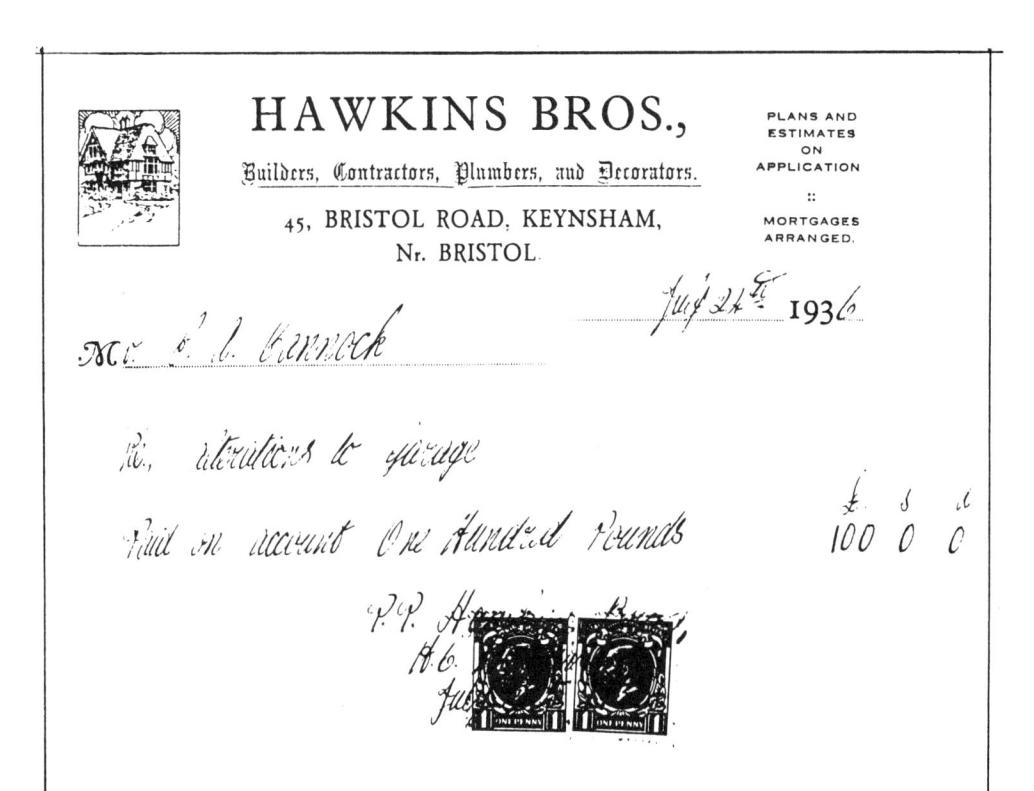

Re. alterations to garage

Paid on account One Hundred Pounds — £100 0 0

The Hawkins Brother's invoice for alterations to Mr E A Cannock's garage in Bristol Road, in July 24 1936. It is the property of Mr E Cannock.

Circa 1930, some employees of the Tangent Tool Company meet together for a firm's outing, outside the Lamb and Lark Hotel. The starting point for many work's outings, it is still remembered with affection. The late Mrs G Newman wrote that on the photo was Mr E A Cannock and Mr Hacker who drove the first of the new Royal Mail vans to Temple Mead.

the left of it, towards the nursery, was the separate newly-built brick fitting-department. The main factory had overhead shafting, which meant that all the machinery was driven from one main engine, which had a great fly wheel with spokes. To start the machinery the spokes had to be pulled down to get the fly wheel moving, which was a difficult job to do early in the morning on a cold frosty day.

'Before my time the firm made the early 'Fairy Motor Cycle'. I don't know if they made any other motor bikes.

'They made a simple factory vehicle, the Keynsham Truck, with wheels of some 12–14 inch diameter with solid tyres. It had one wheel at the front and two behind, and a large motor-bike saddle. Above the wheels was simply a flat metal base without sides. There was no hood or anything like that. It had a 5 horse power JAP side-valve engine. We obtained these engines from a firm in Tottenham, London, and we also used them in our mowers. I actually drove a truck to the Jackson's iron foundry at Kingswood to collect the castings and came back under the Avon Mill bridge. The truck was green and only went slowly. A few other Bristol firms used our Keynsham Trucks, though really these were only a side line for us. Lister's had similar trucks to us. Tangent did not build any other types of trucks or vans.

'My main job was on the lathes. The men would set these up for me to operate. I worked on the capstan lathe, the milling machine with its steel cutters and on the grinding machine. We made all our own products apart from the engines.

'I was there until the firm closed in 1932. Possibly it went into liquidation due to the national Depression. The building lay empty for a long while till a Mr H E Brecknell from Bristol took the business over later in 1932, but that failed as well. I think I'm the last of the Tangent men alive.'

During those years, changes were taking place in the High Street. The Picture House, started in 1904 and so very popular, closed in 1918 and by 1919 Mr Bede had a garage there. Later, in 1926, Bailey and Mattick took over the premises and started the St Keyna Motor Works.

Digressing slightly, Mr R Parsons, in his letter mentioned earlier, also wrote, 'Did you ever hear about the cinema in Keynsham opposite Dr Harrison's house? It was opened by a cycle repairer, and for a short while I was the second operator, when machines were turned by hand.'

The motoring businesses listed in the 1927 edition of Kelly's Directory are 'Cannock, E A, motor garage, 26 Bristol Road; Keynsham Motor Company, motor engineers, Bristol Road; St Keyna Motor Works, motor engineers, 49 High Street; Hancock, Ernest H. motor engineer, Bath Road.' It recorded further that 'Motor omnibuses from Bristol Centre to Saltford and Bitton pass through the town at frequent intervals.'

The 1939 Kelly's Directory, in addition to mentioning some of the above businesses, refers in effect to the disused former Tangent Tool Company building. 'Grove Garage, (W H Hedges & A R Sanders, proprietors) motor engineers, Bath Road, Longreach.' Also listed, and presumably sharing part of the large premises, was, 'Somerdale Motor Company (Roland Heal, proprietor) motor engineer, Bath Road, Longreach.'

But Mr Robe qualified the above paragraph, writing that, 'The Grove Gar-

The lovely photo of 'Homeleigh' around 1934, the home of the Cannock brothers. The apple tree on the left was a Kentish Pippin, and both trees had a circle of earth around them on a concrete forecourt. Behind them are the oil cabinets. An earth path led down to the house. On the left is the Dutch barn, built around 1932. There was a small lawn at the back.

The unusual sight of a tank in St Ladoc Road towards the end of 1939–45 war. It was in town to help raise money in the annual War Weapon's Week. Both photos belong to Mr E Cannock.

age was not in the former Tangent Tool Company buildings; it was where the 'Elf' filling station now is. The Somerdale Motor Company was on the Tangent site, later Henly's and now Shell petrol.'

Expansion

If the Avon Motor Company was the first firm in Keynsham to be engaged in the motor trade, Mr E A Cannock was the second. His son Edward now takes up the story. 'The business started in 1919 at 'Homeleigh', 36 Bristol Road, from a former stable converted into a workshop. Car and motor-bike repairs were carried out. As a trained machinist EAC set up drilling machines etc to make spare parts. There was a great variety of cars often made by small manufacturers who had ceased business, hence there were no factory 'spares' available.

A hiring business was also in being, a large Napier car being used for several years. Petrol was supplied initially in two-gallon cans, though later through hand operated pumps. Second-hand cars and motorcycles were sold in small numbers and the occasional lorry and van.

About 1928 the Morris Agency was taken up and new cars sold. By 1932 the hand-operated petrol pumps were replaced by four electric pumps, and are believed to have been the first installed between Bristol and Bath. The Wayne Pumps were continued in use until after World War Two. In 1937/38 the main workshop was extended to the rear and a facia and small showroom built. Mr Cannock felt that the facia should be long-lasting, hence the name was cast in reconstituted Bath stone. It still exists behind a later addition.

A between-the-wars customer with an Austin 7 was Miss Lucy Webber, who was the operator at the original Keynsham Telephone Exchange in Rock Road.

[Another early customer was Mr B Robe himself. Recalling the occasion, he wrote, 'In 1938 I had eyes on a new blue Morris 8 in the small showroom of Mr Eddie Cannock Senior, and towards the end of the year, returned to buy it. Mr Cannock took me for a trial drive up the Wellsway and agreed to let me have it for £114 because it was showroom soiled. The full price was, I believe, £122. It was EYA 286 and had a wonderful smell of new leather'.]

Around 1937 a lay-by was built opposite the 'Rest a while' café in Bristol Road to be used by steam waggons to take on water from the brook running between the soccer ground and the school playing fields. There were two makes of steam waggons prominent, 'Foden' and 'Sentinel'. The latter, I believe, were favoured by Fry's.

In 1937/38 the Keynsham Bypass was first mooted. Mr Cannock for business reasons, with other residents, particularly those in Station Road whose homes were to be demolished, opposed the plan. The imminence of, and then the outbreak of war, shelved all plans for many years.

During the 1939–46 period, the motor business continued. Petrol was rationed. Brands were discontinued in favour of one blend, namely 'Pool'. The illuminated globes topping the pumps were painted black. The ability to use the electric pumps by hand became important during power failures. Maintenance work was done for the new KUDC vehicles in use. An element of 'make do and mend' became necessary as the war depleted resources. Doctors' cars, ambulances and other vehicles on essential works had to be kept in operation.

A section of the premises was sandbagged and used to house the garage breakdown waggon, an Austin 20 with a crane, which was nominated the ARP 'Heavy Rescue Vehicle'. The crew was often on duty, their kit being kept in the old house. Until recently the names of the members were inscribed above

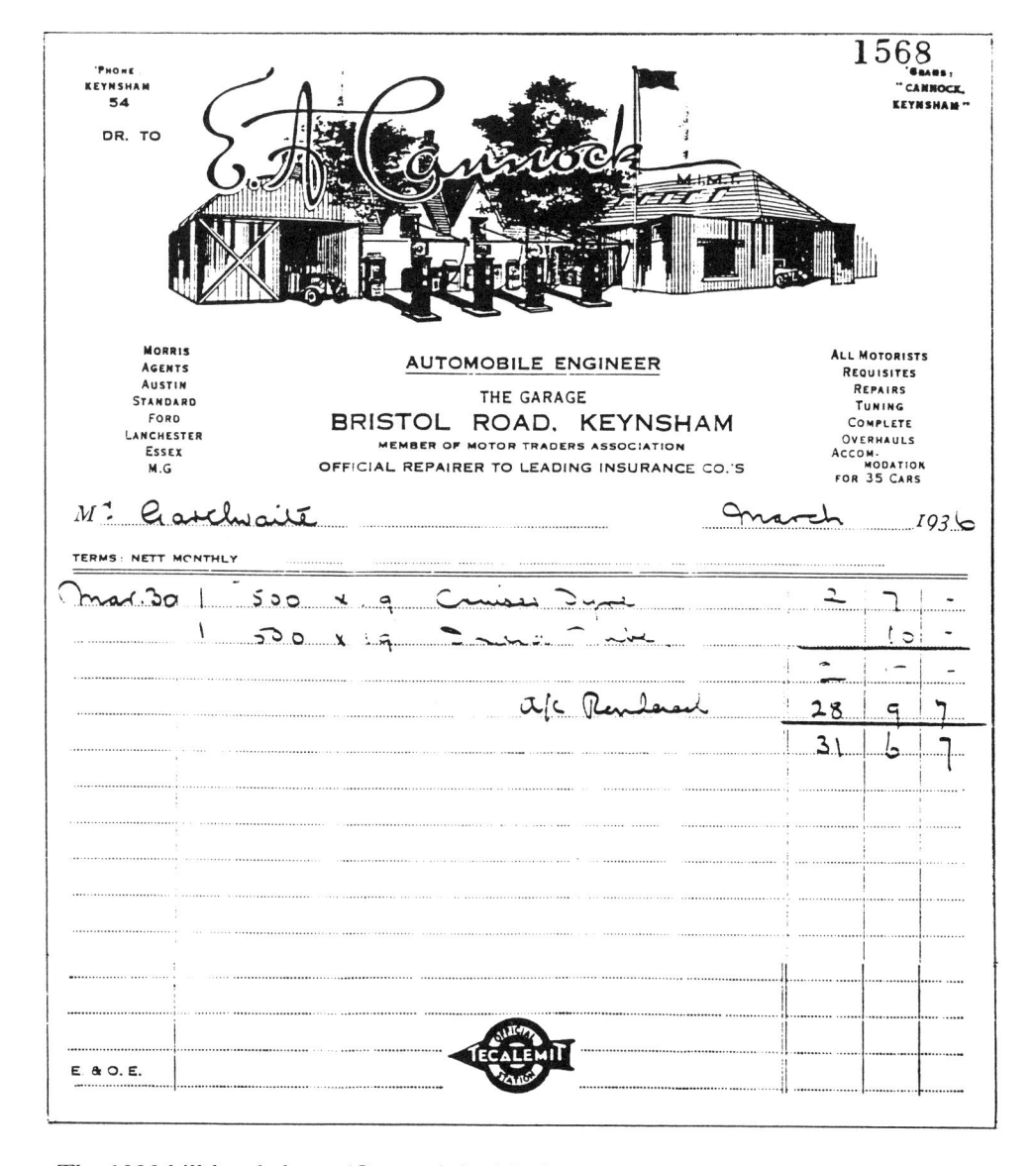

The 1936 bill head shows 'Cannocks' with the new oval roof, barn type shed on the left, and on the right, the addition of the car display showroom. Two trees and a flag complete the scene.

the locker hooks'. The LDV, later the Home Guard, were provided with a scrap car, a Trojan, towed to Queen Charlton for Mills Grenades practice.

Part of the repair workshop was divided to form a machine shop. Mr Cannock had been appointed an officer in charge of the Keynsham ARP Report Centre, but in the time left from these duties he used his knowledge and talents to set up a small unit making components for aircraft, military and naval use. Air Ministry approval was given in 1941 and some quarter of a million items were produced. These included pulleys for Beaufighter undercarriage doors, pipe connections for Bristol Hercules Engines, and numerous small threaded parts for all services. Another item was a mine 'sinker' for the Navy, to position the mine at just the right distance below the surface of the sea.

Plug gauges were machined initially to near size, then passed to the Horstmann Gear Company for hardening and final grinding. Here was an example of the way in which many thousands of small workshops assisted in the War Effort.

By 1945 the ARP operations had already been run down. The machine shop turned to less war-like products. A device was designed and built to seal the packets containing 'Groaten' Porridge Oats, the miller's original plant having been 'blitzed' in Bristol. Later, components were made and assembled to construct a turntable designed to display a car rotating in showrooms and exhibition halls. This was promoted by a firm called Technigraphic in Crews Hole, Bristol. I believe one was used to display the first Austin A40 Somerset in about 1948.

Around 1950 work was carried out for the Forestry Commission, based at Brislington. Maintenance was critical for the F.C. vehicles. Many were ex-Army Hillman and Austin Utilities, together with BSA motorcycles and combinations and Fordson vans. Another assignment for the Commission was the conversion of an ex-Army Q-type Bedford lorry into a fire truck.

The normal body was removed and replaced with a 1,500 gallon water tank, with a platform for two pumps and a hose. The wooden platform bearers to support the tank were made by Mr A F Tucker, who ran a body shop in Temple Street. The safety grill protecting the front was fabricated by Mr L A Dunn, then in business as a coach builder on a site near Beech House, now Old Vicarage Green. The remaining metal work was completed in our machine shop and forge, mainly by E J Cannock.

As well as Morris the firm held agencies for Ford and also Standard. Sales were not high owing to shortage of vehicles, with extremely long waiting lists. But as supplies became more plentiful the firm realised it would be difficult to run competing franchises as the manufacturer's requirements increased. Consequently it was decided to concentrate on the Morris, together with related models in the British Motor Corporation group.'

The second generation

We have seen that Mr E A Cannock's business was able to endure the Depression of the 1930's and World War Two, and outlasted all other local motoring businesses. During that time, his sons were growing up. Edward, the elder boy, was educated at Mrs Jollyman's School in Charlton Road, until he was nine, when he started at the Bristol Grammar School. An uncle of his, Mr Ralph G Taylor, his mother's brother, came to live temporarily at Homeleigh and stayed till he died. But at least he drove to Bristol every day and so Edward

CITY AND COUNTY OF BRISTOL.

MOTOR CAR ACT. 1903.

LICENCE TO DRIVE A MOTOR Cycle.

No. 3378

Edward Arthur Cannock
of 69 Sandringham Road, Brislington,

is hereby Licensed to drive a Motor Car for the period of twelve months from the Twelfth day of May 1910.
until the Eleventh day of May 1911 inclusive.

Dated 12th May 1910.

Signed _____ Town Clerk.

N.B.—Particulars of any endorsement of any Licence previously held by the person licensed must be entered on the back of this Licence.

IMPORTANT.

N.B.—This Licence should always be carried, as failure by the Driver of a Motor Car to produce a Licence when demanded by a Police Constable renders him liable to a fine not exceeding £5. (Sec. 3 (4).)

In the event of the loss or defacement of this Licence a duplicate can be obtained from the Council on the payment of a fee of One Shilling.

Renewals of Licence.

This Licence (Licence No. 3378, granted by the City and County of Bristol under the Motor Car Act, 1903, is hereby renewed, so as to be in force for twelve months from the 12th day of May 1911 until the 11th day of May 1912 inclusive.

Signed Edmund J Taylor
Town Clerk.
Dated 12th May 1911.

This Licence (Licence No. 3378, granted by the City and County of Bristol under the Motor Car Act, 1903, is hereby renewed, so as to be in force for twelve months from the 12th day of May 1912 until the 11th day of May 19.. inclusive.

Signed _____ Town Clerk.
Dated 14th May 1912.

In the halcyon days of the Edwardian era, the cost of a driving licence for a motor cycle was on £1, as seen here on Mr E A Cannock's licence.

was able to go to school by car, unlike the Keynsham 'train boys', with their mischievous adventures.

In due course Mr E A Cannock's two sons took over the business, which is now the longest-established firm of its type in Keynsham, and older even than the long-established firm of E W Joll. There are a few other local businesses that continue the firms that their father's started, and in market gardening, one even reaches into a third generation.

'Cannock's of Keynsham Ltd' is conspicuously placed, where it still supplies a good and reliable service to the community, during the ever-changing face of Keynsham.

Mr E A Cannock outside his sandbagged garage around 1940, with a Coventry 'Singer Cycle Co Ltd's' Motor Wheel, a three wheeler with the motor being entirely within the front wheel, circa 1904, number plate AM 309. It had a small petrol tank within the spokes of the front wheel and an auxiliary larger one hung from the cross bar of the frame bearing Singer's name. It had pneumatic tyres, 'ignition of low tension type, cam working magneto machine and interrupter gear' and a surface type carburettor. Pedals and an ordinary cycle drive helped the small engine. At the back were the brackets and framework for a pillion.

Chapter 25

Old Keynsham recalled in verse

Horace Batchelor lived at Longreach House, which he renamed 'Infra-Grange'. He brought Keynsham to the attention of radio listeners throughout the country with his advertising of his 'Infra-draw' football pools system. Today Longreach House, returned to its former name, is a residential home.

Mrs Jill Renshaw described her following poem as, 'A resumé – with considerable poetic licence – of people, places and things which I do not wish to forget: as a comparative newcomer, most of the names mentioned existed at the time of my arrival in 1958. Two are left, the Trout and the Ship, and also the Park Road clinic is still there.'

'K-E-Y-N-S-H-A-M', a poetic recall by Jill Renshaw

Over Luxembourg air waves I heard spelt the name,
Leaving Liverpool behind to the country I came
To a quiet sleepy village, nineteen at the time,
Where small boys went fishing with rod, hook and line.

A new way of life: for as a wife
I took a husband and began a new life.
He played in fields where houses now stand,
The trees in 'Fry's' drive by his father were planned.

Somerdale then was most families's employer,
For short back and sides, men called on Charles Sawyer.
Packed steam trains brought trippers here for the day,
The river, Bees tea gardens – nice places to play.

Who can remember the shops on Bath Hill,
Or the Fox and Hounds pub, though the name is there still?
Apartments now stand where the market was held,
And the mellow arched bridges by floodwater were felled.

With iron railings removed in wartime alarm,
One way or another we've lost its old charm.
Tate and Lyle tankers would roar up the hill,
Somerset Pickle factory smell lingers still.

Sorry Woodbine Cottages clung behind the New Inn,
Blue-coated T & L lassies had their week's pay day fling.
Firemen responding to the siren's shrill call,
Brought their engine from the High Street, halting all.

The Post-Office-floor creaked, while you waited in line,
Next door the cheerful ladies sold their dairy wares fine.
The Lamb and Lark, Saturday, was the postman's last call,
And the firemen, practice over, the Trout had them all.

Friday evening saw the pigeon baskets piled behind the Ship,
And Thursday night bell ringers made bats from belfry flit.
Smell chocolate on the air and you knew that it would rain,
Leave by the Bitton road – and wait for the Fry's train.

Old Mr Ollis sold nails in the gloom,
And Smart's repaired watches in their tiny room.
Our meat came from Old's, and Pearsall's and Fray's,
And Clark's sandals from Gilbert's forecast sunny days.

Provisions from Reynolds', courteous service with smiles,
Well-wrapped staff served fruit-and-vegetables from cold, outdoor piles.
Keynsham Fisheries plied trade near the Lamb and Lark,
And children played in fields before we made Keynsham Park.

Damp clothed couples, rainy Saturdays, in the Tudor Café met,
Where at mid-day for lunches the tables were set;
And those who required it Jarrett's mobile shop came to see:
The Willow-Pattern Restaurant and Highland Café were where we had tea.

Hartnell Taylor, Cooper and Tanner, with houses for sale;
Mills and Mills; and Church Bakery, where nothing was stale.
Jack Day at the Charlton was queue organiser;
Hedge's chip shop cooked chips to go with the Tizer.

Harvey's for papers, and Rawlings for Raleigh,
Ronto's and Miss Mitzi continue the tally;
Bernard and Woodruff, Stafford and Beale,
Organ and Davis, and Laneham reveal

More names, such as Wiltshire, and Hickling for sure,
And Strudwick and Carter – two names more.
Percy Baker, Lowell Baldwin, Willoughby's and Young's;
Reed's Supermarket Santa was a stop for all mums.

Victor Value and Tesco, David Grieg and Fine Fare,
With the Co-op served our needs with something to spare.
In addition to businesses, certain people I recall:
Sisters Rogers and Bowden, the Gerrish family and all.

Dr. Claude and Dr. Bennett, Mrs. Melbourne, Dr. Ree,
And the Park Road Clinic for weekly checks and vitamin C. . . .

There are people, places, gone for ever,
But memories remain for us to treasure.

INDEX

abattoir 121
Abbey 12, 29
Abbey lintel 13
Abbot Charles, town clerk 26, 40, 278
Abbot Nicholas 12
Abbot Stourton 15
airship 149
Alfred – King 8, 26
Almshouses 17, 19, 67
Andrews – Isabel 63, 195, 200, 201
Anstey Cornelius – saddler 84, 108
Armistice Day 108, 143
Arras 162, 165, 172
Avon Mill Lane (now Avon Rd) 103, 104, 105, 109
Avon Motor Works 286
Avon River 3, 4, 6, 108
Ayres – Rev. 42

Back Lane, house in 84, 85
Baker – Lucy 57
Baker – Percy 269
Bailey and Mattick 296
Band – German 217
Baptist Church 40, 84
barges 122
Barter – Joe 288, 293
Batchelor – Horace 303
Bath Hill East 113
Bath Hill West 114, 116
Battery Mill, Saltford 57
bear – dancing 79. 217
Beck – blacksmith 270
Bedford – Duke of 78
Belgian refugees 79
Belston – H 223
bier 56, 74, 250
Bilbie – Thomas 31
billeting 147
Bishop of Wells 44
Bitton 47
black death 14
Board of Guardians 42, 44, 46, 69
Bolwells 278
Bond – Mitchell 145
Bonsall – P.M. 62
Boston – Mrs 215
boundary stone 47
Bowden T.L. pharmacist 81, 212
Bowditch – Police sgt. 203
Bowring – Rock Hill Hs 117, 135, 236
brass bowl 60
brass mills 21, 30, 54, 65, 85, 226

Bricktown 137, 219
bridges 12, 17, 19, 29
Bridges family 14, 15, 17, 21, 26, 31,
Bridges, Sir Thomas 235, 236
Bristol riots 32
Britain – Harriet 219
Brookman – Arthur 120
Brownsey Bros. – butcher 84, 230
Brunel – I.K. 118
Burial Register 34, 41, 43, 45
Burnett 99
Burnett Hill 63, 66
buses – coming of 144
Bush family 235
Butt – Mrs 157

Cannam – Joy 226–243
Cannock – Edward A 288–302
Cannock – Edward junior 121, 286, 290, 293, 298
Cantle – Wm. confectioner 86
Carbery – Diana 185, 193
Carpenter – Tom 117, 134–5, 270
Carter – Edward 62, 67
Carter – John 81, 83, 118, 223
Carter – William 77, 83, 119, 120, 231
Census 1851 51, 52
Chapman – Eldred 115
Chappell Brothers, grocers 222, 228, 233,
Chappell – George, grocers 83, 219, 223, 228, 234
Chandos – Duke of 15, 21, 236.
Chandos Lodge 18, 30, 235
Chard – Tom 116
Charles – I , King 15, 16, 18, 235
Charles – 2 , King 17, 30
choir members 79
cholera 40, 44
Civil War 17, 26
Clark – Stan 135
Clayfield – Phyllis 119, 120
Clothier – F & L, farmers 117, 136
Coles – Mr 145
Colour mill 31, 85, 108
Connett – Mrs 234
Conygre Farm II, 126, 127, 134, 135, 259
Cook – Michael, watch repairer 81
cotton mill 31
County bridge 4, 11, 17
Cox – Miss, Homeleigh 288, 290, 292, 293
Cox – Ruben 134, 220
Crease – Harry 121
Crease – Mrs 143

Crew – Mr   135
Cridland – Rbt. Henry, grocer   232, 283
Cromwell – Oliver   17
Crowther – Leslie   121, 122, 247

Danes – invasion by   8
Davis – Miss   293
Davis – Tom   121
Densleys – Miss   237
diphtheria   85, 137, 138, 270
Dissolution, of the Abbey   14, 15
Doctors – local   79
Domesday Book   8, 30
Dorey – Fred   63, 86
Dorey – Madge   148, 234
Dowling – Clifford   46, 67, 74
Dowling – Hilda   67, 73, 74
Downey, Sgt.   75
Downs – newsgents   230
Dragon's Hill, and Quarry   17, 27, 276
Dutch workers   30

Edith – Queen   8
Edward the Confessor   8
Edward I ,   11, 27
Edwards, Mr, Medical Oficer   42
eels –   57, 59, 256, 271
Electric Works; electricity,   66, 81, 93, 114
Elizabeth, Queen,   15, 30, 33 281
Ellis – Leonard   138, 142, 215–225
Elm Tree Inn   278, 279
Exon – Mr,   108, 269
Eyelet factory   81, 85

Fairclough – Mary, sketches by, 9, 10, 19, 20, 22, 25
Fairclough – Mary, quoted,   40, 51, 84, 115, 150, 218, 227, 278, 281
Fairfield Terr – Mission hut   255
FANYS – picture of   193
fishing –   116, 270
Fitter, C.J., Dr.   155
ford   12, 281, 282
Flanders House –   114, 134, 221, 236, 281
Flood – Great, 1968   115
Ford – Mrs.   283
Forest – Mr   135
Fowler – farmer   285
Fox – Dr. Brislington   199, 244, 269
Fray – David, butcher   118, 234
Fry – 'Fishy'   83, 231
Fry – Francis   185, 279, 280, 281
Fry's – factory   26, 85, 93, 122, 136, 203

gas lighting/chandeliers   62, 79, 143
George V and Queen Mary   174–179
George VI ,   63

Gibbons – William, Jonathan   28, 148, 149, 151, 201
Gibbs – Miss, sweets/papers   106, 230
Gifford – Joseph, farmer   126
Glover – Charlie   67, 124, 128
Godfrey – Jonas, haulier   218, 219, 223, 270
Grace – Dr   83
grave digging/grave stones   35, 37, 40
Grimes – Mr. grocer   222, 233
Grimes – Sidney, sweep   223
Guyan – Mrs.   57
Gyles – Doreen   65, 73, 115

Hale – p.c.   130
Handel – George F   21, 27
Hannay – Mr. gravedigger   269
Harding – G.R. Rev.   42, 44
Harding – Leslie   63, 65, 75, 113, 246
Harford and Bristol Brass Coy.   57
Harrison – Charles, Dr. father   83, 84, 115, 220, 267, 270
Harrison – Claude, Dr. son   117, 137
Harrison – Lily   73, 86–102, 244
Harvey – Mrs. headteacher   86, 103, 215
Harvey – Green and Grey   272, 273, 274
Harvey – John   149, 150
Harvey – Pamela   272, 275
Harvey – William   34, 38, 228
Hatcher – Rev   79
Hayman – Charles   118, 119
Headington – John, markt.gard.   276
Headington – Louise   57, 275
Headington – Ronald   29, 34, 38, 40, 57, 59, 85, 113, 114, 118, 149, 186, 205, 278, 283
Heahmund – Bishop of Sherborne   8
Henry I,   8
Henry VII,   14
Henry VIII,   15
Henshaw – George   288, 290
Hickling – mangr.colour works   81, 223
Hickling – Rob. D., ironmongers,   83, 130, 231
Hine – 'Henry', sweep   106, 115, 223
Hoddinot   217
Hospice – of St.John   12, 26, 28

ice skating   118
internal combustion engine   286
Isolation Hospital   80, 93, 137, 138, 261, 270

James – Susan   141, 153, 154, 235, 236
Jarrett's bakery   22, 34, 205, 215, 276, 278
Jeffries – Judge   236
Joll – Edward, outfitters   76, 77.
Jollyman – Mrs, school of   226, 228, 301

Keeling Harry   244

306

Keynsham Abbey   9, 26
Keynsham Bypass   298
Keynsham Cemetery Chapel   74
Keynsham Cricket Club   117, 236
Keynsham Flower Show   92
Keynsham Gas Company   93, 282
Keynsham Hundred   15
Kynsham Pictorial map of   25–27
Keynsham Town Guide, 1930   64, 68
Keynsham Town Silver Band   244–248
Keynsham Urban District Council 75, 116, 142, 146, 225
Kinnersley – Captain   135
Kipling – Rudyard   177
Kirkuk   152

Labbot – The   12, 44, 57
Labour Exchange   63
lacrosse – team   85
Lamb and Lark – hotel   79, 143, 151, 219, 235, 247, 270
Lennard's shop   234
Leyland – John, c1533   29
Linham – Bros.   234
Logwood Mill   135, 271, 283
Longreach House   237, 303
Longton House   66, 79, 81
Lord – of the Manor   9, 17, 51
Loxton – Edward, & others   76, 145, 146, 150, 151, 152, 231

Macey – Jim   120
Mann – Rev.   278
Manor – of Keynsham   8, 21, 26
Mansey – Mr. headteacher   86
market – local   14
Martin – Mr.   249
Matilda – Queen   8
Mattick – brothers   81
May – Barney   219
Mayfields   120
Mead – White's   270
medieval footpaths/tracts   4, 84, 117
mills – local   66, 271
Milner – 'Bob'   51
Milwood House/Lodge   79, 235/121, 235
Monmouth Rebellion   17, 27, 236
Moreton – battle of   8
Morris – Patrick, sexton   56
mortuary   71
mules   78, 127, 143, 147, 150
munition factory   143

Newman – Edith   213
Newman – Ed. yeo,   236
Newman – Gwen, nee Glover   123, 250– 268
Newport – Richard H   59, 76– 85
Newport – Tom, Glouc.Reg.   80

Norman – Conquest   8
Norris – John   286
North Som. Yeomanry   23, 32, 145, 151

occupations – in 1851   48–50
Ogborns   84
Old Court House   17, 23, 236
Old Manor House   79, 235
Ollis – Benjamin/Grace   63/282, 284
Ollis – carrier/Fred, baker   78/276
Ollis – Jim   116, 122, 293, 296
Ollis – William Charles   57, 58, 149, 278
Ollis – references to –   30, 51 55, 59, 116, 230, 275
On finding dead hedgehog   241
Orchard – F.M. photographer   147, 229
Oxford–Thomas, clerk to B of G.   69

Packer – Frank   75
Paget – farmer   86
Parker – Beatrice   141
Parker – Guy, Lt.Colonel   154
Parker – John S. Captain   153, 155–184
Parker – Joseph, 'Squire'   235
Parr – Katherine, Queen   15
Parsons – Albert/Raymond   271/290
paupers –   35, 41, 53, 75
Pearce – William, baker   228, 233
Penetta – William   61
Peters – Ivo   122
Phelps – Percy   293
Picture House   81, 106, 230, 296,
pigs –   66, 134, 135, 259, 283–285
Pines   116, 235
plague –   29
Pocock – Mr, muler   78
Police – Station, old   82, 130, 202, 203
Police – Station, WW2   200
Polysulphin – factory   22, 66, 122
Pool – Barton   III, 149
Poor Law Guardians   62
Poor – Rate/the poor   38, 39 /40, 65
Poples – family of   116, 234
population – in 1851   51, 52
pupils – at Jollymans   227

Queen Charlton   7, 11, 15, 69, 99, 127, 147

rabbit – coursing/poaching   144/67, 129, 250
Railways – GWR   23, 24, 63, 110, 111, 144, 283
Rawlings – cycles/'Coffee'   230/101
Red Cross – in WW1   189, 190, 191, 193, 194
Red Mill – Memorial Park   31, 85, 108, 223, 271, 278,
Reed – Gordan   97, 223
Renshaw – Jill   303, 304

307

'Road to Heaven'/roads   240/33, 92
Robe – B. J.   59, 103, 122, 145–6, 230–7, 246, 276, 290
Robinson – Phyllis   121, 122
Rockhill Farm   185, 188
Rockhill House   236, 279, 280, 281
Rogers – James, basket maker   60
Rogers – Isaac, watch repairer   231
Romans – occupation by   4, 5, 6
Royal Coat Arms/R. Mail   18/113, 270
Royal Park and Chace   10, 11, 23, 27

St John's – Church   15, 16, 31, 79, 143, 222
St.Keyna – of Wales   7, 8, 26
St.Keyna – Tennis Club   267
Salmon – Police Sgt.   130
Saunders – Violet   61
Scears – Martin   28, 83
Schools – first/Methodist   21/23, 30
   – Infants, Temple St.   95, 96, 217, 226
   – 'Big Sc' Bath Hill   60, 96, 98, 196, 269
   – Private/dentists   101, 151, 215, 226/106
Shellabear – Fred. Chas., drapery   233
Sherborne – Bishop of   8
Sherer – William   65, 72–4, 137, 281, 284
shopkeepers– local /shop smells 81–84/110
Short – David, carrier   147
Skuse – Mr.   231
Smith – Seymour   148, 149
Somerset – Light Infantry   195, 207 – 214
Spring Cottage, Bath Hill   59, 116, 275, 276
Stickler – Jessie   94, 144, 228
Stokes and Son   83–5, 145–7, 218, 231–5
stone breaking   61, 72, 134, 147
Stone – Walter   121
strike – general   63, 66, 269
Stuart – Charles Shaw   237
Sweet – 'Job', sweep   106, 114, 115, 223

Tangent Tool Company   290, 293, 295, 296, 298
tarmack   113, 147
Taylor – Frank   117, 236
teacher's names   97, 103
Tetley – Jack, poulterer   280
Thomas – William   135, 150
tramps   70, 71, 72, 134, 146, 257
Trimobile   270, 286–9, 290, 291
Troops – convoys, WW1   79, 82
Trott – Bill, blacksmith   27, 110
Tudor – Jasper   14
turnpike roads   19, 32, 33, 281
Tyler & Son, basket–maker   57, 84
typhoid and T.B.   270

undertakers   46, 118, 119
unemployment   63, 269
Usher – J, headmaster   95
Veale – Harry butcher   117
Veale – Monty   269 – 271
Verdun   169
Victoria – Methodist Church   28, 93, 94, 145, 147, 150

Wansborough – Mr   271
War Graves Commission   154–184
Watts – 'Butty'   129
Watts – George   219
Watts – George, San. Inspector   137
Webb – Charlie   138, 244
weighbridge   258, 282, 283
wells –   65, 76, 85, 88, 127, 145
Wesley – John   21, 30
Weston – donkey farm   218
Wheeler – G.E., head teacher,   143, 217
White – Elizabeth   40
White – Ernest, coal   87, 90, 96
White – Lily (Harrison Mrs.   89, 91
White – Herbert   100
Whiting – Lamb & Lark   131
Whitmore – Ann/Sir Thomas   17, 21
Whittock – Jeff/Leslie   60/117
Wiggins – Christopher   65, 84
Wilkin's – bakery   233
Willcox – Charles/John   205, 276/195, 198
Willcox – Dorothy/Jessie   199/199, 200
Willcox – Eleanor/Jack   197, /197
Willcox – Frank/Henry   195/196
Willcox – George/Peter   203/199
Willett – Dr G.G.D.   148, 235
Williams – Jean   212, 244, 246, 249
Williams – Sgt. SL1   210, 212, 213, 214
Williams – Mrs, Temple St.   137
Willougby Bros. grocers   233, 283
Wills – Captain   244, 247
Wilson – Hettie/Lionel   148/148
Withers – Miss, drapers   230
Wood – Alfred/Charles   236/186, 187, 188
Wood – Bessie   190, 191, 192
Wood – Corena/John   185/188
Wood – Harris/C.A.   188.189
Woodham – Brian   67, 71
Workhouse –   40, 53, 56, 69, 93, 98, 133, 144, 219
Workhouse – children of   69, 70, 73, 133, 220

Ypres –   173, 188

Zeppelin   146
Zion – Methodist church   73

1422	Henry VI	Eton & King's College Cambs. founded	Hospital of St. John, from 15th–16th Century, is believed stood where West End House is.
			1447 John St. Loe left Abbey a silver cup and cover.
			Abbey's distinguished seven 15th century Ledgers (coffin slabs), with floriated crosses.
	House of York		
1461	Edward IV	William Caxton	1455 At a Visitation by Bishop, Abbot ordered not to allow his canons to sell wine at public fairs and markets – among other injunctions.
1483	Edward V	Murdered in Tower	
1483	Richard III	1485 Battle of Bosworth Field	
	House of Tudor		
1485	Henry VII	John Cabot	1495 Funeral of Sir Jasper Tudor at Abbey.
			1498 Henry VII's Pilgrimage to St. Anne's, Brislington.
1509	Henry VIII		1534 Abbot acknowledged Royal Supremacy.
		Dissolution of the Monasteries	1534 Break with Rome.
			1539 Dissolution of Keynsham Abbey.
		Break with Rome	Abbot and 11 Canons given pensions.
1547	Edward VI	1st English Book of Common Prayer	c.1540 John Leland's visit.
1553	Jane	9 days' reign	*1552 Sir Thomas Bridges* bought Abbey site. Manor of Keynsham stayed in Royal Hands until 1613 when sold to Anne Whitmore.
1553	Mary	300 Protestant Martyrs	
			The Abbey mills were leased to tenants.
1558		Calais lost	1559 Sir Thomas Bridges left £40 and stone from Abbey to repair County Bridge.
1558	Elizabeth I	1588 Spanish Armada William Shakespeare	1574 Queen Elizabeth reputed to have passed through Keynsham en route for Bristol, traditionally over Dapps Hill bridge. Stayed night at "Queen" Charlton.
	House of Stuart		
1603	James I	Authorised Version Gunpowder Plot	c.1614 Park House Farm built?
1625	Charles I	*Civil War*	c.1616 Old Manor House?
		King beheaded 1649	
		11 year Interregnum Oliver Cromwell	1632 Tower of St. John's crashed.
		John Milton	c.1637 Old Court House built.
			August 1645 Cromwell's troops in Keynsham
1660	Charles II	1665 Great Plague 1666 Great Fire	
1685	James II	*1685 Monmouth Rebellion*	1685 Monmouth's troops camped at Sydenham Mead.
		Judge Jeffreys	1685 King's troops destroyed County Bridge. Monmouth repaired it. 11 men hanged at top of Bath Hill East. Skirmish at and origin of name "Dragoon's Hill"?
			1685 onwards – arrival Flemish/German brass workers.
			1685 Sir Thomas Bridges Almshouses, Bristol Road.
			1695 New Inn (a house).